REEDS
MARINA GUIDE
2009

The source directory for all sail & power boat owners

© Adlard Coles Nautical 2008

Adlard Coles Nautical,
38 Soho Square, London W1D 3HB
Tel: 0207 758 0200
Fax: 0207 758 0222/0333
e-mail: info@reedsalmanac.co.uk
www.reedsalmanac.co.uk

Cover photo: Dean & Reddyhoff Ltd
Tel: 023 9260 1201
www.deanreddyhoff.co.uk

Section 1

The Marinas and Services Section has been fully updated for the 2009 season. These useful pages provide chartlets and facility details for some 175 marinas around the shores of the UK and Ireland, including the Channel Islands, the perfect complement to any *Reeds Nautical Almanac*.

Section 2

The Marine Supplies & Services section lists more than 500 services at coastal and other locations around the British Isles. It provides a quick and easy reference to manufacturers and retailers of equipment, services and supplies both nationally and locally together with emergency services.

Advertisement Sales

Enquiries about advertising space should be addressed to:

**MS Publications, 2nd Floor
Ewer House, 44-46 Crouch Street
Colchester, Essex, CO3 3HH
Tel: +44(0)1206 506227**
Fax: +44 (0)1206 500228

Section 1
Marinas and Services Section

Section 2

Area Guide
Showing Coastal Divisions

Shetland Islands

NORWAY

8

Cape Wrath

7
Orkney Islands

Rattray Head

SCOTLAND

6

Skagen

Crinan Canal

Eyemouth

DENMARK

13

9

Berwick-on-Tweed

5

NORTHERN IRELAND

Mull of Galloway

Sylt

10

REPUBLIC OF IRELAND

ENGLAND

Emden

Delfzijl

Bardsey Island

Great Yarmouth

12

WALES

4

11

Anvil Point

Selsey Bill

3

Land's End

2

Nieuwpoort

BELGIUM

Isles of Scilly

1

14

Port-en-Bessin

Important Note

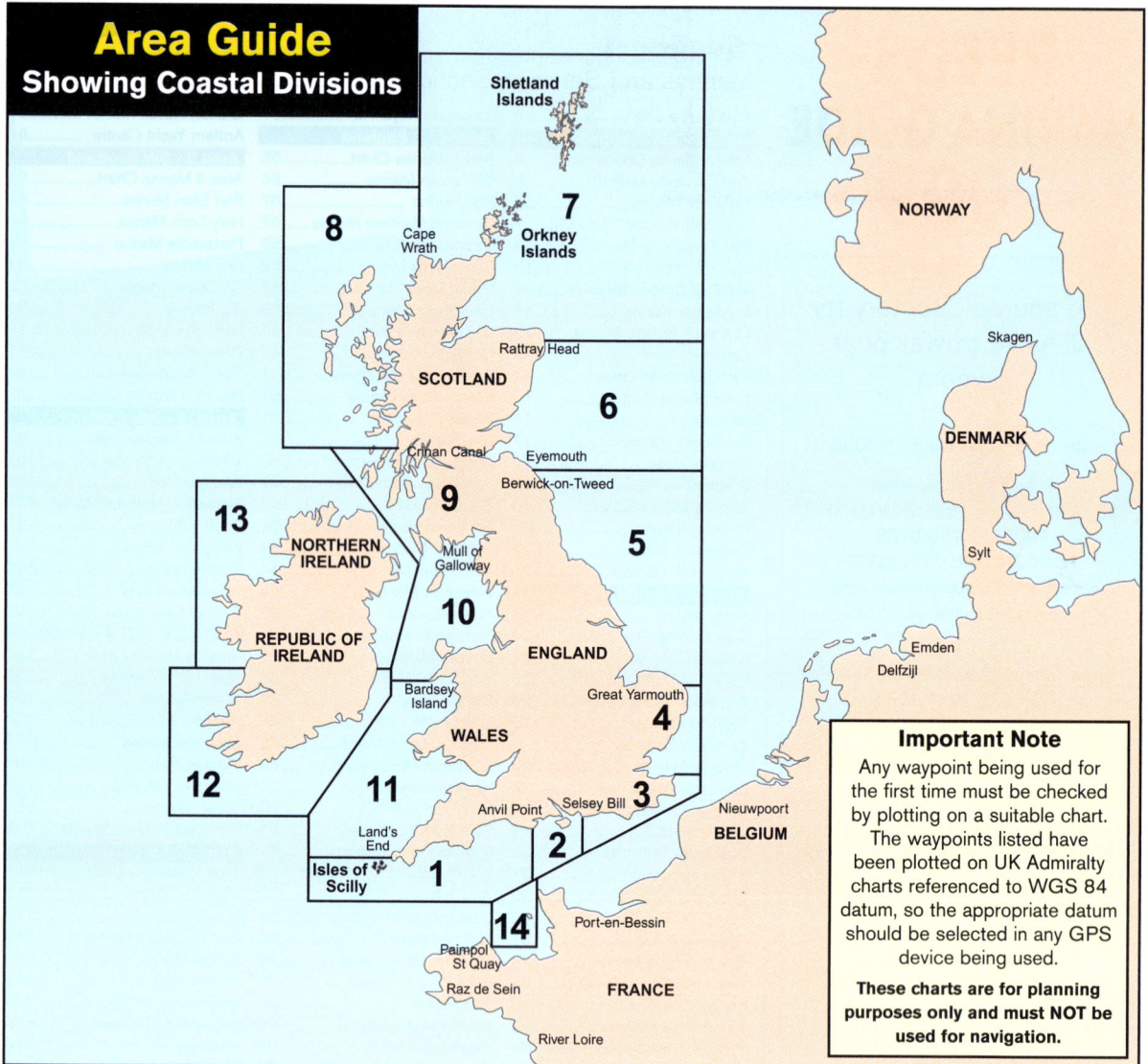

Any waypoint being used for the first time must be checked by plotting on a suitable chart. The waypoints listed have been plotted on UK Admiralty charts referenced to WGS 84 datum, so the appropriate datum should be selected in any GPS device being used.

These charts are for planning purposes only and must NOT be used for navigation.

Paimpol St Quay

Raz de Sein

FRANCE

River Loire

Area 1 ......**South West England** ....Isles of Scilly to Anvil Point

Area 2 ......**Central Southern England** ....Anvil Point to Selsey Bill

Area 3 ......**South East England** ....Selsey Bill to North Foreland

Area 4 ......**East England** ....North Foreland to Great Yarmouth

Area 5 ......**North East England** ....Great Yarmouth to Berwick-upon-Tweed

Area 6 ......**South East Scotland**...Eyemouth to Rattray Head

Area 7 ......**North East Scotland** ....Rattray Head to Cape Wrath including Orkney & Shetland Is

Area 8 ......**North West Scotland** ....Cape Wrath to Crinan Canal

Area 9 ......**South West Scotland**...Crinan Canal to Mull of Galloway

Area 10 ....**North West England** ....Isle of Man & N Wales, Mull of Galloway to Bardsey Is

Area 11 ....**South Wales & Bristol Channel** ....Bardsey Island to Land's End

Area 12 ....**South Ireland**...Malahide, south to Liscanor Bay

Area 13 ....**North Ireland** ....Lambay Island, north to Liscanor Bay

Area 14 ....**Channel Islands** ....Guernsey, Jersey & Alderney

ADLARD COLES NAUTICAL
WEATHER FORECASTS
BY FAX & TELEPHONE

Coastal/Inshore	2-day by Fax	5-day by Phone
Bristol	09065 222 349	09068 969 649
South West	09065 222 348	09068 969 648
Mid Channel	09065 222 347	09068 969 647
N France	09065 501 612	09064 700 422
N Brittany	09065 501 613	09064 700 423
National (3-5 day)	09065 222 340	09068 969 640

Offshore	2-5 day by Fax	2-5 day by Phone
English Channel	09065 222 357	09068 969 657
Irish Sea	09065 222 359	09068 969 659
Biscay	09065 222 360	09068 969 660

09064/68 CALLS COST 60P PER MIN. 09065 CALLS COST £1.50 PER MIN.

Key to Marina Plans symbols

Bottled gas		Parking	
Chandler		Pub/Restaurant	
Disabled facilities		Pump out	
Electrical supply		Rigging service	
Electrical repairs		Sail repairs	
Engine repairs		Shipwright	
First Aid		Shop/Supermarket	
Fresh Water		Showers	
Fuel - Diesel		Slipway	
Fuel - Petrol		Toilets	
Hardstanding/boatyard		Telephone	
Internet Café		Trolleys	
Laundry facilities		Visitors berths	
Lift-out facilities		Wi-Fi	

Area 1 - South West England

MARINAS
Telephone Numbers
VHF Channel
Access Times

Bristol Channel

Ilfracombe
Watchet
Burnham-on-Sea
Appledore

Port Falmouth Marina
01326 212161 Ch 80 H24
Falmouth Marina
01326 316620 Ch 80 H24
Falmouth Visitors' Yacht Haven
01326 310991 Ch 12 H24
Port Pendennis Marina
01326 211211 Ch 80 H24
Mylor Yacht Harbour
01326 372121 Ch 80 H24

Dartside Quay
01803 845445 Ch 80 H24
Dart Marina
01803 832580 Ch 80 H24
Noss Marina
01803 839087 Ch 80 H24
Darthaven Marina
01803 752545 Ch 80 H24

Lyme Regis
Bridport
Exeter
R.Exe
Teignmouth
Exmouth
Portland Marina
08454 302012
Ch 80 H24
Weymouth
Portland Bill

Padstow
Torquay
Torquay Marina
01803 200210
Ch 80 H24
Brixham

Looe
Plymouth
R Yealm
R Erme
R Avon
R Dart
Dartmouth
Brixham Marina
01803 882929
Ch 80 H24

Fowey
Salcombe

Weymouth Harbour
01305 838423 Ch 12
Weymouth Marina
01305 767576
Ch 80 H24

Mevagissey
Newlyn
Falmouth
R.Helford

Torpoint Yacht Harbour 01752 813658 Ch 80 H24
Multihull Centre 01752 823900 HW±3
Mayflower Marina 01752 556633 Ch 80 H24
Q Anne's Battery Marina 01752 671142 Ch 80 H24
Sutton Harbour 01752 204702 Ch 12 H24
Plymouth Yacht Haven 01752 404231 Ch 80 H24

St Mary's
Isles of Scilly

N

Adlard Coles Nautical THE BEST SAILING BOOKS

Blue Water Sailing Manual
Barry Pickthall **£25.00** 978 0 7136 7602 4

Tel: **01256 302699** email: **direct@macmillan.co.uk** or **www.adlardcoles.com**

TO ORDER

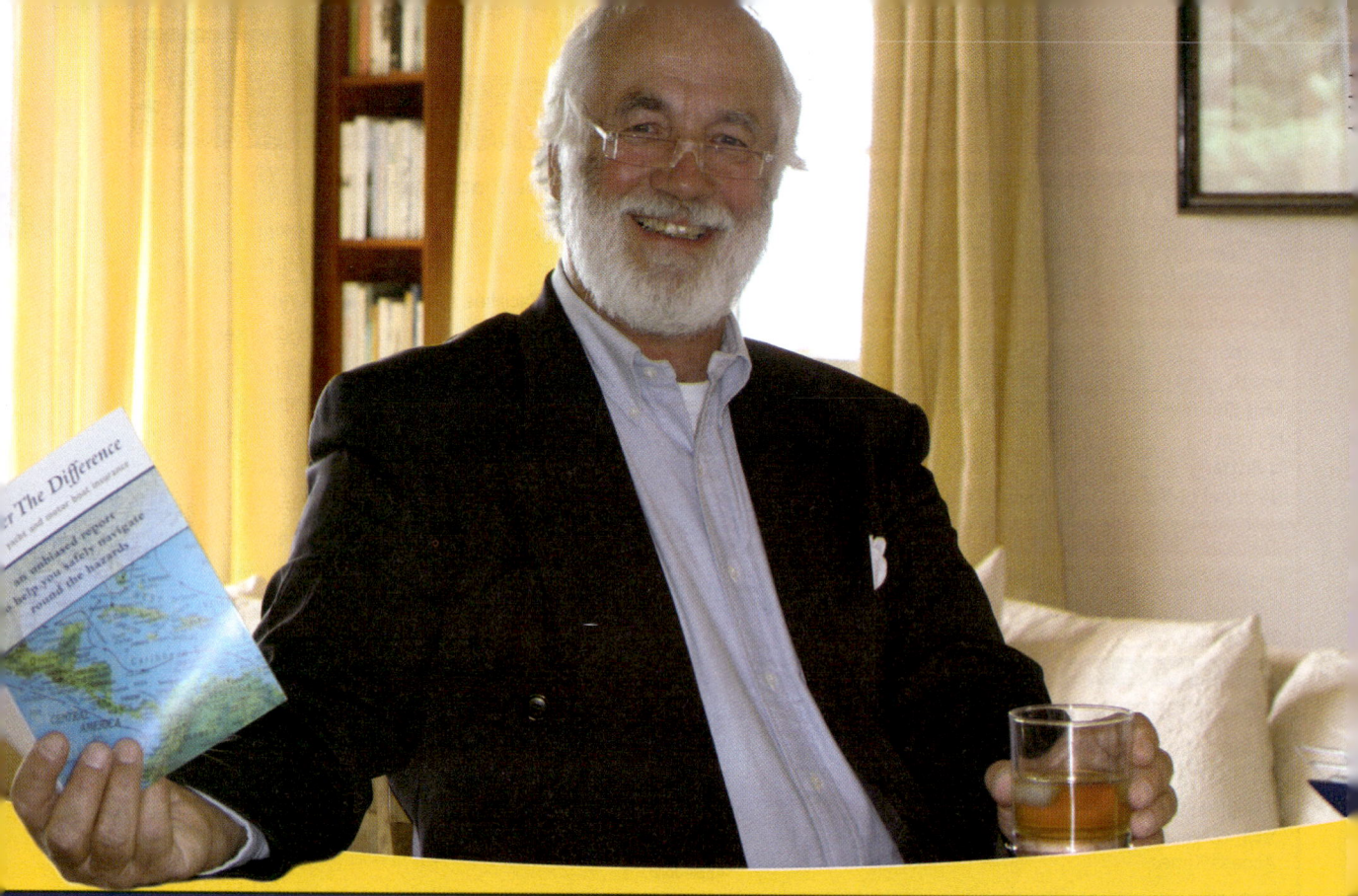

We Discovered the Difference

Sir Anthony Greener

"I hope we are at the end of a very long road and I would like to thank you and Pantaenius for your outstanding service and support. It has been an exemplary (and very unusual) experience for a client."

Mr. David Evans

"Why would I ever try to buy the cheapest insurance? I now have a self-satisfied glow that I made the right decision by buying the BEST insurance. This was brought about by listening to a friend who had a claim with yourselves. His claim was equally well handled by Pantaenius and that experience persuaded me that what I needed was the best, not the cheapest!"

Dr. H. Chadwick

"I would like to thank Pantaenius and especially yourself for the way in which you have dealt with things, as losing one's boat, especially in such dangerous circumstances is quite a traumatic event. I was very grateful for both the immediate help and advice that I received and the subsequent help with managing the situation and the rapid settlement of the insurance issues."

Mr. Dave Leaning

"Thanks for all your help throughout this claim, one reads all sorts of insurance horror stories in the yachting press but I don't think I could possibly have received any better service. It made a difficult process painless."

Why don't you contact us

2009/Mg9/v

PANTAENIUS
Yacht Insurance

Hamburg · Plymouth · Monaco · Skive · Vienna · Palma de Mallorca · Zagreb · New York

Marine Building · Victoria Wharf · Plymouth · Devon PL4 0RF · Phone +44-1752 22 36 56 · Fax +44-1752 22 36 37
Authorised and regulated by the Financial Services Authority

www.pantaenius.com

PORT FALMOUTH MARINA

Port Falmouth Marina
The Docks, Falmouth, TR11 4NR
Tel: 01326 212161 Fax: 01326 319433
Email: info@portfalmouth.com

VHF	Ch 80
ACCESS	H24

Port Falmouth Marina is an exciting new, world-class facility in the heart of Falmouth town.

The state-of-the-art 300-berth marina offers direct access to the sheltered waters of the Fal Estuary. A floating breakwater will protect the marina from prevailing winds and provide additional berthing for visitors and super-yachts. The inner pontoons will have finger berths to accommodate boats up to 18m LOA.

The marina plans include a drive on facility for the provisioning and servicing of yachts and high amp electricity outlets in addition to water and pump out facilities.

FACILITIES AT A GLANCE

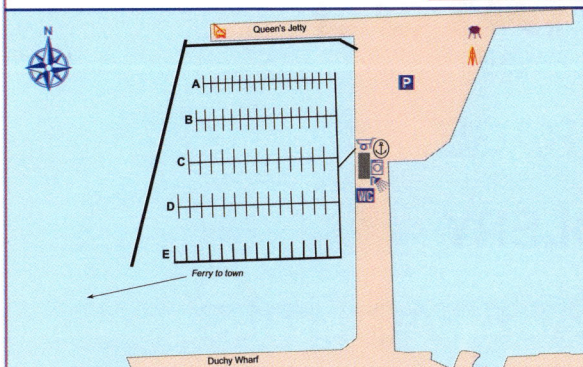

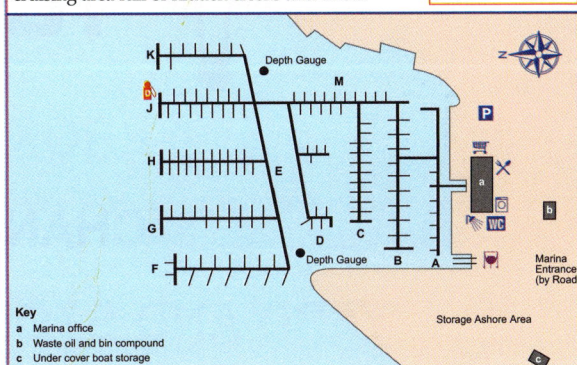

FALMOUTH MARINA

Falmouth Marina
North Parade, Falmouth, Cornwall, TR11 2TD
Tel: 01326 316620 Fax: 01326 313939
Email: falmouth@premiermarinas.com
www.premiermarinas.com

VHF	Ch 80
ACCESS	H24

Falmouth Marina lies tucked away in sheltered waters at the southern end of the Fal Estuary. Welcoming to both visiting and residential yachts, its comprehensive facilities include a restaurant, convenience store and hairdresser, while just a 20-minute walk away is Falmouth's town centre where you will find no shortage of shops and eating places. Comprising more than 70 sq miles of navigable water, the Fal Estuary is an intriguing cruising area full of hidden creeks and inlets.

FACILITIES AT A GLANCE

Key
a   Marina office
b   Waste oil and bin compound
c   Under cover boat storage

PENROSE
SAILMAKERS

For Performance
Sails and Service

▼ **Sails**

▼ **Yacht covers**

▼ **24 hr repair service**

▼ **Yacht upholstery**

01326 312705

50 Church Street, Upton Slip, Falmouth, Cornwall
www.penrosesails.co.uk

2009/Mg107/v

SEAFIT MARINE SERVICES LTD
Falmouth Marina, North Parade, Falmouth,
Cornwall TR11 2TD
Tel: (01326) 313713 Fax: (01326) 313713
Mob: 07971 196175
e-mail: marytownshend@tiscali.co.uk
For installation maintenance and repair work - electrical,
plumbing, hulls, rigs etc.

L12/s

We stock a huge range of
Marine Clothing, Footwear, Books & Charts
Plus
Chandlery including
Paint, Antifouling, Rope, GPS, VHF Radios
Friendly Expert Advice
Open 7 days a week
Shipmates Chandlers
2 Newcomen Road, DARTMOUTH
✆ 01803 839292
SHOP ONLINE NOW AT
www.chandlery.co.uk

FALMOUTH MARINA
North Parade, Falmouth, Cornwall TR11 2TD
Tel: (01326) 316620 Fax: (01326) 313939
e-mail: falmouth@premiermarinas.co.uk
www.permiermarinas.com
Ideal for West country cruising, Falmouth Marina boats fully
servied berths and an onsite boatyard.

2009/L2a/z

CHALLENGER MARINE Ltd

VOLVO PENTA

MerCruiser

TOHATSU

BROKERAGE

CHANDLERY

YARD AND STORAGE FACILITIES

MARINE ENGINEERS INBOARD AND OUT BOARD

Challenger Marine Ltd
Freemans Wharf, Falmouth Road, Penryn
Cornwall TR10 8AD
Tel 01326 377222
www.challengermarine.co.uk

2009/MG66/2

1

FALMOUTH VISITORS' YACHT HAVEN

Falmouth Visitors Yacht Haven
44 Arwenack Street
Tel: 01326 310991 Fax: 01326 211352
Email: admin@falmouthport.co.uk

| VHF | Ch 12 |
| ACCESS | H24 |

Run by Falmouth Harbour Commissioners (FHC), Falmouth Visitors' Yacht Haven has become increasingly popular since its opening in 1982, enjoying close proximity to the amenities and entertainments of Falmouth town centre. Sheltered by a breakwater, the Haven caters for 100 boats and offers petrol and diesel supplies as well as good shower and laundry facilities.

Falmouth Harbour is considered by some to be the cruising capital of Cornwall and its deep water combined with easily navigable entrance – even in the severest conditions – makes it a favoured destination for visiting yachtsmen.

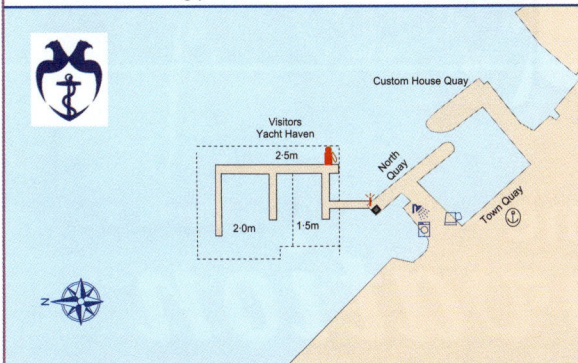

FACILITIES AT A GLANCE

Custom House Quay
Visitors Yacht Haven
2·5m
2·0m   1·5m
North Quay
Town Quay

Visitors Yacht Haven Falmouth

2009/MG74/V

Fresh water & electricity on pontoons.
Close proximity to town centre.
Toilets, showers & laundry.
Fuel barge dispensing diesel & petrol.

"WiFi internet hotspot"

Berthing available all year

FALMOUTH HARBOUR COMMISSIONERS

44 Arwenack Street,
Falmouth TR11 3JQ
Tel: 01326 312285/310991
Fax: 01326 211352

www.falmouthport.co.uk

MDL Dry Stack

The UK's leading Dry Stack provider

- Unlimited Launching on Demand ● 7 Days a Week ● 1 Hour Turn Around
- Secure Out of Water Storage ● Better Fuel Economy ● Use of Superb Marina Facilities

Visit www.mdldrystack.co.uk

2009/MG152/Z

Weems & Plath®

Manufacturer of Fine Nautical Instruments

In Time ~
innovation
Becomes
tradition

Annapolis · MD · USA since 1928

www.weems-plath.com

Kelvin Hughes distributes Weems & Plath products in the UK and
Europe. Contact Southampton@kelvinhughes.co.uk to find a local
authorised stockist, *visit* www.bookharbour.com · *call* 023-80634911

KELVIN HUGHES

2009/Mg1/v

1

PORT PENDENNIS MARINA

Port Pendennis Marina
Challenger Quay, Falmouth, Cornwall, TR11 3YL
Tel: 01326 211211 Fax: 01326 311116
www.portpendennis.com

| VHF | Ch 80 |
| ACCESS | H24 |

Easily identified by the tower of the National Maritime Museum, Port Pendennis Marina is a convenient arrival or departure point for trans-Atlantic or Mediterranean voyages. Lying adjacent to the town centre, Port Pendennis is divided into an outer marina, with full tidal access, and inner marina, accessible three hours either side of HW. Among its impressive array of marine services is Pendennis Shipyard, one of Britain's most prestigious yacht builders, while other amenities on site include car hire, tennis courts and a yachtsman's lounge, from where you can send faxes or e-mails.

FACILITIES AT A GLANCE

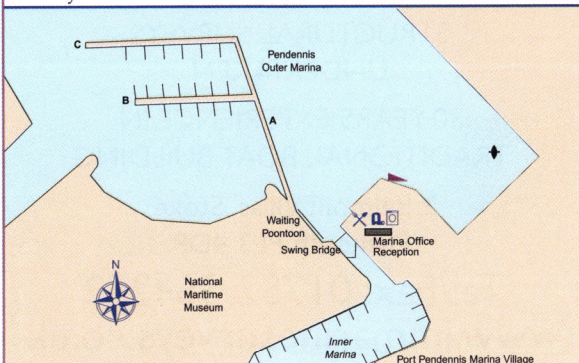

Shamrock Chandlery
What ever your budget, we've got it covered!

seago SP GOTOP BALTIC XM spinlock SEBAGO WEST SYSTEM ECHOMAX Barton MARINE ADMIRALTY LEISURE PLASTIMO SHURHOLD BLAKES Paints LALIZAS International

To buy these and many other brands visit our new on-line shop

www.shamrock.co.uk - then click on GO SHOPPING

Tel: 023 8063 2725

2009/MG128/e

ENJOY EVERY SEVENTH NIGHT FREE AT AN MDL MARINA
WITH MDL CRUISING CLUB
Membership is free and joining is easy.
Join today at www.mdlmarinas.co.uk or call 023 8045 0218

2009/MG152/z

port pendennis

CHALLENGER QUAY • FALMOUTH
CORNWALL • TR11 3YL
Tel: 01326 211211 • Fax: 01326 311116
E-mail: marina@portpendennis.com

A friendly marina, adjacent to the centre of Falmouth, bounded by areas of outstanding beauty.
The ideal centre for cruising the West Country, the Isles of Scilly, Brittany, the Channel Islands and south coast of Ireland.
All facilities available for the discerning yachtsman & family.
Also the perfect stopover for Transatlantic & Biscay passages with berthing for yachts to over 70m l.o.a. & 4m + draft.
Home to the new NATIONAL MARITIME MUSEUM

PLEASE VISIT OUR WEBSITE
www.portpendennis.com

2009/MG108/v

MYLOR YACHT HARBOUR

Mylor Yacht Harbour Marina
Mylor, Falmouth, Cornwall, TR11 5UF
Tel: 01326 372121 Fax: 01326 372120
Email: enquiries@mylor.com

VHF Ch M, 80
ACCESS H24

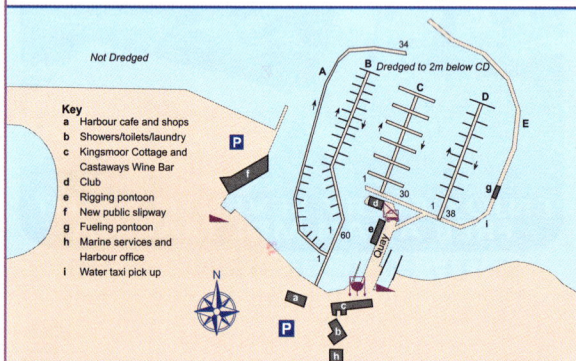

Situated on the western shore of Carrick Roads in the beautiful Fal Estuary, Mylor Yacht Harbour has been improved and expanded in recent years, now comprising two substantial breakwaters, three inner pontoons and approximately 250 moorings. With 24 hour access, good shelter and excellent facilities, it ranks among the most popular marinas on the SW Coast of England.

Formerly the Navy's smallest dockyard, established in 1805, Mylor is today a thriving yachting centre as well as home to the world's only remaining sailing oyster fishing fleet. With Falmouth just 10 mins away, local attractions include the Eden Project in St Austell and the National Maritime Museum in Falmouth.

FACILITIES AT A GLANCE

Key
a Harbour cafe and shops
b Showers/toilets/laundry
c Kingsmoor Cottage and Castaways Wine Bar
d Club
e Rigging pontoon
f New public slipway
g Fueling pontoon
h Marine services and Harbour office
i Water taxi pick up

MULTIHULL CENTRE, TORPOINT

Multihull Centre
Foss Quay, Millbrook, Torpoint, Cornwall, PL10 1EN
Tel: 01752 823900 Fax: 01752 823200
Email: info@multihullcentre.co.uk
www.multihullcentre.co.uk

VHF
ACCESS HW±3

Multihull Centre lies on the Cornish side of the River Tamar up the sheltered tidal inlet of Millbrook lake. The village of Millbrook has shops, pubs, fuel and public transport to Torpoint and Plymouth, the villages of Kingsand and Cawsand are less than 2 miles away. Mt Edgecumbe Country Park is close by.

The centre specialises in catamarans, trimarans, bilge keels and shoal draft craft. There are quay and pontoon berths and swinging moorings, all tidal (half tide). The Multihull Centre can provide moorings and storage ashore on its five acre site; facilities include a small chandlery, repairs, crane and lifting equipment.

FACILITIES AT A GLANCE

MYLOR CHANDLERY & RIGGING SERVICES
Mylor Yacht Harbour, Mylor Church Town, Falmouth, Cornwall. TR11 5UF
Tel: (01326) 375482
Email: info@mylorchandlery.co.uk
Website: www.mylorchandlery.co.uk
The best Stocked Chandlery & Rigging company in the South West.

2009/L10/v

JOHN MERRETT
I.ENG., A.M.R.I.N.A.
MARINE SURVEYOR

APPROVED SURVEYOR TO LEADING INSURANCE COMPANIES

ENGINEERING & STRUCTURAL SURVEYS UNDERTAKEN

30 YEARS EXPERIENCE IN TRADITIONAL BOAT BUILDING

2 Belmont Villas, Stoke, Plymouth PL3 4DP

Tel/Fax: 01752 564252
www.jmmarinesurveys.co.uk

2009/MG117/e

OCEAN ENGINEERING (FIRE) LTD
Unit 8A, Kernick Industrial Estate, Penryn, Cornwall TR10 9EP
Tel: 01326 378878
Fax: 01326 378870
Mob: 07814 879809
Email: errolhopkins@oceanengineering.co.uk
www.oceanengineering.co.uk
Lloyds approved marine fire engineers. Design, supply, installation and servicing of fire suppression systems, Co2, FM200, Pyrogen etc and portables throughout the south west.

2009/L11/v

R. PEARCE AND CO
St. Mary's House, Commercial Road, Penryn, Cornwall TR10 8AG
Tel: (01326) 375500
Fax: (01326) 374777
e-mail: admin@rpearce.co.uk
www.rpearce.co.uk
Marine surveyors & consulting engineers, UK & international services provided.

2009/Ext4/e

PADSTOW HARBOUR COMMISSIONERS
Tel: 01841 532239 Fax: 01841 533346
E-mail: padstowharbour@btconnect.com
Services include showers, toilets, diesel, water and ice, CCTV security.
Inner harbour controlled by tidal gate – open HW ±2hours – minimum depth 3 metres
Harbour Office, Padstow, Cornwall PL28 8AQ.
Website: www.padstow-harbour.co.uk

2009/MD1/e

1

MAYFLOWER MARINA

Mayflower International Marina
Ocean Quay, Richmond Walk, Plymouth, PL1 4LS
Tel: 01752 556633 Fax: 01752 606896
Email: info@mayflowermarina.co.uk

VHF	Ch 80
ACCESS	H24

Sitting on the famous Plymouth Hoe, with the Devon coast to the left and the Cornish coast to the right, Mayflower Marina is a friendly, well-run marina. Facilities include 24 hour access to fuel, gas and a launderette, full repair and maintenance services as well as an on site bar and brasserie. The marina is located only a short distance from Plymouth's town centre, where there are regular train services to and from several major towns and cities.

FACILITIES AT A GLANCE

Key
a Marina office
b Brokerage, chandlery
c Cafe
d Bar
e Brasserie
f Berth holders toilets and showers
g Harbour Master's office
h Riggers shop
i Engineers shop
j Picnic/BBQ area

Northern approach

Southern approach

ENDEAVOUR MARINE

2009/MG113/e

Mobile Marine Services

- Remote Underwater Inspections
- Antifouling
- Painting & Varnishing
- Boat Washing & Polishing
- Valeting
- Boat Management Packages
- Skippering and Crew Services

Your Pride, Our Passion

Phone: 07866561897
Email: info@endeavour-marine.co.uk

www.endeavour-marine.co.uk

Environmentally friendly

BioJet
Surface Preparation
We restore the original surface

MOBILE SODA BLASTING UNIT
ANTIFOULING REMOVAL SPECIALIST
REMOVAL OF ANTIFOULING COATINGS

Back to original gel, aluminium, wood, ferro or steel, or back to Epoxy System coating (Epoxy stays intact) from out-drives, sail-drives, jet-drives & other stern gear, without damage to rubber seals or hoses

REMOVAL OF PAINT COATINGS

From topsides and superstructures
From diesel, petrol or gas engines(kills grease & oil)

FIRE / MOULD DAMAGE

Cleans smoke and soot from fire damaged vessels, or mould from previously flooded or submerged vessels, plus its deoderising properties will neutralise the accompanying odours.

Mike Peonides   Mobile : 07866 019 178
Tel/Fax : 01752 297 461
email: biojet@blueyonder.co.uk

2009/MG116/e

WAYPOINT 1
MARINE ELECTRONICS LTD

Main Agents for:
Raymarine, Simrad, Silva, Mcmurdo,
Lowrance, Icom, Garmin, Mastervolt,
CMap, Navionics, Webasto, Penguin,
Frigoboat and many more.

We can supply and install Marine PC/
Software, Radar and Navigational Aids,
Instruments and Autopilots, Fishfinders,
Communications and Safety Equipment,
Audio - Visual, Heating, Air Con,
Refrigeration and more.

Your first port of call for
Marine Electronics

Ocean Building,
Queen Anne's Battery,
Plymouth, Devon, PL4 0LP
Tel 01752 661913 Fax 01752 661931
enquiries@waypoint-1.co.uk

Shop on-line at
www.waypoint-1.co.uk

2009/MG51/z

QUEEN ANNE'S BATTERY MARINA

Queen Anne's Battery
Plymouth, PL4 0LP
Tel: 01752 671142 Fax: 01752 266297
www.marinas.co.uk Email: qab@mdlmarinas.co.uk

VHF Ch 80
ACCESS H24

At the centre of Plymouth lies Queen Anne's Battery, comprising 280 resident berths as well as a visitor's basin with alongside pontoon berthing. All berths are well protected by a breakwater and double wavescreen.

As Plymouth Sound frequently provides the starting point for many prestigious international yacht races as well as the finish of the Fastnet Race, the marina is often crowded with racers during the height of the season and its vibrant atmosphere can at times resemble a mini 'Cowes'.

FACILITIES AT A GLANCE

Key
a Toilets and showers
b Royal Western Yacht Club
c Marina office and provisions shop
d Bar/restaurant
e Cafe

YACHT PARTS PLYMOUTH
01752 252489
www.yachtparts.co.uk
sales@yachtparts.co.uk
Queen Anne's Battery Marina
Plymouth PL4 0LP
TWO SHOPS - ONE AIM TO GET YOU - AND KEEP YOU ON THE WATER
YAMAHA 225 FOUR STROKE
AVON ZODIAC
The DINGHY & RIB Warehouse
01752 222265
www.dinghyandrib.co.uk
sales@dinghyandrib.co.uk
YAMAHA
2009/MG90/v

WestWays JEANNEAU FINNMASTER BOATS
QAB Marina, Plymouth, PL4 0LP • 01752 670770 • 45 Arwenack St, Falmouth, TR11 3JH • 01326 211771 • info@westways.co.uk
✔ South West Importers of New Jeanneau and Finnmaster Boats
✔ International Brokerage plus Used Yacht & Motorboat Sales
✔ Boat and Marina Berth Packages available in the South West
✔ Boat Maintenance and Management, Export Specialists
✔ Part Exchange, Finance & Insurance arranged, Chandlery
✔ Largest Boat Sales Operation in South West England
www.westways.co.uk
2009/MG149/e
Rigiflex • Cap Camarat • Leader • Merry Fisher • Prestige • Sun • Sunfast • Sun Odyssey • Finnmaster • Grandezza

SUTTON HARBOUR

Sutton Harbour
The Jetty, Sutton Harbour, Plymouth, PL4 0DW
Tel: 01752 204702 Fax: 01752 204693
Email: marina@sutton-harbour.co.uk
www.sutton-harbour.co.uk

VHF Ch 12
ACCESS H24

Boasting a superb location alongside Plymouth's famous Barbican centre, Sutton Harbour lies just north of Queen Anne's Battery Marina. The harbour can be entered 24 hours a day via a lock which is marked by green and red chevrons. Affording good shelter in 3.5m of water, it offers a comprehensive range of marine services, including a fuel berth that opens from 0800 to 1800.

Situated within a minute's walk from the marina is a Tourist Information Centre, providing all the necessary details of how best to explore the surrounding Devon countryside.

FACILITIES AT A GLANCE

Key
a Fish market
b National Marine Aquarium
c Customs House
d The Cove
e Marina office
f Lock tower

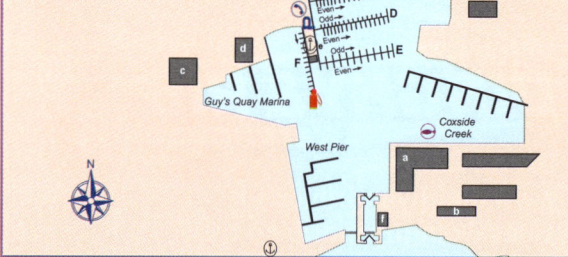

PLYMOUTH YACHT HAVEN

Plymouth Yacht Haven Ltd
Shaw Way, Mount Batten, Plymouth, PL9 9XH
Tel: 01752 404231 Fax: 01752 484177
www.yachthavens.com Email: plymouth@yachthavens.com

VHF Ch 80
ACCESS H24

Situated at the mouth of the river Plym, Plymouth Yacht Haven offers good protection from the prevailing winds and is within close proximity of Plymouth Sound. This 450 berth marina can accommodate vessels up to 45m in length and 7m draught. Members of staff are on site 24/7 to welcome you as a visitor and to serve diesel. 2008 sees the opening of a brand new bar and restaurant at the heart of the marina. Within easy access are coastal walks, a golf course, and health centre with heated swimming pool. The city of Plymouth and historic Barbican are a short water-taxi ride away.

With a 65ton travel hoist, undercover storage, and extensive range of marine services onsite, Plymouth Yacht Haven has the perfect yard for

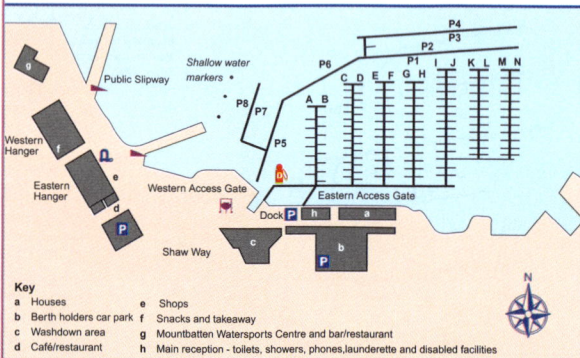

FACILITIES AT A GLANCE

Key
a Houses
b Berth holders car park
c Washdown area
d Café/restaurant
e Shops
f Snacks and takeaway
g Mountbatten Watersports Centre and bar/restaurant
h Main reception - toilets, showers, phones, launderette and disabled facilities

PLYMOUTH YACHT HAVEN

THE BRIDGE
BAR AND RESTAURANT

Now open at Plymouth Yacht Haven
Spectacular Views
Fine Dining
Open all day from 8am

Mount Batten, Plymouth
01752 403888
www.thebridgerestaurant.co.uk

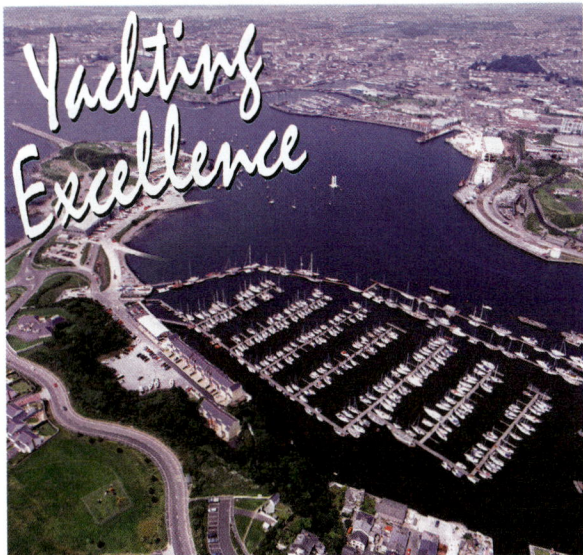

Yachting Excellence

PLYMOUTH YACHT HAVEN

Shaw Way
Mount Batten
PLYMOUTH PL9 9XH

Telephone: (01752) 404231
Fax: (01752) 484177

e-mail: plymouth@yachthavens.com
Website: www.yachthavens.com

2009/MG8/r

LIFERAFTS AND INFLATABLES

Service - Sales - Hire

Approved Service Centre

WE CAN COLLECT FROM AND RETURN TO YOUR VESSEL OR THE MARINA. ALL WORK GUARANTEED.

FOR FURTHER DETAILS:

C.E. Banyard Ltd.
Tamar Inflatables
01208 873777

ce.banyard@btconnect.com

2009/MG115/e

Dicky B Marine

Traditional shipwrights with over 30 years experience

Specialists in repairs and refits in wood and GRP

Professional project management · Teak decking-Teak joinery-Wooden spar makers · Blake's approved osmosis's treatment centre

Hull polishing-Varnishing-Anti fouling-Copper coating-Re paints · Bow and stern thrusters fitted · Bespoke stainless steel and aluminium fabrications

dickybmarine@aol.com   07780975806

Located in The Eastern Hanger at Plymouth Yacht Haven Marina

2009/MG114/e

NOSS MARINA

Noss Marina
Bridge Road, Kingswear, Devon, TQ6 0EA
Tel: 01803 839087 Fax: 01803 835620
Email: info@nossmarina.com
www.nossmarina.com

VHF	Ch 80
ACCESS	H24

Upstream of Dartmouth on the east shore of the River Dart is Noss Marina. Enjoying a peaceful rural setting, this marina is well suited to those who prefer a quieter atmosphere. Besides 180 fully serviced berths, 50 fore-and-aft moorings in the middle reaches of the river are also run by the marina, with mooring holders entitled to use all the facilities available to berth holders. During summer, a passenger ferry service runs regularly between Noss-on-Dart and Dartmouth, while a grocery service to your boat can be provided on request.

FACILITIES AT A GLANCE

Key
a Marina office
b Amenities

Higher Noss Creek

Noss Quay

Dinghy Park

Wardens Cottage

Lower Noss Creek

DART MARINA

Dart Marina
Sandquay Road, Dartmouth
Devon, TQ6 9PH
Tel: 01803 832580 Fax: 01803 835040
Email: yachtharbour@dartmarina.com www.dartmarina.com

VHF	Ch 80
ACCESS	H24

Annual berth holders enjoy the finest marina location in the West Country, with the atmosphere and facilities of an exclusive club. The Yacht Harbour on the River Dart is a perfect retreat for simply relaxing and an ideal base for local boating and more ambitious cruising further afield. During the season there are a limited number of visitors' berths available and a waiting list for the 110 annual berths. The berths are accessible at any tide and are located in peaceful surroundings, just a short walk along the riverfront from Dartmouth's historic centre.

The showers and bathrooms are of high quality and some first class facilities are conveniently onsite - the Wildfire Bistro, Health Spa, River Restaurant and quayside dining.

FACILITIES AT A GLANCE

Dart Marina Hotel

Waterside properties   Waterside properties

Hotel Terrace

Marine Engineering Looe

VOLVO PENTA
MARINE CENTRE

Unit 1 & 2, The Maypool Building, Dartside Quay, Galmpton Creek, Brixham, Devon. TQ5 0GL

Telephone No: 01803 844777
Fax No: 01803 845684

email: torbay@marine-engineering-looe.co.uk

Also at: Looe 01503 263009
Q.A.B. Plymouth 01752 226143

2008/M&WC24/e

Experience the delights of South Devon with

Plain Sailing
SAIL · MOTOR · POWER

- **RYA Training, for all your needs**
- **New Boat Sales Bavaria Yachts**
- **Brokerage, we can sell your yacht for you**
- **Chartering, come sail a yacht in the west country**
- **RBE, sail around Britain and qualify as a Yachtmaster**
- **Corporate Hospitality, we can organise fantastic sailing events**

for more information please visit www.plainsailing.co.uk
Tel: 01803 853 843 Email: enquiries@plainsailing.co.uk
Brixham Marina, Devon TQ5 9BP

2009/MG119/e

1

DARTHAVEN MARINA

Darthaven Marina
Brixham Road, Kingswear, Devon, TQ6 0SG
Tel: 01803 752545 Fax: 01803 752722
Email: darthaven@darthaven.co.uk
www.darthaven.co.uk

VHF	Ch 80
ACCESS	H24

Darthaven Marina is a family run business situated in the village of Kingswear on the east side of the River Dart. Within half a mile from Start Bay and the mouth of the river, it is the first marina you come to from seaward and is accessible at all states of the tide. Darthaven prides itself on being more than just a marina, offering a high standard of marine services with both electronic and engineering experts plus wood and GRP repairs on site. A shop, post office and five pubs are within a walking distance of the marina, while a frequent ferry service takes passengers across the river to Dartmouth.

FACILITIES AT A GLANCE

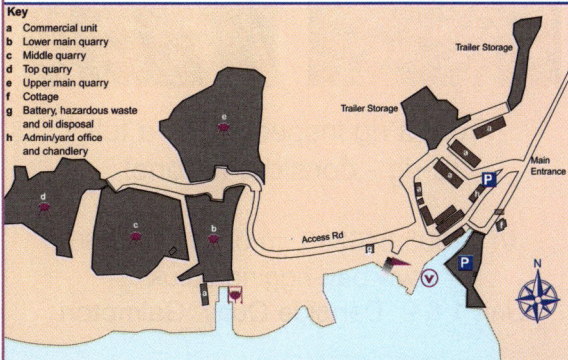

Key
a Main office
   Chandlery
   Electricians
b Shipwrights
c Engineers
d Passenger ferry pontoon
e Berthing office
f Welding workshop

The Ship Inn
"The Village Inn"
Higher Street KINGSWEAR TQ6 0AG
Tel: 01803 752348

2009/MG118/e

15th Century Inn with a superb local atmosphere.

CAMRA South Devon *Pub of the Year* 2006.
Good Beer Guide 2008.

Excellent local and national real ales, fine wines, traditional ciders and speciality whiskeys and cognacs.

Eat in the Ship Restaurant or on the Terrace Deck with spectacular views of the River Dart and Dartmouth – the very best of local fish, shellfish, farm meats and poultry.

Booking essential

It's where the locals eat and meet

Darthaven
... the full-service marina

Electrical & electronics

Engineering

35 tonne travel hoist

Fuel bug elimination

Chandlery

Shipwright & repair

VOLVO PENTA   DOOSAN   GARMIN   Raymarine   B&G   express lube   British Marine Federation

Darthaven Marina, Brixham Road, Kingswear, Dartmouth, Devon TQ6 0SG

Main office	01803 752242	Electrical & electronics	07767 250787
Berthing	01803 752545	Engineering	07973 280584
		Chandlery	01803 752733

www.darthaven.co.uk

2009/MG7/e

DARTSIDE QUAY

Dartside Quay
Galmpton Creek, Brixham, Devon, TQ5 0EH
Tel: 01803 845445 Fax: 01803 843558
Email: dartsidequay@mdlmarinas.co.uk

VHF	Ch 80
ACCESS	H24

Located at the head of Galmpton Creek, Dartside Quay lies three miles up river from Dartmouth.

In a sheltered position and with beautiful views across to Dittisham, it offers extensive boatyard facilities. The 7-acre dry boat storage area has space for over 300 boats and is serviced by a 65-ton hoist operating from a purpose-built dock, a 16-ton trailer hoist and 25-ton crane.

There are also a number of summer mud moorings available and a well stocked chandlery, in fact if the item you want is not in stock we can order it in for you.

FACILITIES AT A GLANCE

Key
a Commercial unit
b Lower main quarry
c Middle quarry
d Top quarry
e Upper main quarry
f Cottage
g Battery, hazardous waste and oil disposal
h Admin/yard office and chandlery

Trailer Storage
Trailer Storage
Main Entrance
Access Rd

2009/MG7/e

BRIXHAM MARINA

Brixham Marina
Berry Head Road, Brixham
Devon, TQ5 9BW
Tel: 01803 882929 Fax: 01803 882737
www.marinas.co.uk Email: brixham@mdlmarinas.co.uk

| VHF | Ch 80 |
| ACCESS | H24 |

Home to one of Britain's largest fishing fleets, Brixham Harbour is located on the southern shore of Tor Bay, which is well sheltered from westerly winds and where tidal streams are weak. Brixham Marina, housed in a separate basin to the work boats, provides easy access in all weather conditions and at all states of the tide. Established in 1989, it has become increasingly popular with locals and visitors alike, enjoying an idyllic setting right on the town's quayside.

Local attractions include a walk out to Berry Head Nature Reserve and a visit to the replica of Sir Francis Drake's ship, the *Golden Hind*.

FACILITIES AT A GLANCE

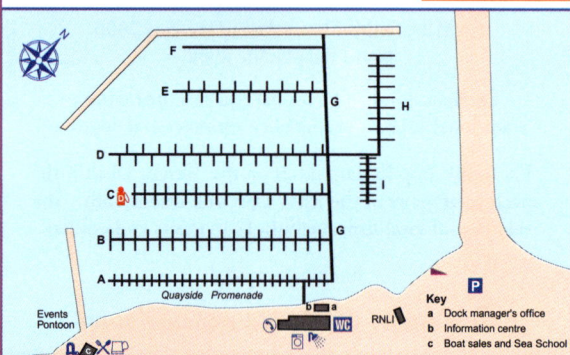

Key
a Dock manager's office
b Information centre
c Boat sales and Sea School

BRIXHAM MARINA

www.findmeaberth.co.uk

Don't miss out on the MDL experience. With 19 marinas in the UK, we're sure to be able to find your perfect berth

Bay Rigging

Yacht rigging services

From a rig inspection to a full re-rig - consider it done!

t/f 01803 846333 m 07816 925666
www.bay-rigging.co.uk
Unit 1 & 2 Dartside Quay Galmpton

2009/Mg14/v

WESTAWAY Sails

The Sail Loft,
Erme Bridge,
Ivybridge, Devon, PL21 9DU

Tel: 01752 892 560 Fax: 01752 895 575
sails@westawaysails.co.uk
www.westawaysails.co.uk

Manufacturers of racing, cruising and traditional sails

- Covers and Spray Hoods
- Repairs and alterations
- Collection, delivery and advice

1st for service and quality, design and technology

'The global company with the local accent'

2009/MG57/s

TORQUAY MARINA

Torquay Marina
Torquay, Devon, TQ2 5EQ
Tel: 01803 200210 Fax: 01803 200225
Emails: torquaymarina@mdlmarinas.co.uk

VHF Ch 80
ACCESS H24

Tucked away in the north east corner of Tor Bay, Torquay Marina is well sheltered from the prevailing SW'ly winds, providing safe entry in all conditions and at any state of the tide. Located in the centre of Torquay, the marina enjoys easy access to the town's numerous shops, bars and restaurants.

On the starboard hand near the harbour entrance is the borough council-owned Town Dock with limited visitor berths.

Torquay is ideally situated for either exploring Tor Bay itself, with its many delightful anchorages, or else for heading further west to experience several other scenic harbours such as Dartmouth and Salcombe. It also provides a good starting point for crossing to Brittany, Normandy or the Channel Islands.

FACILITIES AT A GLANCE

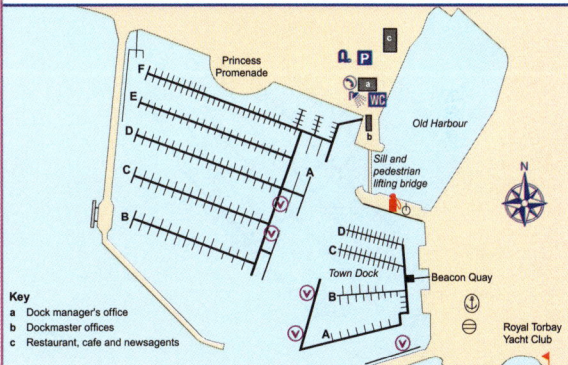

Key
a Dock manager's office
b Dockmaster offices
c Restaurant, cafe and newsagents

TORQUAY MARINA
www.findmeaberth.co.uk

Call **01803 200 210** for berthing here at Torquay, or at any other MDL Marina, and we'll let you know what's available right away.

or visit www.findmeaberth.co.uk and submit your request online.

2009/MG152/z

UPPER DECK MARINE/OUTRIGGERS

Chandlery, paint, rope, life jacket. Situated on visitors pontoon. Leading names in waterproofs and marine casuals.

Albert Quay, Fowey, Cornwall PL23 1AQ
Tel: 01726 832287 and 833233 Fax: 01726 833265
Website www.upper-deck.co.uk

2009/MD12/z

Shamrock Chandlery

What ever your budget, we've got it covered!

seaGo   SP   GOTOP   BALTIC LIFEJACKETS SWEDEN   XM
spinlock   SEBAGO
WEST SYSTEM   ECHOMAX   Barton MARINE   ADMIRALTY
PLASTIMO   SHAKESPEARE   BLAKES Paints   G   LALIZAS   International

To buy these and many other brands visit our new on-line shop

www.shamrock.co.uk

Then click on GO SHOPPING

Our extensively stocked Chandlery is open 7 days a week Winter and Summer
Shamrock Quay William Street
Southampton SO14 5QL

VISA   Maestro   MasterCard

Tel: 023 8063 2725

2009/MG128/e

PORTLAND MARINA

Portland Marina
Osprey Quay, Portland, Dorset, DT5 1DX
Tel: 08454 302012 Fax: 08451 802012
www.deanreddyhoff.co.uk
Email: sales@portlandmarina.co.uk

VHF	Ch 80
ACCESS	H24

Brand new for 2009, Portland Marina is an ideal location for both year-round berthing and weekend stopovers. The marina offers first class facilities including the highest quality washrooms, on-site bar and restaurant, sewage pump out, lift out up to 320t and storage, dry stack up to 10m, marine engineering, chandlery and rigging services, to name but a few, and 24-hour on-site security and CCTV. The 600 berth marina officially opens on 1 April 2009 but at the time of writing (July 2008) it has not been confirmed that the fuel berth will be open for the 2009 season so it is best to call ahead.

In the Olympic context, preparations are well advanced. The adjacent National Sailing Academy, a focal point for the Olympics, works closely with the marina to provide additional facilities on reclaimed land and berths for keelboats in the lee of a second rock breakwater.

FACILITIES AT A GLANCE

WEYMOUTH MARINA

Weymouth Marina
70 Commercial Road, Dorset, DT4 8NA
Tel: 01305 767576 Fax: 01305 767575
www.weymouth-marina.co.uk
Email: sales@weymouth-marina.co.uk

VHF	Ch 80
ACCESS	H24

With more than 280 permanent and visitors' berths, Weymouth is a modern, purpose-built marina ideally situated for yachtsmen cruising between the West Country and the Solent. It is also conveniently placed for sailing to France or the Channel Islands. Accessed via the town's historic lifting bridge, which opens every even hour 0800–2000 (plus 2100 Jun–Aug), the marina is dredged to 2.5m below chart datum. It provides easy access to the town centre, with its abundance of shops, pubs and restaurants, as well as to the traditional seafront where an impressive sandy beach is overlooked by an esplanade of hotels. More details can be found at www.weymouthmarina.co.uk.

FACILITIES AT A GLANCE

DEAN & REDDYHOFF LTD -
WEYMOUTH MARINA
Commercial Rd, Weymouth, Dorset DT4 8NA
Tel: (01305) 767576 Fax: (01305) 767575
e-mail: sales@weymouthmarina.co.uk
www.deanreddyhoff.co.uk
With its sandy beaches, beautiful Georgian esplanade and charming old harbour Weymouth is one of the South Coast's must-visit ports. The marina is conveniently located in the centre of town, only minutes from local pubs, restaurants and transport links, and offers excellent washroom facilities and 24-hour CCTV security.

2009/Ext2/z

PRIME
MOTOR YACHTS
BENETEAU
MAIN DEALER
www.primemotoryachts.co.uk
01305 766660
2009/MG169/z

MARINE ENGINES AND PARTS
BUKH - VOLVO - IVECO - LISTER / PETTER - JOHNSON - JABSCO
VETUS PARTS, M G DUFF ANODES
PROPELLOR & STERN GEAR SUPPLIES & REPAIRS
MARINE PAINTS - ANTI-FOULING ETC

ROVER MARINE SERVICES
Tel: 01305 781612

2009/MG86/z

ROVER MARINE SERVICES / W.L.B. COMPANY
SOUTH PARADE WEYMOUTH DORSET DT4 8DU • 01305 781612

DEAN & REDDYHOFF LTD -
PORTLAND MARINA
Osprey Quay, Portland, Dorset DT5 1DX
Tel: 08454 30 2012 Fax: 08451 80 2012
e-mail: sales@portlandmarina.co.uk
www.deanreddyhoff.co.uk
Brand new for 2009, Portland Marina is an ideal location for both year-round berthing and weekend stopovers. Part of the venue for the sailing events of the London 2012 Olympic and Paralympic Games, the marina offers first class facilities including the highest quality washrooms, on-site bar and restaurant, fuel pontoon, sewage pump out, lift out up to 320t and storage, dry stack up to 10m, marine engineering, chandlery and rigging services, to name but a few, and 24-hour on-site security and CCTV.

2009/Ext2/z

KINGFISHER MARINE
CHANDLERS • MARINE ENGINEERS • RIGGERS
BOAT BUILDING & REPAIRS • BOAT LIFTING

Kingfisher Marine is the one-stop chandlery store based on the waterfront in the heart of Weymouth.

Come in and browse through our impressive range of boat maintenance products, Admiralty charts and publications, electronics, clothing and safety products, rigid dinghies and inflatable boats; or **talk to the local experts** in marine engineering about our extensive on-site workshop facilities.

Boat building, repairs and boat lifting complete the comprehensive range of services all under one roof.

Whatever your boating requirements you're sure of a warm welcome.

MERCURY OUTBOARDS | Morse Controls | WALKER BAY | MERCURY MerCruiser
YANMAR marine | BLAKES Paints | HOLT | ADMIRALTY LEISURE

OPEN 7 DAYS A WEEK - ALL YEAR ROUND

51 Commercial Road, WEYMOUTH, Dorset, DT4 8AQ

Fax: 01305 766502 Email: sales@kingfishermarine.co.uk
or visit our website at www.kingfishermarine.co.uk
2009/MG106/v

A. D. GORDON
MODERN & TRADITIONAL YACHT RIGGING

Hand Splicing in Wire & Rope
Talurit Splicing
Roll Swaging
N.D.T. Rigging Terminal Testing

Tel/Fax: 01305 821569
Mobile: 07774 633419
Email: adgrigging@ukonline.co.uk
Units 8,9&10 St. Georges Centre, Reeforne, Portland, Dorset DT5 2HN

A. D. GORDON YACHT RIGGING
AGENT FOR SELDÉN Masts, Spars & Fittings
2009/MG49/s

Bussells Yacht Chandlers
SUPPLIERS OF ALL MARINE EQUIPMENT
30 Hope Street, Weymouth, Dorset DT4 8TU
Tel: (01305) 785633
2009/MG099/v

RemovALL ™
THE NAME SAYS IT ALL

Remove antifoul
& other marine coatings safely and effectively with
RemovAll 620

Eco-friendly - 100% biodegradable Safe on GRP, gel coat & skin!

For more details contact:
Cirrus Systems Ltd
136 South Way
Southwell Park
Portland
Dorset DT5 2NL
Tel: 01305 822659
www.cirrus-systems.co.uk
Cirrus SYSTEMS LTD
2009/mg166/v

WEYMOUTH HARBOUR

Weymouth & Portland Borough Council
North Quay, Weymouth, Dorset, DT4 8TA
Tel: 01305 838423 Fax: 01305 767927
Email: berthingoffice@weymouth.gov.uk

VHF Ch 12
ACCESS H24

Weymouth Harbour, which lies to the NE of Portland in the protected waters of Weymouth Bay, benefits from deep water at all states of the tide. If wishing to moor in the old Georgian outer harbour, you should contact the harbour authority, which also controls several municipal pontoons above the bridge. In recent years the facilities have been improved and now include electricity and fresh water on both quays, as well as free showers and a coin-operated launderette. Visiting yachtsmen are very welcome both at the Royal Dorset Yacht Club, situated on Customs House Quay in the inner harbour, and the Weymouth Sailing Club, on the south pier of the outer harbour.

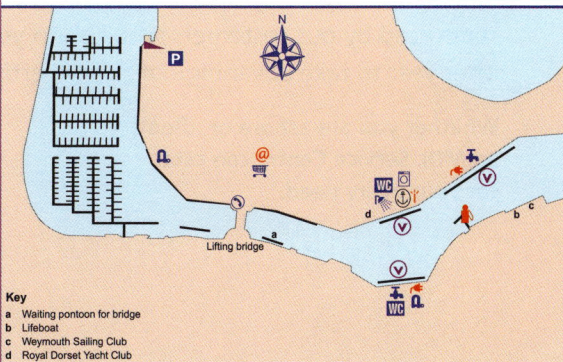

FACILITIES AT A GLANCE

Key
a Waiting pontoon for bridge
b Lifeboat
c Weymouth Sailing Club
d Royal Dorset Yacht Club

Lifting bridge

MDL Marine Service Centres

MAINTENANCE • REFITTING • MANAGEMENT
LIFTING • REPAIRS • STORAGE • BERTHING

Hamble Point

For sheer location alone, Hamble Point Marina is hard to beat. At the mouth of the River Hamble, with easy access to the world famous waters of the Solent, it's a favourite with racers and cruising yachtsmen alike.

☎ (023) 8045 2464

Saxon Wharf

Situated on Southamton's River Itchen, Saxon Wharf is a marine service centre offering outstanding facilities for superyachts and other large craft. It boasts a 200 ton boat hoist – the largest in the UK – and heavy duty, fully serviced pontoons.

☎ (023) 8033 9490

Dartside Quay

Tucked away at the head of Galmpton creek, Dartside Quay lies some three miles up river from Dartmouth. In a sheltered position and with beautiful views accros to Dittisham, it offers extensive facilities along with a chandlery.

☎ (01803) 845445

Each centre is recognised for its long tradition and experience in motorboat and yacht care, reinforced by our customers who return year after year to take advantage of this expertise.

Whether you are ashore or afloat, an MDL Service Centre can cater for your every need.

www.mdlmarinas.co.uk

2009/MG152/z

CENTRAL SOUTHERN ENGLAND - Anvil Point to Selsey Bill

2

ADLARD COLES NAUTICAL
WEATHER FORECASTS
BY FAX & TELEPHONE

Coastal/Inshore	2-day by Fax	5-day by Phone
South West	09065 222 348	09068 969 648
Mid Channel	09065 222 347	09068 969 647
Channel East	09065 222 346	09068 969 646
NE France	09065 501 611	09064 700 421
N France	09065 501 612	09064 700 422
N Brittany	09065 501 613	09064 700 423
Offshore	**2-5 day by Fax**	**2-5 day by Phone**
English Channel	09065 222 357	09068 969 657
Southern North Sea	09065 222 358	09068 969 658
Biscay	09065 222 360	09068 969 660

09064/68 CALLS COST 60P PER MIN. 09065 CALLS COST £1.50 PER MIN.

Key to Marina Plans symbols

Bottled gas		Parking
Chandler		Pub/Restaurant
Disabled facilities		Pump out
Electrical supply		Rigging service
Electrical repairs		Sail repairs
Engine repairs		Shipwright
First Aid		Shop/Supermarket
Fresh Water		Showers
Fuel - Diesel		Slipway
Fuel - Petrol		Toilets
Hardstanding/boatyard		Telephone
Internet Café		Trolleys
Laundry facilities		Visitors berths
Lift-out facilities		Wi-Fi

Area 2 - Central Southern England

MARINAS
Telephone Numbers
VHF Channel
Access Times

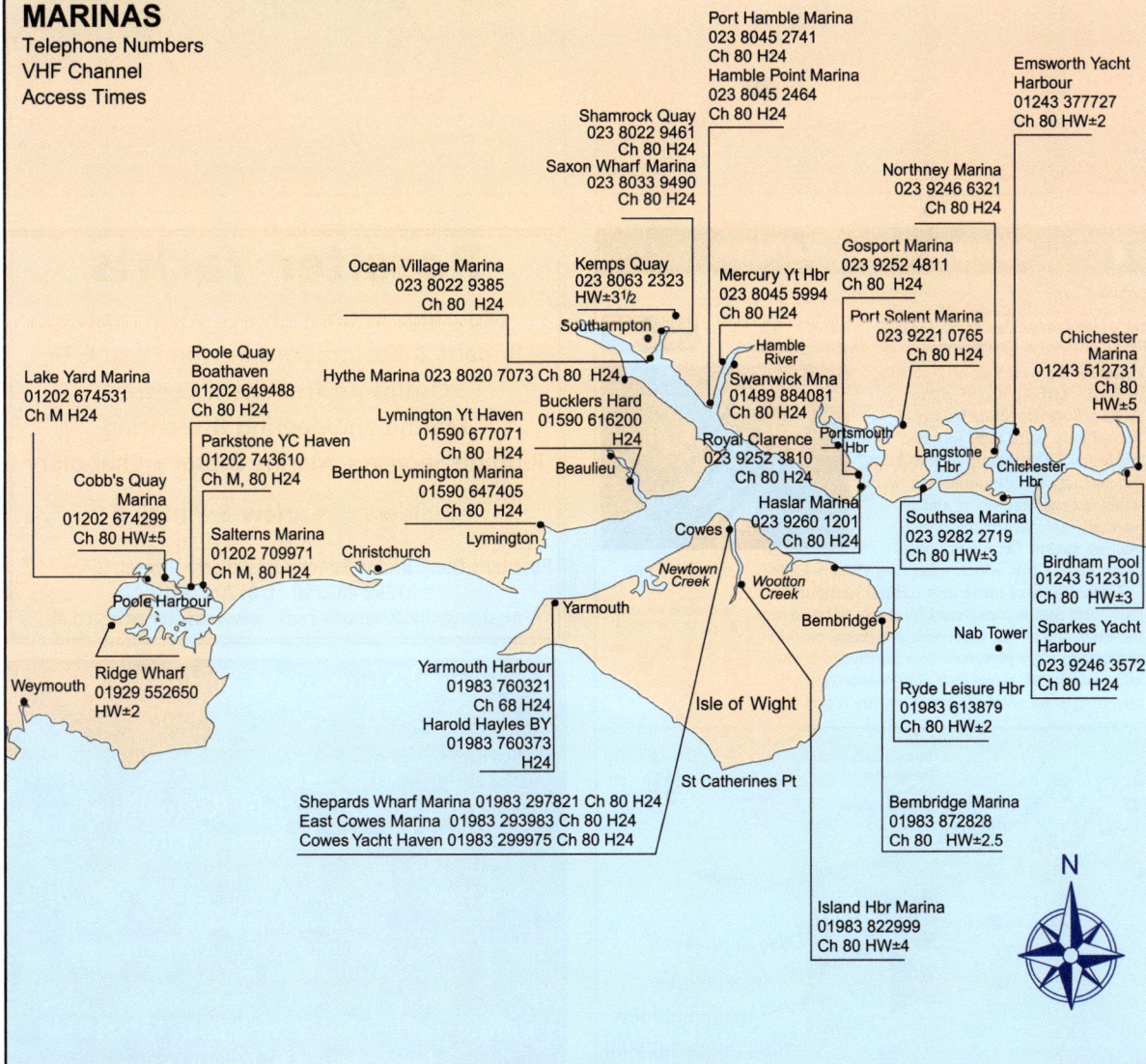

Port Hamble Marina
023 8045 2741
Ch 80 H24
Hamble Point Marina
023 8045 2464
Ch 80 H24

Emsworth Yacht
Harbour
01243 377727
Ch 80 HW±2

Shamrock Quay
023 8022 9461
Ch 80 H24
Saxon Wharf Marina
023 8033 9490
Ch 80 H24

Northney Marina
023 9246 6321
Ch 80 H24

Gosport Marina
023 9252 4811
Ch 80 H24

Ocean Village Marina
023 8022 9385
Ch 80 H24

Kemps Quay
023 8063 2323
HW±3½

Mercury Yt Hbr
023 8045 5994
Ch 80 H24

Port Solent Marina
023 9221 0765
Ch 80 H24

Chichester
Marina
01243 512731
Ch 80
HW±5

Southampton

Hamble
River

Lake Yard Marina
01202 674531
Ch M H24

Poole Quay
Boathaven
01202 649488
Ch 80 H24

Hythe Marina 023 8020 7073 Ch 80 H24,

Swanwick Mna
01489 884081
Ch 80 H24

Parkstone YC Haven
01202 743610
Ch M, 80 H24

Lymington Yt Haven
01590 677071
Ch 80 H24
Berthon Lymington Marina
01590 647405
Ch 80 H24

Bucklers Hard
01590 616200
H24

Royal Clarence
023 9252 3810
Ch 80 H24

Portsmouth
Hbr

Langstone
Hbr

Chichester
Hbr

Beaulieu

Cobb's Quay
Marina
01202 674299
Ch 80 HW±5

Salterns Marina
01202 709971
Ch M, 80 H24

Lymington

Christchurch

Haslar Marina
023 9260 1201
Ch 80 H24

Cowes

Southsea Marina
023 9282 2719
Ch 80 HW±3

Birdham Pool
01243 512310
Ch 80 HW±3

Weymouth

Ridge Wharf
01929 552650
HW±2

Poole Harbour

Newtown
Creek

Wootton
Creek

Yarmouth

Bembridge

Nab Tower

Sparkes Yacht
Harbour
023 9246 3572
Ch 80 H24

Yarmouth Harbour
01983 760321
Ch 68 H24
Harold Hayles BY
01983 760373
H24

Isle of Wight

Ryde Leisure Hbr
01983 613879
Ch 80 HW±2

Shepards Wharf Marina 01983 297821 Ch 80 H24
East Cowes Marina 01983 293983 Ch 80 H24
Cowes Yacht Haven 01983 299975 Ch 80 H24

St Catherines Pt

Bembridge Marina
01983 872828
Ch 80 HW±2.5

Island Hbr Marina
01983 822999
Ch 80 HW±4

N

RIDGE WHARF YACHT CENTRE

Ridge Wharf Yacht Centre
Ridge, Wareham, Dorset, BH20 5BG
Tel: 01929 552650 Fax: 01929 554434
Email: office@ridgewharf.co.uk

VHF	
ACCESS	HW±2

On the south bank of the River Frome, which acts as the boundary to the North of the Isle of Purbeck, is Ridge Wharf Yacht Centre. Access for a 1.5m draught is between one and two hours either side of HW, with berths drying out to soft mud. The Yacht Centre cannot be contacted on VHF, so it is best to phone up ahead of time to inquire about berthing availability.

A trip upstream to the ancient market town of Wareham is well worth while, although owners of deep-draughted yachts may prefer to go by dinghy. Tucked between the Rivers Frome and Trent, it is packed full of cafés, restaurants and shops.

LAKE YARD MARINA

Lake Yard Marina
Lake Drive, Hamworthy, Poole, Dorset BH15 4DT
Tel: 01202 674531 Fax: 01202 677518
Email: office@lakeyard.com www.lakeyard.com

VHF	Ch M
ACCESS	H24

Lake Yard is situated towards the NW end of Poole Harbour, just beyond the SHM No 73. The entrance can be easily identified by 2FR (vert) and 2FG (vert) lights. Enjoying 24 hour access, the marina has no designated visitors' berths, but will accommodate visiting yachtsmen if resident berth holders are away. Its on site facilities include full maintenance and repair services as well as hard standing and a 50 ton boat hoist, although for the nearest fuel go to Corralls (Tel 01202 674551), opposite the Town Quay. Lake Yard's Waterfront Club, offering spectacular views across the harbour, opens seven days a week for lunchtime and evening meals.

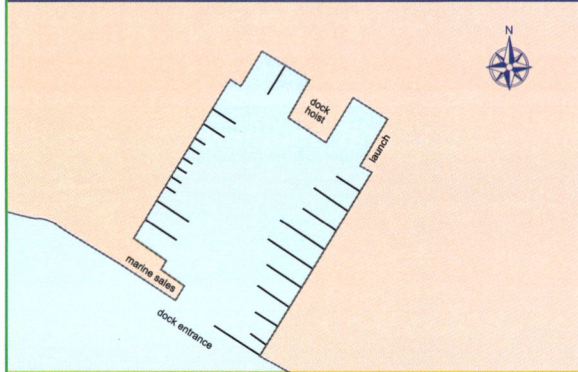

COBB'S QUAY MARINA

Cobb's Quay
Hamworthy, Poole, Dorset, BH15 4EL
Tel: 01202 674299 Fax: 01202 665217
Email: cobbsquay@mdlmarinas.co.uk www.marinas.co.uk

VHF	Ch 80
ACCESS	HW±5

Lying on the west side of Holes Bay in Poole Harbour, Cobb's Quay is accessed via the lifting bridge at Poole Quay. With fully serviced pontoons for yachts up to 25m LOA, the marina can be entered five hours either side of high water and is normally able to accommodate visiting yachts. On site is Cobb's Quay Yacht Club, which welcomes visitors to its bar and restaurant.

Poole is one of the largest natural harbours in the world and is considered by many to be among the finest. Its N side incorporates several modern marinas in close proximity to a multitude of shops and restaurants, while its S side boasts tranquil anchorages set within unspoilt nature reserves.

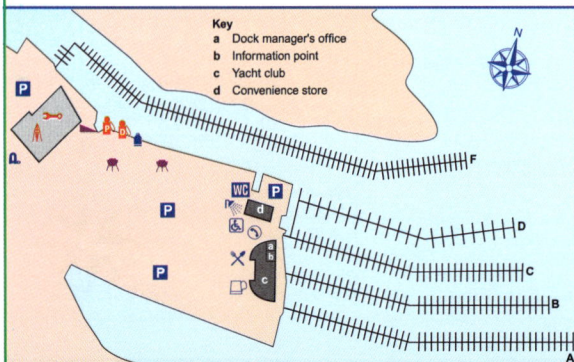

Rossiter Yachts

Moorings in Christchurch town centre
Repairs & Restorations in wood and GRP
Osmosure Treatment Centre
Marine engineering & servicing
Rigging Service + Marine Diesel + Chandlery

Builders of **Curlew** & **Pintail II**

Rossiter's Quay, Bridge Street, Christchurch, Dorset, BH23 1DZ.
t: 01202 483250 f: 01202 490164
rossiteryachts@hotmail.com www.rossiteryachts.co.uk

Traditional Shipwright Services Limited

Boat Building, Yacht Restoration and Marine Associated Joinery.
All aspects of wooden boat work undertaken.
New builds restoration and repairs using modern and traditional methods.
Painting, varnishing and general maintenance.
Mast and spar making.
Insurance and survey work welcome.
Office: 01202 748029 Mobile: 07723 319346
Email: paulk0611@aol.com

POOLE QUAY BOAT HAVEN

Poole Quay Boat Haven
Poole Town Quay, Poole, Dorset, BH15 1BT
Tel: 01202 649488 Fax: 01202 649488
Email: poolequayboathaven@phc.co.uk

VHF	Ch 80
ACCESS	H24

Once inside the Poole Harbour entrance small yachts heading for Poole Quay Boat Haven should use the Boat Channel running parallel south of the dredged Middle Ship Channel, which is primarily used by ferries sailing to and from the Hamworthy terminal. The marina can be accessed via the Little Channel and is easily identified by the large breakwater alongside the Quay. With deep water at all states of the tide the marina has berthing available for 125 yachts up to 30m, but due to its central location the marina can get busy so it is best to reserve a berth.

There is easy access to all of Poole Quay's facilities including restaurants, bars, Poole Pottery and the Waterfront Museum.

FACILITIES AT A GLANCE

Key
a Berthing office
b Showers/Toilets
c The Quay Hotel
d Fish landing area

Even nos - port side of pontoon
Odd nos - starboard side of pontoon

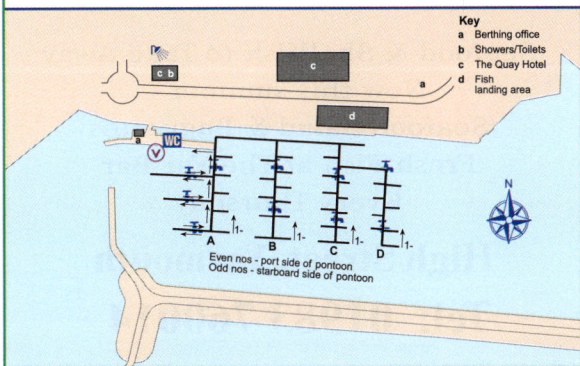

STEVENSON MOORINGS & MARINE SERVICES

DEEP WATER MOORINGS FOR HIRE

AVAILABLE LAKE PIER, HAMWORTHY PARK, ADJACENT TO WAREHAM CHANNEL(OPPOSITE LAKE PIER), POOLE YACHT CLUB, HOLES BAY
YACHTS UP TO 45FT ACCOMMODATED

ALSO MOORINGS SERVICED & LAID

CONTACT JOHN OR SARAH STEVENSON
TEL 01202 675738
MOBILE 07860 907663
FAX 01202 681944
EMAIL INFO@POOLEMOORINGS.CO.UK
14 LULWORTH AVENUE, POOLE BH15 4DQ
WWW.POOLEMOORINGS.CO.UK

2009/MG84/r

Ultimately, There Is Pursuit

New to the UK ! Pursuit Boats will be at the Southampton Show

Tel : 01202 890070
www.pursuit.boats.co.uk
sales@pursuitboats.co.uk

The award - winning range of Pursuit Boats are top quality craft built in Ft Pierce, Florida. Pursuit is a family-owned company with a long history going back to the early 1950s. There are Pursuit Centre Console and Offshore Cruisers from 23ft to 37ft (6.5m - 11m). Boats are in stock now at Salterns Marina in Poole. Full details and brochures are available from sales@pursuitboats.co.uk or come along and visit us at Berth 173 on the marina at the Southampton show.

2009/mg125/y

PARKSTONE YACHT CLUB HAVEN

Parkstone Yacht Club
Pearce Avenue, Parkstone, Poole, Dorset, BH14 8EH
Tel: 01202 743610 Fax: 01202 716394
Email: haven@parkstoneyachtclub.co.uk

| VHF | Ch M, 80 |
| ACCESS | H24 |

Situated on the north side of Poole Harbour between Salterns Marina and Poole Quay Boat Haven, Parkstone Yacht Club Haven can be entered at all states of the tides. Its approach channel has been dredged to 2.0m and is clearly marked by buoys. Run by the Parkstone Yacht Club, the Haven provides 200 deep water berths for members and visitors' berths. Other facilities include a bar, restaurant, new shower/changing rooms and wi-fi. With a busy sailing programme for over 2,500 members, the Yacht Club plays host to a variety of events including Poole Week, which is held towards the end of August.

FACILITIES AT A GLANCE

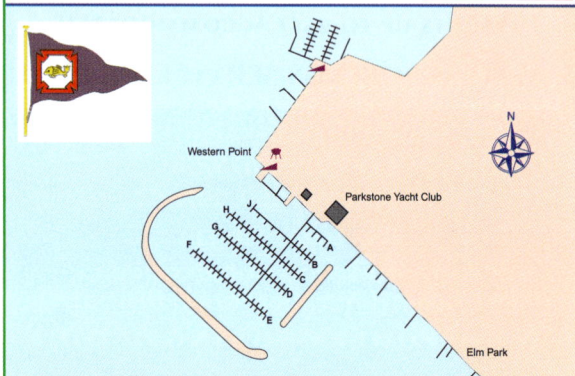

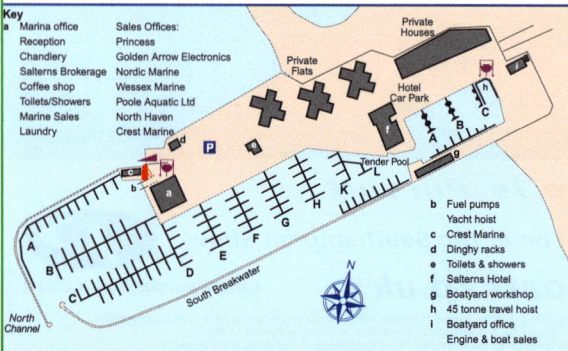

SALTERNS MARINA

Salterns Marina
40 Salterns Way, Lilliput, Poole
Dorset, BH14 8JR
Tel: 01202 709971 Fax: 01202 700398
Email: marina@salterns.co.uk www.salterns.co.uk

| VHF | Ch M, 80 |
| ACCESS | H24 |

Holding both the Blue Flag and Five Gold Anchor awards, Salterns Marina provides a service which is second to none. Located off the North Channel, it is approached from the No 31 SHM and benefits from deep water at all states of the tide. Facilities include 220 alongside pontoon berths as well as 75 swinging moorings with a free launch service. However, with very few designated visitors' berths, it is best to contact the marina ahead of time for availability. Fuel, diesel and gas can all be obtained 24 hours a day and the well-stocked chandlery, incorporating a coffee shop, stays open seven days a week.

FACILITIES AT A GLANCE

The Blue Crab Restaurant

Coffee, Light Lunches & Evening Meals
Specialising in Seafood & Game
Open 11am - 3pm &
6.30pm - 11pm

The Yar Bar

Seafood & Shellfish to Take Away
New this summer -
Seafood Salad & Baguettes
Fresh Fish at The Yar Bar
Every Thursday

High Street, Yarmouth
Tel: 01983 760014

SALTERNS ·CHANDLERY·

DIESEL   PETROL

Full Chandlery Facilities including Fuel, Gas, Clothing, Charts and Books

Ice ~ Food ~ Coffee Shop

Telephone: (01202) 701556
Facsimilie: (01202) 701556

Unit 4 Salterns Marina ~ Salterns Way
Lilliput ~Poole ~Dorset BH14 8JR

YARMOUTH HBR/HAROLD HAYLES BY

Yarmouth Harbour
Yarmouth, Isle of Wight, PO41 0NT
Tel: 01983 760321 Fax: 01983 761192
info@yarmouth-harbour.co.uk
www.yarmouth-harbour.co.uk

| VHF | Ch 68 |
| ACCESS | H24 |

Harold Hayles Ltd
The Quay, Yarmouth, Isle of Wight, PO41 0RS
Tel: 01983 760373 Fax: 01983 760666
Email: info@spurscutters.co.uk
www.spurscutters.co.uk

| VHF | |
| ACCESS | H24 |

The most western harbour on the Isle of Wight, Yarmouth is not only a convenient passage stopover but has become a very desirable destination in its own right, with virtually all weather and tidal access, although strong N to NE'ly winds can produce a considerable swell. The HM launch patrols the harbour entrance and will direct visiting yachtsmen to a pontoon berth or pile. The pretty harbour and town offer plenty of fine restaurants and amenities.

Walkashore pontoon moorings are available from the local boatyard, Harold Hayles Ltd, in the SW corner of the harbour. Pre-booking is preferred for both individuals or rallies.

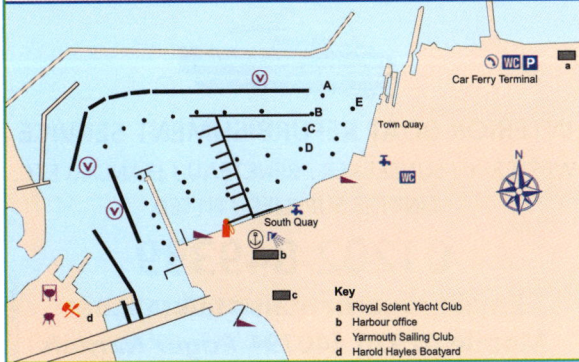

FACILITIES AT A GLANCE

Key
a   Royal Solent Yacht Club
b   Harbour office
c   Yarmouth Sailing Club
d   Harold Hayles Boatyard

Poole Harbour Sea Survival Ltd

COMPLETE SURVIVAL

6 PERS

- RYA Sea Survival
- VHF (SRC) Radio
- Radar
- First Aid
- ISAF Offshore Safety
- Diesel Engine
- RYA Theory

RYA Training Centre

Tel: 07766 222797
www.phsea-survival.co.uk

2009/MG48/s

CHRIS TEMPLE

MA (Cantab), I Eng, AMRINA, MYDSA

YDSA SURVEYOR

Over 30 years of experience

Prompt Professional Surveys & Consultancy

MCA Code of Practice Compliance Examinations

Tonnage Measurement for British Registration

Tel/Fax: 01983 760947 Mobile: 07980 550708
Email: chris@christemple@wanado.co.uk
Website: www.chris-temple-surveys.co.uk

2009/MG120/z

Maritime Enterprises (IoW) Ltd

Maritime Enterprises IoW

Mast, Spar and Block Making
Custom and Production Joinery
Cabinet and Pattern Making
Custom Bronzeware

Tel / Fax: 01983 761784

Saltern Wood Quay, Gasworks Lane
Yarmouth, Isle of Wight PO41 0SE

Mobile: 07979 686888
www.maritimeiow.co.uk
maritime.enterprises@btconnect.com

2009/MG122/e

LYMINGTON YACHT HAVEN

Lymington Yacht Haven
King's Saltern Road, Lymington, S041 3QD
Tel: 01590 677071 Fax: 01590 678186
Email: lymington@yachthavens.com www.yachthavens.com

VHF | Ch 80
ACCESS | H24

The attractive old market town of Lymington lies at the western end of the Solent, just three miles from the Needles Channel. Despite the numerous ferries plying to and from the Isle of Wight, the river is well sheltered and navigable at all states of the tide, proving a popular destination with visiting yachtsmen. LPG is available.

Lymington Yacht Haven is the first of the two marinas from seaward, situated on the port hand side. Offering easy access to the Solent, it is a 10-minute walk to the town centre and supermarkets.

FACILITIES AT A GLANCE

P Berth Holders

Key
c Owners store
d LYH office, brokerage, showers and laundry
e Haven Bar Bistro
f Yacht charter and sales
g Rigger
h Power boat sales
i Electronics
a Royal Lymington Yacht Club
b Lymington Town Sailing Club

LYMINGTON YACHT HAVEN

Perfectly situated at the mouth of the Lymington river giving instant access to the western Solent. Full marina services, boatyard, brokerage, diesel and petrol.

SPECIAL WINTER RATE NOV-FEB (Inclusive)

Tel: (01590) 677071• Fax: (01590) 678186
email: lymington@yachthavens.com
King's Saltern Rd, Lymington, Hampshire SO41 3QD

MARINE HEADLININGS

INTERIOR BOAT REFURBISHMENT SERVICE
WESTERLY / SUNSEEKER / BENETEAU / JEANEAU ETC.
LININGS SUPPLIED / FITTED

01202 849339

Email: rogernantais@talktalk.net
Mobile 07970 440794 *Roger Nantais*

GREENHAM REGIS

Means a Great Deal in
marine electronics

WWW.GREENHAM-REGIS.COM

SALES * SERVICE * INSTALLATION

MAIN SALES OFFICES

**KINGS SALTERN ROAD
LYMINGTON**
HANTS. SO41 3QD
TEL: 01590 671144
FAX: 01590 679517

**SHAMROCK QUAY
SOUTHAMPTON**
HANTS. SO14 5QL
TEL: 023 8063 6555
FAX: 023 8023 1426

ALSO AT

MAIN AGENTS FOR ALL THE LEADING MANUFACTURERS :- INCLUDING
Raymarine FURUNO SIMRAD
ICOM B&G tacktick
GARMIN BMEA

**EMSWORTH YACHT HARBOUR
EMSWORTH**
HAMPSHIRE
PO10 8BP
TEL: 01243 378314
FAX: 01243 378120

**UNIT 3, WEST QUAY ROAD
POOLE**
DORSET
BH15 1HX
TEL: 01202 676363
FAX: 01202 671031

**ITCHENOR SHIPYARD
CHICHESTER**
WEST SUSSEX
PO20 7AE
TEL: 01243 511070
FAX: 01243 511070

British Marine Federation

MEMBERS OF BOTH THE BRITISH MARINE ELETRONICS ASSOCIATION AND THE BRITISH MARINE FEDERATION

2

BERTHON LYMINGTON MARINA

Berthon Lymington Marina Ltd
The Shipyard, Lymington, Hampshire, SO41 3YL
Tel: 01590 647405 Fax: 01590 676353
www.berthon.co.uk Email: marina@berthon.co.uk

VHF Ch 80 ACCESS H24

Situated approximately half a mile up river of Lymington Yacht Haven, on the port hand side, is Lymington Marina. Easily accessible at all states of the tide, it offers between 60 to 70 visitors' berths, although its close proximity to the town centre and first rate services mean that it can get very crowded in summer.

Besides the numerous attractions and activities to be found in the town itself, Lymington also benefits from having the New Forest, with its wild ponies and picturesque scenery, literally on its doorstep. Alternatively, the Solent Way footpath provides an invigorating walk to and from Hurst Castle.

FACILITIES AT A GLANCE

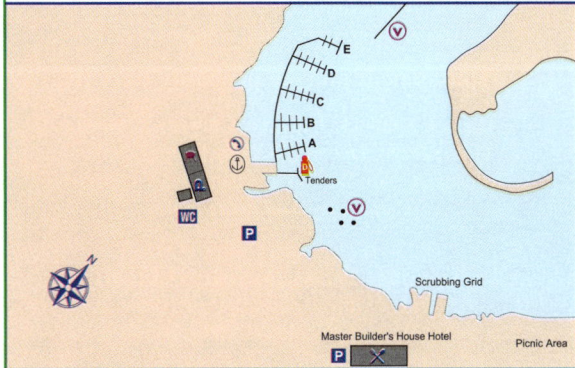

Key
a Dockmaster's office
b Berthon International
c Yacht maintenance & repair
d Building refit shed
e Anchor House
f Seaforth House
g Refueller

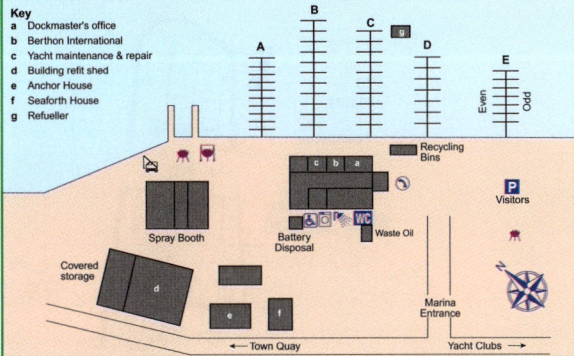

BUCKLERS HARD MARINA

Bucklers Hard
Beaulieu, Brockenhurst, Hampshire, SO42 7XB
Tel: 01590 616200 Fax: 01590 616211
www.bucklershard.co.uk Email: river@beaulieu.co.uk

VHF ACCESS H24

Meandering through the New Forest, the Beaulieu River is considered by many to be one of the most attractive harbours on the mainland side of the Solent. Two miles upstream from the mouth of the river lies Bucklers Hard, an historic 18th century village where shipwrights skilfully constructed warships for Nelson's fleet. The Maritime Museum, showing the history of boat-building in the village, is open throughout the year.

The marina is manned 24/7 and offers deep water to visitors at all states of the tide, although the bar at the river's entrance should be avoided two hours either side of LW.

FACILITIES AT A GLANCE

Bucklers Hard
BOAT YARD SERVICES

"The Little Yard with the Big Reputation"

- Classic Restoration
- Marine Engineering
- Yacht Painting
- CORGI LPG Engineering
- Raymarine/Simrad Dealers
- Lewmar Agent

"Catch them while you can!" Expert boat builders, marine engineers & yacht painting/varnishing technicians with hundreds of years combined knowledge & experience are available to work on your yachts.
Projects may be undertaken at discounted rates during late summer period.
Call for a free estimate. Contact Chris Clayton or Dave Blachford.

2009/MG136/z

Bucklers Hard Boat Builders Ltd
The Agamemnon Boat Yard, Bucklers Hard, Beaulieu, Hampshire SO42 7XB
Phone: (01590) 616214 Fax:: (01590) 616267
E-mail: info@bucklers.co.uk - Web site: http//www.bucklers.co.uk

When responding to adverts please mention the 2009 Marina Guide →

REEDS
DIRECTORY OF MARINAS, MARINE SUPPLIES & SERVICES
MARINA GUIDE 2009

PASCALL ATKEY & SON,
LIMITED. SHIP CHANDLERS
COWES, I.W.
ESTABLISHED 1799

Come to the longest established Ship Chandlers on the Island for the largest stocks of quality, branded sailing clothing, safety equipment, Admiralty and Imray Charts, shoes, code flags, fenders, ropes, shackles, compasses etc.

You name it and we probably have it!

Harken, Spinlock, Plastimo, Crewsaver, Musto, Gill, Sebago, Dubarry, XM Yachting, Lewmar, Ronstan, Casio, Watson, Leatherman, Victorinox, Canterbury *And many more*.

29 & 30 High Street, Cowes PO31 7RS
Tel: 01983 292381   Fax: 01983 292381
Email: info@pascallatkey.co.uk
Web: www.pascallatkey.com

2009/MG11/e

THE ISLAND SAILING CLUB

With the largest membership, the ISC is a friendly and very popular sailing club

We welcome all visiting sailors and new members to come and enjoy the ambience, hospitality, sailing and spectacular views

- Organiser of JPMorgan Asset Management Round-the-Island Race with 1,800 entrants.
- Tuesday night racing and supper throughout the Season
- Bar and Restaurant and balcony overlooking the Harbour
- 9 matched Sonar keel boats for hire
- Scrubbing slip up to 5 tons
- Refurbished accommodation available throughout the year

70 High Street Cowes   PO31 7RE   Tel 01983 296621

Email: admin@islandsc.org.uk   www.islandsc.org.uk

TO ADVERTISE PLEASE CALL 01983 245505
2009/MG94/z

"FOR ALL YOUR RIGGING & CHANDLERY NEEDS"

CHRIS HORNSEY
(Chandlery) Ltd

152 -154 EASTNEY ROAD
SOUTHSEA
HAMPSHIRE
PO4 8DY
Tel: 02392 734728
Fax: 02392 611500
E-mail: sales@chishornsey.com

2009/MG16/v

COWES YACHT HAVEN

Cowes Yacht Haven
Vectis Yard, Cowes, Isle of Wight, PO31 7BD
Tel: 01983 299975 Fax: 01983 200332
www.cowesyachthaven.com
Email: berthing@cowesyachthaven.com

VHF Ch 80
ACCESS H24

Situated virtually at the centre of the Solent, Cowes is best known as Britain's premier yachting centre and offers all types of facilities to yachtsmen. Cowes Yacht Haven, operating 24 hours a day, has very few permanent moorings and is dedicated to catering for visitors and events. At peak times it can become very crowded and for occasions such as Skandia Cowes Week you need to book up in advance.

FACILITIES AT A GLANCE

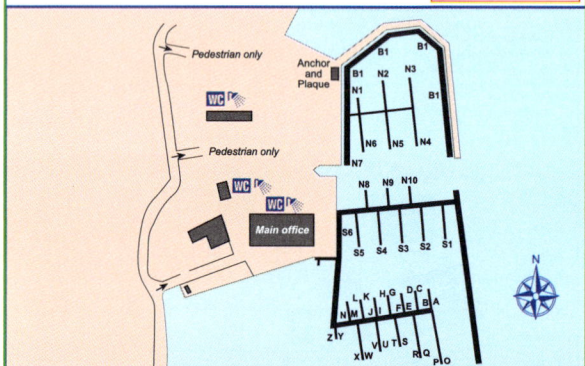

COWES YACHT HAVEN
the home of international boating since 1800

The Reputation The Location The People

Boatyard Facilities Include...
- 250 fully serviced berths
- 30 ton hoist & 15 ton mobile crane
- Free Wireless Broadband Internet access
- Seasonal packages for winter berthing & dry sailing

Shoreside Activities Include...
- Haven Events Centre for all your Hospitality & Events needs
- Conferences
- Seminars & Meetings
- Product Launches
- Exhibitions
- Parties & Weddings
- Boatshed Bar & Terrace

For more information visit:
www.cowesyachthaven.com
Tel: +44 (0) 1983 299975 or
Email: info@cowesyachthaven.com

2009/MG99/v

2

LIGNU MARIS

Wooden Boat Specialists

Repairs, Refits, Fits Outs & Restorations

4 Kingston Works
Kingston Road
East Cowes
I.O.W Po32 6HE

Tel:
0787 1824671
0788 0894275

2009/mG75/v

EAST COWES MARINA

East Cowes Marina
Britannia Way, East Cowes, Isle of Wight, PO32 6UB
Tel: 01983 293983 Fax: 01983 299276
www.eastcowesmarina.co.uk
Email: miket@eastcowesmarina.co.uk

VHF Ch 80
ACCESS H24

Accommodating around 230 residential yachts and 160 visiting boats, East Cowes Marina is situated on the quiet and protected east bank of the Medina River, about a quarter mile above the chain ferry. The on-site chandlery stocks essential marine equipment and a small convenience store is just five minutes walk away. The brand new *club style* centrally heated shower and toilet facilities ensure the visitor a warm welcome at any time of the year, as does the on-site bar and restaurant.

Several water taxis provide a return service to Cowes, ensuring a quick and easy way of getting to the town centre.

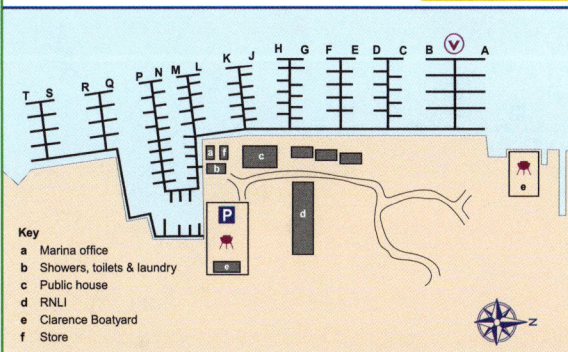

FACILITIES AT A GLANCE

Key
a   Marina office
b   Showers, toilets & laundry
c   Public house
d   RNLI
e   Clarence Boatyard
f   Store

KEVIN MOLE
OUTBOARDS & CHANDLERY

• Customer Mooring and Parking • Chandlery
• Outboard Sales and Service • Electrical Repairs and Installations • Inflatable/Tube Repairs
• Sales of RIBS, Tenders, Dinghies, Canoes, Kayaks

Agents for Yamaha, Suzuki Outboards, XS, Ribeye, Valiant, Avon, Zodiac, Quicksilver RIBS, Plastimo/XM Dinghies & Tenders, West Port Fishing Boats, Emotion, Pelican, Prijon, Typhoon, Teksport Canoes & Kayaks. All this and much more.

10 Medina Court, Cowes, Isle of Wight PO31 7XD
01983 289699   kevinmole@outboards.uk.com   www.outboards.uk.com

2009/MG105/v

Welcome to chandlerystore.co.uk brought to you by Aquatogs chandlery of Cowes

Our website covers all aspects of boating, specialising in marine clothing, footwear and chandlery with free delivery to the UK.

Products stocked in our store are Musto, Henri Llloyd, Gill, Dubarry, Sebago, Quayside, Crewsaver, Spinlock, Harken, Lewmar, Marlow, Gerber, Leatherman, Tilley and Seago.

Our top brands of deck shoes and sailing boots include Dubarry, Sebago, Quayside, Musto, Gill and Henri Lloyd.

Now, Chandlerystore.co.uk offers you the exciting opportunity to purchase your choice of foul weather clothing, footwear, chandlery and accessories easily and securely, and have it delivered to you

2009/MG324/e

ROWLOCKS CHANDLERY
Tel 01983-299800
Email rowlockschandler@aol.com

Chandlery, Provisions, Gas

"If we don't have it, we can get it"

In East Cowes Marina,
55-57 Britannia Way, East Cowes,
Isle of Wight PO32 6DG

2009/MG83/e

DEAN & REDDYHOFF LTD - EAST COWES MARINA
Britannia Way, East Cowes, Isle of Wight PO32 6HA
Tel: (01983) 293983
Fax: (01983) 299276
e-mail: sales@eastcowesmarina.co.uk
www.deanreddyhoff.co.uk

Perfectly situated upstream of Cowes town centre, the marina offers sheltered berthing, luxurious washroom facilities and an excellent on-site pub/restaurant. With dedicated visitors' berths, barbeques, marquee and children's grass play area, visiting boats will receive a warm welcome.

2009/Ext2/z

SHEPARDS WHARF MARINA

Shepards Wharf Boatyard
Medina Road, Cowes, Isle of Wight, PO31 7HT
Tel: 01983 297821 Fax: 01983 294814
www.shephards.co.uk

VHF Ch 80
ACCESS H24

A cable upstream of Cowes Yacht Haven, still on the starboard side, is Shepards Wharf. Incorporating several visitor pontoon berths, its facilities include water as well as full boatyard services ranging from a chandler and sailmaker to a 20-ton boat hoist. Fuel can be obtained from Lallows Boatyard (Tel 01983 292111) or Cowes Yacht Haven. For berthing availability, visiting yachtsmen should contact Cowes Harbour Control on VHF Ch 69 or Tel 01983 293952.

Shepards Wharf is within easy walking distance of Cowes town centre, where among the restaurants to be highly recommended are the Red Duster and Murrays Seafoods on the High Street and Tonino's on Shooters Hill. Also worth visiting are the Maritime Museum, exhibiting the Uffa Fox boats *Avenger* and *Coweslip*, and the Sir Max Aitken Museum. Sir Max contributed enormously to ocean yacht racing and the museum is dedicated to his collection of nautical instruments, paintings and maritime artefacts.

FACILITIES AT A GLANCE

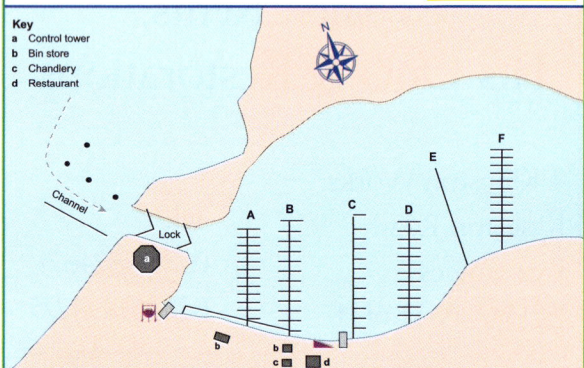

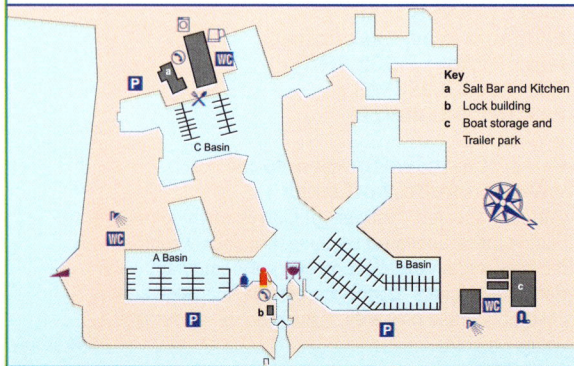

ISLAND HARBOUR MARINA

Island Harbour Marina
Mill Lane, Binfield, Newport, Isle of Wight, PO30 2LA
Tel: 01983 822999 Fax: 01983 526020
Email: info@island-harbour.co.uk

VHF Ch 80
ACCESS HW±4

Situated in beautiful rolling farmland about half a mile south of Folly Inn, Island Harbour Marina provides around 200 visitors' berths. Protected by a lock that is operated daily from 0700 – 2100 during the summer and from 0800 – 1730 during the winter, the marina is accessible for about four hours either side of HW for draughts of 1.5m.

Due to its remote setting, the marina's on site restaurant also sells essential provisions and newspapers. A half hour walk along the river brings you to Newport, the capital and county town of the Isle of Wight.

FACILITIES AT A GLANCE

Key
a   Control tower
b   Bin store
c   Chandlery
d   Restaurant

HYTHE MARINA

Hythe Marina Village
Shamrock Way, Hythe, Southampton, SO45 6DY
Tel: 023 8020 7073 Fax: 023 8084 2424
www.marinas.co.uk Email: d.wilson@mdlmarinas.co.uk

VHF Ch 80
ACCESS H24

Situated on the western shores of Southampton Water, Hythe Marina Village is approached by a dredged channel leading to a lock basin. The lock gates are controlled 24 hours a day throughout the year, with a waiting pontoon to the south of the approach basin.

Hythe Marina Village incorporates full marine services as well as on site restaurants and shops. Forming an integral part of the New Forest Waterside, Hythe is the perfect base from which to explore Hampshire's pretty inland villages and towns, or alternatively you can catch the ferry to Southampton's Town Quay.

FACILITIES AT A GLANCE

Key
a   Salt Bar and Kitchen
b   Lock building
c   Boat storage and Trailer park

ATLANTIC REFRIGERATION LTD

Refrigeration and Air-Conditioning

Atlantic Refrigeration Ltd. designs, manufactures, and installs a wide range of refrigeration equipment throughout the marine industry and used by many of the leading shipping lines. Since its inception in 1984 Atlantic refrigeration Ltd. has accumulated experience spanning all aspects of industrial and commercial refrigeration and air conditioning through the successful completion of many varied contracts on all types of vessels including:- Major installations on cruise ships, design and building of specialist cooling equipment for the sub-sea cable industry and the installation of yacht refrigeration equipment. Contact us now or visit our website for more information

www.atlanticrefrigeration.co.uk

ATLANTIC REFRIGERATION LTD
Peel Street, Northam, Southampton SO14 5QT
Tel:023 8033 9141 Fax:023 8022 9840 Email:office@atlantic-refrig.co.uk

ATLANTIC REFRIGERATION
Since 1984, many of the world's leading shipping lines have relied on Atlantic Refrigeration Ltd for design, manufacture, supply and installation of a wide range of refrigeration equipment and associated spares.
Atlantic Refrigeration Ltd will respond quickly and efficiently to emergency and service requirements throughout the marine industry in the UK and overseas.

2009/MG140/z

OCEAN VILLAGE MARINA

Ocean Village Marina
2 Channel Way, Southampton, SO14 3TG
Tel: 023 8022 9385 Fax: 023 8023 3515
www.marinas.co.uk Email: oceanvillage@mdlmarinas.co.uk

VHF	Ch 80
ACCESS	H24

The entrance to Ocean Village Marina lies on the port side of the River Itchen, just before the Itchen Bridge. With the capacity to accommodate large yachts and tall ships, the marina, accessible 24 hours a day, is renowned for hosting the starts of the Volvo and BT Global Challenge races. Situated at the heart of a waterside development incorporating shops, cinemas, restaurants and housing as well as The Royal Southampton Yacht Club, Ocean Village offers a vibrant atmosphere along with high quality service.

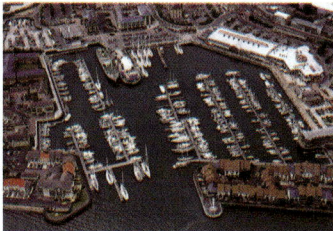

FACILITIES AT A GLANCE

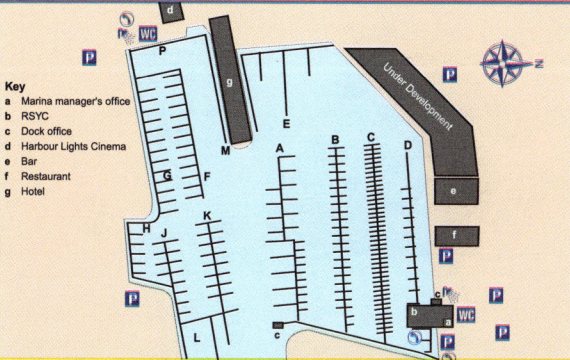

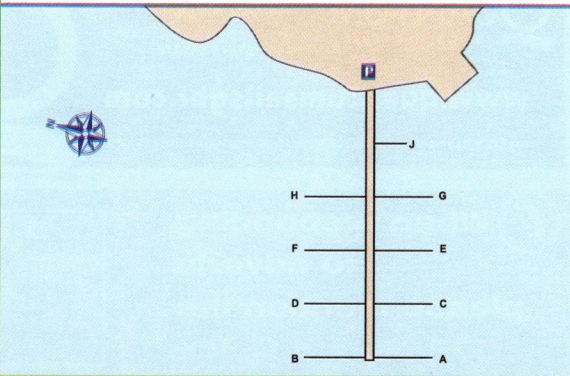

Key
a Marina manager's office
b RSYC
c Dock office
d Harbour Lights Cinema
e Bar
f Restaurant
g Hotel

SHAMROCK QUAY MARINA

Shamrock Quay Marina
William Street, Northam, Southampton, Hants, SO14 5QL
Tel: 023 8022 9461 Fax: 023 8021 3808
Email: shamrockquay@mdlmarinas.co.uk

VHF	Ch 80
ACCESS	H24

Shamrock Quay, lying upstream of the Itchen Bridge on the port hand side, offers excellent facilities to yachtsmen. It also benefits from being accessible 24 hours a day, although the inside berths can get quite shallow at LWS. Note that it is best to arrive at slack water as the cross tide can be tricky when close quarter manoeuvring.

The city centre is about two miles away, where among the numerous attractions are the Maritime Museum at Town Quay, the Medieval Merchant's House in French Street and the Southampton City Art Gallery in the Civic Centre.

FACILITIES AT A GLANCE

Key
a Office, bar and restaurant
b Marina office
c Cafe

KEMPS QUAY

Kemp's Shipyard Ltd
Quayside Road, Southampton, SO18 1BZ
Tel: 023 8063 2323 Fax: 023 8022 6002
Email: enquiries@kempsquay.com

VHF	
ACCESS	HW±3.5

At the head of the River Itchen on the starboard side is Kemps Quay, a family-run marina with a friendly, old-fashioned feel. Accessible only 3½ hrs either side of HW, it has a limited number of deep water berths, the rest being half tide, drying out to soft mud. Its restricted access is, however, reflected in the lower prices.

Although situated on the outskirts of Southampton, a short bus or taxi ride will soon get you to the city centre. Besides a nearby BP Garage selling bread and milk, the closest supermarkets can be found in Bitterne Shopping Centre, which is five minutes away by bus.

FACILITIES AT A GLANCE

MP marinapower
electrical installation & repairs

Along with Sargent Marine, we carried out the electrical & electronic refit of 'GEE', the winner of the Historic Class in the 2008 round of Britain's Power Boat Race.

185

- Batteries
- Electronic Installations
- Radar & GPS
- Re-wires

- Audio & TV
- Chargers & Inverters
- Generators Solar and Wind

APPROVED SUPPLIERS & INSTALLERS FOR:

STUDER   Raymarine
MASTERVOLT   SIMRAD

Shamrock Quay, Southampton, Hampshire SO14 5QL
Contact David Mclean: +44 (0)7919 522226 or 02380 332123
fax 02380 331956

2009/MG129/azz

SAXON WHARF MARINA

Saxon Wharf Marina
Lower York Street, Northam
Southampton, SO14 5QF
Tel: 023 8033 9490 Fax: 023 8033 5215
www.marinas.co.uk Email: m.leigh@mdlmarinas.co.uk

VHF Ch 80
ACCESS H24

Saxon Wharf is a relatively new development which is situated towards the top of the River Itchen at the head of Southampton Water. Equipped with 50-metre marina berths and heavy duty pontoons, it is intended to accommodate superyachts and larger vessels. Boasting a 200-ton boat hoist and several marine specialists, including Southampton Yacht Services, it is the ideal place for the refit and restoration of big boats, whether it be a quick liftout or a large scale project. Located close to Southampton city centre and airport, Saxon Wharf is easily accessible by road, rail or air.

FACILITIES AT A GLANCE

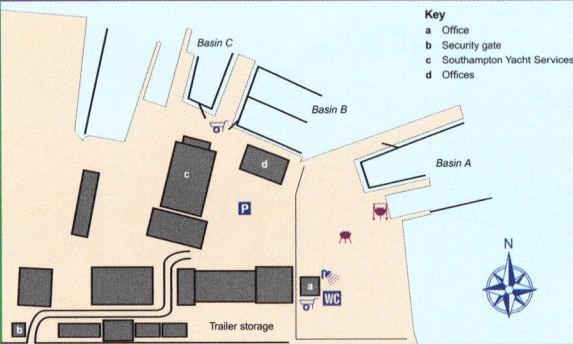

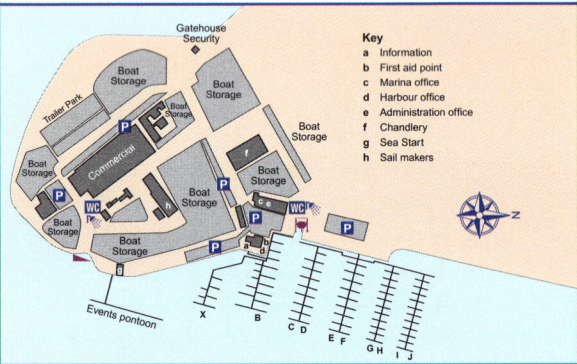

Key
a Office
b Security gate
c Southampton Yacht Services
d Offices

HAMBLE POINT MARINA

Hamble Point Marina
School Lane, Hamble, Southampton, SO31 4NB
Tel: 023 8045 2464 Fax: 023 8045 6440
Email: hamblepoint@mdlmarinas.co.uk

VHF Ch 80
ACCESS H24

Situated virtually opposite Warsash, this is the first marina you will come to on the western bank of the Hamble. Accommodating yachts up to 20m and power boats to 25m in length, it offers easy access to the Solent.

As with all the berths in the Hamble, be careful when manoeuvring at certain states of the tide and if possible try to avoid berthing when the tide is ebbing strongly. Boasting extensive facilities, the marina is within a 15-minute walk of Hamble Village, where services include a plethora of pubs and restaurants as well as a post office, bank and general store.

FACILITIES AT A GLANCE

Key
a Information
b First aid point
c Marina office
d Harbour office
e Administration office
f Chandlery
g Sea Start
h Sail makers

YACHT & MOTOR BOAT SERVICES

M D L T E N A N T

- Professional Boat & Vehicle Valating, Buff Up & Polishing
- Painting, Varnishing
- Anti Foul Stripping & Anti Fouling
- Osmosis Prevention
- Teak Deck Brightening
- Step Un Step Mast
- Minor Fibre Glass Repairs
- Keel Repairs
- Race Boat Preparations
- General Maintenance
- Install Bow Thrusters & Holding Tanks
- Copper Bottoms

~ Competitive Service with no VAT ~

Also Powerboat Charters
INSURED UPTO £2,000,000

Tel: 07802 442671
Email: yachtservices@btconnect.com

Hamble Sailing Services in association with Hamble Cover Services Ltd
Upholstery Boat Covers
Tel: 023 8045 5868
Tel: 023 8045 6354
sales@hamblesailingservices.co.uk
Mercury Yacht Harbour, Satchell Lane, Hamble, SO31 4HQ
www.hamblesailingservices.co.uk
2009/MG26/v

QUANTUM SAIL DESIGN GROUP
Quantum GBR South (Hamble) +44 (0)23 8045 8213
Quantum GBR East (Ipswich) +44 (0)1473 659878
www.quantumsailsgbr.com
Find Quantum sail lofts worldwide at www.quantumsails.com
2009/md10/v

When responding to adverts please mention the 2009 Marina Guide
REEDS

PORT HAMBLE MARINA

Port Hamble Marina
Satchell Lane, Hamble, Southampton, SO31 4QD
Tel: 023 8045 2741 Fax: 023 8045 5206
Email: porthamble@mdlmarinas.co.uk www.marinas.co.uk

VHF Ch 80
ACCESS H24

On the west bank of the River Hamble, Port Hamble is the closest marina to the picturesque Hamble Village, therefore proving extremely popular with visiting yachtsmen. However, with no dedicated places for visitors, berthing availability is often scarce in the summer and it is best to contact the marina ahead of time.

Besides exploring the River Hamble, renowned for its maritime history which began as far back as the ninth century when King Alfred's men sank some 20 Viking long ships at Bursledon, other nearby places of interest include the 13th century Netley Abbey, allegedly haunted by Blind Peter the monk, and the Royal Victoria Country Park.

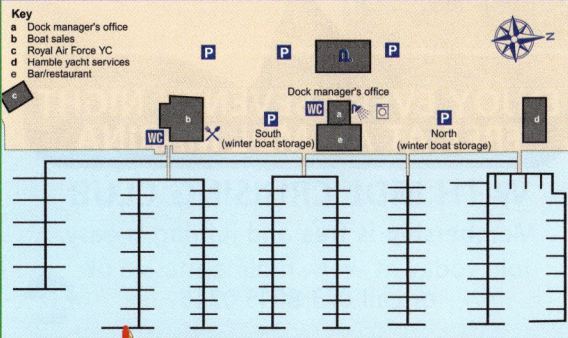

FACILITIES AT A GLANCE

Key
a Dock manager's office
b Boat sales
c Royal Air Force YC
d Hamble yacht services
e Bar/restaurant

Dock manager's office

South
(winter boat storage)

North
(winter boat storage)

MERCURY YACHT HARBOUR

Mercury Yacht Harbour
Satchell Lane, Hamble, Southampton, SO31 4HQ
Tel: 023 8045 5994 Fax: 023 8045 7369
Email: mercury@mdlmarinas.co.uk www.marinas.co.uk

VHF Ch 80
ACCESS H24

Mercury Yacht Harbour is the third marina from seaward on the western bank of the River Hamble, tucked away in a picturesque, wooded site adjacent to Badnam Creek. Enjoying deep water at all states of the tide, it accommodates yachts up to 24m LOA and boasts an extensive array of facilities.

Hamble Village is at least a 20-minute walk away, although the on site chandlery does stock a small amount of essential items, and for a good meal you need look no further than the Oyster Quay bar and restaurant whose balcony offers striking of the water.

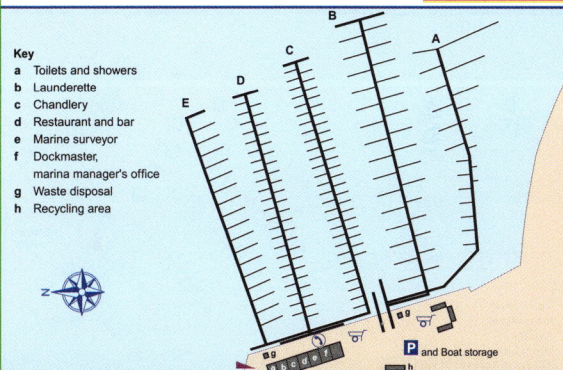

FACILITIES AT A GLANCE

Key
a Toilets and showers
b Launderette
c Chandlery
d Restaurant and bar
e Marine surveyor
f Dockmaster,
    marina manager's office
g Waste disposal
h Recycling area

P and Boat storage

PORT HAMBLE MARINA

www.findmeaberth.co.uk

Don't miss out on the MDL experience. With 19 marinas in the UK we're sure to be able to find you a berth.

Call (023) 8045 2741 for enquiries
• Berthing at any MDL Marina
• Dry stack berthing
• Boat lifting and yard services

And we'll let you know what's available right away.

or visit www.findmeaberth.co.uk and submit your request online.

2009/MG152/z

SWANWICK MARINA

Swanwick Marina
Swanwick, Southampton, Hampshire, SO31 1ZL
Tel: 01489 884081 Fax: 01489 579073
Email: swanwick@premiermarinas.com
www.premiermarinas.com

VHF Ch 80
ACCESS H24

Situated on the east bank of the River Hamble next to Bursledon Bridge, Swanwick Marina is accessible at all states of the tide and can accommodate yachts up to 20m LOA.

The marina's fully-licensed bar and bistro, Velshedas, overlooking the river, is open for breakfast, lunch and dinner during the summer. Alternatively, just a short row or walk away is the celebrated Jolly Sailor pub in Bursledon on the west bank, made famous for being the local watering hole in the British television series *Howard's Way*.

FACILITIES AT A GLANCE

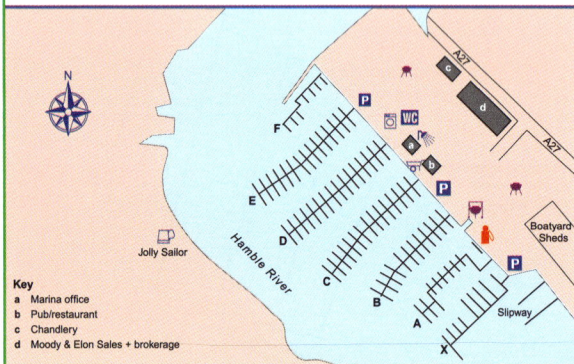

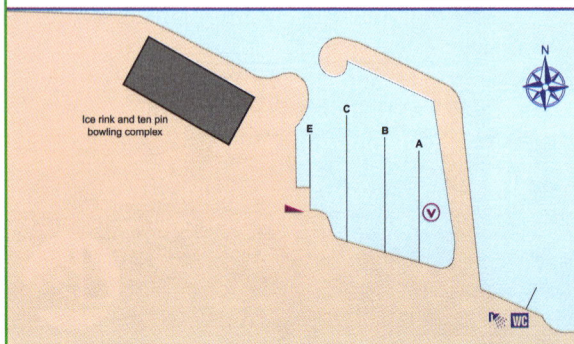

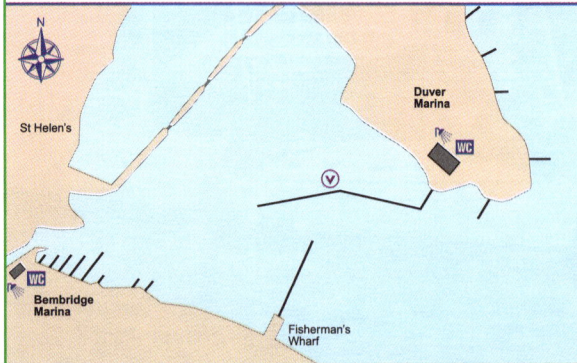

Key
a Marina office
b Pub/restaurant
c Chandlery
d Moody & Elon Sales + brokerage

When responding to adverts please mention the 2009 Marina Guide →

REEDS

ENJOY EVERY SEVENTH NIGHT FREE AT AN MDL MARINA
WITH MDL CRUISING CLUB
Membership is free and joining is easy.
Join today at www.mdlmarinas.co.uk or call 023 8045 0218

2009/MG152/z

RYDE LEISURE HARBOUR

Ryde Harbour
The Esplanade, Ryde, Isle of Wight, PO33 1JA
Tel: 01983 613879 Fax: 01983 613903
www.rydeharbour.com Email: ryde.harbour@iow.gov.uk

VHF Ch 80
ACCESS HW±2

Known as the 'gateway to the Island', Ryde, with its elegant houses and abundant shops, is among the Isle of Wight's most popular resorts. Its well-protected harbour is conveniently close to the exceptional beaches as well as to the town's restaurants and amusements.

Drying to 2.5m and therefore only accessible to yachts that can take the ground, the harbour accommodates 90 resident boats as well as up to 75 visiting yachts. Fin keel yachts may dry out on the harbour wall.

Ideal for family cruising, Ryde offers a wealth of activities, ranging from ten pin bowling and ice skating to crazy golf and tennis.

FACILITIES AT A GLANCE

BEMBRIDGE MARINA

Bembridge Marina
Harbour Office, The Duver, St Helens, Ryde
Isle of Wight, PO33 1YB
Tel: 01983 872828 Fax: 01983 872922
Email: chris@bembridgeharbour.co.uk
www.bembridgeharbour.co.uk

VHF Ch 80
ACCESS HW±2.5

Bembridge is a compact, pretty harbour whose entrance, although restricted by the tides (recommended entry for a 1.5m draught is 2½hrs before HW), is well sheltered in all but north north easterly gales. Offering excellent sailing clubs, beautiful beaches and fine restaurants, this Isle of Wight port is a first class haven with plenty of charm. With approximately 100 new visitors' berths on the Duver Marina pontoons, the marina at St Helen's Quay, at the western end of the harbour, is now allocated to annual berth holders only.

FACILITIES AT A GLANCE

2

HASLAR MARINA

Haslar Marina
Haslar Road, Gosport, Hampshire, PO12 1NU
Tel: 023 9260 1201 Fax: 023 9260 2201
www.haslarmarina.co.uk Email: sales@haslarmarina.co.uk

VHF Ch 80
ACCESS H24

This modern, purpose-built marina lies to port on the western side of Portsmouth Harbour entrance and is easily recognised by its prominent lightship incorporating a bar and restaurant. Accessible at all states of the tide, Haslar's extensive facilities do not however include fuel, the nearest being at the Camper and Nicholsons jetty only a few cables north.

Within close proximity is the Royal Navy Submarine Museum and the Museum of Naval Firepower 'Explosion' both worth a visit.

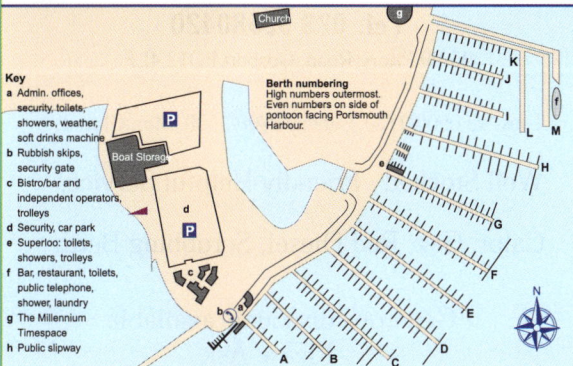

FACILITIES AT A GLANCE

Key
a Admin. offices, security, toilets, showers, weather, soft drinks machine
b Rubbish skips, security gate
c Bistro/bar and independent operators, trolleys
d Security, car park
e Superloo: toilets, showers, trolleys
f Bar, restaurant, toilets, public telephone, shower, laundry
g The Millennium Timespace
h Public slipway

Berth numbering
High numbers outermost. Even numbers on side of pontoon facing Portsmouth Harbour.

ROYAL CLARENCE MARINA

Royal Clarence Marina, Royal Clarence Yard
Weevil Lane, Gosport, Hampshire PO12 1AX
Tel: 023 9252 3810 Fax: 023 9252 3980
Email: enquiries@royalclarencemarina.co.uk
www.royalclarencemarina.co.uk

VHF Ch 80
ACCESS H24

Royal Clarence Marina benefits from a unique setting within a deep-water basin in front of the Royal Navy's former victualling yard. Only 10 minutes from the entrance to Portsmouth Harbour, it forms part of a £100 million redevelopment scheme which will incorporate residential homes, waterfront bars and restaurants as well as shopping outlets. Among its facilities are fully serviced finger pontoon berths up to 18m in length, while over 200m of alongside berthing will accommodate Yacht Club rallies and other maritime events.

FACILITIES AT A GLANCE

Bembridge Harbour

Bembridge Harbour welcomes visiting yachts which are now accommodated at the new Duver Marina providing access to the shore on the north side of the harbour. Rafting will be necessary at busy times. Showers and toilets, formerly in the Marina Office, are now located on the old Duver Boatyard site.

Water Taxi

The Water Taxi operates a service to ferry visitors to other parts of the harbour where there are various pick-up points.

Reservations

Reservations are not accepted for visitors' berths which are allocated strictly on a first-come, first-served basis. Visitors should call VHF Channel 80 for berthing instructions before entering the harbour.

ASSURING YOU OF A WARM AND FRIENDLY WELCOME

Harbour Master: Chris Turvey
Bembridge Harbour Improvements Company Limited.
Harbour Office, The Duver, St Helens, Ryde, Isle of Wight, PO33 1YB
Tel: 01983 872828 · Fax: 01983 872922
email: chris@bembridgeharbour.co.uk
web: www.bembridgeharbour.co.uk

When responding to adverts please mention the **2009 Marina Guide**

REEDS
DIRECTORY OF MARINAS, MARINE SUPPLIES & SERVICES
MARINA GUIDE 2009

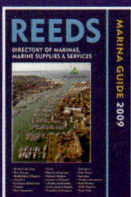

ENJOY EVERY SEVENTH NIGHT FREE AT AN MDL MARINA

CRUISING CLUB

WITH MDL CRUISING CLUB
Membership is free and joining is easy.
Join today at www.mdlmarinas.co.uk
or call 023 8045 0218

DEAN & REDDYHOFF LTD - WEYMOUTH MARINA
Commercial Rd, Weymouth, Dorset DT4 8NA
Tel: (01305) 767576 Fax: (01305) 767575
e-mail: sales@weymouthmarina.co.uk
www.deanreddyhoff.co.uk
With its sandy beaches, beautiful Georgian esplanade and charming old harbour Weymouth is one of the South Coast's must-visit ports. The marina is conveniently located in the centre of town, only minutes from local pubs, restaurants and transport links, and offers excellent washroom facilities and 24-hour CCTV security.

2009/Ext2/z

GOSPORT MARINA

Premier Gosport Marina
Mumby Road, Gosport, Hampshire, PO12 1AH
Tel: 023 9252 4811 Fax: 023 9258 9541
Email: gosport@premiermarinas.com
www.premiermarinas.com

| VHF | Ch 80 |
| ACCESS | H24 |

A few cables north of Haslar Marina, again on the port hand side, lies Gosport Marina. Boasting 519 fully-serviced visitors' berths, its extensive range of facilities incorporates a fuel barge on its southern breakwater as well as shower and laundry amenities. Numerous boatyard and engineering specialists are also located in and around the premises.

Within easy reach of the marina is Gosport town centre, offering a cosmopolitan selection of restaurants along with several supermarkets and shops.

FACILITIES AT A GLANCE

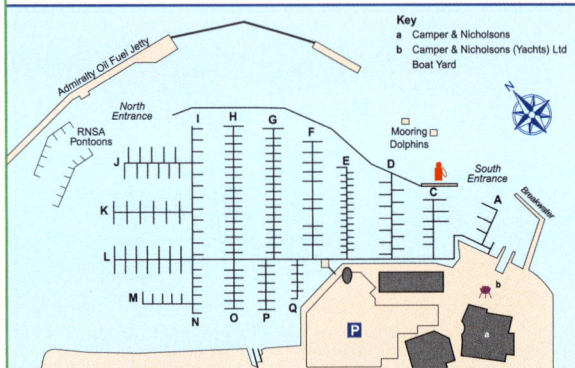

Key
a Camper & Nicholsons
b Camper & Nicholsons (Yachts) Ltd Boat Yard

GOSPORT MARINA
Mumby Road, Gosport, Hampshire PO12 1AH
Tel: (023) 9252 4811 Fax: (023) 9258 9541
e-mail: gosport@premiermarinas.co.uk
www.permiermarinas.com
Located at the entrance to Portsmouth Harbour with 24 hour access. 519 fully serviced berths varying in size from 5m to 20m. Ideal for easy access to the Solent.
2009/L2b/z

Hardway Marine CHANDLERY

www.hardwaychandlery.co.uk
e-mail:hardwaymarine@hotmail.co.uk
Tel: 023 92580420
95-99 Priory Road, Gosport. PO12 4LF

Tues-Sat 0900-1730. Sunday 0900-1500. Mon-Closed

Well Stocked , Friendly Helpful Service,
Calor, Gaz, Red Diesel, Scrubbing Berth

Generous discounts available
Please Ask
2009/MG151/z

TECSEW

THE YACHT CANOPY COMPANY

COCKPIT CANOPIES | COCKPIT COVERS
SPRAYHOODS | SUN AWNINGS
BIMINIS | WINTER COVERS
TONNEAU COVERS | LETTERED DODGERS

'Tailored to Perfection'

We hold standard patterns for most Jeanneau, Beneteaus, Moodys, Bavarias, Legends, Westerlys, Hunters, Rodmans, Dufours, Southerlys and many others.

"The cockpit enclosure fitted to my Moody 36 is a great success. It effectively lengthens the boat providing a "room in the cockpit". The fixtures and fittings are robust and precise, ensuring we can sail the boat in all conditions with it folded in the cockpit, as we have done for hundreds of hours. Most yachtsmen do not realise this and think fitting a cockpit enclosure means constant removal and reassembly. The design is so effective that I have never needed another pair of hands in order to fold and erect the cover! All our winches can be operated with it remaining permanently in the cockpit, greatly increasing our sailing pleasure. *Jim Flanagan "Xtraduty". Port Hamble*"

Original equipment suppliers to:
ANCASTA, SEAVENTURES, PREMIER YACHTS, PORTWAY, NORTHSHORE YACHTS, DISCOVERY YACHTS

TECSEW LIMITED
Units 3 & 4 Camden Street,
Gosport, Hampshire, PO12 3LU

Tel: 0845 402 4310
Fax: 0845 402 4311
Email: sales@tecsew.com

PAY US A VISIT...
www.tecsew.com
2009/MG145/ez

adrenaline
sailing school

Professional Yachtmaster

2000 Miles from only **£4995** inclusive

2500 Miles from only **£5995** inclusive

New Yachts & Friendly Instructors

RYA Start Yachting
RYA Competent Crew
RYA Day Skipper Theory
RYA Day Skipper Practical
RYA Coastal Skipper Theory
RYA Coastal Skipper Practical
RYA Yachtmaster Theory
RYA Yachtmaster Practical
RYA Powerboat Level 1 to Advanced

RYA Training Centre

Yacht Charter, Motor Boat Charter, RIB Charter

Bavaria 34, 36, 42, 49, Jeanneau 35, 37, 40, 49

Tel: **02392 587755** or **07793 944700**

www.adrenalinesailing.co.uk

PORT SOLENT MARINA

Port Solent Marina
South Lockside, Portsmouth, PO6 4TJ
Tel: 023 9221 0765 Fax: 023 9232 4241
www.premiermarinas.com
Email: portsolent@premiermarinas.com

VHF	Ch 80
ACCESS	H24

Port Solent Marina is located to the north east of Portsmouth Harbour, not far from the historic Portchester Castle. Accessible via a 24-hour lock, this purpose built marina offers a full range of facilities. The Boardwalk comprises an array of shops and restaurants, while close by is a David Lloyd Health Centre and a large Odeon cinema.

No visit to Portsmouth Harbour is complete without a trip to the Historic Dockyard, home to Henry VIII's *Mary Rose*, Nelson's HMS *Victory* and the first iron battleship, HMS *Warrior*, built in 1860.

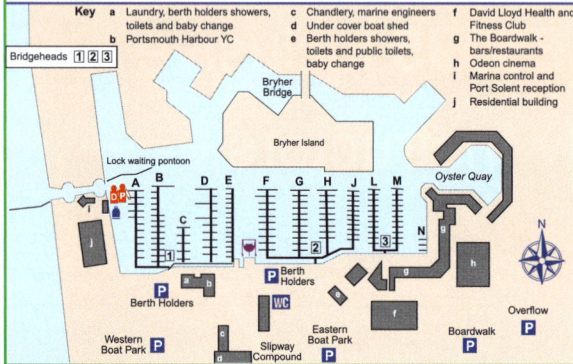

FACILITIES AT A GLANCE

Key
a Laundry, berth holders showers, toilets and baby change
b Portsmouth Harbour YC
c Chandlery, marine engineers
d Under cover boat shed
e Berth holders showers, toilets and public toilets, baby change
f David Lloyd Health and Fitness Club
g The Boardwalk - bars/restaurants
h Odeon cinema
i Marina control and Port Solent reception
j Residential building

SOUTHSEA MARINA

Southsea Marina
Fort Cumberland Road, PO4 9RJ
Tel: 02392 822719 Fax: 02392 822220
Email: southsea@premiermarinas.com
www.premiermarinas.com

VHF	Ch 80
ACCESS	HW±3

Southsea Marina is a small and friendly marina located on the western shore of Langstone Harbour, an expansive tidal bay situated between Hayling Island and Portsmouth. The channel is clearly marked by seven starboard and nine port hand markers. A tidal gate allows unrestricted movement in and out of the marina up to 3 hours either side of HW operates the entrance. The minimum depth in the marina entrance during this period is 1.6m and a waiting pontoon is available. There are excellent on site facilities including a bar, restaurant and chandlery.

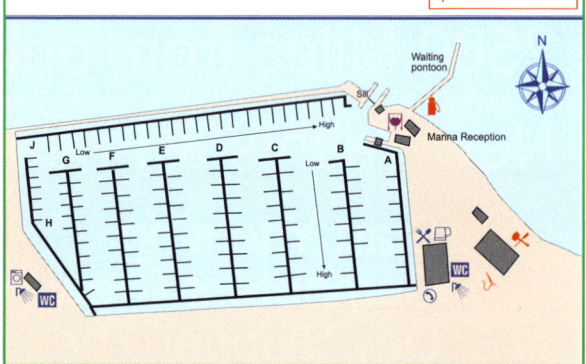

FACILITIES AT A GLANCE

SHIPSHAPE SERVICES LTD

Boat Management & Valet Service
Across The South Coast

The industry's choice....

Serving both the marine industry and private boat owners for all their valet needs. A reliable and professional service allowing you to make the most of your time on the water.

Why settle for less?

- Hot wash & deck steam cleaning
- High quality teak cleaning & sealing
- Cutting back & wax polishing
- Full detailed interior valets
- One-off & regular wash service
- Heater & Dehumidifier Hire
- Professional carpet & upholstery cleaning with state-of-the-art equipment
- Shrink wrapping
- Advice & help in general boat related topics.

Tel: 023 92 324 500
Fax: 023 92 324 550
Email: info@shipshapeservices.co.uk
2 The Slipway Port Solent
Portsmouth PO6 4TR

2009/MG88/e

Members of
British Marine Federation

www.shipshapeservices.co.uk

SPARKES YACHT HARBOUR

Sparkes Yacht Harbour
Wittering Road, Hayling Island, Hampshire, PO11 9SR
Tel: 023 9246 3572 Fax: 023 9246 5741
Email: info@sparkes.co.uk www.sparkes.co.uk

VHF	Ch 80
ACCESS	H24

Just inside the entrance to Chichester Harbour, on the eastern shores of Hayling Island, lies Sparkes Marina and Boatyard. Its approach channel has been dredged to 2m MLW and can be identified by an unlit ECM. One of two marinas in Chichester to have full tidal access, its facilities include a wide range of marine services as well as a well-stocked chandlery and first class restaurant. Within close proximity are a newsagent, farm shop and various takeaways, while a taxi ride away are Capers and Jaspers, two restaurants on Hayling Island renowned for their top quality cuisine.

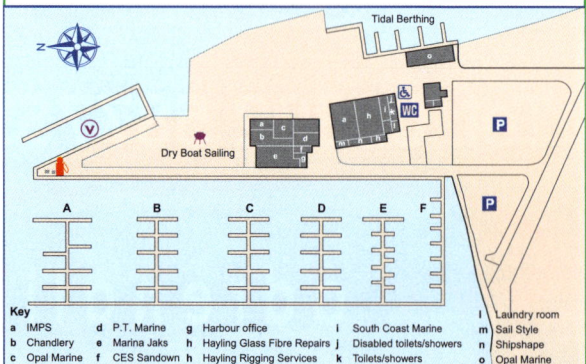

FACILITIES AT A GLANCE

Key
a IMPS
b Chandlery
c Opal Marine
d P.T. Marine
e Marina Jaks
f CES Sandown
g Harbour office
h Hayling Glass Fibre Repairs
h Hayling Rigging Services
i South Coast Marine
j Disabled toilets/showers
k Toilets/showers
l Laundry room
m Sail Style
n Shipshape
o Opal Marine

PORT SOLENT MARINA
South Lockside, Port Solent, Portsmouth, Hampshire PO6 4TJ
Tel: (023) 9221 0765 Fax: (023) 9232 4241
e-mail: portsolent@premiermarinas.co.uk
www.permiermarinas.com
Situated in Portsmouth Harbour, Port Solent offers every facility a boatowner could wish for.

2009/L2c/z

SOUTHSEA MARINA
Fort Cumberland Marina, Portsmouth, Hampshire PO4 9RJ
Tel: (023) 9282 2719 Fax: (023) 9282 2220
e-mail: southsea@premiermarinas.co.uk
www.permiermarinas.com
A small and friendly Marina on the doorstep of the Solent.

2009/L2d/z

NORTHNEY MARINA

Northney Marina
Northney Road, Hayling Island, Hampshire, PO11 0NH
Tel: 023 9246 6321 Fax: 023 9246 1467
www.marinas.co.uk Email: northney@mdlmarinas.co.uk

| VHF | Ch 80 |
| ACCESS | H24 |

One of two marinas in Chichester Harbour to be accessible at all states of the tide, Northney Marina is on the northern shore of Hayling Island in the well marked Sweare Deep Channel, which branches off to port almost at the end of the Emsworth Channel. With a new facilities block having recently been completed, the marina now incorporates a very basic grocery store as well as improved ablution facilities. There is an events area for rallies.

FACILITIES AT A GLANCE

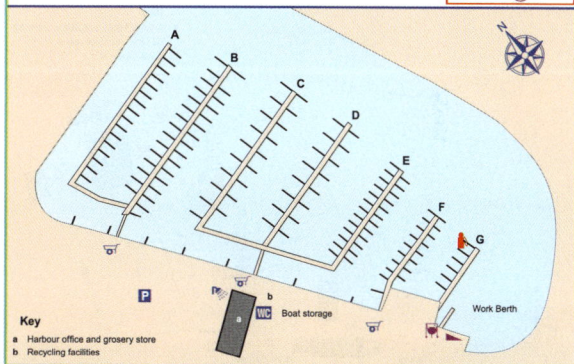

Key
a Harbour office and grosery store
b Recycling facilities

SPARKES MARINA
www.findmeaberth.co.uk
(023) 9246 3572

2009/MG152/z

RJ WELLS *marine*

Heating and Refrigeration Installations, Servicing & Repairs

ROB WELLS

Tel: 07909 950979

robertjwells@ntlworld.com

MIKUNI
MARINE & VEHICLE HEATING

frigoboat
MARINE REFRIGERATION

2009/MG19/z

MDL **Dry Stack**

The UK's leading Dry Stack provider
www.mdldrystack.co.uk

2009/MG152/z

HOLMAN RIGGING

Professional Rigging Services

- Visual rig checks
- Electronic non-destructive rig checks
- Roller reefing
- In-mast reefing
- In-boom reefing
- Single line reefing
- Masts
- Life lines
- Guard wires

Contact Chris Holman
Chichester Marina
Chichester, W. Sussex PO20 7EJ
Email: enquiries@holmanrigging.co.uk
Web: www.holmanrigging.co.uk
Tel/Fax: 01243 514000

Agents for Hyde Sails and all major mast and reefing suppliers

2009/MG131/z

EMSWORTH YACHT HARBOUR

Emsworth Yacht Harbour
Thorney Road, Emsworth, Hants, PO10 8BP
Tel: 01243 377727 Fax: 01243 373432
Email: info@emsworth-marina.co.uk
www.emsworth-marina.co.uk

| VHF | Ch 80 |
| ACCESS | HW±2 |

Accessible about one and a half to two hours either side of high water, Emsworth Yacht Harbour is a sheltered site, offering good facilities to yachtsmen.

Created in 1964 from a log pond, the marina is within easy walking distance of the pretty little town of Emsworth, which boasts at least 10 pubs, several high quality restaurants and two well-stocked convenience stores.

FACILITIES AT A GLANCE

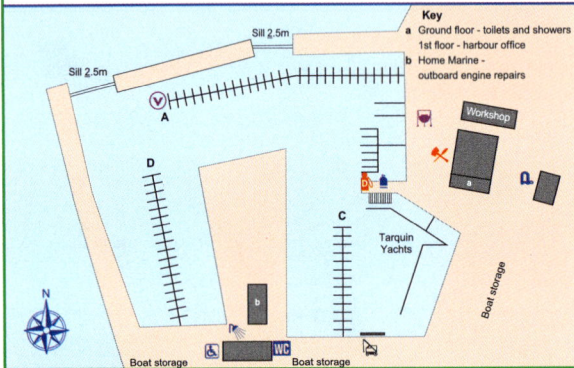

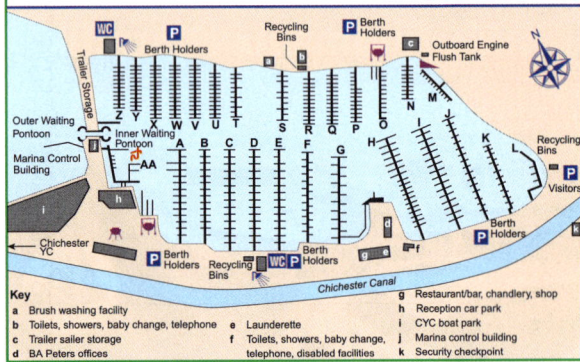

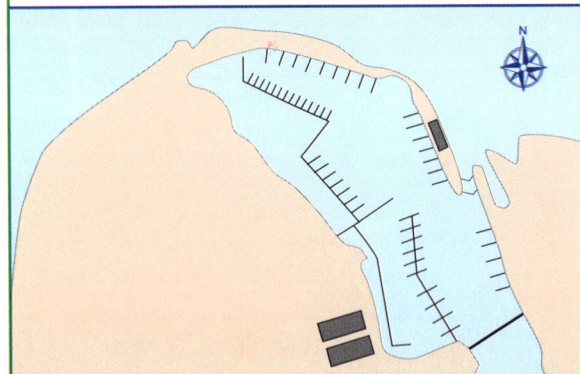

Key
a Ground floor - toilets and showers
   1st floor - harbour office
b Home Marine -
   outboard engine repairs

CHICHESTER MARINA

Chichester Marina
Birdham, Chichester, West Sussex, PO20 7EJ
Tel: 01243 512731 Fax: 01243 513472
Email: chichester@premiermarinas.com
www.premiermarinas.com

| VHF | Ch 80 |
| ACCESS | HW±5 |

Chichester Marina, nestling in an enormous natural harbour, has more than 1,000 berths, making it one of the largest marinas in the UK. Its approach channel can be easily identified by the CM SHM pile. The channel was dredged to 0.5m below CD in 2004, giving access of around five hours either side of HW at springs. Besides the wide ranging marine facilities, there are also a restaurant and small convenience store on site. Chichester, which is only about a five minute bus or taxi ride away, has several places of interest, the most notable being the cathedral.

FACILITIES AT A GLANCE

Key
a Brush washing facility
b Toilets, showers, baby change, telephone
c Trailer sailer storage
d BA Peters offices
e Launderette
f Toilets, showers, baby change,
   telephone, disabled facilities
g Restaurant/bar, chandlery, shop
h Reception car park
i CYC boat park
j Marina control building
k Security checkpoint

BIRDHAM POOL MARINA

Birdham Pool Marina
Birdham Pool, Chichester, Sussex
Tel: 01243 512310 Fax: 01243 513163
Email: info@birdhampool.co.uk

| VHF | Ch 80 |
| ACCESS | HW±3 |

Birdham Pool must be among Britain's most charming and rustic marinas. Only accessible three hours either side of HW via a lock, any visiting yachtsman will not be disappointed by its unique and picturesque setting. To get to Birdham Pool, enter the channel at the Birdham SHM beacon. The channel is marked by green piles that should be left no more than 3m to starboard. There is a wide range of marine facilities on hand, including a small chandlery that opens six days a week.

FACILITIES AT A GLANCE

HOLMAN RIGGING Tel/Fax:
Chichester Marina, Chichester, 01243
West Sussex PO20 7EJ 514000
Insurance Rig Checks
Expert inspection, report and recommendation. Mast, Rigging and reefing systems. Agents for major suppliers in this field. Also for Hyde Sails. Purpose designed mast trailer for quick and safe transportation. 2009/MD8/s
E-mail: enquiries@holmanrigging.co.uk www.holmanrigging.co.uk

Birdham Pool Marina
one of the earliest marinas built in the UK in one of the loveliest settings.

Annual berths available

Facilities:
Marina berths up to 18m with Wi-Fi
Slipway & Crane
Winter storage
All boatyard services

Contact: 01243 512310
or email: info@birdhampool.co.uk for details

Birdham Pool Marina, Birdham, Chichester, PO20 7BG

2009/MG1153/z

CHICHESTER MARINA
Birdham, Chichester, West Sussex PO20 7EJ
Tel: (01243) 512731 Fax: (01243) 513472
e-mail: chichester@premiermarinas.co.uk
www.permiermarinas.com
A peaceful and relaxing Marina situated in a stunning natural harbour.

2009/L2e/z

Make a **winning** decision.

Your choice of marine electronics is one of the most important decisions you will have to make as a boat owner, next to choosing the boat itself of course. Thousands of sailors head to the water everyday, confident in the performance and accuracy of their chosen Raymarine equipment.

When you buy Raymarine equipment, you are buying into world-class performance, top-notch integration, and the latest proven design technologies. Years of research and development, and customer feedback have resulted in the 'simple-on-the-outside, sophisticated-on-the-inside' design philosophy that is behind all our intuitive easy-to-use equipment.

Worldwide support and warranty

That's why Raymarine has a worldwide network of product-trained distributors and service dealers and offers a comprehensive warranty to handle the unexpected… wherever you decide to go.

Every change in direction. Every shift in the wind. Every change in depth. Every port you pass. Every ship on your ocean. Every fish in your sea…

2009/Mg98/v

www.raymarine.co.uk

Raymarine®

… with you every degree of the way.

Experience the fine art of sailing with In2Sail

in2sail

"Seriously Good Sail Training On-Board Quality Yachts with Friendly Professional Skippers, Served with Good Food and Fun."

RYA Training Courses

☐ Practical Sailing Courses in the Solent.

☐ Theory Courses in Central London.

☐ Solent Combined Theory & Practical.

☐ Patient and Personable Instructors to help you Learn Skills & Improve Existing Knowledge.

☐ Personalised for Families & Couples.

Blue Water & Long Distance

☐ Fun Long Weekend Trips to Cherbourg & St Vaast.

☐ Discover UK & Irish Sailing Waters.

☐ Normandy & Brittany Coastlines.

☐ Adventure Sailing to Spain & Portugal.

☐ Customised Skippered Charter to Locations of your Choice.

Specialist Courses

☐ Racing Yacht Training and Race Participation.

☐ Specialised Boat Handling and Technical Sailing Courses.

☐ Yacht Maintenance Programme.

☐ Fast Track Yachtmaster.

Racing Events

☐ Fastnet Yacht Race 2009.

☐ Round the Island 2008.

☐ Cowes Week 2008.

☐ Cork Week.

☐ Spring and Winter Series.

"New or Experienced - In2Sail Welcomes You."

RYA Training Centre

+44 (0) 1983 615557 | INFO@IN2SAIL.COM | WWW.IN2SAIL.COM

ONLINE BOOKING | SUBSCRIBE TO E- NEWSLETTER TO HEAR ABOUT SPECIAL OFFERS

2009/mg171/v

ADLARD COLES NAUTICAL
WEATHER FORECASTS
BY FAX & TELEPHONE

Coastal/Inshore	2-day by Fax	5-day by Phone
Mid Channel	09065 222 347	09068 969 647
Channel East	09065 222 346	09068 969 646
NE France	09065 501 611	09064 700 421
Anglia	09065 222 345	09068 969 645
East	09065 222 344	09068 969 644
National (3-5 day)	09065 222 340	09068 969 640

Offshore	2-5 day by Fax	2-5 day by Phone
English Channel	09065 222 357	09068 969 657
Southern North Sea	09065 222 358	09068 969 658
Northern North Sea	09065 222 362	09068 969 662

09064/68 CALLS COST 60P PER MIN. 09065 CALLS COST £1.50 PER MIN.

Key to Marina Plans symbols

Bottled gas		P	Parking
Chandler			Pub/Restaurant
Disabled facilities			Pump out
Electrical supply			Rigging service
Electrical repairs			Sail repairs
Engine repairs			Shipwright
First Aid			Shop/Supermarket
Fresh Water			Showers
Fuel - Diesel	D		Slipway
Fuel - Petrol	P	WC	Toilets
Hardstanding/boatyard			Telephone
Internet Café	@		Trolleys
Laundry facilities		V	Visitors berths
Lift-out facilities			Wi-Fi

3

Area 3 - South East England

MARINAS
Telephone Numbers
VHF Channel
Access Times

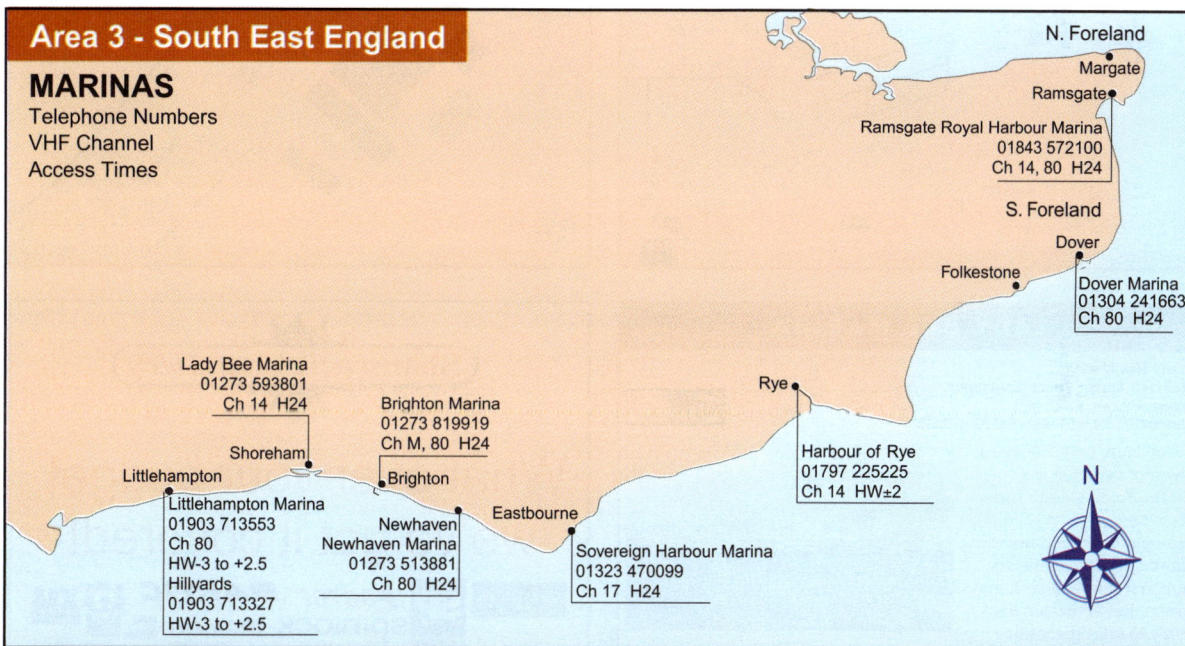

N. Foreland

Margate

Ramsgate

Ramsgate Royal Harbour Marina
01843 572100
Ch 14, 80 H24

S. Foreland

Dover

Folkestone

Dover Marina
01304 241663
Ch 80 H24

Rye

Harbour of Rye
01797 225225
Ch 14 HW±2

Lady Bee Marina
01273 593801
Ch 14 H24

Brighton Marina
01273 819919
Ch M, 80 H24

Shoreham

Littlehampton

Brighton

Eastbourne

Littlehampton Marina
01903 713553
Ch 80
HW-3 to +2.5
Hillyards
01903 713327
HW-3 to +2.5

Newhaven
Newhaven Marina
01273 513881
Ch 80 H24

Sovereign Harbour Marina
01323 470099
Ch 17 H24

N

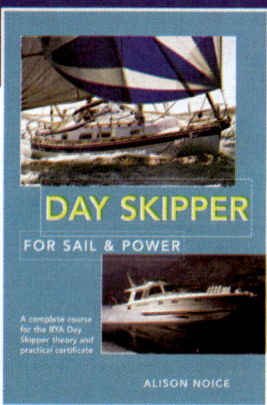

Courses

Adlard Coles Nautical
THE BEST SAILING BOOKS

Day Skipper
for Sail and Power

Covering the theory and practical aspects of the RYA
Day Skipper Certificate, this text offers an introduction
to pilotage, navigation and general boatwork for anyone
intending to make coastal passages in a small boat.
Alison Noice   **£19.99**   978 0 7136 8272 4

DAY SKIPPER
FOR SAIL & POWER

A complete course
for the RYA Day
Skipper theory and
practical certificate

ALISON NOICE

TO ORDER   Tel: **01256 302699** email: **direct@macmillan.co.uk** or **www.adlardcoles.com**

LITTLEHAMPTON MARINA

**Littlehampton Marina
Ferry Road, Littlehampton, W Sussex
Tel: 01903 713553 Fax: 01903 732264
Email: sales@littlehamptonmarina.co.uk**

VHF Ch 80
ACCESS HW-3 to +2.5

A typical English seaside town with funfair, promenade and fine sandy beaches, Littlehampton lies roughly midway between Brighton and Chichester at the mouth of the River Arun. It affords a convenient stopover for yachts either east or west bound, providing you have the right tidal conditions to cross the entrance bar with its charted depth of 0.7m. The marina lies about three cables above Town Quay and Fisherman's Quay, both of which are on the starboard side of the River Arun, and is accessed via a retractable footbridge that opens on request to the HM (note that you should contact him by 1630 the day before you require entry).

FACILITIES AT A GLANCE

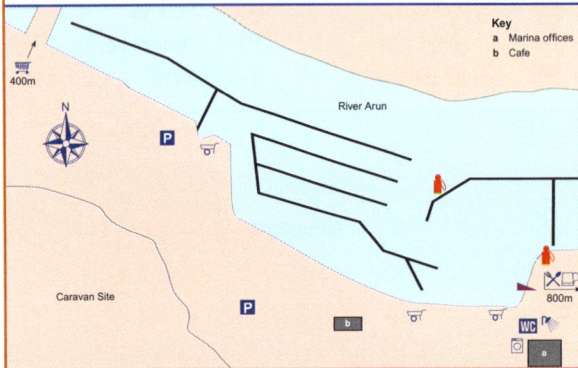

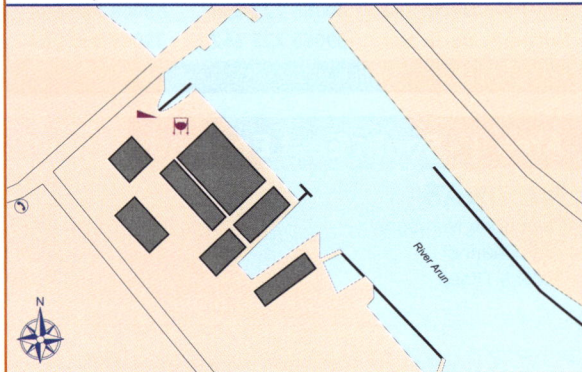

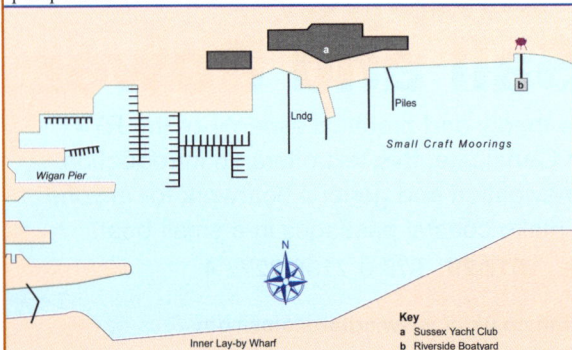

Key
a Marina offices
b Cafe

River Arun

400m

Caravan Site

800m

HILLYARDS

**Hillyards
Rope Walk, Littlehampton, West Sussex, BN17 5DG
Tel: 01903 713327 Fax: 01903 722787
www.hillyards.co.uk Email: info@hillyards.co.uk**

VHF
ACCESS HW-3 to +2.5

Established for more than 100 years Hillyards is a full service boatyard with moorings and storage for up to 50 boats. Based on the south coast within easy reach of London and the main yachting centres of the UK and Europe, Hillyards provides a comprehensive range of marine services.

The buildings of the boatyard are on the River Arun, a short distance from the English Channel. They provide the ideal conditions to accommodate and service craft up to 36m in length and with a maximum draft 3.5m. There is also craning services for craft up to 40 tons and the facilities to slip vessels up to 27m. In addition there are secure facilities to accommodate vessels up to 54m in dry dock.

FACILITIES AT A GLANCE

River Arun

LADY BEE MARINA

**Lady Bee Marina
138-140 Albion Street, Southwick
West Sussex, BN42 4EG
Tel: 01273 593801 Fax: 01273 870349**

VHF Ch 14
ACCESS H24

Shoreham, only five miles west of Brighton, is one of the South Coast's major commercial ports handling, among other products, steel, grain, tarmac and timber. On first impressions it may seem that Shoreham has little to offer the visiting yachtsman, but once through the lock and into the eastern arm of the River Adur, the quiet Lady Bee Marina, with its Spanish waterside restaurant, can make this harbour an interesting alternative to the lively atmosphere of Brighton Marina. Run by the Harbour Office, the marina meets all the usual requirements, although fuel is available in cans from Southwick garage or from Corral's diesel pump situated in the western arm.

FACILITIES AT A GLANCE

Lndg
Piles
Small Craft Moorings
Wigan Pier
Inner Lay-by Wharf

Key
a Sussex Yacht Club
b Riverside Boatyard

Shamrock Chandlery

What ever your budget, we've got it covered!

seago SP GOTOP BALTIC LIFEJACKETS SWEDEN XM
spinlock SEBAGO
WEST SYSTEM ECHOMAX Bar on MARINE ADMIRALTY LEISURE
SHURHOLD BLAKES Paints LALIZAS International

To buy these and many other brands visit our new on-line shop
www.shamrock.co.uk
Then click on GO SHOPPING

Our extensively stocked Chandlery is open 7 days a week Winter and Summer
Shamrock Quay William Street Southampton SO14 5QL

VISA Maestro MasterCard

Tel: 023 8063 2725

2009/MG128/e

BRIGHTON MARINA

Brighton Marina
West Jetty, Brighton, East Sussex, BN2 5UP
Tel: 01273 819919 Fax: 01273 675082
Email: brighton@premiermarinas.com
www.premiermarinas.com

VHF	Ch M, 80
ACCESS	H24

Brighton Marina is the largest marina in the country and with its extensive range of shops, restaurants and facilities, is a popular and convenient stop-over for east and west-going passagemakers. Note, however, that it is not advisable to attempt entry in strong S to SE winds.

Only half a mile from the marina is the historic city of Brighton itself, renowned for being a cultural centre with a cosmopolitan atmosphere. Among its numerous attractions are the exotic Royal Pavilion, built for King George IV in the 1800s, and the Lanes, with its multitude of antiques shops.

FACILITIES AT A GLANCE

Key
a David Lloyd Heath & Fitness Club
b Bowling alley
c Casino/night club
d Multiplex cinema
e Yacht club
f Petrol station
g Mariners Quay
h Marina reception

SMR MARINE LIMITED

Tel:01273 668900
Email:sales@smrmarine.co.uk

2009/MG80/e

SMR is the friendly face of boating. We can help with any marine enquiry and offer you a prompt & professional service.
Come visit us at either of our two Chandlery's in Brighton Marina, alternatively you can order online on our newly designed, easy to use website!

- Chandlery
- Online Chandlery
- Rigging
- Sail Loft
- Boat Sales
- Brokerage

www.smrchandlery.co.uk

BRIGHTON MARINA
West Jetty, Brighton Marina, Brighton, East Sussex BN2 5UQ
Tel: (01273) 819919
Fax: (01273) 675082
e-mail: brighton@premiermarinas.co.uk
The UK's largest fully serviced Marina, accessible at all states of the tide.

2009/L2f/z

When responding to adverts please mention the **2009 Marina Guide** →

REEDS

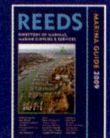

Adlard Coles Nautical
THE BEST SAILING BOOKS

Sailmate

How to Design a Boat
John Teale
978 0 7136 7572 6
£11.99

How to Choose the Right Yacht
J Muhs
978 0 7136 7581 8
£11.99

How to Paint Your Boat
Nigel Clegg
978 0 7136 7571 9
£11.99

How to Cope with Storms
D von Haeften
978 0 7136 7582 5
£11.99

How to Trim Sails
Peter Schweer
978 0 7136 7570 2
£11.99

How to Install a New Diesel Engine
Peter Cumberlidge
978 0 7136 7580 1
£11.99

TO ORDER MDL, Brunel Road, Houndmills, Basingstoke RG21 6XS
Tel: **01256 302699** email: **direct@macmillan.co.uk** or **www.adlardcoles.com**

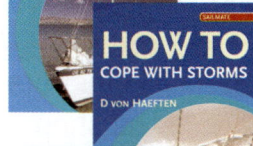

NEWHAVEN MARINA

Newhaven Marina
The Yacht Harbour, Fort Road, Newhaven
East Sussex, BN9 9BY
Tel: 01273 513881 Fax: 01273 510493
Email: john.stirling@seacontainers.com

VHF Ch 80
ACCESS H24

Some seven miles from Brighton, Newhaven lies at the mouth of the River Ouse. With its large fishing fleet and regular ferry services to Dieppe, the harbour has over the years become progressively commercial, therefore care is needed to keep clear of large vessels under manoeuvre. The marina lies approximately quarter of a mile from the harbour entrance on the west bank and was recently dredged to allow full tidal access except on LWS.

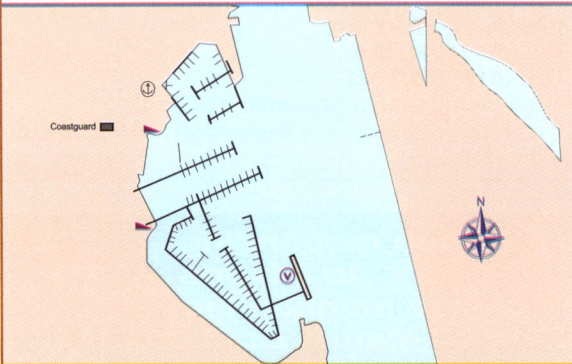

FACILITIES AT A GLANCE

Coastguard

WEST MARINE SERVICES LTD

mickwestmarine.com   marinecare.biz

We provide a highly professional, personal service to our customers, offering the following services:
- **Cummings mercruiser dealer** CM
- Marclear antifouling centre
- Webasto heating dealer
- Beta Marine engine dealer
- Boat valeting service
- Boat management services
- Skippering services

Mick West: 07990 683267
Mike West: 07769 677835
Office: 01273 626656
or email: mick@mickwestmarine.com

2009/MG56/v

Shamrock Chandlery

What ever your budget, we've got it covered!

seago SP GOTOP BALTIC XM
spinlock SEBAGO
WEST SYSTEM ECHOMAX Barton MARINE ADMIRALTY
SHURHOLD BLAKES Paints G LALIZAS International

To buy these and many other brands visit our new on-line shop

www.shamrock.co.uk

Then click on GO SHOPPING

Our extensively stocked Chandlery is open 7 days a week Winter and Summer
Shamrock Quay William Street
Southampton SO14 5QL
VISA

Tel: 023 8063 2725

2009/MG128/e

The Yacht Harbour, Fort Road, NEWHAVEN, East Sussex, BN9 9BY
Telephone (01273) 513881
Fax (01273) 510493

newhavenmarina

2009/MG81/r

Adlard Coles Nautical
THE BEST SAILING BOOKS

Safety Sail safely with
Adlard Coles Nautical
First Aid at Sea
5th edition
Colin Berry and Douglas Justins
978 1 4081 0599 3
£9.99

FIRST AID AT SEA

TO ORDER Tel: 01256 302699 or visit www.adlardcoles.com

SOVEREIGN HARBOUR MARINA

Sovereign Harbour Marina Ltd
Pacific Drive, Eastbourne, East Sussex, BN23 5BJ
Tel: 01323 470099 Fax: 01323 470077
Email: taylor.janet@carillianplc.com
www.sovereignharbour.co.uk

| VHF | Ch 17 |
| ACCESS | H24 |

Opened in 1993, Sovereign Harbour is situated a few miles NE of Eastbourne and is accessible at all states of the tide and weather except for in strong NE to SE'ly winds. Entered via a lock at all times of the day or night, the marina is part of one of the largest waterfront complexes in Britain, enjoying close proximity to shops, restaurants and a multiplex cinema. A short bus or taxi ride takes you to Eastbourne, where again you will find an array of shops and eating places to suit all tastes and budgets.

FACILITIES AT A GLANCE

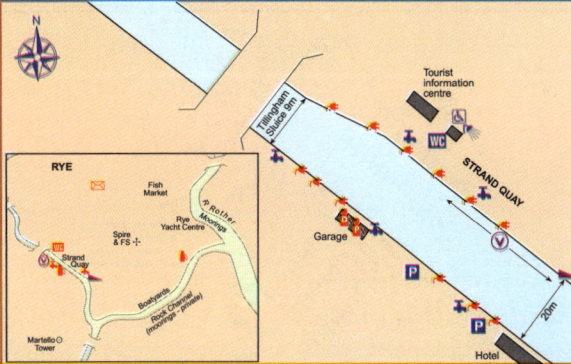

Key
a   The Waterfront, shops, restaurants, pubs and offices
b   Harbour office - weather information and visitor's information
c   Cinema
d   Retail park - supermarket and post office
e   Restaurant
f   Toilets, showers, telephone, launderette and disabled facilities
g   24 hr fuel pontoon (diesel, petrol and holding tank pump out)
h   Recycling centre
i   Boatyard, boatpark, marine engineers, riggers and electricians

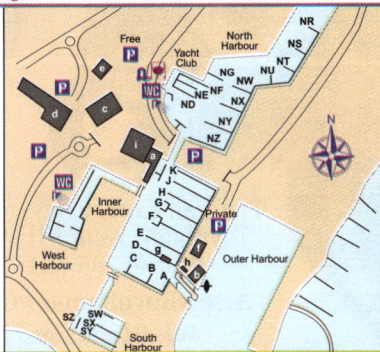

HARBOUR OF RYE

Harbour of Rye
New Lydd Road, Camber, E Sussex, TN31 7QS
Tel: 01797 225225 Fax: 01797 227429
Email: rye.harbour@environment-agency.gov.uk
www.environment-agency.gov.uk/harbourofrye

| VHF | Ch 14 |
| ACCESS | HW±2 |

The Strand Quay moorings are located in the centre of the historic town of Rye with all of its amenities a short walk away. The town caters for a wide variety of interests with the nearby Rye Harbour Nature Reserve, a museum, numerous antique shops and plentiful pubs, bars and restaurants. Vessels, up to a length of 15 metres, wishing to berth in the soft mud in or near the town of Rye should time their arrival at the entrance for not later than one hour after high water. Larger vessels should make prior arrangements with the Harbour Master. Fresh water, electricity, shower and toilet facilities are available.

FACILITIES AT A GLANCE

2009/MG2/v

Environment Agency

next time you visit Rye, why not bring your boat...

Visitor's berths are available from £16 per night including power, water, shower and toilet facilities. Permanent moorings are also available. The yearly charge for a 9 metre boat is just £978.61. Contact the Harbour Office for more details.

Rye Harbour Office, New Lydd Road, Camber, Rye, East Sussex TN31 7QS. Tel: 01797 225225.
Email: rye.harbour@environment-agency.gov.uk Website: www.environment-agency.gov.uk/harbourofrye

DOVER MARINA

Dover Harbour Board
Harbour House, Dover, Kent, CT17 9TF
Tel: 01304 241663 Fax: 01304 242549
Email: marina@doverport.co.uk

VHF Ch 80
ACCESS H24

Nestling under the famous White Cliffs, Dover sits between South Foreland to the NE and Folkestone to the SW. Boasting a maritime history stretching back as far as the Bronze Age, Dover is today one of Britain's busiest commercial ports, with a continuous stream of ferries and cruise liners plying to and from their European destinations. However, over the past years the harbour has made itself more attractive to the cruising yachtsman, with the marina, set well away from the busy ferry terminal, offering three sheltered berthing options in the Tidal Harbour, Granville Dock and Wellington Dock.

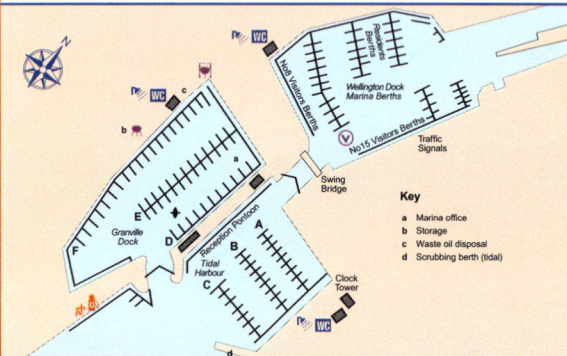

FACILITIES AT A GLANCE

Key
a Marina office
b Storage
c Waste oil disposal
d Scrubbing berth (tidal)

Wilkinson Sails
For Cruising Sails

Superb quality, fast and durable. Made to your own requirements.
Also covers, valeting & alterations.

W Conyer

The Sail Loft, Conyer Wharf
Teynham, Kent ME9 9HN
Tel: 01795 521503
Also@Burnham-on-Crouch
Tel: 01621 786770

2009/MG54/v

HAMMOND
GEORGE HAMMOND PLC

MARINE GAS OIL AVAILABLE 24 HOURS PER DAY AT CROSSWALL QUAY

TELEPHONE: 01304 206809

PETROL FILLING STATION OPEN 24 HRS SELLS FRESH FOOD, CIGARETTES, HOUSEHOLD PRODUCTS, NEWSPAPERS AND HAS AN 'ATM' CASH DISPENSER

M20 & ASHFORD LONDON

A20

FUEL

BOAT HOIST

Swing Bridge

WELLINGTON DOCK MARINA BERTHS

GRANVILLE DOCK MARINA BERTHS

FUEL BERTH

Two fast pumps of Marine Gas Oil.
ALSO PUMP-OUT FACILITY FOR HOLDING TANKS

MARINA BERTHS

TUG HAVEN

DOLPHIN HARD

CLARENCE QUAY

NORTH PIER

SOUTH PIER

2009/MG87/v

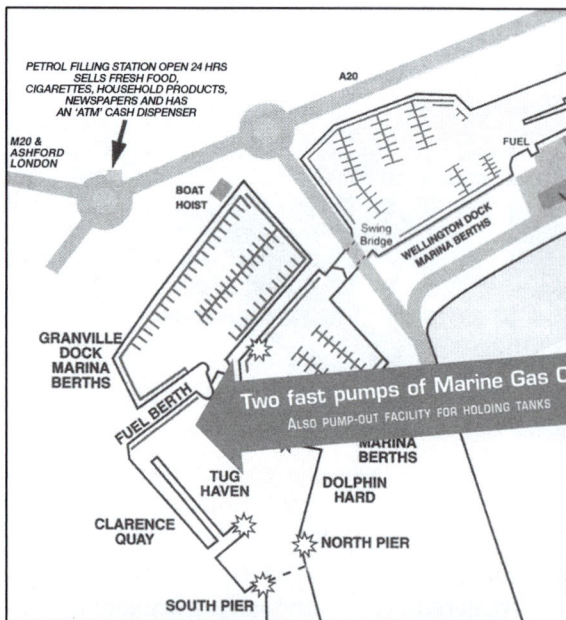

3

WHITSTABLE MARINE

For all your Sailing & Powerboat needs

3 shops to cater for all your sailing needs

Ramsgate	Whitstable
01843 597158	01227 262525/ 01227 274168

Three shops with over 10,000 product lines, including *Musto, Henri Lloyd, Douglas Gill, Crewsaver, Gul wetsuits, Barton Blocks, Plastimo, Marlow Ropes, paints, West Systems, fastenings, books, Harken, RWO, Holt, Ronstan, Whale, Rule, Icom radios, Perception & Bic Kayaks, Garmin GPS, inflatable tenders, Mercury outboards.*

You name it we have probably got it!

Largest selection of Imray and Admiralty charts in Kent.

www.whitstablemarine.co.uk

2009/MG163/z

ROYAL HARBOUR MARINA

Royal Harbour Marina, Ramsgate
Harbour Office, Military Road, Ramsgate, Kent, CT11 9LQ
Tel: 01843 572100 Fax: 01843 590941
Email: portoframsgate@thanet.gov.uk
www.portoframsgate.co.uk

VHF Ch 14, 80
ACCESS H24

Steeped in maritime history, Ramsgate was awarded 'Royal' status in 1821 by George IV in recognition of the warm welcome he received when sailing from Ramsgate to Hanover with the Royal Squadron. Offering good shelter and modern facilities, the Royal Harbour can be accessed in all conditions except in strong E'ly winds and comprises an inner marina, entered approximately HW±2, a western marina in 3m of water and an eastern marina with a 2m depth. Permission to enter or leave the Royal Harbour must be obtained from Ramsgate Port Control on Ch 14.

FACILITIES AT A GLANCE

Key
a Harbour office
b Port Control (VHF 14)
c Dock office
d Showers/toilets laundry
e RNLI
f Dockmasters office
g Fuel barge (VHF 14)
h Museum

Town Centre
Beach
Inner Marina
East Marina
West Marina

Adlard Coles Nautical

THE BEST SAILING BOOKS

New

Reeds Astro Navigation Tables 2009

ASTRO NAVIGATION TABLES

REEDS 2009
LT CDR HARRY J BAKER

Lt Cdr Harry Baker

An established book of annual astro-navigation tables for yachtsmen.
978 0 7136 8996 9
£17.99

Reeds Astro Navigation Tables 2009 can be obtained from your normal supplier - or please contact www.adlardcoles.com.

Shamrock Chandlery

What ever your budget, we've got it covered!

seago SP GOTOP BALTIC XM
spinlock SEBAGO
WEST SYSTEM ECHOMAX Barton MARINE ADMIRALTY
PLASTIMO SHURHOLD BLAKES Paints LALIZAS International

To buy these and many other brands visit our new on-line shop

www.shamrock.co.uk

Then click on GO SHOPPING

Our extensively stocked Chandlery is open 7 days a week Winter and Summer
Shamrock Quay William Street
Southampton SO14 5QL

VISA Maestro

Tel: 023 8063 2725

2009/MG128/e

When responding to adverts please mention the **2009 Marina Guide**

REEDS
DIRECTORY OF MARINAS, MARINE SUPPLIES & SERVICES
MARINA GUIDE 2009

MarineStore Chandlers

Maldon Chandlery

Shipways, North Street, Maldon, Essex. CM9 5HL
Tel +44(0) 1621 854280 • Fax 01621 843849 • Email chandler@marinestore.co.uk
http://marinestore.co.uk

MALDON - NORTH STREET

Maldon Marinestore,
Shipways, North St,
Maldon, Essex.
CM9 5HL
Tel 01621 854280
Fax 01621 843849

BURNHAM ON CROUCH - BURNHAM YACHT HARBOUR

Marinestore
Burnham, Burnham
Yacht Harbour,
Burnham on Crouch,
Essex. CM0 8BL
Tel 01621 783090

East coast based mail order chandlery with shops at:

WEST MERSEA - COAST ROAD

128 Coast Road, West Mersea, Essex. CO5 8PA
Tel 01206 384745

WALTON ON THE NAZE - TITCHMARSH MARINA

Marinestore Walton, Coles lane ,
Walton on the Naze, Essex.
Tel 01255 677775 Fax 01255 679028

MarineStore Rubicon S.L.
C/EL Berrugo, Marina Rubicon,
Local 78 B. CP;35570,
Yaiza, Lanzarote.
CIF B35973171

All major brands stocked

http://marinestore.co.uk

Mail order line: 01621 854280

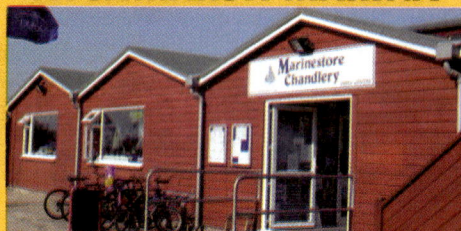

3

FAMBRIDGE YACHT HAVEN

Widely regarded as the finest marina facility on the River Crouch, Fambridge Yacht Haven is nestled within our surrounding salt marsh's providing naturally sheltered swinging moorings, pontoon berths and extensive hard standing. Visitors are always welcome, whether staying over night afloat or wintering ashore.

Undercover & Indoor Boat Storage Units

- New indoor boat storage facilities available for long or short term hire. These secure, well lit units are suitable for vessels up to 16m LOA and 5m beam. The units can be hired for painting, GRP repairs, welding, osmosis treatment and new builds.

- Valet Berthing, with just a few hours notice we will collect your boat from its river mooring and place it alongside our new visitor pontoon, you can then just step aboard and go sailing. On return you leave your boat alongside the pontoon and we will return it to its river mooring.

- Secure 'Bosuns Lockers' available to rent for the storage of general boat maintenance equipment, outboards, sails etc

- Long term & project boat storage in secure compound at reduced rates

- Modern boat handling and lifting equipment

- 120 deep-water swinging moorings
- 180 berth marina with 24 hours access
- Thames and Dutch barges welcome any time of year on fully serviceable mud berths
- Extensive hardstanding for long and short term storage, visitors welcome
- WISE 25 ton slipway hoist

- Mobile crane and pressure washing
- 24 hour CCTV
- 120 meter, deep water visitors' pontoon
- Valet berthing service, contact us for further information
- 2 x concrete slipways

2009/MG28/r

Fambridge Yacht Haven
Church Road, North Fambridge, Essex, CM3 6LR
Telephone 01621 740370

www.yachthavens.com
email: fambridge@yachthavens.com

wildlife TRUSTS
ESSEX
Wildlife Trust
Corporate Members

SAFETY WATER MOORINGS

on pontoons, 24 hr security, cranage & slipway nearby, hardstanding, valeting, surveys, repairs, access to Thames 5 hrs each side of high water. £193 per mtr. P.A. inc VAT.

Gallions Point Marina
Tel: 020 7476 7054 Fax: 020 7474 7056

Gallions Point Marina Ltd,
Gate 14, Royal Docks, Royal Albert Basin
Woolwich Manor Way, North Woolwich, London E16 2QY

www.gallionspointmarina.co.uk
info@gallionspointmarina.co.uk

2007/MgT0/v

ADLARD COLES NAUTICAL
WEATHER FORECASTS
BY FAX & TELEPHONE

Coastal/Inshore	2-day by Fax	5-day by Phone
Channel East	09065 222 346	09068 969 646
NE France	09065 501 611	09064 700 421
Anglia	09065 222 345	09068 969 645
East	09065 222 344	09068 969 644
North East	09065 222 343	09068 969 643
National (3-5 day)	09065 222 340	09068 969 640

Offshore	2-5 day by Fax	2-5 day by Phone
English Channel	09065 222 357	09068 969 657
Southern North Sea	09065 222 358	09068 969 658
Northern North Sea	09065 222 362	09068 969 662

09064/68 CALLS COST 60P PER MIN. 09065 CALLS COST £1.50 PER MIN.

Key to Marina Plans symbols

Bottled gas		P	Parking
Chandler			Pub/Restaurant
Disabled facilities			Pump out
Electrical supply			Rigging service
Electrical repairs			Sail repairs
Engine repairs			Shipwright
First Aid			Shop/Supermarket
Fresh Water			Showers
Fuel - Diesel			Slipway
Fuel - Petrol		WC	Toilets
Hardstanding/boatyard			Telephone
@ Internet Café			Trolleys
Laundry facilities		V	Visitors berths
Lift-out facilities			Wi-Fi

4

Area 4 - East England

MARINAS
Telephone Numbers
VHF Channel
Access Times

Gallions Pt Marina
020 7476 7054
Ch M, 80 HW±5
South Dock Marina
020 7252 2244
Ch M HW-2½ to +1½
Poplar Dock Marina
020 7308 9930
Ch 13 HW±1
St Katharine Haven
020 7264 5312
Ch 80 HW-2 to +1½
Chelsea Harbour
020 7225 9157
Ch 80 HW±1½
Brentford Dock Marina
020 8232 8941 HW±2½
Penton Hook Marina
01932 568681
Ch 80 H24
Windsor Marina
01753 853911
Ch 80 H24

Fox's Marina 01473 689111 Ch 80 H24
Neptune Marina 01473 215204 Ch M, 80 H24
Ipswich Haven Marina 01473 236644 Ch M, 68, 80 H24
Woolverstone Marina 01473 780206 Ch 80 H24
Royal Harwich YC Marina 01473 780319 Ch 77 H24
Suffolk Yacht Hbr 01473 659240 Ch 80 H24

Burnham Yacht Harbour 01621 782150 Ch 80 H24
Essex Marina 01702 258531 Ch 80 H24
Fambridge Yacht Haven 01621 740370 Ch 80 H24
Bridgemarsh Marina 01621 740414 Ch 80 HW±4

Limehouse Marina
020 7308 9930
Ch 80 HW±3

Hoo Marina 01634 250311 Ch 80 HW±3

Chatham Maritime Marina
01634 899200

Gt Yarmouth
Lowestoft
Southwold
Orford
Ipswich
Harwich
R Thames
N. Foreland
Ramsgate

Royal Norfolk & Suffolk YC
01520 566726 Ch 14, 80 H24
Lowestoft Haven Marina
01520 580300 Ch M, 80 H24

Shotley Marina
01473 788982
Ch 80 H24

Titchmarsh Marina   Walton Yacht Basin
01255 672185   01255 675873
Ch 80 HW±5   Ch 80 HW-¾ to +¼

Bradwell Marina 01621 776235 Ch M, 80 HW±4½
Blackwater Marina 01621 740264 Ch M HW±2
Tollesbury Marina 01621 869202 Ch 80 HW±2
Heybridge Basin 01621 853506 Ch 80 HW±1

Gillingham Marina
01634 280022
Ch 80 HW±4½

N

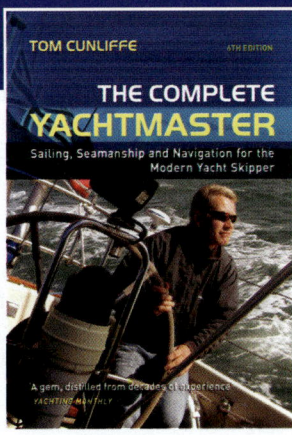

Adlard Coles Nautical
THE BEST SAILING BOOKS

Courses

TOM CUNLIFFE   4TH EDITION
THE COMPLETE
YACHTMASTER
Sailing, Seamanship and Navigation for the
Modern Yacht Skipper

A gem, distilled from decades of experience
YACHTING MONTHLY

The Complete
Yachtmaster™

6th edition *Tom Cunliffe*
978 0 7136 8948 8
£24.99

TO ORDER Tel: **01256 302699** email: **direct@macmillan.co.uk** or **www.adlardcoles.com**

GILLINGHAM MARINA

Gillingham Marina
173 Pier Road, Gillingham, Kent, ME7 1UB
Tel: 01634 280022 Fax: 01634 280164
Email: berthing@gillingham-marina.co.uk
www.gillingham-marina.co.uk

| VHF | Ch 80 |
| ACCESS | HW±4.5 |

Gillingham Marina comprises a locked basin, accessible four and a half hours either side of high water, and a tidal basin upstream which can be entered approximately two hours either side of high water. Deep water moorings in the river cater for yachts arriving at other times.

Visiting yachts are usually accommodated in the locked basin, although it is best to contact the marina ahead of time. Lying on the south bank of the River Medway, the marina is approximately eight miles from Sheerness, at the mouth of the river, and five miles downstream of Rochester Bridge. Facilities include a well-stocked chandlery, brokerage and an extensive workshop.

FACILITIES AT A GLANCE

Key
a Workshop
b Showers & toilets
c Shop
d Laundry
e Play area
f Reception & club
g Tender storage
h Lead in pontoon
i Petrol & diesel
j Leisure centre

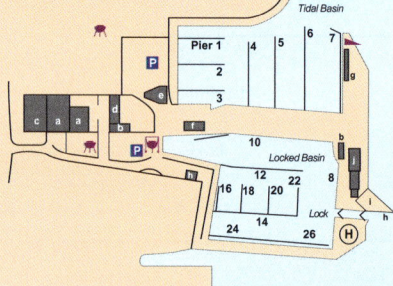

marine solutions YACHT CHARTER SERVICE

Charter a comfortable 4 berth performance sailing yacht in some of the most historic and fascinating waters of the British Isles.

Based near the Historical Port of Harwich on the Orwell River our Marine Coastguard Agency approved vessel will be waiting for you, fully equipped with all the latest knobs and whistles!
For details telephone: Peter or Angela now on mobile: 07961 296023.

2009/MG37/s

Shamrock Chandlery What ever your budget, we've got it covered!

seaGo SP GOTOP BALTIC LIFEJACKETS SWEDEN XM
spinlock SEBAGO
PLASTIMO WEST SYSTEM ECHOMAX Barton MARINE ADMIRALTY LEISURE
SHURHOLD BLAKES Paints BLUE GEE LALIZAS International

To buy these and many other brands visit our new on-line shop

www.shamrock.co.uk - then click on GO SHOPPING

Tel: 023 8063 2725

2009/MG128/e

Adlard Coles Nautical
THE BEST SAILING BOOKS

Courses

Pass Your Day Skipper
3rd edition *David Fairhall & Mike Peyton*
978 1 4081 0380 7
£12.99

Day Skipper for Sail & Power
Alison Noice
978 0 7136 8272 4
£19.99

Day Skipper Exercises for Sail and Power
Alison Noice
978 0 7136 8271 7
£19.99

Yachtmaster™ for Sail and Power
Alison Noice
978 0 7136 6988 6
£19.99

Yachtmaster™ Exercises for Sail and Power
Alison Noice
978 0 7136 7126 1
£17.99

The Complete Yachtmaster™
6th edition *Tom Cunliffe*
978 0 7136 8948 8
£24.99

TO ORDER MDL, Brunel Road, Houndmills, Basingstoke RG21 6XS
Tel: **01256 302699** email: **direct@macmillan.co.uk** or **www.adlardcoles.com**

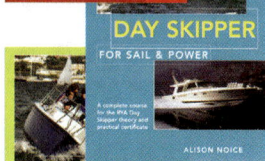

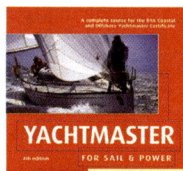

HOO MARINA

Hoo Marina
Vicarage Lane, Hoo, Rochester, Kent, ME3 9LE
Tel: 01634 250311 Fax: 01634 251761
Email: jcmarine@btconnect.com

VHF Ch 80
ACCESS HW±3

Hoo is a small village on the Isle of Grain, situated on a drying creek on the north bank of the River Medway approximately eight miles inland from Sheerness. Its marina was the first to be constructed on the East Coast and comprises finger berths supplied by all the usual services. It can be approached either straight across the mudflats near HW or, for a 1.5m draught, three hours either side of HW via a creek known locally as Orinoco. The entrance to this creek, which is marked by posts that must be left to port, is located a mile NW of Hoo Ness. Note that the final mark comprises a small, yellow buoy which you should pass close to starboard just before crossing the marina's sill.

Grocery stores can be found either in the adjacent chalet park or else in Hoo Village, while the Hoo Ness Yacht Club welcomes visitors to its bar and restaurant. There are also frequent bus services to the nearby town of Rochester.

FACILITIES AT A GLANCE

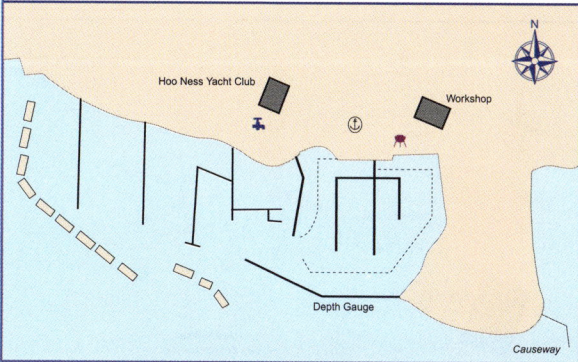

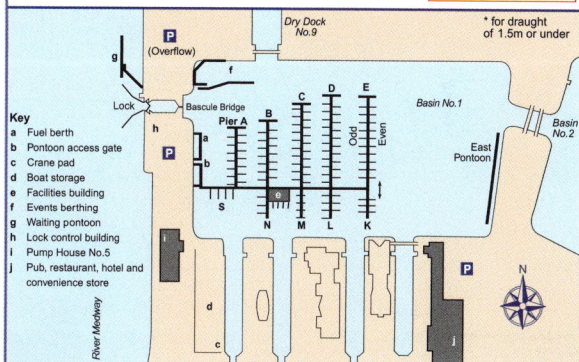

CHATHAM MARITIME MARINA

MDL, The Lock Building, Chatham Maritime Marina
Leviathan Way, Chatham Maritime, Chatham, Medway, ME4 4LP
Tel: 01634 899200 Fax: 01634 899201
Email: chatham@mdlmarinas.co.uk www.marinas.co.uk

VHF Ch 80
ACCESS H24

Chatham Maritime Marina is situated on the banks of the River Medway in Kent, providing an ideal location from which to explore the surrounding area. There are plenty of secluded anchorages in the lower reaches of the Medway Estuary, while the river is navigable for some 13 miles from its mouth at Sheerness right up to Rochester, and even beyond for those yachts drawing less than 2m. Only 45 minutes from London by road, the marina is part of a multi-million pound leisure and retail development, currently accommodating 300 yachts.

FACILITIES AT A GLANCE

Key
a Fuel berth
b Pontoon access gate
c Crane pad
d Boat storage
e Facilities building
f Events berthing
g Waiting pontoon
h Lock control building
i Pump House No.5
j Pub, restaurant, hotel and
   convenience store

Main Dealers for:
Waeco
Somoya Batteries
Quick Windlasses &
Most Electronics
International & Blakes Paint
Plastimo XM Yachting
Seago
Whale & Jabsco Pumps
Crewsaver Products
Spinlock

Pirates Cave
Chandlery

Tel: 01634 295233
Fax: 01634 722326

e-mail: piratescaveuk@yahoo.co.uk
Web: www.piratescave.co.uk

Unit 14.
Northpoint Business Estate,
Enterprise Close,
Medway City Estate
Frindsbury,
Rochester,
Kent ME2 4LX

Pirates Cave
McDonalds | garage
Medway Tunnel
from Chatham Marina

2009/MG10/r

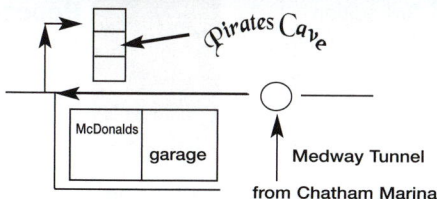

GALLIONS POINT MARINA

Gallions Point Marina, Gate 14, Royal Albert Basin
Woolwich Manor Way, North Woolwich
London, E16 2QY. Tel: 020 7476 7054 Fax: 020 7474 7056
Email: info@gallionspointmarina.co.uk
www.gallionspointmarina.co.uk

VHF Ch M, 80
ACCESS HW±5

Gallions Point Marina lies about 500 metres downstream of the Woolwich Ferry on the north side of Gallions Reach. Accessed via a lock at the entrance to the Royal Albert Basin, the marina offers deep water pontoon berths as well as hard standing. Future plans to improve facilities include the development of a bar/restaurant, a chandlery and an RYA tuition school.

FACILITIES AT A GLANCE

Royal Albert Dock

= Dock Edge Moorings

Bascule Bridge

SOUTH DOCK MARINA

South Dock Marina
Rope Street, Off Plough Way
London, SE16 7SZ
Tel: 020 7252 2244 Fax: 020 7237 3806
Email: gary.bettesworth@southwark.gov.uk

VHF Ch M
ACCESS HW-2.5 to +1.5

South Dock Marina is housed in part of the old Surrey Dock complex on the south bank of the River Thames. Its locked entrance is immediately downstream of Greenland Pier, just a few miles down river of Tower Bridge. For yachts with a 2m draught, the lock can be entered HW-2½ to HW+1½ London Bridge, although if you arrive early there is a holding pontoon on the pier. The marina can be easily identified by the conspicuous arched rooftops of Baltic Quay, a luxury waterside apartment block. Once inside this secure, 200-berth marina, you can take full advantage of all its facilities as well as enjoy a range of restaurants and bars close by or visit historic maritime Greenwich.

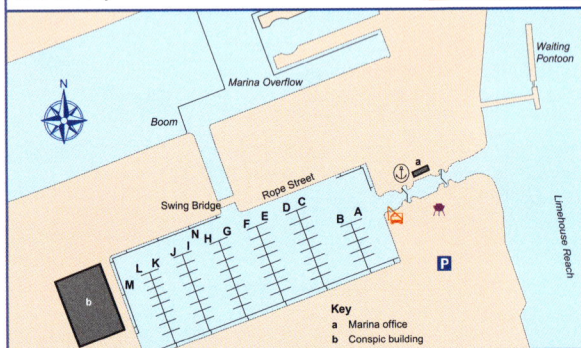

FACILITIES AT A GLANCE

Marina Overflow
Waiting Pontoon
Boom
Swing Bridge
Rope Street
Limehouse Reach

Key
a Marina office
b Conspic building

To book your berth at the South Dock Marina contact:

SOUTH DOCK

Wapping
Royal Docks
Tower Bridge
Thames Bridge
Millennium Site
Surrey Quays
SOUTH DOCK MARINA
Cutty Sark & Historical Greenwich

2009/MG96/e

SOUTH DOCK MARINA
Only a rope's throw away

MARINA

The Berthing Manager, South Dock Marina, South Lock Office, Rope Street, Plough Way LONDON SE16 7SZ. Tel: 020 7252 2244 Fax: 020 7237 3806
Website: www.southwark.gov.uk

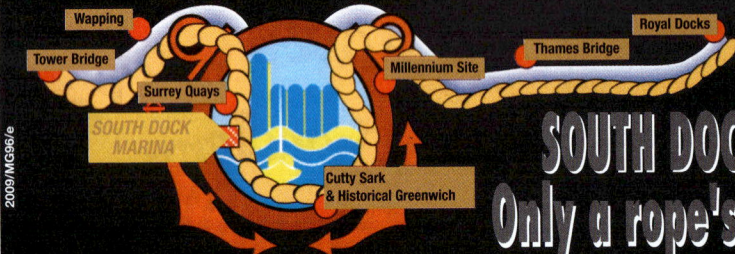

Adlard Coles Nautical THE BEST SAILING BOOKS

Knots Tie Yourself in Knots with Adlard Coles Nautical

Des Pawson's Knot Craft
Des Pawson
978 0 7136 8150 5
£9.99

Knots in Use
3rd edition
Colin Jarman
978 0 7136 6710 3
£8.99

Creative Ropecraft
4th edition, reissue
Stuart Grainger
978 0 7136 7401 9
£10.99

TO ORDER Tel: 01256 302699 email: direct@macmillan.co.uk or www.adlardcoles.com

POPLAR DOCK MARINA

Poplar Dock Marina
c/o Harbourmaster's Office
Limehouse Marina
46 Goodhart Place, London, E14 8EG
Tel: 020 7308 9930 Fax: 020 7363 0428
www.bwml.co.uk

VHF	Ch 13
ACCESS	HW±1 0700-1700

Poplar Dock was originally designed and constructed to maintain the water level in the West India Docks. Nowadays, with Canary Wharf lying to the west and the Millennium Dome to the east, it has been converted into London's newest marina and was officially opened by the Queen in June 1999. Canary Wharf, boasting as many as 90 shops, bars and restaurants, is just a five minute walk away, while slightly further north of this is West India Quay, where Grade I listed warehouses have been converted into waterside eating places, a 12-screen cinema and fitness centre.

FACILITIES AT A GLANCE

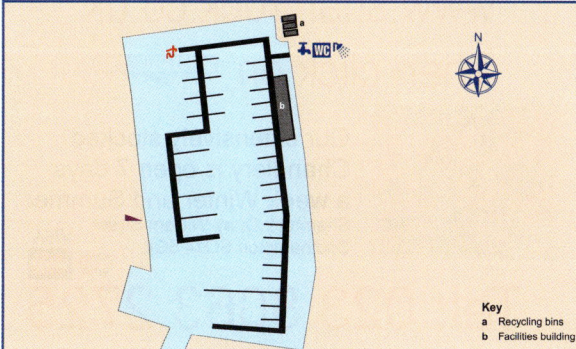

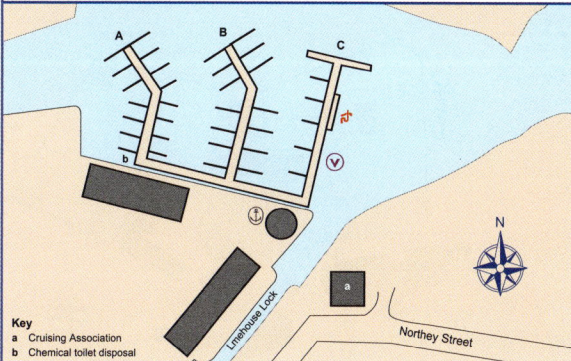

Key
a Recycling bins
b Facilities building

LIMEHOUSE MARINA

Limehouse Marina
46 Goodhart Place, London, E14 8EG
Tel: 020 7308 9930 Fax: 020 7363 0428
www.bwml.co.uk

VHF	Ch 80
ACCESS	HW±3

Limehouse Marina, situated where the canal system meets the Thames, is now considered the 'Jewel in the Crown' of the British inland waterways network. With complete access to 2,000 miles of inland waterway systems and with access to the Thames at most stages of the tide except around low water, the marina provides a superb location for river, canal and sea-going pleasure craft alike. Boasting a wide range of facilities and up to 90 berths, Limehouse Marina is housed in the old Regent's Canal Dock.

FACILITIES AT A GLANCE

Key
a Cruising Association
b Chemical toilet disposal

Limehouse Lock

Northey Street

4

Shamrock Chandlery

What ever your budget,
we've got it covered!

seago   SP   GOTOP   BALTIC LIFEJACKETS SWEDEN   XM Crewsaver

PLASTIMO   WEST SYSTEM BRAND   ECHOMAX   Barton MARINE   ADMIRALTY LEISURE

SHURHOLD   BLAKES Paints   BLUE GEE   LALIZAS   International

To buy these and many other brands visit
our new on-line shop

www.shamrock.co.uk - then click on   GO SHOPPING

Tel: 023 8063 2725

2009/MG128/e

ST KATHARINE HAVEN

St Katharine's Marina Ltd
50 St Katharine's Way, London, E1W 1LA
Tel: 020 7264 5312 Fax: 020 7702 2252
Email: haven.reception@skdocks.co.uk
www.skdocks.co.uk

VHF	Ch 80
ACCESS	HW -2 to +1.5

St Katharine Docks has played a significant role in worldwide trade and commerce for over 1,000 years. Formerly a working dock, today it is an attractive waterside development housing a mixture of shops, restaurants, luxury flats and offices as well as a state-of-the-art marina. St Katharine Haven is ideally situated for exploring central London and taking full advantage of the West End's theatres and cinemas. Within easy walking distance are Tower Bridge, the Tower of London and the historic warship HMS *Belfast*. No stay at the docks is complete without a visit to the famous Dickens Inn, an impressive three storey timber building incorporating a pizza bar and stylish restaurant.

FACILITIES AT A GLANCE

Key
a Ivory House
b Dickens Inn
c Haven office
d Tower Hotel

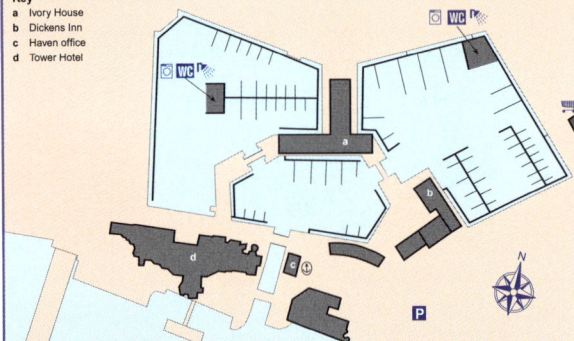

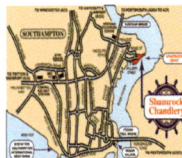

Shamrock Chandlery

What ever your budget, we've got it covered!

seago SP GOTOP BALTIC LIFEJACKETS SWEDEN XM
PLASTIMO spinlock SEBAGO
WEST SYSTEM ECHOMAX Barton MARINE ADMIRALTY LEISURE
SHURHOLD BLAKES Paints BLUE GEE LALIZAS International

To buy these and many other brands visit our new on-line shop

www.shamrock.co.uk

Then click on GO SHOPPING

Our extensively stocked Chandlery is open 7 days a week Winter and Summer
Shamrock Quay William Street Southampton SO14 5QL

VISA Maestro MasterCard

Tel: 023 8063 2725

2009/MG128/e

CHELSEA HARBOUR MARINA

Chelsea Harbour Marina
Estate Managements Office
C2-3 The Chambers, London, SW10 0XF
Tel: 07770 542783 Fax: 020 7352 7868
Email: harboumaster@chelsea-harbour.co.uk

VHF	
ACCESS	HW±1.5

Chelsea Harbour is now widely thought of as one of London's most significant maritime sites. It is located in the heart of South West London, therefore enjoying easy access to the amenities of Chelsea and the West End. On site is the Chelsea Harbour Design Centre, where 80 showrooms exhibit the best in British and International interior design, while offering superb waterside views along with excellent cuisine is the Conrad Hotel.

The harbour lies approximately 48 miles up river from Sea Reach No 1 buoy in the Thames Estuary and is accessed via the Thames Flood Barrier in Woolwich Reach. With its basin gate operating one and a half hours either side of HW (+ 20 minutes at London Bridge), the marina welcomes visiting yachtsmen.

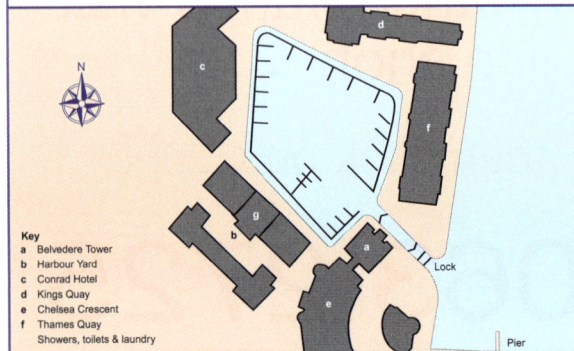

FACILITIES AT A GLANCE

Key
a Belvedere Tower
b Harbour Yard
c Conrad Hotel
d Kings Quay
e Chelsea Crescent
f Thames Quay
Showers, toilets & laundry

Lock
Pier

Sailing Information

CHELSEA HARBOUR

Location and Access:
From the sea, Chelsea Harbour is 48 nautical miles upriver from Sea Reach No: 1 Buoy in the Thames Estuary. For vessels entering or leaving the Thames, the recommended overnight mooring, if required, is at Queenbough at the river entrance to the River Medway. Vessels bound for Chelsea Harbour will pass through the Thames Floor Barrier located in Woolwich Reach. Traffic is controlled by Woolwich Radio (VHF Ch 14), and vessels equipped with VHF are required to call up Barrier Control on passing Margaret Ness when proceeding upstream, or on passing Blackwall Point when heading downstream. There is a speed limit of 8 knots on the tideway above Wandsworth Bridge.

Visitors:
Visitor yachtsmen from home and abroad are most welcome to Chelsea Harbour Marina, and are able to make prior arrangements by telephoning the Harbour Master's office on +44 (0) 7770 542783

Basin Gate Operation:
Approximately 1? hours either side of high water +20 minutes at London Bridge. With spring tide it may be necessary to close the outer gates around high water to control marina level.

Marina Lock Dimensions (Maximum for Craft):
Beam 5.5m (18')
Draught 2.5m (8')

Recommended Charts and Publications:
Admiralty: 1183, 2151 2484, 3319
Imray: C1, C2.

Cruising Opportunities:
Chelsea Harbour is ideally located for day, weekend or longer trips either upstream to Kew, Richmond, Hampton Court, or downstream to Rochester.

2009/MG89/v

BRENTFORD DOCK MARINA

Brentford Dock Marina
2 Justine Close, Brentford, Middlesex, TW8 8QE
Tel: 020 8232 8941 Fax: 020 8560 5486 Mob: 07920 143 987
E-mail: sam.langton@brentford-dock.co.uk

VHF
ACCESS HW±2.5

Brentford Dock Marina is situated on the River Thames at the junction with the Grand Union Canal. Its hydraulic lock is accessible for up to two and a half hours either side of high water, although boats over 9.5m LOA enter on high water by prior arrangement. There is a Spar grocery store on site. The main attractions within the area are the Royal Botanic Gardens at Kew and the Kew Bridge Steam Museum at Brentford.

FACILITIES AT A GLANCE

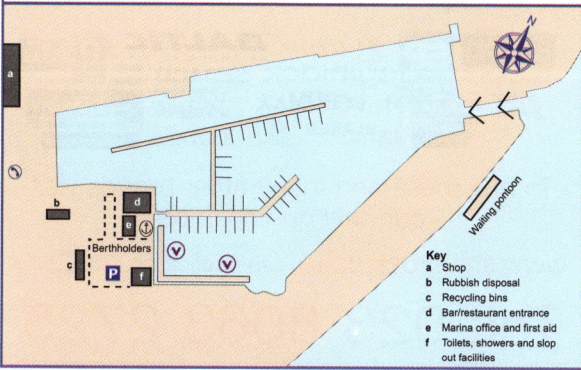

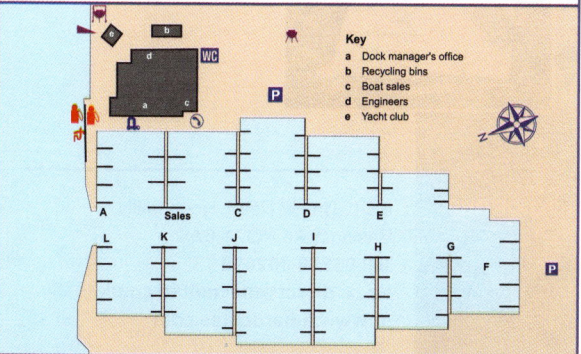

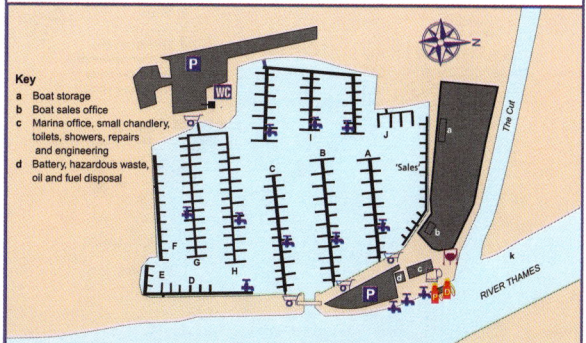

Key
a Shop
b Rubbish disposal
c Recycling bins
d Bar/restaurant entrance
e Marina office and first aid
f Toilets, showers and slop out facilities

PENTON HOOK MARINA

Penton Hook
Staines Road, Chertsey, Surrey, KT16 8PY
Tel: 01932 568681 Fax: 01932 567423
Email: pentonhook@mdlmarinas.co.uk
www.marinas.co.uk

VHF Ch 80
ACCESS H24

Penton Hook Marina is situated on what is considered to be one of the most attractive reaches of the River Thames, close to Chertsey and about a mile downstream of Runnymede. Providing unrestricted access to the River Thames through a deep water channel below Penton Hook Lock, the marina can accommodate ocean-going craft of up to 21m LOA and is ideally placed for a visit to Thorpe Park, reputedly one of Europe's most popular family leisure attractions.

FACILITIES AT A GLANCE

Key
a Information point
b Dock manager's office
c Yacht club
d Repairs and under cover storage

WINDSOR MARINA

Windsor Marina
Maidenhead Road, Windsor
Berkshire, SL4 5TZ
Tel: 01753 853911 Fax: 01753 868195
Email: windsor@mdlmarinas.co.uk www.marinas.co.uk

VHF Ch 80
ACCESS H24

Situated on the outskirts of Windsor town on the south bank of the River Thames, Windsor Marina enjoys a peaceful garden setting. On site are the Windsor Yacht Club as well as boat lifting and repair facilities, a chandlery and brokerage.

A trip to the town of Windsor, comprising beautiful Georgian and Victorian buildings, would not be complete without a visit to Windsor Castle. With its construction inaugurated over 900 years ago by William the Conqueror, it is the oldest inhabited castle in the world and accommodates a priceless art and furniture collection.

FACILITIES AT A GLANCE

Key
a Dock manager's office
b Recycling bins
c Boat sales
d Engineers
e Yacht club

BRAY MARINA

Bray Marina
Monkey Island Lane, Bray
Berkshire, SL6 2EB
Tel: 01628 623654 Fax: 01628 773485
Email: bray@mdlmarinas.co.uk www.marinas.co.uk

VHF Ch 80
ACCESS H24

Bray Marina is situated in a country park setting among shady trees, providing berth holders with a delightfully tranquil mooring. From the marina there is direct access to the Thames and there are extensive well-maintained facilities available for all boat owners. Also on site is the highly acclaimed Riverside Brasserie. Twice winner of the AA rosette award for culinary excellence and short-listed for the Tatler best country restaurant, the Brasserie is especially popular with Club Outlook members who enjoy a 15% discount. The 400-berth marina boasts an active club, which holds social functions as well as boat training lessons and handling competitions, a chandlery and engineering services.

FACILITIES AT A GLANCE

Key
a Boat storage
b Boat sales office
c Marina office, small chandlery, toilets, showers, repairs and engineering
d Battery, hazardous waste, oil and fuel disposal

BURNHAM YACHT HARBOUR MARINA

Burnham Yacht Harbour Marina Ltd
Burnham-on-Crouch, Essex, CM0 8BL
Tel: 01621 782150 Fax: 01621 785848
Email: admin@burnhamyachtharbour.co.uk

VHF Ch 80
ACCESS H24

Boasting four major yacht clubs, each with comprehensive racing programmes, Burnham-on-Crouch has come to be regarded by some as 'the Cowes of the East Coast'. At the western end of the town lies Burnham Yacht Harbour, dredged 2.2m below datum. Offering a variety of on site facilities, its entrance can be easily identified by a yellow pillar buoy with an 'X' topmark.

The historic town, with its 'weatherboard' and early brick buildings, elegant quayside and scenic riverside walks, exudes plenty of charm. Among its attractions are a sports centre, a railway museum and a two-screen cinema.

FACILITIES AT A GLANCE

Key
a Workshop
b Yacht sales
c Marina office
d Shower block
e The Swallowtail
f RNLI shore station
g Country park

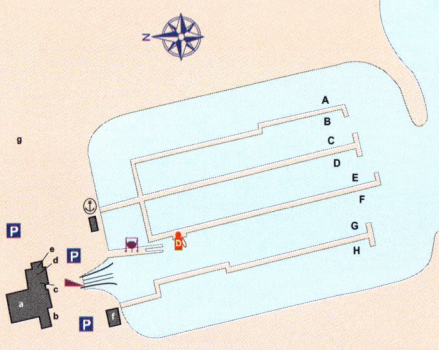

FAMBRIDGE YACHT HAVEN

Fambridge Yacht Haven
Church Road, North Fambridge, Essex, CM3 6LR
Tel: 01621 740370 Fax: 01621 742359
Email: fambridge@yachthavens.com

VHF Ch 80
ACCESS H24

Just under a mile upstream of North Fambridge, Stow Creek branches off to the north of the River Crouch. The creek, marked with occasional starboard hand buoys and leading lights, leads to the entrance to Fambridge Yacht Haven, which enjoys an unspoilt, tranquil setting between saltings and farmland. Home to West Wick Yacht Club, the marina has 180 berths and can accommodate vessels up to 17m LOA.

The nearby village of North Fambridge features the Ferryboat Inn, a favourite haunt with the boating fraternity. Only six miles down river lies Burnham-on-Crouch, while the Essex and Kent coasts are within easy sailing distance.

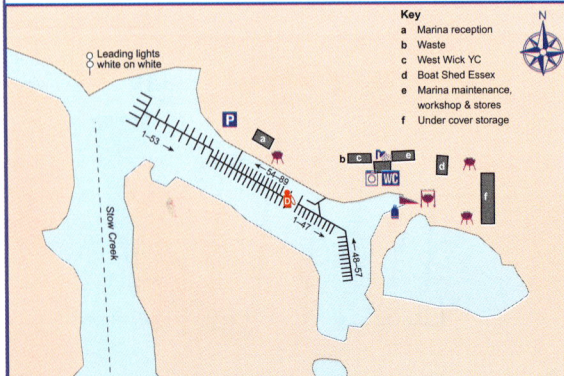

FACILITIES AT A GLANCE

Key
a Marina reception
b Waste
c West Wick YC
d Boat Shed Essex
e Marina maintenance, workshop & stores
f Under cover storage

MarineStore
Burnham-on-Crouch, Essex
www.marinestore.co.uk
Excellent range of day to day chandlery and wide selection of clothing
STOCKIST OF
INTERNATIONAL • BLAKES • S P SYSTEMS • WEST MUSTO • CREWSAVER
THE EASTCOAST CHANDLERY SPECIALISTS
TEL: 01621 783090 EMAIL: chandlery@marinestore.co.uk

Shamrock Chandlery
What ever your budget, we've got it covered!
To buy these and many other brands visit our new on-line shop
www.shamrock.co.uk - then click on GO SHOPPING
Tel: 023 8063 2725

Adlard Coles Nautical
THE BEST SAILING BOOKS
Maintenance
Boatowner's Mechanical & Electrical Manual
3rd edition
Nigel Calder
978 0 7136 7226 8
£45
TO ORDER
MDL, Brunel Road, Houndmills, Basingstoke RG21 6XS
Tel: 01256 302699
email: direct@macmillan.co.uk
or www.adlardcoles.com

ESSEX MARINA

Essex Marina
Wallasea Island, Essex, SS4 2HF
Tel: 01702 258531 Fax: 01702 258227
Email: info@essexmarina.co.uk
www.essexmarina.co.uk

VHF Ch 80
ACCESS H24

Surrounded by beautiful countryside in an area of Special Scientific Interest, Essex Marina is situated in Wallasea Bay, about half a mile up river of Burnham on Crouch. Boasting 500 deep water berths, including 50 swinging moorings, the marina can be accessed at all states of the tide. On site are a 70 ton boat hoist, a chandlery and brokerage service as well as the Essex Marina Yacht Club.

Buses run frequently to Southend-on-Sea, just seven miles away, while a ferry service takes passengers across the river on weekends to Burnham, where you will find numerous shops and restaurants. Benefiting from its close proximity to London (just under an hour's drive away) and Rochford Airport (approximately four miles away), the marina provides a suitable location for crew changeovers.

FACILITIES AT A GLANCE

Key
a Marina office & chandlery
b Essex Marina Yacht Club
c Brokerage & boat sales
d Licenced bar & restaurant

BRIDGEMARSH MARINA

Bridge Marsh Marine
Fairholme, Bridge Marsh Lane, Althorne, Essex
Tel: 01621 740414 Mobile: 07968 696815 Fax: 01621 740414

VHF Ch 80
ACCESS HW±4

On the north side of Bridgemarsh Island, just beyond Essex Marina on the River Crouch, lies Althorne Creek. Here Bridgemarsh Marine accommodates over 100 boats berthed alongside pontoons supplied with water and electricity. A red beacon marks the entrance to the creek, with red can buoys identifying the approach channel into the marina. Accessible four hours either side of high water, the marina has an on site yard with two docks, a slipway and crane. The village of Althorne is just a short walk away, from where there are direct train services (taking approximately one hour) to London.

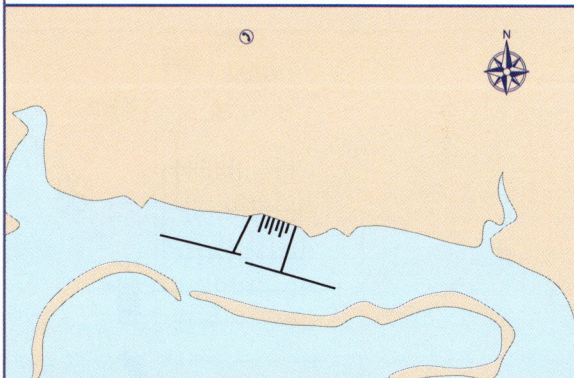

FACILITIES AT A GLANCE

4

Burnham Yacht Harbour Marina Ltd

The finest marina in Essex on the delightful River Crouch offering all services

- Access at all states of the tide
- On site Chandlery, Brokerage, Restaurant/Bar
- 100 ton slipway, 35 ton Travelhoist
- Experienced engineers, shipwrights, riggers and outfitters
- Free wireless internet connectivity
- 10 minutes walk from the picturesque town and all its amenities

Harbourmaster:
01621 786832
VHF Channel 80

Tel: 01621 782150 • Fax: 01621 785848
Email: admin@burnhamyachtharbour.co.uk • www.burnhamyachtharbour.co.uk

2009/MG156/zz

BRADWELL MARINA

Bradwell Marina, Port Flair Ltd, Waterside
Bradwell-on-Sea, Essex, CM0 7RB
Tel: 01621 776235 Fax: 01621 776393
Email: info@bradwellmarina.com
www.bradwellmarina.com

VHF Ch M, 80
ACCESS HW±4.5

Opened in 1984, Bradwell is a privately-owned marina situated in the mouth of the River Blackwater, serving as a convenient base from which to explore the Essex coastline or as a departure point for cruising further afield to Holland and Belgium. The yacht basin can be accessed four and a half hours either side of HW and offers plenty of protection from all wind directions. With a total of 300 fully serviced berths, generous space has been allocated for manoeuvring between pontoons. Overlooking the marina is Bradwell Club House, incorporating a bar, restaurant, launderette and ablution facilities.

FACILITIES AT A GLANCE

Key
a Clubhouse
b Tower office

Bradwell Marina

- 300 Pontoon Berths in Rural Setting
- Access 4hrs either side H.W.
- VHF monitoring 9CH.M,P1,37+80)
- Water/Electricity to all Pontoons
- Fuel jetty – Petrol and Diesel
- Chandlery
- Hot Showers
- 1st Class Workshop/Repairs
- Marine Slip to 20 tons
- Boat Hoistage to 45 tons
- Winter Storage
- Licensed Club (Membership Free)
- Yacht Brokerage

Port Flair Ltd., Waterside, Bradwell-on-Sea, Essex CM0 7RB (01621) 776235/776391

2009/MGM2/e

Adlard Coles Nautical
THE BEST SAILING BOOKS

The Adlard Coles Book of Knots
Peter Owen 978 0 7136 8152 9 £7.99

Knots & Splices
2nd edition
Cyrus L Day, revised by Colin Jarman
978 0 7136 7748 5
£3.99

TO ORDER Tel: **01256 302699** or visit **www.adlardcoles.com**

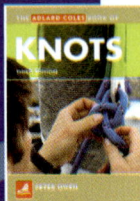

BLACKWATER MARINA

Blackwater Marina
Marine Parade, Maylandsea, Essex
Tel: 01621 740264 Tel: 01621 742122
Email: info@blackwater-marina.co.uk

VHF Ch M
ACCESS HW±2

Blackwater Marina is a place where families in day boats mix with Smack owners and yacht crews; here seals, avocets and porpoises roam beneath the big, sheltering East Coast skies and here the area's rich heritage of working Thames Barges and Smacks remains part of daily life today. But it isn't just classic sailing boats that thrive on the Blackwater. An eclectic mix of motor cruisers, open boats and modern yachts enjoy the advantages of a marina sheltered by its natural habitat, where the absence of harbour walls allows uninterrupted views of some of Britain's rarest wildlife and where the 21st century shoreside facilities are looked after by experienced professionals, who are often found sailing on their days off.

FACILITIES AT A GLANCE

Key
a Maylandsea Bay YC
b Harlow (Blackwater) Sailing Club
c Main office

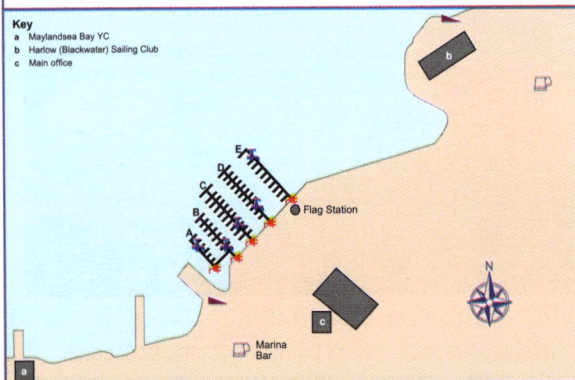

Shamrock Chandlery

What ever your budget, we've got it covered!

seago SP GOTOP BALTIC XM spinlock SEBAGO WEST SYSTEM ECHOMAX Barton SHURHOLD BLAKES Paints G LALIZAS ADMIRALTY International

To buy these and many other brands visit our new on-line shop

www.shamrock.co.uk

Then click on GO SHOPPING

Our extensively stocked Chandlery is open 7 days a week Winter and Summer
Shamrock Quay William Street
Southampton SO14 5QL

Tel: 023 8063 2725

2009/MG128/e

TOLLESBURY MARINA

Tollesbury Marina
The Yacht Harbour, Tollesbury, Essex, CM9 8SE
Tel: 01621 869202 Fax: 01621 868489
email: marina@woodrolfe.com

VHF Ch M, 80
ACCESS HW±2

Tollesbury Marina lies at the mouth of the River Blackwater in the heart of the Essex countryside. Within easy access from London and the Home Counties, it has been designed as a leisure centre for the whole family, with on-site activities comprising tennis courts and a covered heated swimming pool as well as a convivial bar and restaurant. Accommodating over 240 boats, the marina can be accessed two hours either side of HW and is ideally situated for those wishing to explore the River Crouch to the south and the Rivers Colne, Orwell and Deben to the north.

FACILITIES AT A GLANCE

Key
a Brokerage and Chandlery
b Workshop
c Covered Heated Pool and Tennis

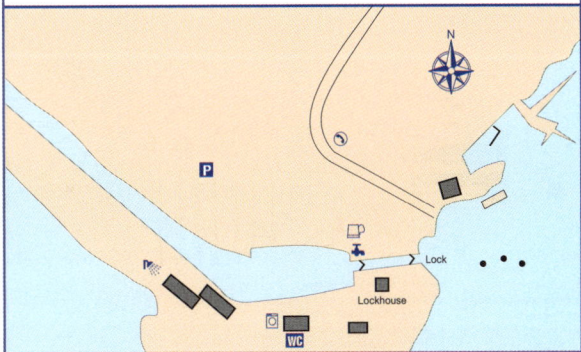

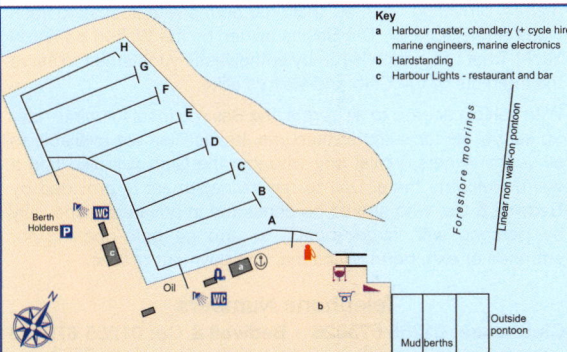

HEYBRIDGE BASIN

Heybridge Basin
Lock Hill, Heybridge Basin, Maldon, Essex, CM9 4RX
Tel: 01621 853506 Fax: 01621 859689
Email: colinandmargeret@lockkeepers.fsnet.co.uk
www.cbn.co.uk

VHF Ch 80
ACCESS HW±1

Towards the head of the River Blackwater, not far from Maldon, lies Heybridge Basin. Situated at the lower end of the 14–mile long Chelmer and Blackwater Navigation Canal, it can be reached via a lock about one hour either side of HW for a yacht drawing around 2m. If you arrive too early, there is good holding ground in the river just outside the lock. Incorporating as many as 200 berths, the basin has a range of facilities, including shower and laundry amenities. It is strongly recommendedthat you book 24 hours in advance for summer weekends.

FACILITIES AT A GLANCE

TITCHMARSH MARINA

Titchmarsh Marina Ltd
Coles Lane, Walton on the Naze, Essex, CO14 8SL
Tel: 01255 672185 Fax: 01255 851901
Email: info@titchmarshmarina.co.uk
www.titchmarshmarina.co.uk

VHF Ch 80
ACCESS HW±5

Titchmarsh Marina sits on the south side of The Twizzle in the heart of the Walton Backwaters. As the area is designated as a 'wetland of international importance', the marina has been designed and developed to function as a natural harbour. The 420 berths are well sheltered by the high-grassed clay banks, offering good protection in all conditions. Access to Titchmarsh is over a sill, which has a depth of about 1m at LWS, but once inside the basin, the depth increases to around 2m. Among the excellent facilities are an on site chandlery as well as the Harbour Lights Restaurant & Bar serving breakfasts, lunch and dinners.

FACILITIES AT A GLANCE

Key
a Harbour master, chandlery (+ cycle hire)
   marine engineers, marine electronics
b Hardstanding
c Harbour Lights - restaurant and bar

TITCHMARSH marina

Friendly service in the peaceful Backwaters.
Visiting yachtsmen welcome.
Sheltered Marina berths with Full Marina facilities:
16 amp electricity supply, diesel, LPG, Calor Gas, Travel-lifts, concrete hard standing, Winter storage - afloat & ashore.
Restaurant and Bar - Harbour Lights Restaurant
Brokerage - Westwater Yacht Sales - www.wwys.co.uk
www.titchmarshmarina.co.uk
Coles Lane, Walton-on-the-Naze, Essex, CO14 8SL
Marina Office Tel: 01255 672 185
Harbour Master Tel/Fax: 01255 851 899 VHF: Channel 80

2009/MG61/Ve

Adlard Coles Nautical
THE BEST SAILING BOOKS

Safety

Sail safely with
Adlard Coles Nautical
First Aid at Sea
5th edition
Colin Berry and Douglas Justins
978 1 4081 0599 3
£9.99

FIRST AID AT SEA

TO ORDER Tel: **01256 302699** or visit **www.adlardcoles.com**

SHOTLEY MARINA

Shotley Marina Ltd
Shotley Gate, Ipswich, Suffolk, IP9 1QJ
Tel: 01473 788982 Fax: 01473 788868
Email: sales@shotleymarina.co.uk
www.shotleymarina.co.uk

| VHF | Ch 80 |
| ACCESS | H24 |

Based in the well protected Harwich Harbour where the River Stour joins the River Orwell, Shotley Marina is only eight miles from the county town of Ipswich. Entered via a lock at all states of the tide, its first class facilities include extensive boat repair and maintenance services as well as a well-stocked chandlery and on site bar and restaurant. The marina is strategically placed for sailing up the Stour to Manningtree, up the Orwell to Pin Mill or exploring the Rivers Deben, Crouch and Blackwater as well as the Walton Backwaters.

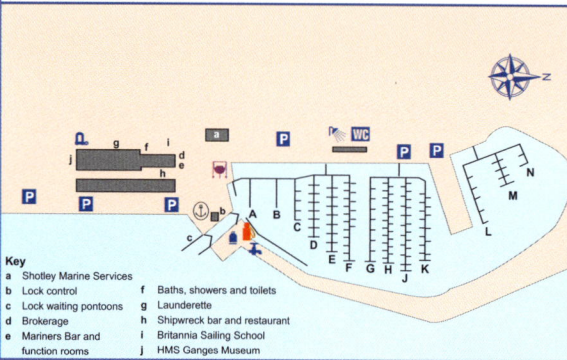

FACILITIES AT A GLANCE

Key
a Shotley Marine Services
b Lock control
c Lock waiting pontoons
d Brokerage
e Mariners Bar and function rooms
f Baths, showers and toilets
g Launderette
h Shipwreck bar and restaurant
i Britannia Sailing School
j HMS Ganges Museum

SHOTLEY MARINA LTD

SHOTLEY GATE, IPSWICH, SUFFOLK IP9 1QJ.
TEL: (01473) 788982
FAX: (01473) 788868

350-berth, modern state of the art marina offering all the services expected. Open 24 hours with full security - Access all states of tide.

CHANDLERY • GENERAL STORE • RESTAURANT • BAR
LAUNDRY & IRONING CENTRE • SHOWERS BATHS TOILETS • CHILDREN'S ROOM • FREE WI-FI CONNECTION
FULLY EQUIPPED BOATYARD OFFERING REPAIRS TO FULL REFITS.
DISABLED FACILITIES AVAILABLE.
E-mail: sales@shotleymarina.co.uk
Website: www.eastcoastmarinas.co.uk

2009/MGM6/e

Shamrock Chandlery

What ever your budget, we've got it covered!

seaGo SP GOTOP BALTIC XM
spinlock SEBAGO
WEST SYSTEM ECHOMAX Barton MARINE ADMIRALTY LEISURE
SHURHOLD BLAKES Paints G LALIZAS International

To buy these and many other brands visit our new on-line shop

www.shamrock.co.uk - then click on GO SHOPPING

Tel: 023 8063 2725

2009/MG128/e

WALTON YACHT BASIN

Walton and Frinton Yacht Trust
Mill Lane, Walton on the Naze, CO14 8PF
Managed by Bedwell & Co Tel: 01255 675873
Fax: 01255 677405 After hours Tel: 01255 672655

| VHF | |
| ACCESS | HW-0.75, HW+0.25 |

Walton Yacht Basin lies at the head of Walton Creek, an area made famous in Arthur Ransome's *Swallows & Amazons* and *Secret Waters*. The creek can only be navigated two hours either side of HW, although yachts heading for the Yacht Basin should arrive on a rising tide as the entrance gate is kept shut once the tide turns in order to retain the water inside. Before entering the gate, moor up against the Club Quay to enquire about berthing availability.

A short walk away is the popular seaside town of Walton, full of shops, pubs and restaurants. Its focal point is the pier which, overlooking superb sandy beaches, offers various attractions including a ten-pin bowling alley. Slightly further out of town, the Naze affords pleasant coastal walks with striking panoramic views.

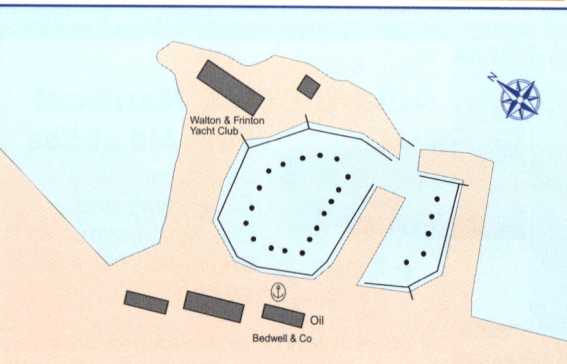

FACILITIES AT A GLANCE

Walton & Frinton Yacht Club

Oil

Bedwell & Co

WALTON Yacht Basin

Mill Lane, Walton-on-the-Naze, Essex CO14 8PF

2008/MG50/s

The Yacht Basin has a gate-controlled minimum depth of 2 metres, providing up to 60 sheltered berths with access to fresh water and electricity. The Basins owned by the Walton & Frinton Yacht Trust Ltd, which is run by enthusiastic yachtsmen to serve the interests of the Club and visitors alike.

With vehicle access to all berths, the Basin is ideal for winter lay-up as well as for summer-time use. Its facilities are available to all yacht-owners, whilst any who join the Club will also find a warm welcome there. Day to day management is provided by Bedwell & Co, who should be contacted in advance (especially by persons with larger boats) to arrange gate-opening for entrance or exit, berth allocation, and payment of fees.

Telephone Numbers
Clubhouse: 01255 675526   Bedwell & Co: 01255 675873

FOX'S MARINA

Fox's Marina Ipswich Ltd
The Strand, Wherstead, Ipswich, Suffolk, IP2 8SA
Tel: 01473 689111 Fax: 01473 601737
Email: foxs@foxsmarina.com

VHF Ch 80
ACCESS H24

One of five marinas on the River Orwell, Fox's provides good shelter in all conditions and, dredged to 2m below chart datum, benefits from full tidal access from Ostrich Creek. Accommodating yachts up to 21m LOA, it has enough storage ashore for over 200 vessels and offers a comprehensive refit, repair and maintenance service. Since becoming part of the Oyster Group of Companies, Fox's facilities have further improved with ongoing investment. Besides several workshops, other services on hand include an osmosis centre, a spray centre, engineering, rigging and electronic specialists as well as one of the largest chandleries on the East Coast. In addition there are regular bus services to Ipswich, which is only about one to two miles away.

Key
a Chandlery
b Harbourmaster office
c Yacht Club

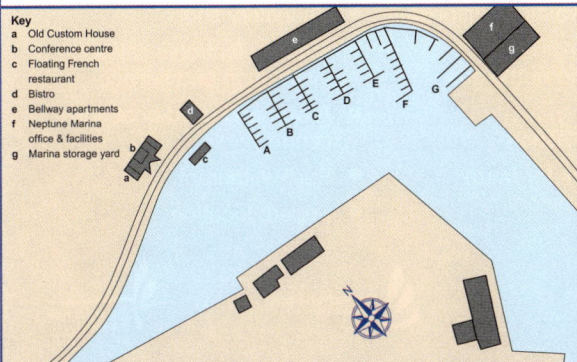

OYSTER BROKERAGE
Specialists in Pre-Owned Oyster Yachts

Visit our website for a wide selection of luxurious Oyster yachts

www.oysterbrokerage.com

Oyster Brokerage Ltd • Fox's Marina • Ipswich • IP2 8SA
E: brokerage@oystermarine.com
T: 01473 695100 F: 01473 695120

FOX'S SINCE 1927
MARINE SERVICE CENTRE

Heated Workshops
Osmosis Treatment
Masts & Rigging
Stainless Steel
Fabrication
Insurance Repairs
Yacht Spray Centre
Electronics
Sales & Service
Engineering
Boat Hoist to 70 tons
Large Chandlery

Fox's Marina Ipswich Ltd
Ipswich Suffolk IP2 8SA
T: +44 (0) 1473 689111
F: +44 (0) 1473 601737
E: foxs@foxsmarina.com
www.foxsmarina.com

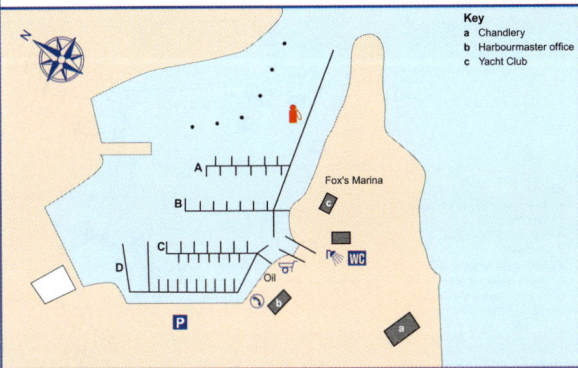

NEPTUNE MARINA

Neptune Marina Ltd
Neptune Quay, Ipswich, IP4 1AX
Tel: 01473 215204 Fax: 01473 215206
Email: enquiries@neptune-marina.com

VHF Ch M, 80
ACCESS H±2.5

The Wet Dock at Ipswich, which was opened in 1850, became the largest in Europe and was in use right up until the 1930s. Now the dock incorporates Neptune Marina, situated at Neptune Quay on the Historic Waterfront, and ever increasing shoreside developments. This 26-acre dock is accessible through a 24-hr lock gate, with a waiting pontoon outside. The town centre is a 10 minute walk away, while Cardinal Park, a relatively new complex housing an 11-screen cinema and several eating places, is nearby. There are also a number of other excellent restaunts along the quayside and adjacent to the Marina. The new Neptune Marina building occupies an imposing position in the NE corner of the dock with quality coffee shop and associated retail units.

Key
a Old Custom House
b Conference centre
c Floating French restaurant
d Bistro
e Bellway apartments
f Neptune Marina office & facilities
g Marina storage yard

Martin Evans, MYDSA
YACHT & SMALL CRAFT SURVEYOR

Full Member of Yacht Designers & Surveyors Association

• Condition surveys for purchase and insurance
• Valuations
• Damage assessment
• Repair and project supervision
• MCA Code of Practice inspections and advice
• Sea trials
• General consultancy

Esplanade House, 32 Kings Quay Street, Harwich, Essex CO12 3ES
Telephone/Fax 01255 556216
Mobile 07887 724055
e-mail shipshape@homecall.co.uk

HARRY KING & SONS LTD

BOAT YARD • BOAT BUILDERS • REPAIRERS

Specialists in construction, restoration and repair of both traditional and modern craft

Harry King & Sons Ltd
Pin Mill, Ipswich, Suffolk IP9 1JN

Telephone & Fax: 01473 780258
E-mail: info.kingsboatyard@virgin.net
www.kingsboatyard.co.uk

2009/MG91/e

IPSWICH HAVEN MARINA

Ipswich Haven Marina
Associated British Ports
New Cut East, Ipswich, Suffolk, IP3 0EA
Tel: 01473 236644 Fax: 01473 236645
Email: ipswichhaven@abports.co.uk

VHF	Ch M, 68 & 80
ACCESS	H24

Lying at the heart of Ipswich, the Haven Marina enjoys close proximity to all the bustling shopping centres, restaurants, cinemas and museums that this County Town of Suffolk has to offer. The main railway station is only a 10-minute walk away, where there are regular connections to London, Cambridge and Norwich, all taking just over an hour to get to.

Within easy reach of Holland, Belgium and Germany, East Anglia is proving an increasingly popular cruising ground. The River Orwell, displaying breathtaking scenery, was voted one of the most beautiful rivers in Britain by the RYA.

FACILITIES AT A GLANCE

Key
a   Toilets, showers, laundry, office
b   Licensed bistro
c   R&J Marine Electronics
d   Boat sales
e   Fairline PDI Shed
f   Future restaurant retail
g   Burton Waters Repair Shop

IPSWICH & LOWESTOFT HAVEN MARINAS

For more information please contact:

IPSWICH
Telephone: +44 (0)1473 236644
Facsimile: +44 (0)1473 236645
Email: ipswichhaven@abports.co.uk

LOWESTOFT
Telephone: +44 (0)1502 580300
Facsimile: +44 (0)1502 581851
Email: lowestofthaven@abports.co.uk
www.lowestofthavenmarina.co.uk

ABP

Welcome to **Ipswich Haven Marina** and **Lowestoft Haven Marina**, (incorporating the new, 46 berth, Hamilton Dock extension) both situated in the heart of the towns they serve.

Both Marinas hold the coveted T.Y.H.A. five gold anchor award and offer the following outstanding facilities:

- 70-tonne boat hoist
- Shower and toilet facilities
- Refuse and waste oil disposal facilities
- Diesel fuel and bottle gas supplies
- Boat storage ashore
- Large car park for berth holders and visitors
- Emergency telephone
- Repair and re-fit workshops
- Chandlery shop
- Marine electronic sales installation and service
- A new and used boat sales centre
- Bar/Restaurant
- Superb location

The Yacht Harbour Association Ltd.

British Marine Federation

2009/MG73/e

4

LOWESTOFT HAVEN MARINA

Lowestoft Haven Marina
School Road, Lowestoft, Suffolk, NR33 9NB
Tel: 01502 580300 Fax: 01502 581851
Email: lowestofthaven@abports.co.uk

VHF	Ch M, 80
ACCESS	H24

Lowestoft HavenLowestoft Haven Marina is phase 1 of a new marina complex for Lowestoft and is based on Lake Lothing and offering easy access to both the open sea and the Norfolk Broads. The town centres of both Lowestoft and Oulton Broad are within a short distance of the marina. The marina's 140 berths can accommodate vessels from 7-20m. Offering a full range of modern facilities the marina welcomes all visitors.

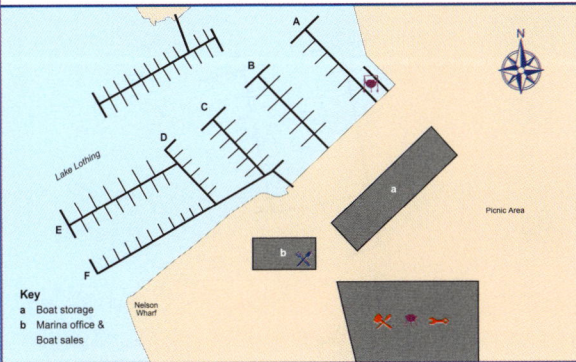

FACILITIES AT A GLANCE

Key
a Boat storage
b Marina office &
    Boat sales

The Marine Safety Centre Limited

NEED A LIFERAFT?
WE ARE SPECIALISTS IN LIFERAFT
SALES • HIRE • SERVICE
Also Fenders, Life Jackets, Pyrotechnics

Unit 4 Colville Road Works, Colville Road
Lowestoft, Suffolk NR33 9QX
Tel: 01502 500940 Fax: 01502 500937
After Hours: 01502 566044

2009/MG35/v

JPCdirect.com

'When only the best will do'

Sales ~ Service ~ Installation
Repair ~ Spare Parts ~ Support

Webasto
Marine Comfort

**Air Heating
Water Heating
Air Conditioning**

Wroxham - Norfolk
01603 784884

Lowestoft Haven Marina
01502 500712

sales@jpcdirect.com

SIDE-POWER
Thruster systems

**Electric and Hydraulic
Bow and Stern Thrusters**

Visit our workshop in
Lowestoft Haven Marina for

GRP repairs ~ Engineering
Antifouling ~ Polishing
Re-Fits ~ New Builds
Painting ~ Electronics

2009/MG162/z

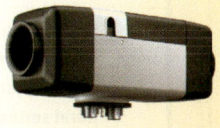

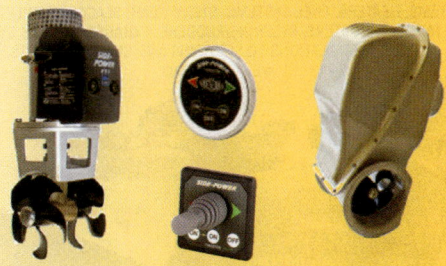

WOOLVERSTONE MARINA

Woolverstone Marina
Woolverstone, Ipswich, Suffolk, IP9 1AS
Tel: 01473 780206 Fax: 01473 780273
Email: t.barnes@mdlmarinas.co.uk www.marinas.co.uk

| VHF | Ch 80 |
| ACCESS | H24 |

Set in 22 acres of parkland, within close proximity to the Royal Harwich Yacht Club, Woolverstone Marina boasts 210 pontoon berths as well as 120 swinging moorings, all of which are served by a water taxi. Besides boat repair services, an on site chandlery and excellent ablution facilities, the marina also incorporates a sailing school and yacht brokerage.

Woolverstone's location on the scenic River Orwell makes it ideally placed for exploring the various cruising grounds along the East Coast, including the adjacent River Stour, the Colne and Blackwater estuaries to the south and the River Deben to the north.

FACILITIES AT A GLANCE

Key
a Marina office, toilets, showers, launderette and boat sales
b Restaurant/bar
c Royal Harwich Yacht Club

ROYAL HARWICH YACHT CLUB MARINA

Royal Harwich Yacht Club Marina
Marina Road, Woolverstone, Suffolk, IP9 1BA
Tel: 01473 780319 Fax: 01473 780919
www.rhyc.demon.co.uk
Email: secretary@rhyc.demon.co.uk

| VHF | Ch 77 |
| ACCESS | H24 |

This 54 berth marina is ideally situated at a mid point on the Orwell between Levington and Ipswich. The facility is owned and run by the Royal Harwich Yacht Club and enjoys a full catering and bar service in the Clubhouse. The marina benefits from full tidal access, and can accommodate yachts up to 4.5m on the hammerhead. Within the immediate surrounds, there are boat repair services, and a well stocked chandlery. The marina is situated a mile's walk from the world famous Pin Mill and is a favoured destination with visitors from Holland, Belgium and Germany. The marina welcomes racing yachts and cruisers, and is able to accommodate multiple bookings.

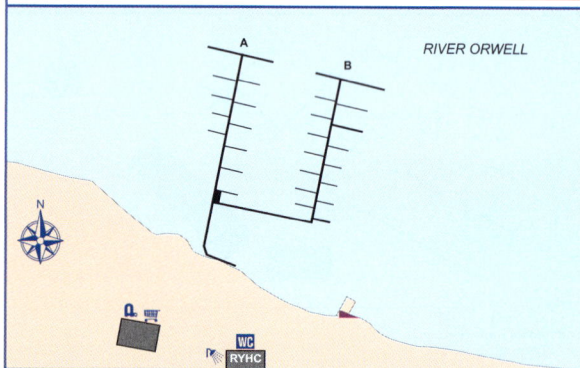

FACILITIES AT A GLANCE

RIVER ORWELL

Harvey Marine Services

CUMMINS MARINE CERTIFIED APPLICATIONS ENGINEER. SPECIALIST IN MARINE ENGINEERING WITH 20 YEARS EXPERIENCE. ATTENDING TO A WIDE RANGE OF TASKS ON ENGINES, GENERATORS, WATER SYSTEMS, HEATERS, FUEL SYSTEMS, SEACOCKS,TOILET/HOLDING TANKS, THRUSTERS, STEERING/RUDDERS, EXHAUST AND GAS SYSTEMS FROM INSTALLATIONS TO SERVICING AND SUPPLY OF UNITS. WE COVER IT ALL.

"FOR DEPENDABLE QUALITY WITH NO HIDDEN EXTRAS"
Tel: 07711 810793   WK: 01473 328870
www.harveymarineservices
email: hmsbilly@btinternet.com

Specialising in . . .
CAT CUMMINS NANNI SABRE PERKINS VOLVO BUKH YANMAR ONAN WESTERBEKE EBERSPACHER WEBASTO JABSCO VETUS

2009/mg143/vvz

THE ROYAL HARWICH YACHT CLUB
Marina & Clubhouse, Woolverstone

Everything To 'Float Your Boat'

Our fabulous, modern marina offers you more than just a place to come alongside. With 54 spacious berths, and excellent on-site facilities, you can relax in the knowledge that you and your boat are in safe and experienced hands!

❖ Fully-licensed bar and catering throughout the year.
❖ Family friendly Clubhouse and lawn
❖ Breathtaking views from a sunny sheltered aspect
❖ Rural setting with countryside walks to nearby villages
❖ On-site services for all your boating needs

Experience the ideal place to enjoy your stay afloat; from one night to several weeks! Visiting Clubs and Cruising Associations are always welcome.

To reserve your berth with us, please contact:
Berth Master Geoff Prentice (07742) 145 994/ VHF CH 77
Clubhouse (01473) 780 219/319*
please access our website for opening times
Or visit www.royalharwichyachtclub.co.uk
Wifi available

RHYC
THE PRIDE OF EAST COAST SAILING

2009/MG102/z

Adlard Coles Nautical
THE BEST SAILING BOOKS

New

Reeds Astro Navigation Tables 2009

Lt Cdr Harry Baker

An established book of annual astro-navigation tables for yachtsmen.

978 0 7136 8996 9

£17.99

REEDS 2009

ASTRO NAVIGATION TABLES

LT CDR HARRY J BAKER

Reeds Astro Navigation Tables 2009 can be obtained from your normal supplier - or please contact www.adlardcoles.com.

SUFFOLK YACHT HARBOUR

Suffolk Yacht Harbour Ltd
Levington, Ipswich, Suffolk, IP10 0LN
Tel: 01473 659240 Fax: 01473 659632
Email: enquiries@syharbour.co.uk
www.syharbour.co.uk

VHF Ch 80
ACCESS H24

A friendly, independently-run marina on the East Coast of England, Suffolk Yacht Harbour enjoys a beautiful rural setting on the River Orwell, yet it is within easy access of Ipswich, Woodbridge and Felixstowe. With approximately 500 berths, the marina offers extensive facilities while the Haven Ports Yacht Club provides a bar and restaurant.

FACILITIES AT A GLANCE

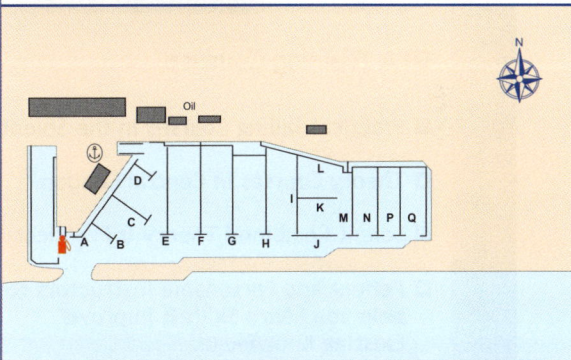

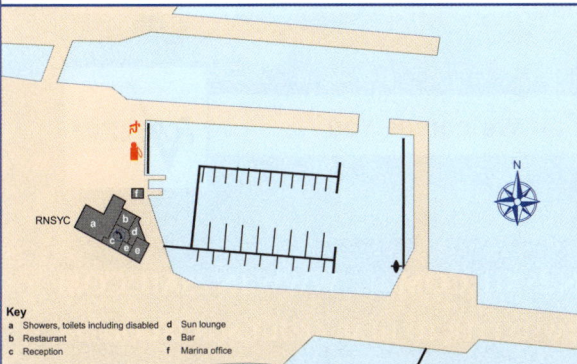

ROYAL NORFOLK & SUFFOLK YACHT CLUB

Royal Norfolk and Suffolk Yacht Club
Royal Plain, Lowestoft, Suffolk, NR33 0AQ
Tel: 01502 566726 Fax: 01502 517981
Email: marinaoffice@rnsyc.org.uk

VHF Ch 14, 80
ACCESS H24

With its entrance at the inner end of the South Pier, opposite the Trawl Basin on the north bank, the Royal Norfolk and Suffolk Yacht Club marina occupies a sheltered position in Lowestoft Harbour. Lowestoft has always been an appealing destination to yachtsmen due to the fact that it can be accessed at any state of the tide, 24 hours a day. Note, however, that conditions just outside the entrance can get pretty lively when the wind is against tide. The clubhouse is enclosed in an impressive Grade 2 listed building overlooking the marina and its facilities include a bar and restaurant as well as a formal dining room with a full *à la carte* menu.

FACILITIES AT A GLANCE

RNSYC

Key
a Showers, toilets including disabled
b Restaurant
c Reception
d Sun lounge
e Bar
f Marina office

QUANTUM SAIL DESIGN GROUP

Quantum GBR South (Hamble)
+44 (0)23 8045 8213

Quantum GBR East (Ipswich)
+44 (0)1473 659878

www.quantumsailsgbr.com

Find Quantum sail lofts worldwide at www.quantumsails.com

2009/md10/v

LECTROTAB Faria SHERWOOD A-ZAP

PERKO QUIETLIFE RACOR Fuel Filtration SEAFLOW CENTEK

www.asap-supplies.com

A.S.A.P. SUPPLIES LTD

Anodes | Controls | DTI Soundproofing | Engine Cooling
Electrical | Exhaust Systems | Fuel Systems | Instruments & Panels
Marinisation Kits | Pumps & Spares | Steering | Sterngear

See us at... LONDON BOAT SHOW BIG SOUTHAMPTON BOAT SHOW Keep an eye out for... Clean life Environmental Products

Tel: 0845 1300 870 Fax: 0800 316 2727
Intl Tel: +44 1502 716 993 Intl Fax: +44 1502 711680
Email: sales@asap-supplies.com

2009/MG71/e

in2sail

Experience the fine art of sailing with In2Sail

"Seriously Good Sail Training On-Board Quality Yachts with Friendly Professional Skippers, Served with Good Food and Fun."

RYA Training Courses

- ☐ Practical Sailing Courses in the Solent.
- ☐ Theory Courses in Central London.
- ☐ Solent Combined Theory & Practical.
- ☐ Patient and Personable Instructors to help you Learn Skills & Improve Existing Knowledge.
- ☐ Personalised for Families & Couples.

Blue Water & Long Distance

- ☐ Fun Long Weekend Trips to Cherbourg & St Vaast.
- ☐ Discover UK & Irish Sailing Waters.
- ☐ Normandy & Brittany Coastlines.
- ☐ Adventure Sailing to Spain & Portugal.
- ☐ Customised Skippered Charter to Locations of your Choice.

Specialist Courses

- ☐ Racing Yacht Training and Race Participation.
- ☐ Specialised Boat Handling and Technical Sailing Courses.
- ☐ Yacht Maintenance Programme.
- ☐ Fast Track Yachtmaster.

Racing Events

- ☐ Fastnet Yacht Race 2009.
- ☐ Round the Island 2008.
- ☐ Cowes Week 2008.
- ☐ Cork Week.
- ☐ Spring and Winter Series.

"New or Experienced - In2Sail Welcomes You."

RYA Training Centre

+44 (0) 1983 615557 | INFO@IN2SAIL.COM | WWW.IN2SAIL.COM

ONLINE BOOKING | SUBSCRIBE TO E- NEWSLETTER TO HEAR ABOUT SPECIAL OFFERS

2009/mg171/v

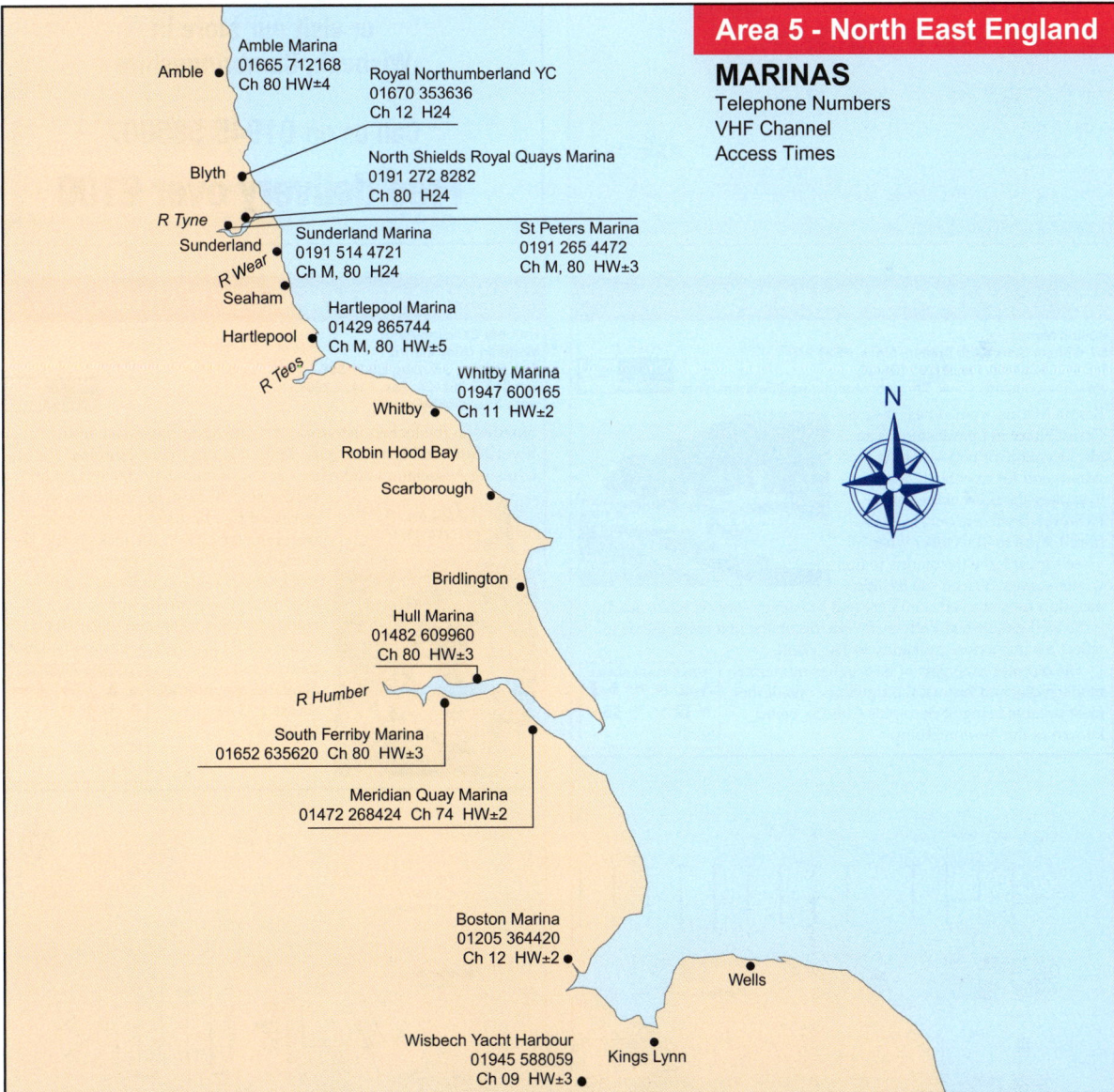

NORTH EAST ENGLAND - Great Yarmouth to Berwick-upon-Tweed

ADLARD COLES NAUTICAL
WEATHER FORECASTS
BY FAX & TELEPHONE

Coastal/Inshore	2-day by Fax	5-day by Phone
Anglia	09065 222 345	09068 969 645
East	09065 222 344	09068 969 644
North East	09065 222 343	09068 969 643
Scotland East	09065 222 342	09068 969 642
National (3-5 day)	09065 222 340	09068 969 640

Offshore	2-5 day by Fax	2-5 day by Phone
English Channel	09065 222 357	09068 969 657
Southern North Sea	09065 222 358	09068 969 658
Northern North Sea	09065 222 362	09068 969 662
North West Scotland	09065 222 361	09068 969 661

09068 CALLS COST 60P PER MIN. 09065 CALLS COST £1.50 PER MIN.

Key to Marina Plans symbols

- Bottled gas
- Chandler
- Disabled facilities
- Electrical supply
- Electrical repairs
- Engine repairs
- First Aid
- Fresh Water
- Fuel - Diesel
- Fuel - Petrol
- Hardstanding/boatyard
- Internet Café
- Laundry facilities
- Lift-out facilities
- Parking
- Pub/Restaurant
- Pump out
- Rigging service
- Sail repairs
- Shipwright
- Shop/Supermarket
- Showers
- Slipway
- Toilets
- Telephone
- Trolleys
- Visitors berths
- Wi-Fi

Area 5 - North East England

MARINAS
Telephone Numbers
VHF Channel
Access Times

Amble
Amble Marina
01665 712168
Ch 80 HW±4

Royal Northumberland YC
01670 353636
Ch 12 H24

Blyth

North Shields Royal Quays Marina
0191 272 8282
Ch 80 H24

R Tyne

Sunderland

Sunderland Marina
0191 514 4721
Ch M, 80 H24

St Peters Marina
0191 265 4472
Ch M, 80 HW±3

R Wear

Seaham

Hartlepool

Hartlepool Marina
01429 865744
Ch M, 80 HW±5

R Tees

Whitby Marina
01947 600165
Ch 11 HW±2

Whitby

Robin Hood Bay

Scarborough

Bridlington

Hull Marina
01482 609960
Ch 80 HW±3

R Humber

South Ferriby Marina
01652 635620 Ch 80 HW±3

Meridian Quay Marina
01472 268424 Ch 74 HW±2

Boston Marina
01205 364420
Ch 12 HW±2

Wells

Wisbech Yacht Harbour
01945 588059
Ch 09 HW±3

Kings Lynn

N

WISBECH YACHT HARBOUR

Wisbech Yacht Harbour
Harbour Master, Harbour Office, Dock Cottage
Wisbech, Cambridgeshire PE13 3JJ
Tel: 01945 588059 Fax: 01945 580589
Email: torbeau@btinternet.com www.fenland.gov.uk

VHF Ch 9
ACCESS HW±3

Regarded as the capital of the English Fens, Wisbech is situated about 25 miles north east of Peterborough and is a market town of considerable character and historical significance. Rows of elegant houses line the banks of the River Nene, with the North and South Brink still deemed two of the finest Georgian streets in England.

Wisbech Yacht Harbour, linking Cambridgeshire with the sea, is proving increasingly popular as a haven for small craft, despite the busy commercial shipping. In recent years the facilities have been developed and improved upon and the HM is always on hand to help with passage planning both up or downstream.

FACILITIES AT A GLANCE

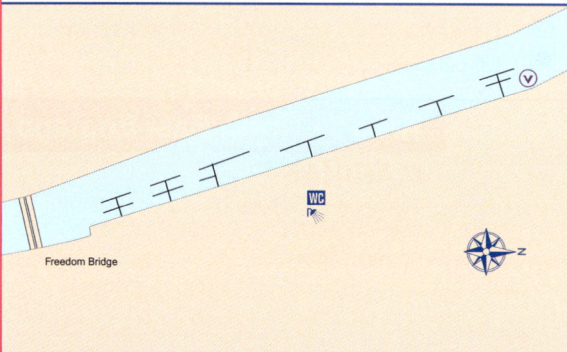

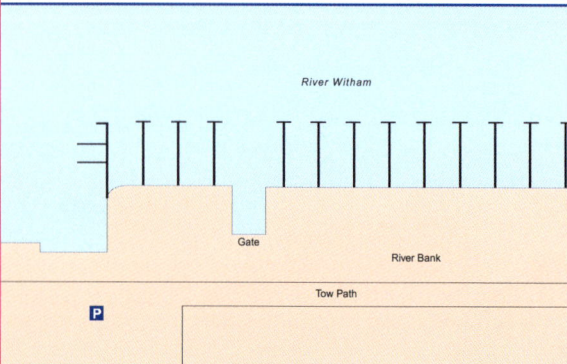

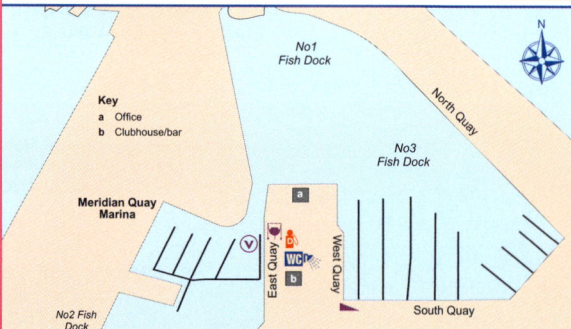

Freedom Bridge

MARINE ESSENTIALS

The place for your boating needs

Unit 29 Boleness Business Units,
Boleness Road, Wisbech, Cambs. PE13 2RB

10am-4:30pm Monday, Tuesday, Thursday & Friday except for Bank Holidays until the Spring.

Low Prices & Fast Delivery

Agents for Flag Marine Paint

MARINE ESSENTIALS

GENERAL CHANDLERY • INTERNATIONAL PAINT

on-line shop
www.marine-essentials.co.uk
or visit our store in
Wisbech, Cambridgeshire

Call us on **01945 585007**

Free delivery over £100

MG8.08/MG164/sZ

BOSTON MARINA

Boston Marina
5/7 Witham Bank East, Boston, Lincs, PE21 9JU
Tel: 01205 364420 Fax: 01205 364420
www.bostonmarina.co.uk Email: bostonmarina@5witham.fsnet

VHF Ch 12
ACCESS H±2

Boston Marina, located near Boston Grand Sluice in Lincolnshire, is an ideal location for both seagoing vessels and for river boats wanting to explore the heart of the Fens. However, berths are only available from 1 April to 31 October when all vessels must leave the marina to find winter storage. The on site facilities include a fully-stocked chandlery and brokerage service, while nearby is the well-established Witham Tavern, decorated in a rustic theme to reflect the pub's close proximity to The Wash.

The old maritime port of Boston has numerous modern-day and historical attractions, one of the most notable being St Botolph's Church, better known as the 'Boston Stump'.

FACILITIES AT A GLANCE

River Witham
Gate
River Bank
Tow Path
P

MERIDIAN QUAY MARINA

Humber Cruising Assn
Meridian Quay Marina
Fish Docks, Grimsby, DN31 3SD
Tel: 01472 268424 Fax: 01472 269832
www.hcagrimsby.co.uk

VHF Ch 74
ACCESS HW±2

Situated in the locked fish dock of Grimsby, at the mouth of the River Humber, Meridian Quay Marina is run by the Humber Cruising Association and comprises approximately 200 alongside berths plus 30 more for visitors. Accessed two hours either side of high water via lock gates, the lock should be contacted on VHF Ch 74 (call sign 'Fish Dock Island') as you make your final approach. The pontoon berths are equipped with water and electricity, while a fully licensed clubhouse boasts a television. Also available are internet access and laundry facilities.

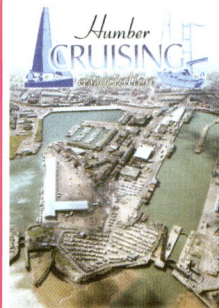

FACILITIES AT A GLANCE

No1 Fish Dock
North Quay
No3 Fish Dock
Key
a Office
b Clubhouse/bar
Meridian Quay Marina
East Quay
West Quay
South Quay
No2 Fish Dock

SOUTH FERRIBY MARINA

South Ferriby Marina
Barton on Humber, Lincolnshire, DN18 6JH
Tel: 01652 635620 (Lock 635219) Fax: 01652 660517
www.clapsons.co.uk Email: marina@clapsons.co.uk

VHF Ch 80
ACCESS HW±3

South Ferriby Marina is run by Clapson & Sons, an established company founded in 1912. The marina site was developed in 1967 and today offers a comprehensive range of services, including heated workshops for osmosis repairs, general boat repairs and ample storage space. Its well stocked on site chandlery is open until 1700 seven days a week.

Situated at Barton upon Humber, the marina lies on the south bank of the River Humber at the southern crossing of the Humber Bridge, approximately eight miles south west of Kingston upon Hull. Good public transport links to nearby towns and villages include train services to Cleethorpes and Grimsby, and bus connections to Scunthorpe and Hull.

FACILITIES AT A GLANCE

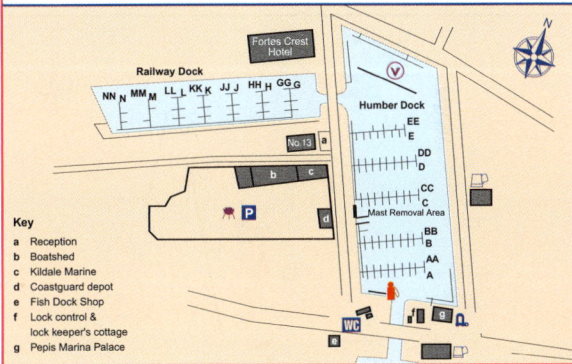

Key
a Chandlery
b Shipwrights workshop

HULL MARINA

Hull Marina
Railway Street, Hull, HU1 2DQ
Tel: 01482 609960 Fax: 01482 224148
www.britishwaterways.co.uk
Email: hullmarina@bwml.co.uk

VHF Ch 80
ACCESS HW±3

Situated on the River Humber, Hull Marina is literally a stone's throw from the bustling city centre with its array of arts and entertainments. Besides the numerous historic bars and cafés surrounding the marina itself, there are plenty of traditional taverns to be sampled in the Old Town, while also found here is the Street Life Museum, vividly depicting the history of the city.

Yachtsmen enter the marina via a tidal lock, operating HW±3, and should try to give 15 minutes' notice of arrival via VHF Ch 80. Hull is perfectly positioned for exploring the Trent, Ouse and the Yorkshire coast as well as across the North Sea to Holland or Belgium.

FACILITIES AT A GLANCE

Key
a Reception
b Boatshed
c Kildale Marine
d Coastguard depot
e Fish Dock Shop
f Lock control &
   lock keeper's cottage
g Pepis Marina Palace

B. COOKE & SON LTD

'KINGSTON OBSERVATORY'
56/59 MARKET PLACE
HULL, HU1 1RH

ESTABLISHED 1863 - 146 YEARS OF SERVICE TO NAVIGATION

INTERNATIONAL ADMIRALTY CHART AGENTS

Chart Folio Management System Maintained
Worldwide stock of Admiralty Charts and Publications
Admiralty Raster (ARCS) Chart Service Navigator and Skipper - programmes to suit your Individual Requirements
Full Chart Correction and Customised Service for Tracings and Notices to Mariners
All Nautical Publications Stocked - Visitors Welcome

MANUFACTURE OF
MAGNETIC COMPASSES AND BINNACLES

For All Classes of Vessel
Azimuth Mirrors, Pelorus, Sextants, Clinometers, Clocks and Barometers.
Supply and Service Electronic Repeaters, Off Course Alarms, Auto Pilots, Latest GPs etc.
All Engine Room Requirements.
Parallel Rulers and Dividers, Chartroom Instruments.
MCA Certified Compass Adjusters available 24 hours a day

MARINE PROGRAMMES FOR
IBM PC & COMPATIBLE COMPUTERS

Voyage Planner, PC Stability, Draft & Trim, PC Sightmaster, PC Oilsurvey, Container Ship Stability, MArine Surveyor's Compilation, Showtide++ and PC Draft Survey
LAtest Psion Computers, Accessories & Software

All Enquiries Welcome, no matter how small

Tel: 01482 223454 / 224412

Fax: 01482 219793 Telex: 597636
E-mail: bcs@cooke.karoo.co.uk
Web: www.bcookeandsonsltd.co.uk

2009/Mg12/v

GILL   CREWSAVER

KILDALE MARINE

HULL MARINA, HULL HU1 3DQ
Tel: (01482) 227464 Fax: (01482) 329217

Kildale Marine stocks the largest range of Chandlery, Ropes, Marine Paints and Deck Fittings for all sizes of yacht and motorcruiser in the North East

EXTENSIVE RANGE OF BOOKS, CHARTS AND NAVIGATION AIDS

SERVICES INCLUDE:
LIFERAFT HIRE
• GAS REFILLS
• STANDARD & RUNNING RIGGING
& ROPE SPLICING

We are open 6 days a week 9.30 to 5.30
Sunday 10.00 - 4.00 • Closed all day Tuesday

BLAKES PAINTS
INTERNATIONAL PAINTS
BARTON
HARKEN
WHALE
JABSCO
WALLAS HEATERS

2009/MG72/k

WEST SYSTEMS   MUSTO   HENRI LLOYD

WHITBY MARINA

Whitby Marina
Whitby Harbour Office, Endeavour Wharf
Whitby, North Yorkshire YO21 1DN
Harbour Office: 01947 602354 Marina: 01947 600165
Email: lesley.dale@scarborough.gov.uk

VHF	Ch 11, 16
ACCESS	HW±2

The only natural harbour between the Tees and the Humber, Whitby lies some 20 miles north of Scarborough on the River Esk. The historic town is said to date back as far as the Roman times, although it is better known for its abbey, which was founded over 1,300 years ago by King Oswy of Northumberland. Another place of interest is the Captain Cook Memorial Museum, a tribute to Whitby's greatest seaman.

A swing bridge divides the harbour into upper and lower sections, with the marina being in the Upper Harbour. The bridge opens on request (VHF Ch 11) each half hour for two hours either side of high water.

FACILITIES AT A GLANCE

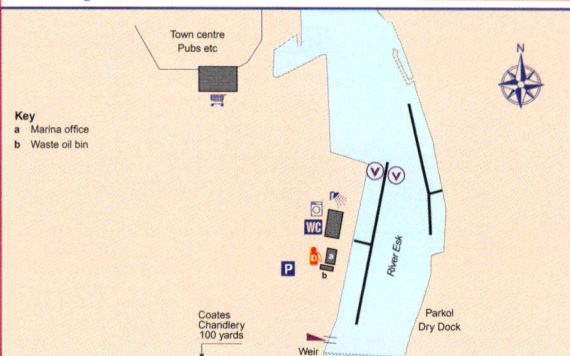

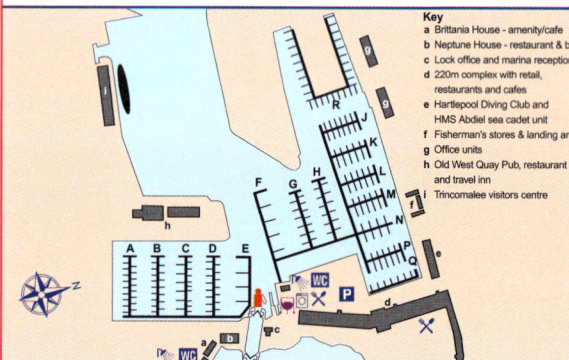

Key
a Marina office
b Waste oil bin

HARTLEPOOL MARINA

Hartlepool Marina
Lock Office, Slake Terrace, Hartlepool, TS24 0UR
Tel: 01429 865744 Fax: 01429 865947
Email: allan@hartlepool-marina.com

VHF	Ch M, 80
ACCESS	HW±5

Hartlepool Marina is a major boating facility on the North East coast with over 500 fully serviced berths surrounded by a cosmopolitan mix of bars restaurants and hotels. The Historic Quay is nearby with the 17th Century warship, Trincomelee. A tourist town with shopping centre is an easy walk away. Beautiful crusing water north and south access channel dredged to chart datum.

The marina can be accessed five hours either side of high water via a lock: note that yachtsmen wishing to enter should contact the marina on VHF Ch 80 about 15 minutes before arrival.

FACILITIES AT A GLANCE

Key
a Brittania House - amenity/cafe
b Neptune House - restaurant & bar
c Lock office and marina reception
d 220m complex with retail, restaurants and cafes
e Hartlepool Diving Club and HMS Abdiel sea cadet unit
f Fisherman's stores & landing area
g Office units
h Old West Quay Pub, restaurant and travel inn
i Trincomalee visitors centre

Shamrock Chandlery

What ever your budget, we've got it covered!

seaGo SP GOTOP BALTIC LIFEJACKETS SWEDEN XM Crewsaver
spinlock SEBAGO
WEST SYSTEM ECHOMAX Barton MARINE ADMIRALTY LEISURE
PLASTIMO SHURHOLD BLAKES Paints G LALIZAS International

To buy these and many other brands visit our new on-line shop

www.shamrock.co.uk

Then click on GO SHOPPING

2009/MG128/e

Our extensively stocked Chandlery is open 7 days a week Winter and Summer
Shamrock Quay William Street
Southampton SO14 5QL

VISA Maestro MasterCard

Tel: 023 8063 2725

HARTLEPOOL MARINA
Lock Office, Slake Terrace, Hartlepool, Cleveland

A prestigious 500 berth marina alive with busy shops, cafes bars and a wealth of international restaurants. Adjoining the marina site is a retail park, multi screen cinema, health club and a selection of the usual fast food outlets. Visit the Historic Quay and step back through history and enjoy the experience of life at the time of Lord Nelson and step on board HMS Trincomalee 1817 the oldest fighting ship afloat in the UK

In addition to fully serviced pontoon berthing [including broadband internet connection] there are quay wall facilities, a fully equipped boat yard and 40 tonne travel hoist. Our in house Chandlery, sail repairs, outboard and diesel inboard dealerships make the marina complete. We are proud to fly our 4 anchor award as assessed by the British Marine Federation.

2009/MG627/v

Tel: 01429 865744 Fax: 01429 865947

SUNDERLAND MARINA

The Marine Activities Centre
Sunderland Marina, Sunderland, SR6 0PW
Tel: 0191 514 4721 Fax: 0191 514 1847
Email: mervyn.templeton@marineactivitiescentre.co.uk

VHF Ch M, 80
ACCESS H24

Sunderland Marina sits on the north bank of the River Wear and is easily accessible through the outer breakwater at all states of the tide. Among the extensive range of facilities on site are a newsagent, café, hairdresser and top quality Italian restaurant. Other pubs, restaurants, hotels and cafés are located nearby on the waterfront. Both the Wear Boating Association and the Sunderland Yacht Club are also located in the vicinity and welcome yachtsmen to their respective bars and lounges.

FACILITIES AT A GLANCE

Key
a. Marina Reception
b. Marine News - Newsagent & Shop
c. Snow Goose - Café
d. Hairdresser
e. Trattoria Due - Italian Restaurant
f. Wear Boating Association
g. Hard stand compound
h. Refuse Compound

QUAY MARINAS LTD
A & W Building, The Docks, Portishead, N. Somerset BS20 7DF
Tel: (01275) 841188 Fax: (01275) 841189
e-mail: sriggs@quaymarinas.com
A wholly owned subsidiary of Quay Marinas, operate comprehensive yachting facilities at 5 locations in the UK and are marketing agents for Malahide Marina in Dublin Bay.

2009/EXT3/e

Shamrock Chandlery

What ever your budget, we've got it covered!

seago · SP · GOTOP · BALTIC LIFEJACKETS SWEDEN · XM
WEST SYSTEM · SEBAGO · spinlock
PLASTIMO · ECHOMAX · Barton MARINE · ADMIRALTY LEISURE
SHURHOLD · BLAKES Paints · LALIZAS · International

To buy these and many other brands visit our new on-line shop

www.shamrock.co.uk

Then click on GO SHOPPING

Our extensively stocked Chandlery is open 7 days a week Winter and Summer
Shamrock Quay William Street
Southampton SO14 5QL

VISA · Maestro · MasterCard

Tel: 023 8063 2725

2009/MG128/e

5

NORTH SHIELDS ROYAL QUAYS MARINA

North Shields Royal Quays Marina
Coble Dene Road, North Shields, NE29 6DU
Tel: 0191 272 8282 Fax: 0191 272 8288
www.quaymarinas.com
Email: royalquaysmarina@quaymarinas.com

VHF Ch 80
ACCESS H24

North Shields Royal Quays Marina enjoys close proximity to the entrance to the River Tyne, allowing easy access to and from the open sea as well as being ideally placed for cruising further up the Tyne. Just over an hour's motoring upstream brings you to the heart of the city of Newcastle, where you can tie up on a security controlled visitors' pontoon right outside the Pitcher and Piano Bar.

With a reputation for a high standard of service, the marina accommodates 300 pontoon berths, all of which are fully serviced. It is accessed via double sector lock gates which operate at all states

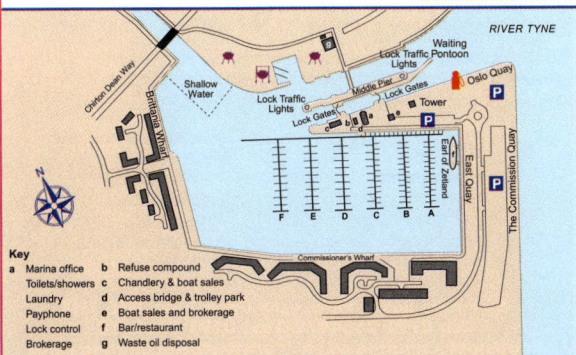

FACILITIES AT A GLANCE

Key
a Marina office
   Toilets/showers
   Laundry
   Payphone
   Lock control
   Brokerage
b Refuse compound
c Chandlery & boat sales
d Access bridge & trolley park
e Boat sales and brokerage
f Bar/restaurant
g Waste oil disposal

Adlard Coles Nautical
THE BEST SAILING BOOKS

Maintenance

Boatowner's Mechanical & Electrical Manual

Third Edition
BOATOWNER'S Mechanical AND Electrical Manual
How to Maintain, Repair, and Improve Your Boat's Essential Systems
Nigel Calder

3rd edition
Nigel Calder
978 0 7136 7226 8
£45

TO ORDER
MDL, Brunel Road, Houndmills, Basingstoke RG21 6XS
Tel: **01256 302699**
email: **direct@macmillan.co.uk**
or **www.adlardcoles.com**

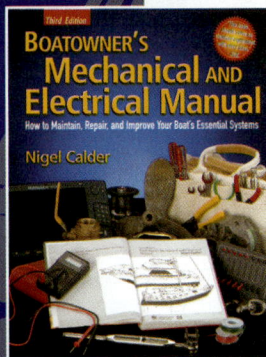

ST PETERS MARINA

St Peters Marina, St Peters Basin
Newcastle upon Tyne, NE6 1HX
Tel: 0191 2654472 Fax: 0191 2762618
Email: info@stpetersmarina.co.uk
www.stpetersmarina.co.uk

VHF	Ch 80, M
ACCESS	HW±3

Nestling on the north bank of the River Tyne, some eight miles upstream of the river entrance, St Peters Marina is a fully serviced, 150-berth marina with the capacity to accommodate large vessels of up to 37m LOA. Situated on site is the Bascule Bar and Bistro, while a few minutes away is the centre of Newcastle. This city, along with its surrounding area, offers an array of interesting sites, among which are Hadrian's Wall, the award winning Gateshead Millennium Bridge and the Baltic Art Centre.

FACILITIES AT A GLANCE

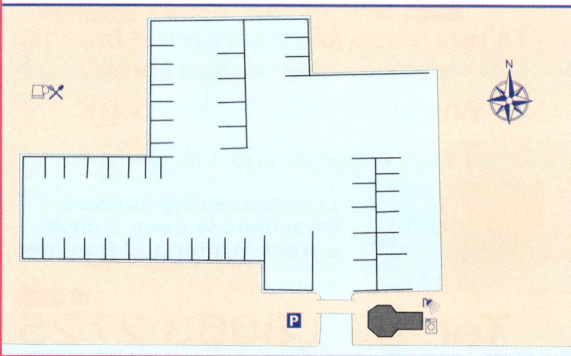

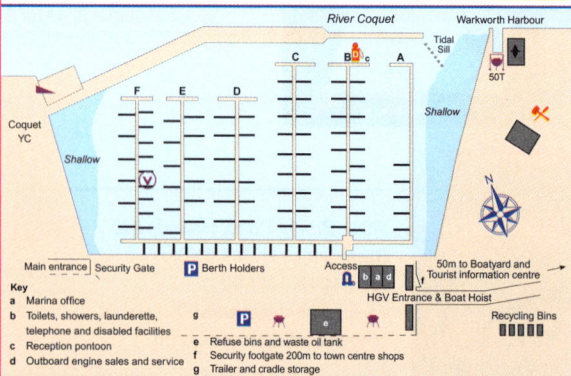

ROYAL NORTHUMBERLAND YACHT CLUB

Royal Northumberland Yacht Club
South Harbour, Blyth, Northumberland, NE24 3PB
Tel: 01670 353636

VHF	Ch 12
ACCESS	H24

The Royal Northumberland Yacht Club is based at Blyth, a well-sheltered port that is accessible at all states of the tide and in all weathers except for when there is a combination of low water and strong south-easterly winds. The yacht club is a private club with some 75 pontoon berths and a further 20 fore and aft moorings.

Visitors usually berth on the north side of the most northerly pontoon and are welcome to use the clubship, HY *Tyne* – a wooden lightship built in 1880 which incorporates a bar, showers and toilet facilities. The club also controls its own boatyard, providing under cover and outside storage space plus a 20 ton boat hoist.

FACILITIES AT A GLANCE

Key
a H.Y. Tyne

AMBLE MARINA

Amble Marina Ltd
Amble, Northumberland, NE65 0YP
Tel: 01665 712168 Fax:01665 713363
Email: marina@amble.co.uk   www.amble.co.uk

VHF	Ch 80
ACCESS	HW±4

Amble Marina is a small family run business offering peace, security and a countryside setting at the heart of the small town of Amble. It is located on the banks of the beautiful River Coquet and at the start of the Northumberland coast's area of outstanding natural beauty. Amble Marina has 250 fully serviced berths for residential and visiting yachts. Cafes, bars, restaurants and shops are all within a short walk.

From your berth watch the sun rise at the entrance to the harbour and set behind Warkworth Castle or walk on wide empty beaches. There is so much to do or if you prefer simply enjoy the peace, tranquillity and friendliness at Amble Marina.

FACILITIES AT A GLANCE

Key
a Marina office
b Toilets, showers, launderette, telephone and disabled facilities
c Reception pontoon
d Outboard engine sales and service
e Refuse bins and waste oil tank
f Security footgate 200m to town centre shops
g Trailer and cradle storage

ST. PETERS MARINA

Nestling on the North Bank of the River Tyne - 7.5 miles upstream of the river entrance but only minutes away from the heart of the city - St. Peters Marina offers quality facilities and a personal service.

The marina basin contains around 150 pontoon berths, all with electricity and water, and can accommodate vessels up to 120 feet LOA. Maintained depth in the marina is in excess of 2 metres, with access over the sill 0.8 metres about chart datum.

Access to the visitors waiting pontoon is available at all states of the tide. The marina building, with its toilets, shower and laundry, is available to berth holders 24 hours a day, 365 days a year.

As well as a call-out service for stranded boats, the marina services include the following facilities, which are either available on site or can be arranged on request:

Berthing
CCTV security
Engine servicing
Electrical repairs
Crane lift
Mast stepping
Rigging & Sail repairs
Hull repairs

Pressure washing
Antifoulding Valeting
Valeting
Boat deliveries
Sludge pump-out
Chandlery
Petrol & Diesel
RYA Training Centre

St. Peters Basin, Newcastle Upon Tyne, NE6 1HX
Tel: 0191 2654472 Fax: 0191 2762618
info@stpetersmarina.co.uk   www.stpetersmarina.co.uk

2008/MG159/z

5

YPP

YACHT PARTS PLYMOUTH

QUEEN ANNE'S BATTERY MARINA
PLYMOUTH
PL4 0LP

01752 252489
www.yachtparts.co.uk
sales@yachtparts.co.uk

International

ANTIFOULING • ANTI-INCRUST
Cruiser UNO

LEWMAR

2 SHOPS - 1 AIM
TO GET YOU & KEEP YOU ON THE WATER

YAMAHA
FOUR STROKE

YAMAHA

AVON

ZODIAC

TERHI

The DINGHY & RIB Warehouse

DISTRIBUTORS FOR YAMAHA - AVON - ZODIAC - TERHI

QUEEN ANNE'S BATTERY MARINA, PLYMOUTH, PL4 0LP
01752 222265   www.dinghyandrib.co.uk   sales@dinghyandrib.co.uk

2009/MG170/z

Shamrock Chandlery

What ever your budget, we've got it covered!

seaGo **SP** **GOTOP** **BALTIC** LIFEJACKETS SWEDEN **Crewsaver** **XM**

spinlock **SEBAGO**

PLASTIMO **WEST SYSTEM** BRAND **ECHOMAX** **Barton MARINE** **ADMIRALTY LEISURE**

SHURHOLD **BLAKES Paints** **BLUE GEE** **LALIZAS** **International**

To buy these and many other brands visit our new on-line shop

www.shamrock.co.uk

Then click on GO SHOPPING

Our extensively stocked
Chandlery is open 7 days
a week Winter and Summer
Shamrock Quay William Street
Southampton SO14 5QL

VISA **Maestro** **MasterCard**

Tel: 023 8063 2725

2009/MGIFC/e

SOUTH EAST SCOTLAND - Eyemouth to Rattray Head

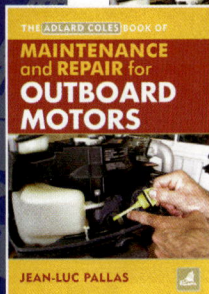

ADLARD COLES NAUTICAL
WEATHER FORECASTS
BY FAX & TELEPHONE

Coastal/Inshore	2-day by Fax	5-day by Phone
East	09065 222 344	09068 969 644
North East	09065 222 343	09068 969 643
Scotland East	09065 222 342	09068 969 642
Scotland North	09065 222 341	09068 969 641
National (3-5 day)	09065 222 340	09068 969 640

Offshore	2-5 day by Fax	2-5 day by Phone
English Channel	09065 222 357	09068 969 657
Southern North Sea	09065 222 358	09068 969 658
Northern North Sea	09065 222 362	09068 969 662
North West Scotland	09065 222 361	09068 969 661

09068 CALLS COST 60P PER MIN. 09065 CALLS COST £1.50 PER MIN.

Key to Marina Plans symbols

Symbol	Description	Symbol	Description
	Bottled gas	P	Parking
	Chandler		Pub/Restaurant
	Disabled facilities		Pump out
	Electrical supply		Rigging service
	Electrical repairs		Sail repairs
	Engine repairs		Shipwright
	First Aid		Shop/Supermarket
	Fresh Water		Showers
	Fuel - Diesel		Slipway
	Fuel - Petrol	WC	Toilets
	Hardstanding/boatyard		Telephone
@	Internet Café		Trolleys
	Laundry facilities	V	Visitors berths
	Lift-out facilities		Wi-Fi

Area 6 - South East Scotland

MARINAS
Telephone Numbers
VHF Channel
Access Times

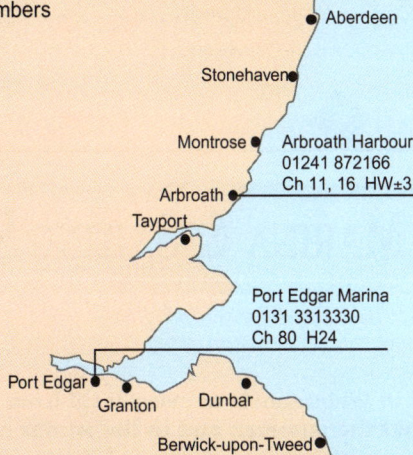

Aberdeen

Stonehaven

Montrose

Arbroath Harbour
01241 872166
Ch 11, 16 HW±3

Arbroath

Tayport

Port Edgar Marina
0131 3313330
Ch 80 H24

Port Edgar

Granton   Dunbar

Berwick-upon-Tweed

N

6

Adlard Coles Nautical
THE BEST SAILING BOOKS

Practical

The Adlard Coles Book of Maintenance and Repair for Diesel Engines
Jean-Luc Pallas
£22.99   978 0 7136 7614 3

The Adlard Coles Book of Maintenance and Repair for Outboard Motors
Jean-Luc Pallas
£19.99   978 0 7136 7615 0

TO ORDER   Tel: **01256 302699**   email: **direct@macmillan.co.uk** or **www.adlardcoles.com**

PORT EDGAR MARINA

Port Edgar Marina
Shore Road, South Queensferry
West Lothian, EH3 9SX
Tel: 0131 331 3330 Fax: 0131 331 4878
Email: admin.pe@edinburghleisure.co.uk

VHF	Ch 80
ACCESS	H24

Port Edgar is a large watersports centre and marina found on the south bank of the sheltered Firth of Forth. Situated in the village of South Queensferry, just west of the Forth Road Bridge, it is managed by Edinburgh Leisure on behalf of the City of Edinburgh Council and is reached via a deep water channel just west of the suspension bridge.

The nearby village offers a sufficient range of shops and restaurants, while Port Edgar is only a 20-minute walk from Dalmeny Station from where trains run regularly to Edinburgh.

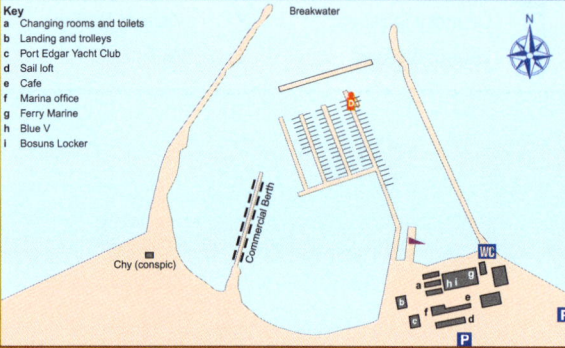

FACILITIES AT A GLANCE

Key
a Changing rooms and toilets
b Landing and trolleys
c Port Edgar Yacht Club
d Sail loft
e Cafe
f Marina office
g Ferry Marine
h Blue V
i Bosuns Locker

ARBROATH HARBOUR

Arbroath Harbour
Harbour Office, Arbroath, DD11 1PD
Tel: 01241 872166 Fax: 01241 878472
Email: harbourmaster@arbroathharbour.sol.co.uk

VHF	Ch 11, 16
ACCESS	HW±3

Arbroath harbour has 59 floating pontoon berths with security entrance which are serviced with electricity and fresh water to accommodate all types of leisure craft. Half height dock gates with walkway are located between the inner and outer harbours, which open and close at half tide, maintaining a minimum of 2.5m of water in the inner harbour.

The town of Arbroath offers a variety of social and sporting amenities to visiting crews and a number of quality pubs, restaurants, the famous twelfth century Abbey and Signal Tower Museum are located close to the harbour. Railway and bus stations are only 1km from the harbour with direct north and south connections.

FACILITIES AT A GLANCE

Key
a Signal Tower Museum
b Tourist Information
c RNLI
d Harbourmaster
e Harbour gates & walkway

Welcome to PORT EDGAR MARINA & SAILING SCHOOL

Our programme has something to offer all types of sailor whatever their experience. To find out more please telephone **0131 331 3330**

What's on offer?

Something for everyone who is interested in Watersports at every level from beginner to instructor. Courses are available throughout the summer, and in the winter months we run a wide range of shore based classes.

Activities include: -

- Dinghy Sailing At All Levels.
- Children's Holiday Sailing Courses
- SPLASH! Multi Activity Courses for Youngsters
- Catamaran Courses
- Dinghy Crusing
- Dinghy Racing

- Powerboating
- Safety Boat Handling
- Advanced Powerboating
- Canoeing - BCU 1 & 2 Star Courses
- SRC/DSC Radio Operators Course
- GPS Operator
- Yachtmaster, Coastal Skipper, Day Skipper

The Marina

The marina is fully serviced with power and water to 300 berths. We have storage facilities for craft in boat sheds or boat parks. Cranage is available throughout the year via our fixed crane for craft up to 4.3/4 tons. Other services on site are Chandlery, Sailmakers, Marine engineers, Electronics, Port Edgar Yacht Club.

PORT EDGAR MARINA

2009/MG18/z

Edinburgh Leisure
www.edinburghleisure.co.uk
This facility is managed for the City of Edinburgh Council by Edinburgh Leisure

RYA Training Centre

The Yacht Harbour Association Ltd.

British Marine Federation

BRITISH CANOE UNION

ADLARD COLES NAUTICAL
WEATHER FORECASTS
BY FAX & TELEPHONE

Coastal/Inshore	2-day by Fax	5-day by Phone
North East	09065 222 343	09068 969 643
Scotland East	09065 222 342	09068 969 642
Scotland North	09065 222 341	09068 969 641
Minch	09065 222 354	09068 969 654
National (3-5 day)	09065 222 340	09068 969 640

Offshore	2-5 day by Fax	2-5 day by Phone
Southern North Sea	09065 222 358	09068 969 658
Northern North Sea	09065 222 362	09068 969 662
North West Scotland	09065 222 361	09068 969 661
Irish Sea	09065 222 359	09068 969 659

09068 CALLS COST 60P PER MIN. 09065 CALLS COST £1.50 PER MIN.

Key to Marina Plans symbols

Bottled gas	Parking
Chandler	Pub/Restaurant
Disabled facilities	Pump out
Electrical supply	Rigging service
Electrical repairs	Sail repairs
Engine repairs	Shipwright
First Aid	Shop/Supermarket
Fresh Water	Showers
Fuel - Diesel	Slipway
Fuel - Petrol	Toilets
Hardstanding/boatyard	Telephone
Internet Café	Trolleys
Laundry facilities	Visitors berths
Lift-out facilities	Wi-Fi

Area 7 - North East Scotland

MARINAS
Telephone Numbers
VHF Channel
Access Times

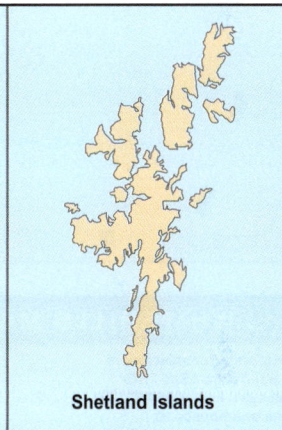

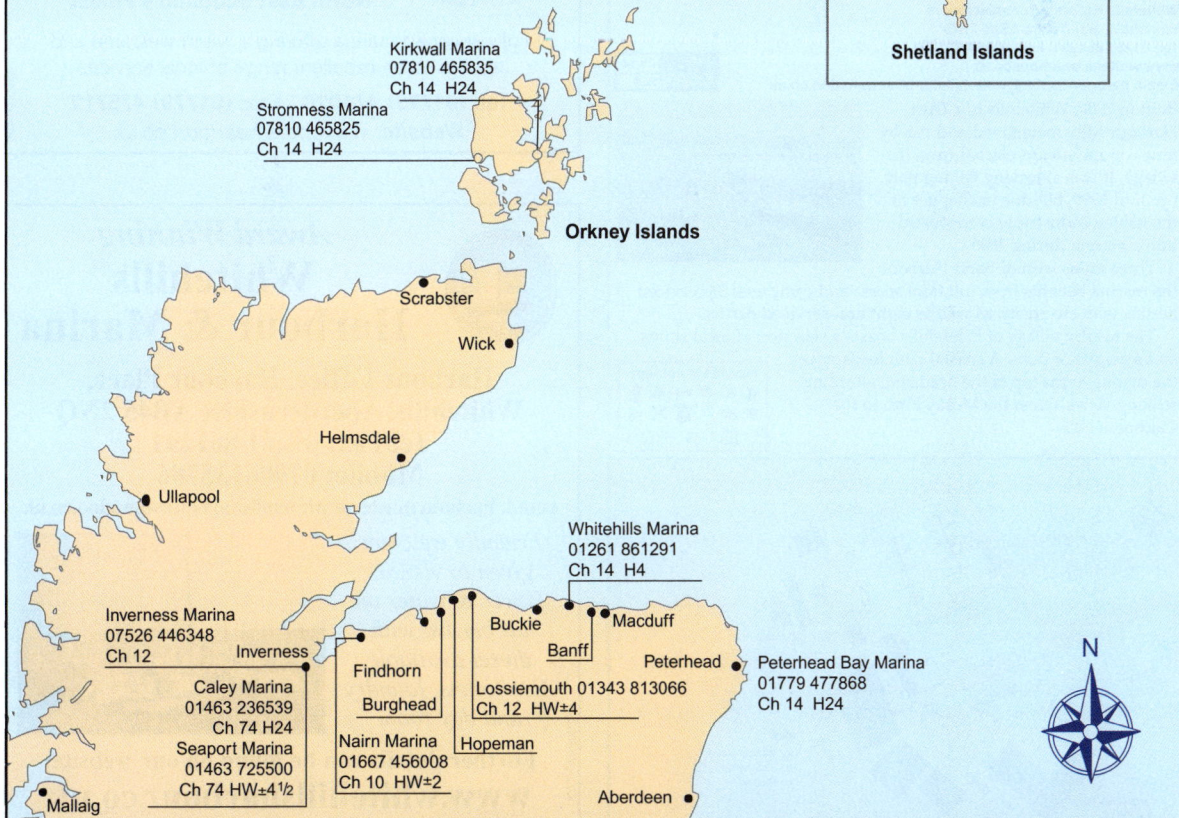

Shetland Islands

Kirkwall Marina
07810 465835
Ch 14 H24

Stromness Marina
07810 465825
Ch 14 H24

Orkney Islands

Scrabster

Wick

Helmsdale

Ullapool

Whitehills Marina
01261 861291
Ch 14 H4

Inverness Marina
07526 446348
Ch 12

Inverness

Buckie

Macduff

Banff

Peterhead

Peterhead Bay Marina
01779 477868
Ch 14 H24

Findhorn

Lossiemouth 01343 813066
Ch 12 HW±4

Caley Marina
01463 236539
Ch 74 H24

Burghead

Seaport Marina
01463 725500
Ch 74 HW±4½

Nairn Marina
01667 456008
Ch 10 HW±2

Hopeman

Mallaig

Aberdeen

N

PETERHEAD BAY MARINA

Peterhead Port Authority
Harbour Office, West Pier, Peterhead, AB42 1DW
Tel: 01779 477868 Fax: 01779 478397
Email: info@peterheadport.co.uk
www.peterheadport.co.uk

VHF Ch 14
ACCESS H24

Based in the south west corner of Peterhead Bay Harbour, the marina provides one of the finest marine leisure facilities in the east of Scotland. In addition to the services on site, there are plenty of nautical businesses in the vicinity, ranging from ship chandlers and electrical servicing to boat repairs and surveying.

Due to its easterly location, Peterhead affords an ideal stopover for those yachts heading to or from Scandinavia as well as for vessels making for the Caledonian Canal.

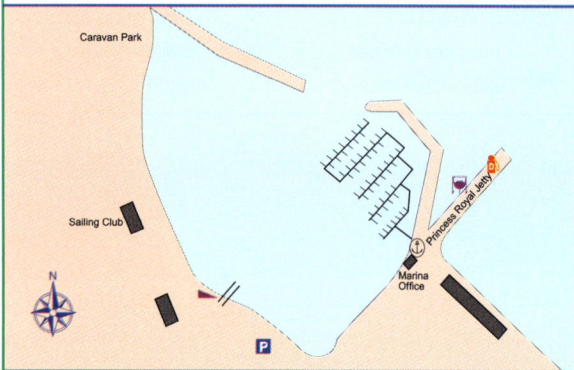

FACILITIES AT A GLANCE

Caravan Park

Sailing Club

Princess Royal Jetty

Marina Office

WHITEHILLS MARINA

Whitehills Harbour Commissioners
Whitehills, Banffshire AB45 2NQ
Tel: 01261 861291 Fax: 01261 861291
www.whitehillsharbour.co.uk
Email: harbourmaster@whitehillsharbour.wanadoo.co.uk

VHF Ch 14
ACCESS H24

Built in 1900, Whitehills is a Trust Harbour fully maintained and run by nine commissioners elected from the village. It was a thriving fishing port up until 1999, but due to changes in the fishing industry, was converted into a marina during 2000.

Three miles west of Banff Harbour the marina benefits from full tidal access and comprises 38 serviced berths, with electricity, as well as eight non-serviced berths.

The nearby village of Whitehills boasts a selection of local stores and a couple of pubs. A coastal path leads from the marina to the top of the headland, affording striking views across the Moray Firth to the Caithness Hills.

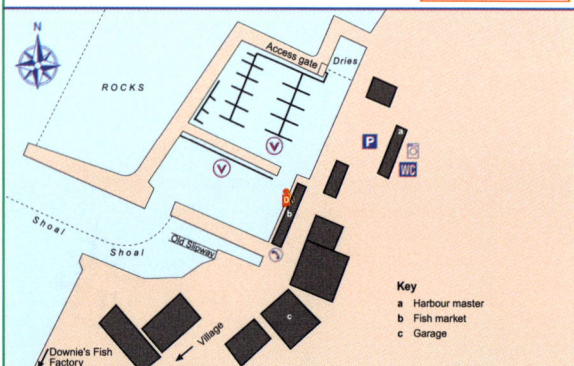

FACILITIES AT A GLANCE

ROCKS
Access gate
Dries
Shoal
Shoal
Old Slipway
Village
Downie's Fish Factory

Key
a Harbour master
b Fish market
c Garage

Elgin & Lossiemouth Harbour Company

Lossiemouth Harbour Marina is in a perfect location in the Moray Firth, ideally situated for vessels heading to/from Inverness or further afield to Norway and the Continent. Berths are fully serviced. Additional facilities including showers, toilets and laundry, diesel/gas sales, telephones and engine repair services, bars, hotels and excellent restaurants. Lossiemouth is an ideal location for visits to the Grampian Mountains and Whisky Trails, and has its own beautiful sandy beaches for walking and relaxing.

Elgin and Lossiemouth Harbour Marina
6 Pitgaveney Quay Lossiemouth IV31 6NT
Telephone: 01343 813066 (Fax & Ans)
E-mail: harbourmaster@lossiemarina.fsnet.co.uk

PETERHEAD BAY MARINA
North East Scotland's Finest
Fully serviced marina offering a warm welcome and access to an excellent range of local services
Tel: (01779) 474020   Fax: (01779) 475712
Website: www.peterheadport.co.uk

Award Winning
Whitehills Harbour & Marina
Harbour Office, Harbour Place, Whitehills, Aberdeenshire AB45 2NQ
Tel/Fax: 01261 861291
Mobile: 07906135786
email: harbourmaster@whitehillsharbour.wanadoo.co.uk
Friendly welcome given to visitors Power & water on all berths, with diesel available Also toilets, laundry and day room
Further details can be found on our website:
www.whitehillsharbour.co.uk

NAIRN MARINA

Nairn Marina
Nairn Harbour, Nairnshire, Scotland
Tel: 01667 456008
Email: nairn.harbourmaster@virgin.net

VHF Ch 10
ACCESS HW±2

Nairn is a small town on the coast of the Moray Firth. Formerly renowned both as a fishing port and as a holiday resort dating back to Victorian times, it boasts miles of award-winning, sandy beaches, famous castles such as Cawdor, Brodie and Castle Stuart, and two championship golf courses. Other recreational activities include horse riding or walking through spectacular countryside.

The marina lies at the mouth of the River Nairn, entry to which should be avoided in strong N to NE winds. The approach is made from the NW at or around high water as the entrance is badly silted and dries out.

FACILITIES AT A GLANCE

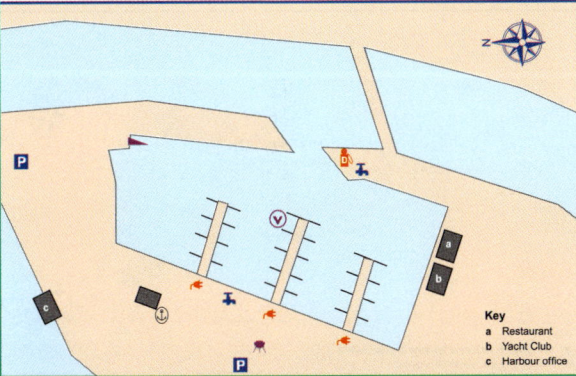

Key
a   Restaurant
b   Yacht Club
c   Harbour office

LOSSIEMOUTH MARINA

The Harbour Office
Lossiemouth, Moray, IV31 6NT
Tel: 01343 813066   Fax: 01343 813066
Email: harbourmaster@lossiemarina.fsnet.co.uk

VHF Ch 12
ACCESS HW±4

Situated on the beautiful Moray Firth coastline, Lossiemouth Marina provides 47 berths in its East Basin and 25 berths for larger vessels in its West Basin. Although the berths are primarily taken up by residential yachts, during the summer months a certain number are allocated to visitors who can benefit from the friendly, efficient service. The marina lies within easy walking distance of the town, which has a good range of shops and restaurants and boasts an array of leisure facilities, two golf courses and acres of sandy beaches. Lossiemouth is also a great starting off point for Scotland's whisky trail.

FACILITIES AT A GLANCE

Engineer
WC
Service station
Bar
Harbour Office
Gift Shops
Theatre
Tea shop
Fisheries Museum
Banks
DIY
Bar
WC

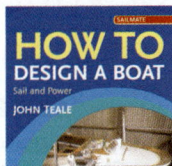

Adlard Coles Nautical
THE BEST SAILING BOOKS

Sailmate

How to Design a Boat
John Teale
978 0 7136 7572 6
£11.99

How to Choose the Right Yacht
J Muhs
978 0 7136 7581 8
£11.99

How to Paint Your Boat
Nigel Clegg
978 0 7136 7571 9
£11.99

How to Cope with Storms
D von Haeften
978 0 7136 7582 5
£11.99

How to Trim Sails
Peter Schweer
978 0 7136 7570 2
£11.99

How to Install a New Diesel Engine
Peter Cumberlidge
978 0 7136 7580 1
£11.99

TO ORDER   MDL, Brunel Road, Houndmills, Basingstoke RG21 6XS
Tel: **01256 302699** email: **direct@macmillan.co.uk** or **www.adlardcoles.com**

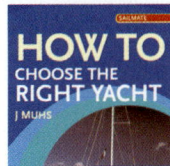

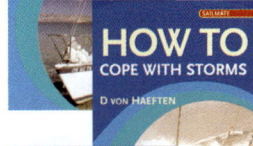

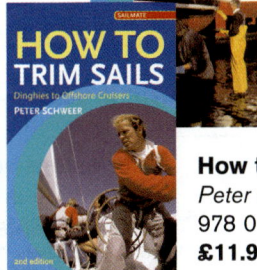

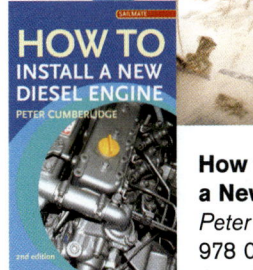

CALEY MARINA

Caley Marina
Canal Road, Inverness, IV3 8NF
Tel: 01463 236539 Fax: 01463 238323
Email: info@caleymarina.com
www.caleymarina.com

VHF	Ch 74
ACCESS	H24

Caley Marina is a family run business based near Inverness. With the four flight Muirtown locks and the Kessock Bridge providing a dramatic backdrop, the marina runs alongside the Caledonian Canal which, opened in 1822, is regarded as one of the most spectacular waterways in Europe. Built as a short cut between the North Sea and the Atlantic Ocean, thus avoiding the potentially dangerous Pentland Firth on the north coast of Scotland, the canal is around 60 miles long and takes about three days to cruise from east to west. With the prevailing winds behind you, it takes slightly less time to cruise in the other direction.

FACILITIES AT A GLANCE

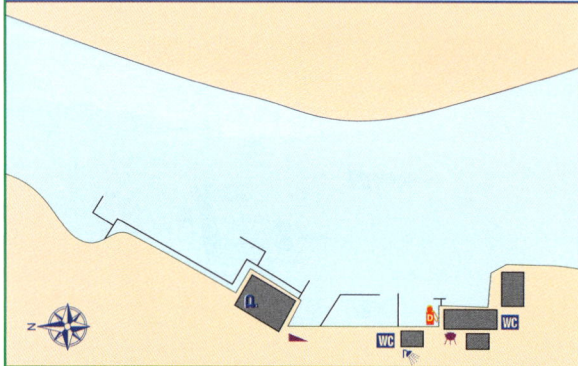

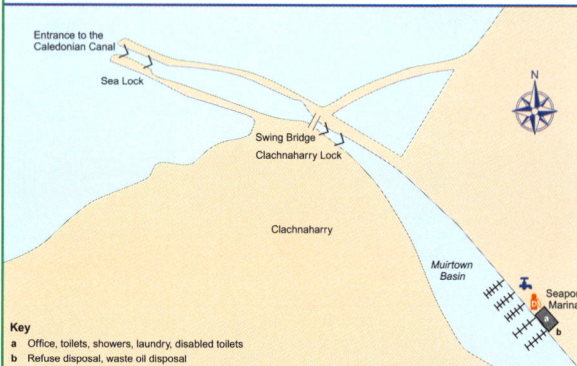

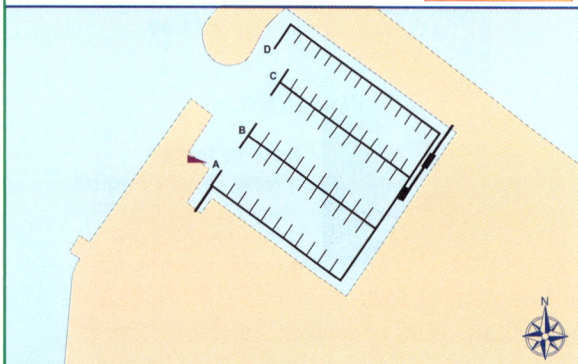

SEAPORT MARINA

Seaport Marina
Muirtown Wharf, Inverness, IV3 5LE
Tel: 01463 725500 Fax: 01463 710942
Email: enquiries.scotland@britishwaterways.co.uk
www.scottishcanals.co.uk

VHF	Ch 74
ACCESS	HW±4

Seaport Marina is situated at Inverness at the head of the Caledonian Canal. Although it only incorporates 80 berths, it proves a popular location for long and short term berthing and is accessible four hours either side of HW. The centre of Inverness is just a 15-minute walk away, where you will find a full range of shops, pubs and restaurants,
while entertainment venues include a theatre, bowling alley and multiplex cinema.

As the capital of the Highlands, Inverness attracts thousands of visitors each year, providing the ideal base from which to explore the surrounding area by road, coach or train. In addition, Inverness airport is only 20 minutes by taxi from the marina.

FACILITIES AT A GLANCE

Entrance to the
Caledonian Canal

Sea Lock

N

Swing Bridge
Clachnaharry Lock

Clachnaharry

Muirtown
Basin

Seaport
Marina

Key
a Office, toilets, showers, laundry, disabled toilets
b Refuse disposal, waste oil disposal

INVERNESS MARINA

Inverness Marina
Longman Drive, Inverness, IV1 1SU
Tel: 07526 446348 Fax: 01463 238323
Email: info@invernessmarina.co.uk
www.invernessmarina.com

VHF	Ch 12
ACCESS	H24

Inverness Marina is a brand new marina (October 2008) situated in the Inverness firth just 1 mile (1.6km) from Inverness city centre and half a mile (0.8km) from the entrance to the Caledonian Canal. The marina has a minimum depth of 2.5m, 24hr access and 150 fully serviced berths. On site are a chandlery and access to full repair services including rigging, engineering, electronics and boat repair.

Inverness is the capital of the highlands with transport networks that link including bus, train, and flights to the rest of the UK and continental Europe, Inverness Airport is less than 7 miles (11km) from the marina and within easy walking distance is the city centre which contains many hotels, restaurants, pubs and excellent shopping. Inverness is the gateway to the Highlands with best possible location as a base for touring with golf courses, historic sites and the Whisky Trail all within easy reach.

FACILITIES AT A GLANCE

D
C
B
A
N

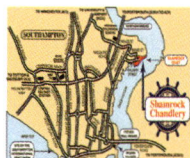

Shamrock Chandlery

What ever your budget, we've got it covered!

seaGo SP GOTOP BALTIC XM
spinlock SEBAGO
WEST SYSTEM ECHOMAX Barton MARINE ADMIRALTY LEISURE
SHURHOLD BLAKES Paints LALIZAS International

To buy these and many other brands visit our new on-line shop

www.shamrock.co.uk

Then click on GO SHOPPING

Our extensively stocked Chandlery is open 7 days a week Winter and Summer
Shamrock Quay William Street
Southampton SO14 5QL

Tel: 023 8063 2725

VISA Maestro MasterCard

2009/MG12B/e

KIRKWALL MARINA

Kirkwall Marina
Harbour Street, Kirkwall, Orkney, KW15
Tel: 07810 465835 Fax: 01856 871313
Email: info@orkneymarinas.co.uk www.orkneymarinas.co.uk

VHF Ch 14
ACCESS H24

The Orkney Isles, comprising 70 islands in total, provides some of the finest cruising grounds in Northern Europe. The Main Island, incorporating the ancient port of Kirkwall, is the largest, although 16 others have lively communities and are rich in archaeological sites as well as spectacular scenery and wildlife.

Kirkwall Marina offers excellent facilities along with 24hr access and good shelter. The marina is very close to the historic Kirkwall, whose original town is one of the best preserved examples of an ancient Norse dwelling.

FACILITIES AT A GLANCE

Breakwater/Pier
Main Pier
Harbour Office
Ferry Berth
Bins
Ferry Berth
Basin
Town Centre
N

STROMNESS MARINA

Stromness Marina
Stromness, Orkney, KW16
Tel: 07810 465825 Fax: 01856 871313
Email: info@orkneymarinas.co.uk
www.orkneymarinas.co.uk

VHF Ch 14
ACCESS H24

Just 16 miles to the west of Kirkwall, Stromness lies on the south-western tip of the Orkney Isles' Mainland. Sitting beneath the rocky ridge known as Brinkie's Brae, it is considered one of Orkney's major seaports, with sailors first attracted to the fine anchorage provided by the bay of Hamnavoe.

Stromness, like Kirkwall, is a brand new marina, offering comprehensive facilities including a chandlery and repair services. Also on hand are an internet café, a fitness suite and swimming pool as well as car and bike hire.

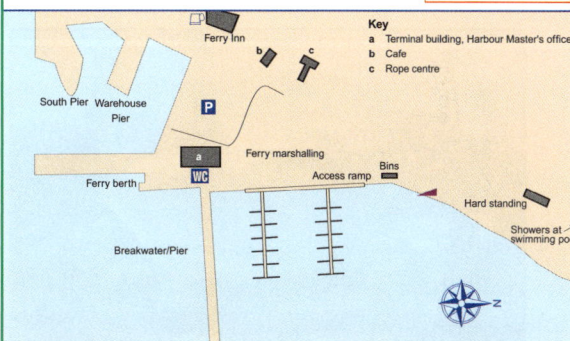

FACILITIES AT A GLANCE

Ferry Inn
Key
a Terminal building, Harbour Master's office
b Cafe
c Rope centre

South Pier Warehouse Pier
P
a
Ferry berth
WC
Ferry marshalling
Access ramp
Bins
Hard standing
Breakwater/Pier
Showers at swimming pool
N

Sail Orkney

Orkney Marinas
126 Victoria Street
Stromness
Orkney KW16 3BU
Tel/Fax 018856 852888   www.orkneymarinas.co.uk   info@orkneymarinas.co.uk

2009/IMG65v

Tel:
01631 566555
Fax:
01631 571044

DUNSTAFFNAGE
MARINA

Dunstaffnage
Marina Ltd,
Dunbeg,
Oban Argyll,
PA37 1PX

Email: info@dunstaffnagemarina.com • Website: www.dunstaffnagemarina.com

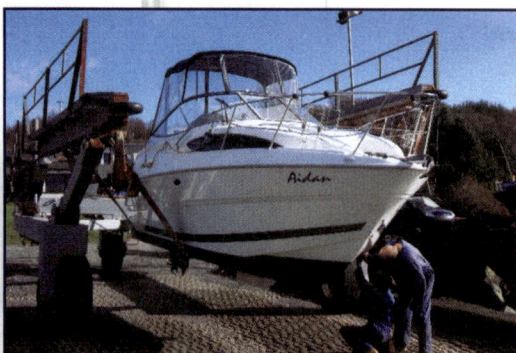

Whether you are a first time visitor or regular customer, we hope you enjoy our recently expanded facilities and the magnificent environment in which we are located.

Dunstaffnage Marina is located on the shores of Dunstaffnage Bay overlooking Dunstaffnage Castle at the entrance to Loch Etive.

Just 3 miles from Oban, the gateway to the Western Isles, Dunstaffnage is easily accessible by road, rail and ferry, or by air from Oban Airport at Connel just 2 miles away.

The Marina has excellent facilities with 150 fully serviced berths able to accommodate yachts or motor vessels up to 25 metres loa.

Operating in tandem with the renowned Wide Mouthed Frog, the Marina provides a unique range of services. The Frog is the social hub of the Marina and includes the acclaimed seafood restaurant, a family bistro, a friendly bar and 9 en-suite rooms.

To enter Dunstaffnage Bay from the Firth of Lorne leave Dunstaffnage Castle to starboard and the island Eilean Mor to port. Navigation Lights are fixed on both the Castle and island foreshores.

Entrance to the marina is by following the fairway in a direction of 150 degrees leaving green marker buoys to the starboard.

After the second buoy, the Marina Fairway should become apparent on a course of 270 degrees.

Strong currents exist in the bay due to the effect of tidal flow in Loch Etive. The prevailing current follows the shores of the Bay in an anti-clockwise direction.

Please do not attempt to cut through the Moorings on your approach to the Marina.

Please show consideration to other users by not exceeding 4 knots within the anchorage and bay.

2009/MG32/v

NORTH WEST SCOTLAND - Cape Wrath to Crinan Canal

ADLARD COLES NAUTICAL
WEATHER FORECASTS
BY FAX & TELEPHONE

Coastal/Inshore	2-day by Fax	5-day by Phone
Scotland North	09065 222 341	09068 969 641
Minch	09065 222 354	09068 969 654
Caledonia	09065 222 353	09068 969 653
Clyde	09065 222 352	09068 969 652
National (3-5 day)	09065 222 340	09068 969 640

Offshore	2-5 day by Fax	2-5 day by Phone
Southern North Sea	09065 222 358	09068 969 658
Northern North Sea	09065 222 362	09068 969 662
North West Scotland	09065 222 361	09068 969 661
Irish Sea	09065 222 359	09068 969 659

09068 CALLS COST 60P PER MIN. 09065 CALLS COST £1.50 PER MIN.

Key to Marina Plans symbols

Bottled gas	Parking
Chandler	Pub/Restaurant
Disabled facilities	Pump out
Electrical supply	Rigging service
Electrical repairs	Sail repairs
Engine repairs	Shipwright
First Aid	Shop/Supermarket
Fresh Water	Showers
Fuel - Diesel	Slipway
Fuel - Petrol	Toilets
Hardstanding/boatyard	Telephone
Internet Café	Trolleys
Laundry facilities	Visitors berths
Lift-out facilities	Wi-Fi

Area 8 - North West Scotland

MARINAS
Telephone Numbers
VHF Channel
Access Times

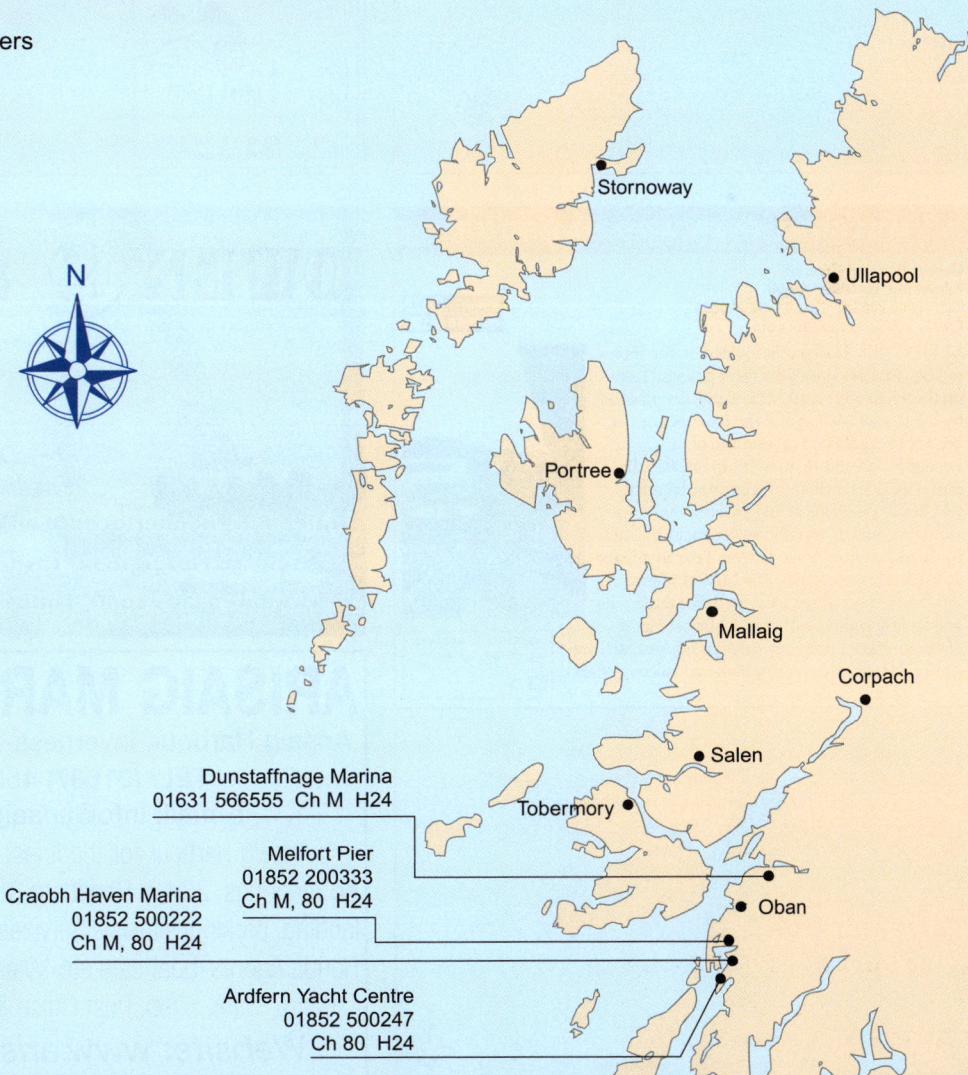

Stornoway

Ullapool

Portree

Mallaig

Corpach

Salen

Tobermory

Oban

Dunstaffnage Marina
01631 566555 Ch M H24

Melfort Pier
01852 200333
Ch M, 80 H24

Craobh Haven Marina
01852 500222
Ch M, 80 H24

Ardfern Yacht Centre
01852 500247
Ch 80 H24

DUNSTAFFNAGE MARINA

Dunstaffnage Marina Ltd
Dunbeg, by Oban, Argyll, PA37 1PX
Tel: 01631 566555 Fax: 01631 571044
Email: lizzy@dunstaffnage.sol.co.uk

VHF Ch M
ACCESS H24

Located just two to three miles north of Oban, Dunstaffnage Marina has recently been renovated to include an additional 36 fully serviced berths, a new breakwater providing shelter from NE'ly to E'ly winds and an increased amount of hard standing. Also on site is the Wide Mouthed Frog, offering a convivial bar, restaurant and accomodation with spectacular views of the 13th century Dunstaffnage Castle.

The marina is perfectly placed to explore Scotland's stunning west coast and Hebridean Islands. Only 10 miles NE up Loch Linnhe is Port Appin, while sailing 15 miles S, down the Firth of Lorne, brings you to Puldohran where you can walk to an ancient hostelry situated next to the C18 Bridge Over the Atlantic.

FACILITIES AT A GLANCE

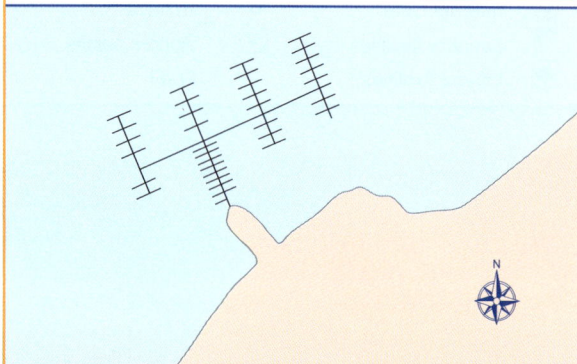

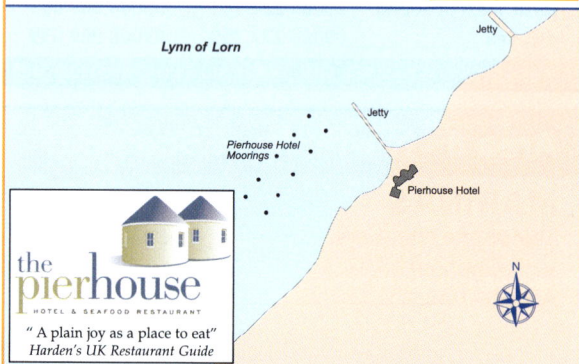

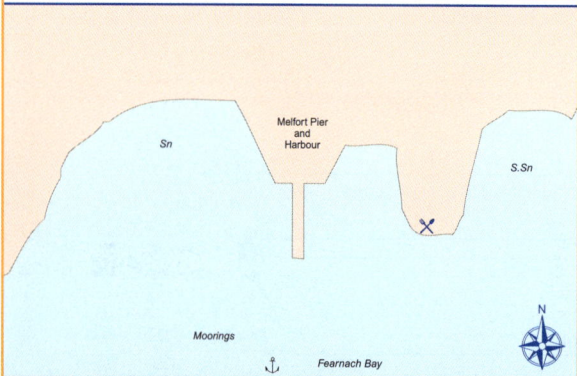

THE PIERHOUSE HOTEL MOORINGS

The Pierhouse Hotel
Port Appin, by Oban, Argyll, PA34 5UL
Tel: 01631 730302 Fax: 01631 730400
Email: reservations@pierhousehotel.co.uk

VHF
ACCESS H24

Situated in one of Argyll's most spectacular destinations on Loch Linnhe, just 10 miles by sea (20 miles by road) north of Oban, The 10 new Pierhouse Hotel Moorings (max. capacity 20 tonnes) offer 5 inner & 5 outer lines at 3 metres & 5 metres depth respectively at low water. A concrete ferry jetty co-located alongside is available for private boat use, providing shelter for landing on the northern side. Marine facilities include sauna, showers/ washing facilities. The Pierhouse Hotel is renowned for its award-winning restaurant serving fresh local seafood, meat & game. Daily lunch and bar dinner menus, home baking and teas/coffees.

FACILITIES AT A GLANCE

the pierhouse
HOTEL & SEAFOOD RESTAURANT
" A plain joy as a place to eat"
Harden's UK Restaurant Guide

MELFORT PIER AND HARBOUR

Melfort Pier and Harbour
Kilmelford, by Oban, Argyll
Tel: 01852 200333 Fax: 01852 200329
Email: melharbour@aol.com

VHF M, 80
ACCESS H24

Melfort Pier & Harbour is situated on the shores of Loch Melfort, one of the most peaceful lochs on the south west coast of Scotland. Overlooked by the Pass of Melfort and the Braes of Lorn, it lies approximately 18 miles north of Lochgilphead and 16 miles south of Oban. Its onsite facilities include hot showers, laundry, telephone, Wi-Fi access and parking – pets are welcome. Fuel, power and water are available at nearby Kilmelford Yacht Haven. Take advantage of the onsite restaurant – The Melfort Mermaid serving freshly cooked local food. For those who want a few nights on dry land, Melfort Pier & Harbour offers luxury self catering houses, each one equipped with a sauna, spa bath and balcony offering

FACILITIES AT A GLANCE

OWEN SAILS
Tralee Bay, Benderloch, Oban, Argyll, PA37 1QR
Tel 01631 720485   Fax 01631 720545
www.owensails.com   info@owensails.com

ARISAIG MARINE LTD
Arisaig Harbour, Inverness-shire PH39 4NH
TEL: (01687) 450224
e-mail: info@arisaig.co.uk
Arisaig Harbour for the finest coastal sailing.
60 moorings, 20 ton Roodberg Boat trailed, Linkspan landing, parking, slipway. Services, wintering, repairs, Honda Agents, boat sale etc. Village amenities: Hotel, Bistro, Café, Shop, Post Office & Railway Station.
Website: www.arisaig.co.uk

CRAOBH HAVEN MARINA

Craobh Haven Marina
By Lochgilphead, Argyll, Scotland, PA31 8UA
Tel: 01852 500222 Fax: 01852 500252
Email: info@craobhmarina.co.uk
www.craobhmarina.co.uk

VHF Ch M, 80
ACCESS H24

Craobh Marina is idyllically situated in the heart of Scotland's most sought after cruising grounds. Not only does Craobh offer ready access to a wonderful choice of scenic cruising throughout the western isles, the marina is conveniently close to Glasgow and its international transport hub.

Craobh Marina has been developed from a near perfect natural harbour, offering secure and sheltered berthing for up to 250 vessels to 22m LOA and with a draft of 4m. With an unusually deep and wide entrance Craobh Marina provides shelter and a warm welcome for all types of craft.

FACILITIES AT A GLANCE

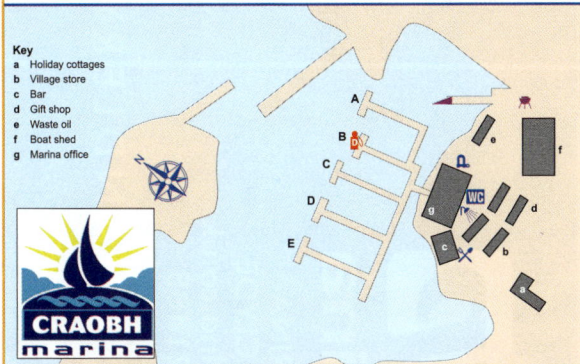

Key
a Holiday cottages
b Village store
c Bar
d Gift shop
e Waste oil
f Boat shed
g Marina office

ARDFERN YACHT CENTRE

Ardfern Yacht Centre
Ardfern, by Lochgilphead, Argyll, PA31 8QN
Tel: 01852 500247 Fax: 01852 500624
www.ardfernyacht.co.uk Email: office@ardfernyacht.co.uk

VHF Ch 80
ACCESS H24

Developed around an old pier once frequented by steamers, Ardfern Yacht Centre lies at the head of Loch Craignish, one of Scotland's most sheltered and picturesque sea lochs. With several islands and protected anchorages nearby, Ardfern is an ideal place from which to cruise the west coast of Scotland and the Outer Hebrides.

The Yacht Centre comprises pontoon berths and swinging moorings as well as a workshop, boat storage and well-stocked chandlery, while a grocery store and eating places can be found in the village. Among the onshore activities available locally are horse riding, cycling, and walking.

FACILITIES AT A GLANCE

Key
a Workshop
b Showers, toilets and launderette
c Chandlery and office

Village (300m)
Waste Oil
Hard Standing

ARDFERN YACHT CENTRE

E-mail: office@ardfernyacht.co.uk Website: www.ardfernyacht.co.uk
The ideal place to visit and keep your boat
while cruising the West of Scotland

Tel: (01852) 500247/636 Fax: (01852) 500624
Ardfern By Lochgilphead, Argyll, Scotland PA31 8QN
COMPREHENSIVE FACILITIES.   2009/Md13/v

ISLE OF SKYE YACHTS
The Boatyard, Ardvasar, Isle of Skye, IV45 8RS
Tel: 01471 844216
Fax: 01471 844387
e-mail: enquiries@isleofskyeyachts.co.uk
www.isleofskyeyachts.co.uk
Bareboat and Skippered Yacht Charter, boat repairs, servicing, moorings, supplies. RYA Practical Cruising courses.

2009/L13/s

There is always a friendly welcome at Craobh Marina • It is the perfect and most attractive location on the West Coast • boatyard with slipway hoist and crane • service and repair facilities • storage yard • well stocked chandlery • café, pub & gift shop • car hire call VHF 80 call sign Craobh Marina.

Craobh is the ideal stopping off cruising base. Please contact Jim Berry about your plans.

Tel: 01852 500222 Fax: 01852 500252
info@craobhmarina.co.uk

Craobh Haven
by Lochgilphead
Argyll PA31 8UD

website: www.craobhmarina.co.uk   2009/MD6a/z

ARDORAN MARINE LTD
Lerags, Oban, Argyll, Scotland PA34 4SE
Tel: 01631 566123
Fax: 01631 566611
e-mail: colin@ardoran.co.uk
www.ardoran.co.uk
West coast Scotland. All marine facilities.   2009/L3/V

DUNCAN'S Scotland's #One

1 For Service   # 1 For Value
1 For Choice
1 For Advice
1 For Price

Why not pay us a visit and see our vast range of chandlery, electronics, inflatables, outboards, clothing, footwear, lifejackets, buoyancy aids and lots lots more...
All at very competitive prices.

OPENING HOURS
Mon - Fri 9am - 5.30pm
Sat 9am - 1pm (Sep - Feb) 9am - 4pm (Mar - Aug)

FREE AND EASY PARKING IN OUR OWN CAR PARK

DUNCAN YACHT CHANDLERS

7 Scotland Street, Glasgow G5 8NL.
Tel: 0141 429 6044 Fax: 0141 429 3078
Email: sales@duncanyachtchandlers.co.uk

2009/MG154/e

8

SCOTLAND'S GATEWAY

SAIL SCOTLAND'S FINEST WATERS FROM SCOTLAND'S PREMIER MARINAS

fairlie QUAY marina
FAIRLIE QUAY MARINA
LARGS
www.fairliequaymarina.co.uk
01475 568267

KIP marina
KIP MARINA
FIRTH OF CLYDE
www.kipmarina.co.uk
01475 521485

CRAOBH marina
CRAOBH MARINA
SOUTH OF OBAN
www.craobhmarina.co.uk
01852 500222

BERTHING STORAGE HOIST CHANDLERY BOAT REPAIRS

PART OF THE HOLT LEISURE GROUP

2009/MG43/e

SOUTH WEST SCOTLAND - Crinan Canal to Mull of Galloway

ADLARD COLES NAUTICAL
WEATHER FORECASTS
BY FAX & TELEPHONE

Coastal/Inshore	2-day by Fax	5-day by Phone
Minch	09065 222 354	09068 969 654
Caledonia	09065 222 353	09068 969 653
Clyde	09065 222 352	09068 969 652
North West	09065 222 351	09068 969 651
National (3-5 day)	09065 222 340	09068 969 640

Offshore	2-5 day by Fax	2-5 day by Phone
Southern North Sea	09065 222 358	09068 969 658
Northern North Sea	09065 222 362	09068 969 662
North West Scotland	09065 222 361	09068 969 661
Irish Sea	09065 222 359	09068 969 659

09068 CALLS COST 60P PER MIN. 09065 CALLS COST £1.50 PER MIN.

Key to Marina Plans symbols

Bottled gas		Parking	
Chandler		Pub/Restaurant	
Disabled facilities		Pump out	
Electrical supply		Rigging service	
Electrical repairs		Sail repairs	
Engine repairs		Shipwright	
First Aid		Shop/Supermarket	
Fresh Water		Showers	
Fuel - Diesel		Slipway	
Fuel - Petrol		Toilets	
Hardstanding/boatyard		Telephone	
Internet Café		Trolleys	
Laundry facilities		Visitors berths	
Lift-out facilities		Wi-Fi	

Area 9 - South West Scotland

MARINAS
Telephone Numbers
VHF Channel
Access Times

Holy Loch Marina 01369 701800
Ch 80 H24

Portavadie Marina
01700 811075
Ch 80 H24

Rhu Marina
01436 820238
Ch 80 H24

Sandpoint Marina
01389 762396
Ch M HW±3

Ardrishaig

Rhu

Inverkip

Kip Marina
01475 521485
Ch 80 H24

Ardrossan

Largs Yacht Haven
01475 675333
Ch M, 80 H24

Port Ellen
01496 300311

N

Lamlash

Troon

Clyde Marina
01294 607077
Ch 80 H24

Campbeltown

Troon Yacht Haven
01292 315553
Ch M, 80 H24

Maryport Marina
01900 814431
Ch 12, 16 HW±2½

Stranraer

Portpatrick

Maryport

9

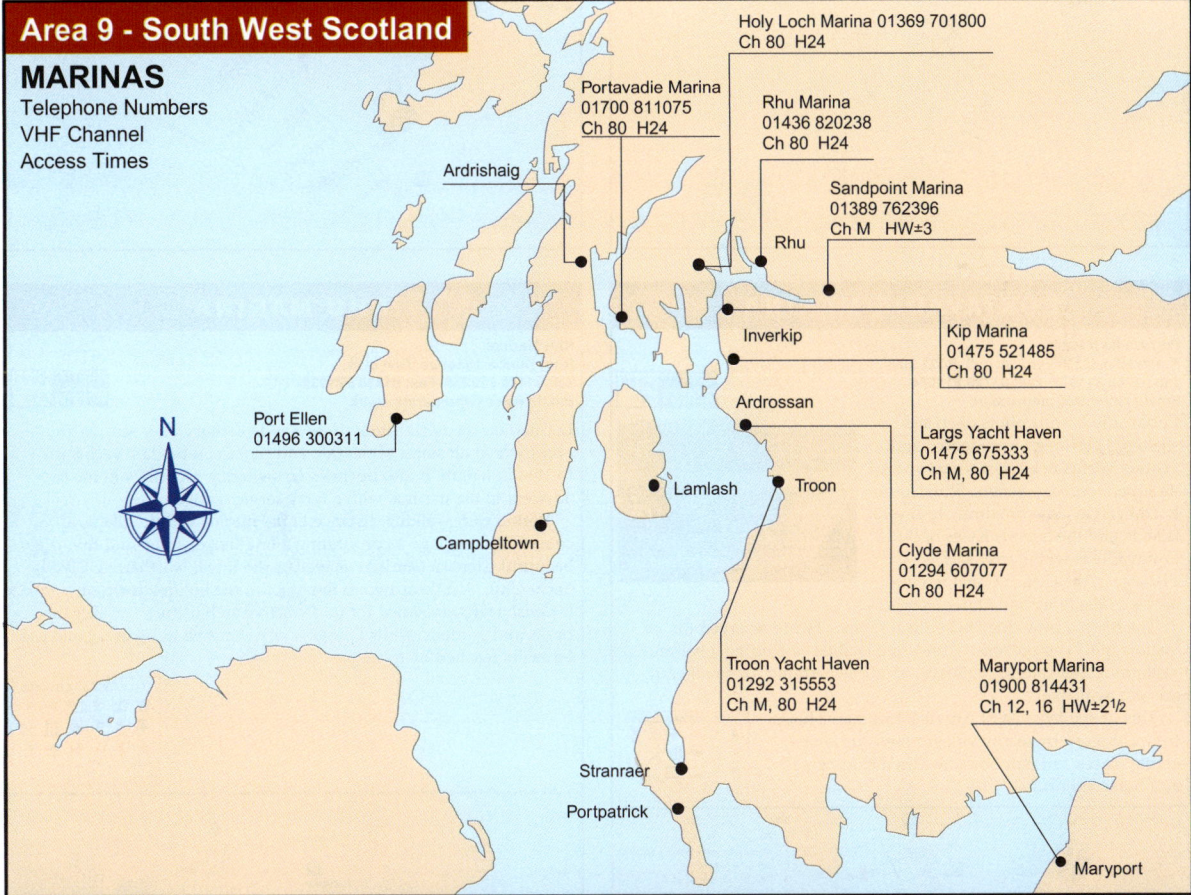

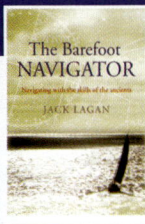

Adlard Coles Nautical THE BEST SAILING BOOKS

The Barefoot NAVIGATOR

Barefoot Navigator
Navigating with the Skills of the Ancients
Jack Lagan £14.99 978 0 7136 7429 3

Tel: 01256 302699 email: direct@macmillan.co.uk or www.adlardcoles.com

PORT ELLEN MARINA

Port Ellen Marina
Port Ellen, Islay, Argyll, PA42 7DB
Tel: 01496 300301 Fax: 01496 300302
www.portellenmarina.com

VHF
ACCESS H24

A safe and relaxed marina for visitors to the *Malt Whisky Island*. There are seven classic distilleries and yet another still (private) to start production soon. If you are planning a cruise to the north then superb sailing will take you onward via Craighouse on Jura. Meeting guests or short term storage is trouble free with the excellent air and ferry services connecting to Glasgow. Once on Islay you will be tempted to extend your stay so be warned, check www.portellenmarina.com for the many reasons to visit, from golf to music.

FACILITIES AT A GLANCE

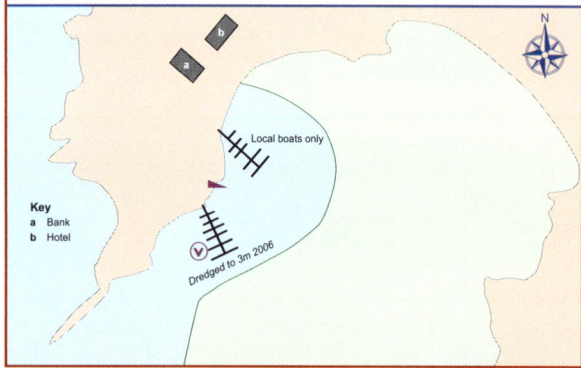

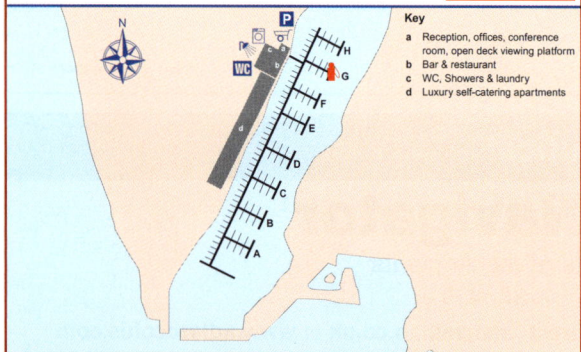

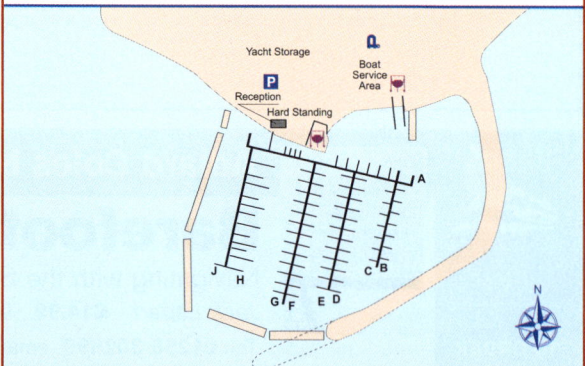

Key
a Bank
b Hotel

Local boats only

Dredged to 3m 2006

HOLY LOCH MARINA

Holy Loch Marina
Rankin's Brae, Sandbank, Dunoon, PA23 8FE
Tel: 01369 701800 Fax: 01369 704749
Email: info@holylochmarina.co.uk

VHF Ch 80
ACCESS H24

Holy Loch Marina, the marine gateway to Loch Lomond and the Trossachs National Park, lies on the south shore of the loch, roughly half a mile west of Lazaretto Point. Holy Loch is among the Clyde's most beautiful natural harbours and, besides being a peaceful location, offers an abundance of wildlife, places of local historical interest as well as excellent walking and cycling through the Argyll Forest Park. The marina can be entered in all weather conditions and is within easy sailing distance of Loch Long and Upper Firth.

FACILITIES AT A GLANCE

HOLY LOCH MARINA

Key
a Office/Harbourmaster
b Boat storage
c Holy Loch Sailing Club
d Pier

Sandbank Village

PORTAVADIE MARINA

Portavadie Marina
Portavadie, Loch Fyne, Argyll, PA21 2DA
Tel: 01700 811075 Fax: 01700 811074
Email: r.kitchin@yahoo.co.uk

VHF Ch 80
ACCESS H24

Portavadie Marina offers deep and sheltered berthing to residential and visiting yachts in an area renowned for its superb cruising waters. Situated on Loch Fyne in close proximity to several islands and the famous Kyles of Bute, Portavadie is within easy sailing distance of the Crinan Canal, giving access to the Inner and Outer Hebrides.

The marina provides 230 berths, of which 50 are reserved for visitors, plus comprehensive on-shore facilities including a bar and restaurant. Self-catering cottages, with free berthing for small craft, are also available.

This unspoiled area of Argyll is less than 2 hours from Glasgow. In nearby villages there are shops, eating places and outdoor activities including golf and horse-riding.

FACILITIES AT A GLANCE

Key
a Reception, offices, conference room, open deck viewing platform
b Bar & restaurant
c WC, Showers & laundry
d Luxury self-catering apartments

RHU MARINA

Rhu Marina
Rhu, Dunbartonshire, G84 8LH
Tel: 01436 820238 Fax: 01436 821039
Email: sales@rhumarina.co.uk

VHF Ch 80
ACCESS H24

Located on the north shore of the Clyde Estuary, Rhu Marina is accessible at all states of the tide and can accommodate yachts up to 18m in length. It also operates 60 swinging moorings in the bay adjacent to the marina, with a ferry service provided.

Within easy walking distance of the marina is Rhu village, a conservation village incorporating a few shops, a pub and the beautiful Glenarn Gardens as well as the Royal Northern & Clyde Yacht Club. A mile or two to the east lies the holiday town of Helensburgh, renowned for its attractive architecture and elegant parks and gardens, while Glasgow city is just 40 miles away and can be easily reached by train.

FACILITIES AT A GLANCE

Yacht Storage
Boat Service Area
Reception
Hard Standing

SANDPOINT MARINA

Sandpoint Marina Ltd
Sandpoint, Woodyard Road, Dumbarton, G82 4BG
Tel: 01389 762396 Fax: 01389 732605
Email: sales@sandpoint-marina.co.uk
www.sandpoint-marina.co.uk

VHF CH M
ACCESS HW±3

Lying on the north bank of the Clyde estuary on the opposite side of the River Leven from Dumbarton Castle, Sandpoint Marina provides easy access to some of the most stunning cruising grounds in the United Kingdom. It is an independently run marina, offering a professional yet personal service to every boat owner. Among the facilities to hand are an on site chandlery, storage areas, a 40 ton travel hoist and 20 individual workshop units.

Within a 20-minute drive of Glasgow city centre, the marina is situated close to the shores of Loch Lomond, the largest fresh water loch in Britain.

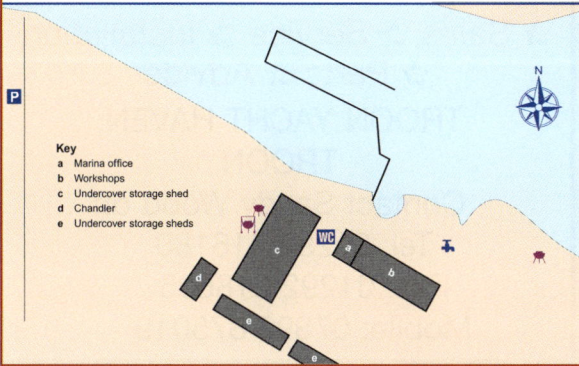

FACILITIES AT A GLANCE

Key
a Marina office
b Workshops
c Undercover storage shed
d Chandler
e Undercover storage sheds

KIP MARINA

Kip Marina, The Yacht Harbour
Inverkip, Renfrewshire, Scotland, PA16 0AS
Tel: 01475 521485 Fax: 01475 521298
www.kipmarina.co.uk Email: enquire@kipmarina.co.uk

VHF Ch 80
ACCESS H24

Inverkip is a small village which lies on the south shores of the River Kip as it enters the Firth of Clyde. Once established for fishing, smuggling and, in the 17th century, witch-hunts, it became a seaside resort in the 1860s as a result of the installation of the railway. Today it is a yachting centre, boasting a state-of-the-art marina with over 600 berths and full boatyard facilities. With the capacity to accommodate yachts of up to 23m LOA, Kip Marina offers direct road and rail access to Glasgow and its international airport, therefore making it an ideal location for either a winter lay up or crew changeover.

FACILITIES AT A GLANCE

Key
a Boat sales, chandlery and reception
b Workshop and contractors
c Chartroom and superloos

SJ Marine Services

Sail Wash

Wash : Polish
Anti - foul
Interior Valet

07740 984146

2009/MG62/r

BOAT COVERS BY

covercraft
INDUSTRIAL

makers of quality sprayhoods, canopies, all types of marine covers & upholstery

celebrating 10 years of quality manufacturing

now at kip marina
tel: 01475 529070 / 07918 641 963
info@covercraftindustrial.com

2009/MG76/z

For the best in Marine Electronics. Kip, Troon, Hull & Argyll.

Boat Electrics & Electronics Ltd

Boat Electrics & Electronics Ltd
The Service Centre - Kip marina - Inverkip - Renfrewshire - PA16 0AW
Tel: 0870 4460143 Fax: 0870 4460145 BMEA
Sales@boatelectronics.com

2009/MG42/e

kip marina

Renown as Scotland's Premier Marina • Beautifully sheltered marina basin with 700 berths • 50t boat hoist • service and repair facilities • storage yard • well stocked chandlery • bar & restaurant • 24hr security • call VHF 80 call sign Kip Marina.

For full details of all our services please visit our website.

The Yacht Harbour
Inverkip
Renfrewshire PA16 0AS

Tel: 01475 521485 Fax: 01475 521298
info@kipmarina.co.uk

website: www.kipmarina.co.uk

2009/MD6b/z

9

LARGS YACHT HAVEN

Largs Yacht Haven Ltd
Irvine Road, Largs, Ayrshire, KA30 8EZ
Tel: 01475 675333 Fax: 01475 672245
www.yachthavens.com Email: largs@yachthavens.com

VHF	Ch M, 80
ACCESS	H24

Largs Yacht Haven offers a superb location among lochs and islands, with numerous fishing villages and harbours nearby. Sheltered cruising can be enjoyed in the inner Clyde, while the west coast and Ireland are only a day's sail away. With a stunning backdrop of the Scottish mountains, Largs incorporates 700 fully serviced berths and provides a range of on site facilities including chandlers, sailmakers, divers, engineers, shops, restaurants and club.

A 20-minute coastal walk brings you to the town of Largs, which has all the usual amenities as well as good road and rail connections to Glasgow.

FACILITIES AT A GLANCE

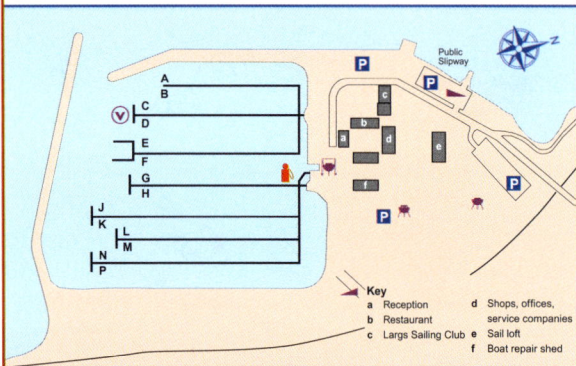

Key
a Reception
b Restaurant
c Largs Sailing Club
d Shops, offices, service companies
e Sail loft
f Boat repair shed

Troon Marine Services

☆ MARINE ENGINEERS
☆ GRP REPAIRS
☆ FITTING OUT
☆ PAINTING AND OSMOSIS TREATMENT

YANMAR DIESEL ENGINES

YOUR FIRST CHOICE FROM 9hp up to 720hp

☆ Sales ☆ Service ☆ Installation
☆ Parts ☆ Advice

TROON YACHT HAVEN, TROON
Contact Sandy Wood on
Tel: 01292 316180
Fax: 01292 318606
Mobile: 07899 875019

2009/MG135/V

CLYDE MARINA

Clyde Marina Ltd
The Harbour, Ardrossan, Ayrshire, KA 22 8DB
Tel: 01294 607077 Fax: 01294 607076
www.clydemarina.com Email: info@clydemarina.com

VHF	Ch 80
ACCESS	H24

Situated on the Clyde Coast between Irvine and Largs, Clyde Marina is a modern bustling yacht harbour with boatyard, 50 Tonne hoist and active boat sales, set in a landscaped environment. A deep draft marina accommodating vessels up to 30m LOA, draft up to 5m. Recent arrivals include tall ships and Whitbread 60s plus a variety of sail and power craft. Fully serviced pontoons plus all the yard facilities you would expect from a leading marina including boatyard and boatshed for repairs or storage. Good road and rail connections and only 30 minutes from Glasgow and Prestwick airports.

FACILITIES AT A GLANCE

key
a Winter storage shed
b Secure winter hard standing area

Jessail

SAIL REPAIRS – CANVAS WORK
UPHOLSTERY – INDUSTRIAL SEWING

58 Glasgow Street, Ardrossan KA22 8EH

Tel/Fax: 01294 467311

Mob: 07771 970578
jessail@btinternet.com

2009/MG133/d

The Harbour Ardrossan Ayrshire KA22 8DB
Tel: (01294) 607077 Fax: (01294) 607076
info@clydemarina.com
The Clyde's Deep Draft Marina
250 berth full service marine, large secure boatyard, undercover storage, 50 ton hoist, visitors welcome.
CLYDE MARINA LTD
Sunbird International Yacht sales
2008/MD4/v

TROON YACHT HAVEN

Troon Yacht Haven Ltd
The Harbour, Troon, Ayrshire, KA10 6DJ
Tel: 01292 315553 Fax: 01292 312836
Email: troon@yachthavens.com
www.yachthavens.com

VHF Ch 80, M
ACCESS H24

Troon Yacht Haven, situated on the Southern Clyde Estuary, benefits from deep water at all states of the tide. Tucked away in the harbour of Troon, it is well sheltered and within easy access of the town centre. There are plenty of cruising opportunities to be had from here, whether it be hopping across to the Isle of Arran, with its peaceful anchorages and mountain walks, sailing round the Mull or through the Crinan Canal to the Western Isles, or heading for the sheltered waters of the Clyde.

FACILITIES AT A GLANCE

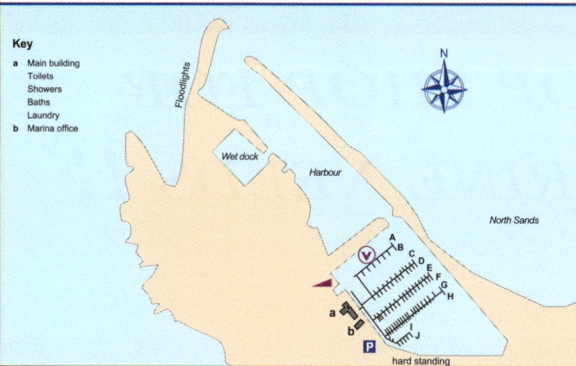

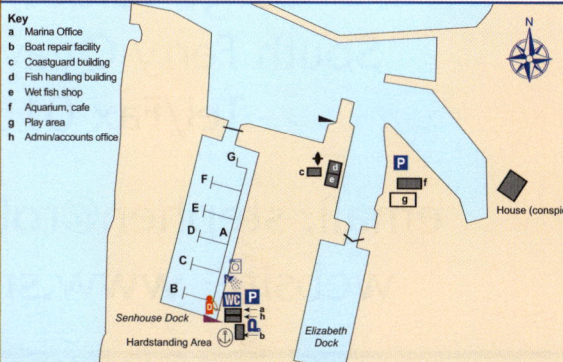

Key
a Main building
  Toilets
  Showers
  Baths
  Laundry
b Marina office

KYLE CHANDLERS

Friendly Chandlers stocking a wide range of clothing and footwear including
HENRY LLOYD • GILL • DUBARRY
HOLBROOK • QUAYSIDE
Quality marine products from top names
INTERNATIONAL • HOLT • LUMAR • NAVIMO
XM YACHTING • EMRAY • ADMILARTY

TEL: 01292 311880
www.kylechandlers.co.uk
Fax: 01292 319910 Email: sales@kylechandlers.co.uk
WE ALSO STOCK CALOR GAS & CAMPING GAS

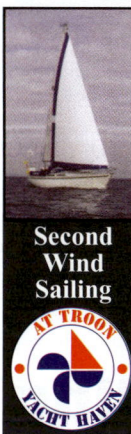

WWW.SECONDWINDSAILING.CO.UK

Second Wind Sailing is based in Troon, Scotland teaching RYA courses from Start Yachting to Yachtmaster preparation + exam.
Also Skippered Charter for up to 6 guests.
Sail in the Clyde and beyond aboard 'Chewsy' our comfortable well equipped Moody 41 with spacious accommodation for 6 guests.

Second Wind Sailing

Email: steve@secondwindsailing.co.uk
Phone: 07980 003098 / 01292 310517

All inclusive courses:
5 day course fees from £395pp
Own boat tuition from £125 per day
Weekend charter £175pp
5 day charter £350pp

RYA Training Centre

Also available: Second Wind Motor Cruising

Maritime Connection
Sailing and Powerboat
Tuition Yacht Charter & Delivery

Courses also available in VHF Radiotelephony.
Diesel Engine Maintenance, RYA First Aid and Radar

Troon Yacht Haven,
The Harbour, Troon KA10 6DJ
Telephone/Fax: 01292 315492
Email: mariconn@dial.pipex.com
Website: www.maritimeconnection.co.uk

Largs CHANDLERS

Specialists in marine clothing, boat hardware, spares and advice.
Mail order service 24hr collection Available

Phone: 01475 686026
Email: shop@largschandlers.co.uk

Open 7 days at Largs Yacht Haven

MARYPORT MARINA

Maryport Development Ltd
Marine Road, Maryport, Cumbria, CA15 8AY
Tel: 01900 814431 Fax: 01900 810212
www.maryportmarina.com
Email: enquires@maryportmarina.com

VHF Ch 12, 16
ACCESS HW±2.5

Maryport Marina lies in the historic Senhouse Dock, which was originally built for sailing clippers. The old stone harbour walls provide good shelter to this 161-berth, Blug Flag marina in all wind directions. Set within a quiet spot, although still within easy walking distance of Maryport town centre, it affords a perfect location from which to explore the west coast of Scotland as well as the Isle of Man and the Galloway Coast. For those who wish to venture inland, then the Lake District is only seven miles away.

FACILITIES AT A GLANCE

Key
a Marina Office
b Boat repair facility
c Coastguard building
d Fish handling building
e Wet fish shop
f Aquarium, cafe
g Play area
h Admin/accounts office

House (conspic)
Senhouse Dock
Hardstanding Area
Elizabeth Dock

S. ROBERTS MARINE LIMITED
at

Liverpool Marina

YOUR ONE STOP SHOP FOR ALL YOUR MARINE NEEDS !!

✔ **Boatbuilding**
✔ **Repairs**
✔ **Surveying**
✔ **Consultancy**
✔ **Chandlery**
✔ **Rigging** up to 12mm

British Marine
Federation

Barge Turbot, Coburg Wharf,
South Ferry Quay, Liverpool L3 4BP
Tel/Fax 0151 707 8300

email: stephen@robmar.freeserve.co.uk
website: www.srobertsmarine.com

2009/MG78/e

NW ENGLAND, ISLE OF MAN & N WALES - Mull of Galloway to Bardsey Is

ADLARD COLES NAUTICAL
WEATHER FORECASTS
BY FAX & TELEPHONE

Coastal/Inshore	2-day by Fax	5-day by Phone
Northern Ireland	09065 222 355	09068 969 655
Clyde	09065 222 352	09068 969 652
North West	09065 222 351	09068 969 651
Wales	09065 222 350	09068 969 650
National (3-5 day)	09065 222 340	09068 969 640

Offshore	2-5 day by Fax	2-5 day by Phone
Northern North Sea	09065 222 362	09068 969 662
North West Scotland	09065 222 361	09068 969 661
Irish Sea	09065 222 359	09068 969 659
English Channel	09065 222 357	09068 969 657

09068 CALLS COST 60P PER MIN. 09065 CALLS COST £1.50 PER MIN.

Key to Marina Plans symbols

Bottled gas		Parking	
Chandler		Pub/Restaurant	
Disabled facilities		Pump out	
Electrical supply		Rigging service	
Electrical repairs		Sail repairs	
Engine repairs		Shipwright	
First Aid		Shop/Supermarket	
Fresh Water		Showers	
Fuel - Diesel		Slipway	
Fuel - Petrol		Toilets	
Hardstanding/boatyard		Telephone	
Internet Café		Trolleys	
Laundry facilities		Visitors berths	
Lift-out facilities		Wi-Fi	

Area 10 - North West England & Wales

MARINAS
Telephone Numbers
VHF Channel
Access Times

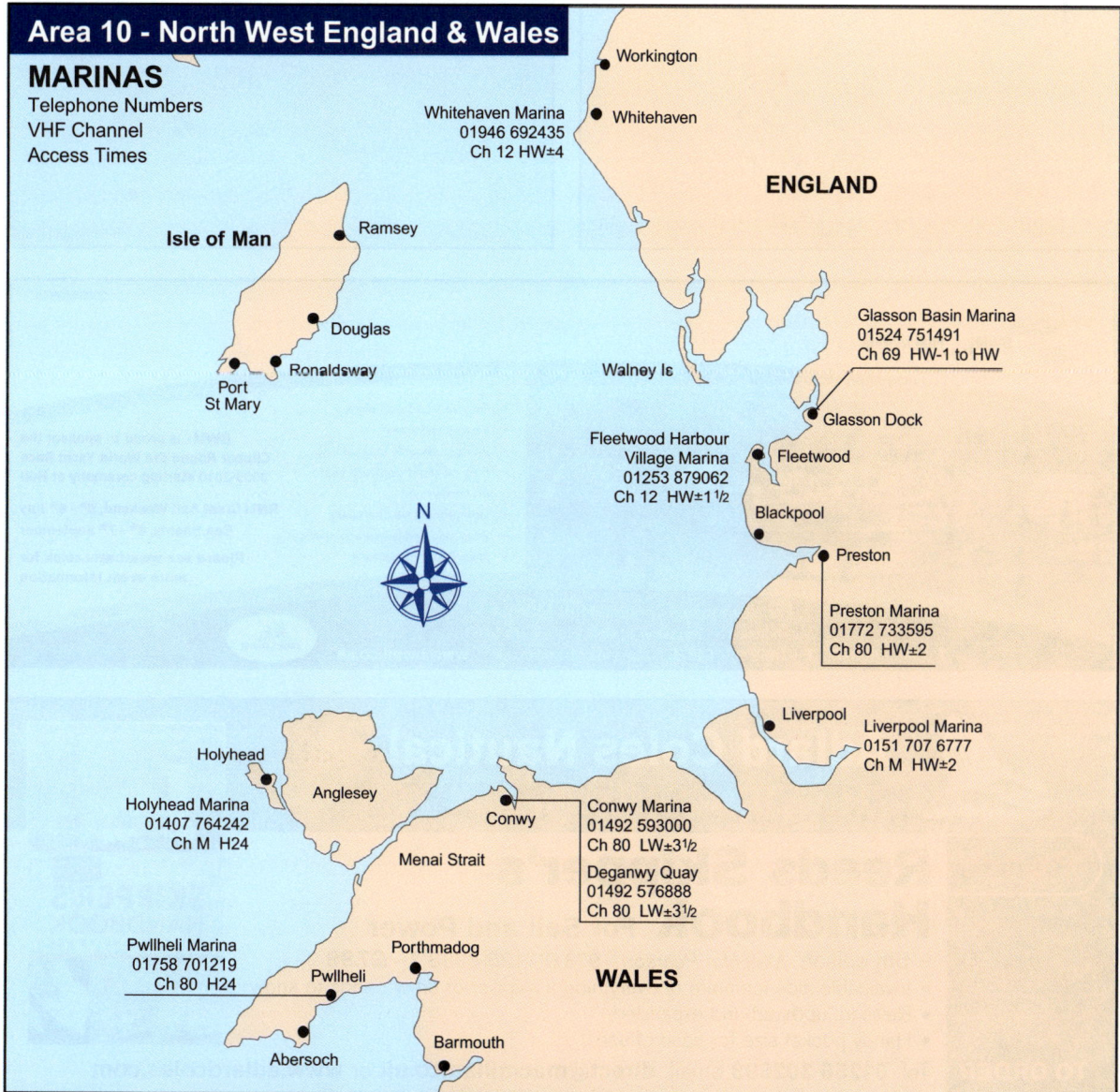

Workington

Whitehaven Marina
01946 692435
Ch 12 HW±4

Whitehaven

ENGLAND

Isle of Man

Ramsey

Douglas

Ronaldsway

Port
St Mary

Walney Is

Glasson Basin Marina
01524 751491
Ch 69 HW-1 to HW

Glasson Dock

Fleetwood Harbour
Village Marina
01253 879062
Ch 12 HW±1 1/2

Fleetwood

Blackpool

Preston

Preston Marina
01772 733595
Ch 80 HW±2

N

Liverpool

Liverpool Marina
0151 707 6777
Ch M HW±2

Holyhead

Anglesey

Holyhead Marina
01407 764242
Ch M H24

Conwy

Conwy Marina
01492 593000
Ch 80 LW±3 1/2

Deganwy Quay
01492 576888
Ch 80 LW±3 1/2

Menai Strait

Pwllheli Marina
01758 701219
Ch 80 H24

Porthmadog

Pwllheli

WALES

Abersoch

Barmouth

WHITEHAVEN MARINA

Whitehaven Harbour Commissioners, Pears House
1 Duke Street, Whitehaven, Cumbria, CA28 7HW
Tel: 01946 692435 Fax: 01946 61455
Email: office@whitehaven-harbour.co.uk
www.whitehaven-harbour.co.uk

| VHF | Ch 12 |
| ACCESS | HW±4 |

Whitehaven Marina can be found at the south-western entrance to the Solway Firth, providing a strategic departure point for those yachts heading for the Isle of Man, Ireland or Southern Scotland. The harbour is one of the more accessible ports of refuge in NW England, affording a safe entry in most weathers. The approach channel across the outer harbour is dredged to about 1.0m above chart datum, allowing entry into the inner harbour via a sea lock at around HW±4.

Conveniently situated for visiting the Lake District, Whitehaven is an attractive Georgian town, renowned in the C18 for its rum and slave imports.

FACILITIES AT A GLANCE

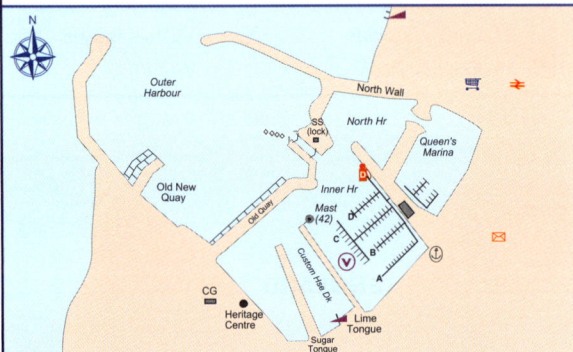

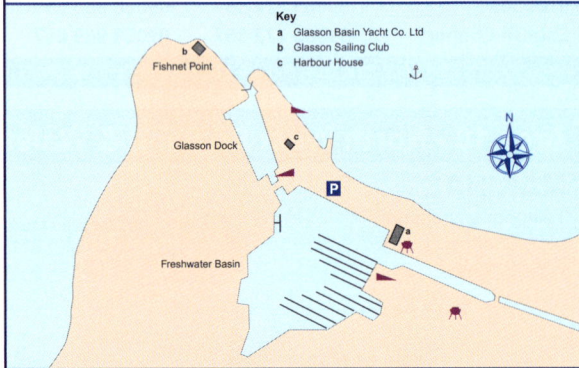

GLASSON BASIN MARINA

Glasson Basin Yacht Company Ltd
Glasson Dock, Lancaster, LA2 0AW
Tel: 01524 751491 Fax: 01524 752626
Email: info@glassonmarina.com
www.glassonmarina.com

| VHF | Ch 69 |
| ACCESS | HW-1 to HW |

Glasson Dock Marina lies on the River Lune, west of Sunderland Point. Access is via the outer dock which opens 45 minutes before H. W.Liverpool and thence via BWB lock into the inner basin. It is recommended to leave Lune No. 1 Buoy approx 11/2 hrs. before H. W.. Contact the dock on Channel 69. The Marina can only be contacted by telephone. All the necessary requirements can be found either on site or within easy reach of Glasson Dock, including boat, rigging and sail repair services as well as a launderette, ablution facilities, shops and restaurants.

FACILITIES AT A GLANCE

Key
a Glasson Basin Yacht Co. Ltd
b Glasson Sailing Club
c Harbour House

2009/MG97/z

BWML Hull Marina

- Fully serviced pontoons
- Visitors welcome
- 24 hour security and parking
- Fully serviced boatyard with 50 tonne hoist
- Comprehensive chandlery
- Boat sale and brokerage service
- New 7000l diesel tank

BWML is proud to sponsor the Clipper Round the World Yacht Race 2009-2010 starting ceremony at Hull

RNLI Great Sail Weekend, 5th - 6th July
Sea Shanty, 6th - 7th September

Please see www.bwml.co.uk for more event information

For all enquiries contact: **Hull Marina**
Warehouse 13 Kingston Street Hull HU1 2DQ
T 01482 609960 **F** 01482 224148 **E** hull.marina@bwml.co.uk   **www.bwml.co.uk**

KENDALE MARINE

Adlard Coles Nautical
THE BEST SAILING BOOKS

Practical

Reeds Skipper's Handbook For Sail and Power
– 5th edition *Malcolm Pearson*   978 0 7136 8338 7 **£7.99**
- Invaluable aide-memoire of everything a skipper or crew needs to know
- Revised, updated and expanded
- Handy pocket size for ease of use

TO ORDER Tel: **01256 302699** email: **direct@macmillan.co.uk** or **www.adlardcoles.com**

MALCOLM PEARSON   RYA Yachtmaster Instructor

REEDS
SKIPPER'S
HANDBOOK
FOR SAIL AND POWER

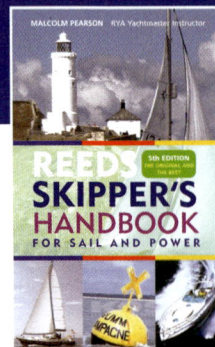

FLEETWOOD HARBOUR MARINA

Fleetwood Harbour Village Marina
The Dock Office, Wyre Dock, Fleetwood, FY7 6PP
Tel: 01253 879062 Fax: 01253 879043
Email: fleetwood@abports.co.uk

VHF Ch 12
ACCESS HW±1.5

Fleetwood Harbour Village Marina provides a good location from which to cruise Morecambe Bay and the Irish Sea. To the north west is the Isle of Man, to the north is the Solway Firth and the Clyde Estuary, while to the south west is Conwy, the Menai Straits and Holyhead.

Tucked away in a protected dock which dates back as far as 1835, Fleetwood Harbour Marina has 300 berths and offers extensive facilities. Overlooking the marina is a 15-acre retail and leisure park laid out in a popular American style.

FACILITIES AT A GLANCE

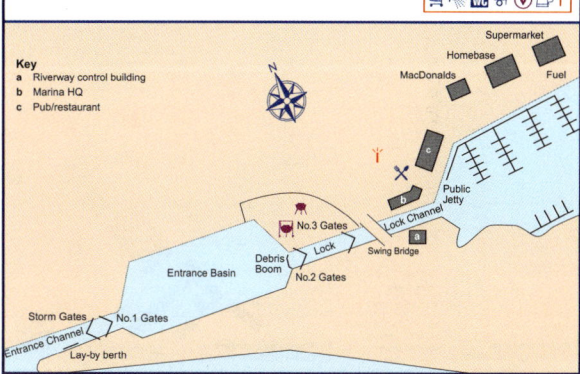

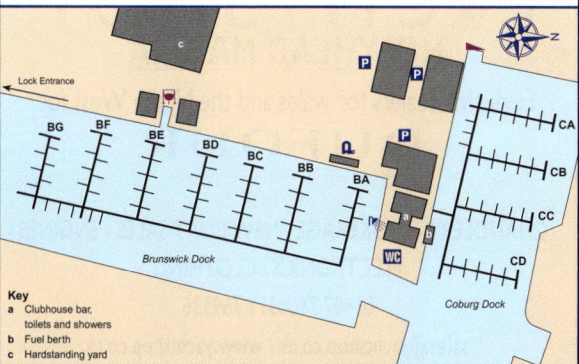

PRESTON MARINA

Preston Marine Services Ltd
The Boathouse, Navigation Way, Preston, PR2 2YP
Tel: 01772 733595 Fax: 01772 733595
Email: info@prestonmarina.co.uk www.prestonmarina.co.uk

VHF Ch 80
ACCESS HW±2

Preston Marina forms part of the comprehensive Riversway Docklands development, meeting all the demands of modern day boat owners. With the docks' history dating back over 100 years, today the marina comprises 40 acres of fully serviced pontoon berths sheltered behind the refurbished original lock gates. Lying 15 miles up the River Ribble, which itself is an interesting cruising ground with an abundance of wildlife, Preston is well placed for sailing to parts of Scotland, Ireland or Wales. The Docklands development includes a wide choice of restaurants, shops and cinemas as well as being in easy reach of all the cultural and leisure facilities provided by a large town.

FACILITIES AT A GLANCE

Key
a Riverway control building
b Marina HQ
c Pub/restaurant

LIVERPOOL MARINA

Liverpool Marina
Coburg Wharf, Sefton Street, Liverpool, L3 4BP
Tel: 0151 707 6777 Fax: 0151 707 6770
Email: harbourside@liverpoolmarina.co.uk

VHF Ch M
ACCESS HW±2

Liverpool Marina is ideally situated for yachtsmen wishing to cruise the Irish Sea. Access is through a computerised lock that opens two and a half hours either side of high water between 0600 and 2200 daily. Once in the marina, you can enjoy the benefits of the facilities on offer, including a first class club bar and restaurant.

Liverpool - recently announced Capital of Culture 2008 - is now a thriving cosmopolitan city, with attractions ranging from numerous bars and restaurants to museums, art galleries and the Beatles Story.

FACILITIES AT A GLANCE

Key
a Clubhouse bar,
   toilets and showers
b Fuel berth
c Hardstanding yard

LIFERAFT SERVICING

£65 + VAT (Carriage £15)

SALES

IS09650-1 STANDARD

SOLAS B PACKS SELF RIGHTING

From £570

Liferaft Hire from £30

NORWEST MARINE LTD
Unit 43 Wellington
Employment Park South
Dunes Way
Liverpool L5 9RJ
Tel: 0151 207 2860
Tel: 0151 207 2861
www.norwestmarine.co.uk

2009/MG36/s

British Marine
INDUSTRIES
FEDERATION

QUAY MARINAS LTD
A & W Building, The Docks, Portishead, N.
Somerset BS20 7DF
Tel: (01275) 841188
Fax: (01275) 841189
e-mail: sriggs@quaymarinas.com

A wholly owned subsidiary of Quay Marinas, operate comprehensive yachting facilities at 5 locations in the UK and are marketing agents for Malahide Marina in Dublin Bay.

2009/EXT3/e

When responding to adverts please mention the 2009 Marina Guide →

REEDS

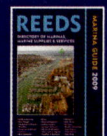

10

CONWY MARINA

Conwy Marina
Conwy, LL32 8EP
Tel: 01492 593000 Fax: 01492 572111
Email: jroberts@quaymarinas.com
www.quaymarinas.co.uk

VHF Ch 80
ACCESS LW±3.5

Situated in an area of outstanding natural beauty, with the Mountains of Snowdonia National Park providing a stunning backdrop, Conwy is the first purpose-built marina to be developed on the north coast of Wales. Enjoying a unique site next to the 13th century Conwy Castle, the third of Edward I's great castles, it provides a convenient base from which to explore the cruising grounds of the North Wales coast. The unspoilt coves of Anglesey and the beautiful Menai Straits prove a popular destination, while further afield are the Llyn Peninsula and the Islands of Bardsey and Tudwells.

The marina incorporates about 500 fully serviced berths which are accessible through a barrier gate between half tide and high water.

FACILITIES AT A GLANCE

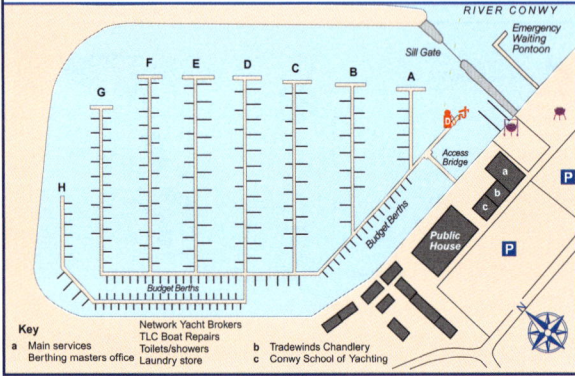

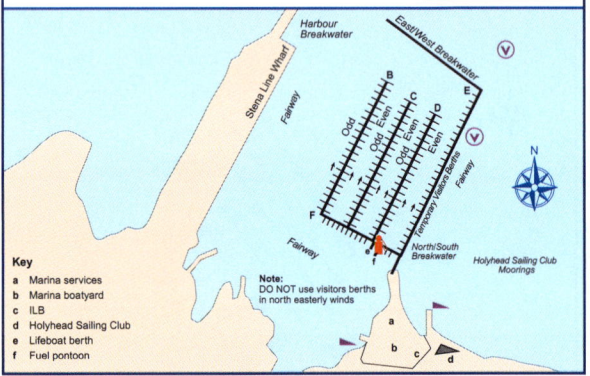

Key
a Main services
   Berthing masters office
   Network Yacht Brokers
   TLC Boat Repairs
   Toilets/showers
   Laundry store
b Tradewinds Chandlery
c Conwy School of Yachting

HOLYHEAD MARINA

Holyhead Marina Ltd
Newry Beach, Holyhead, Gwynedd, LL65 1YA
Tel: 01407 764242 Fax: 01407 769152
Email: info@holyheadmarina.co.uk

VHF Ch M
ACCESS H24

One of the few natural deep water harbours on the Welsh coast, Anglesey is conveniently placed as a first port of call if heading to North Wales from the North, South or West. Its marina at Holyhead, accessible at all states of the tide, is sheltered by Holyhead Mountain as well as an enormous harbour breakwater and extensive floating breakwaters, therefore offering good protection from all directions.

Anglesey boasts numerous picturesque anchorages and beaches in addition to striking views over Snowdonia, while only a tide or two away are the Isle of Man and Eire.

FACILITIES AT A GLANCE

Key
a Marina services
b Marina boatyard
c ILB
d Holyhead Sailing Club
e Lifeboat berth
f Fuel pontoon

Note:
DO NOT use visitors berths in north easterly winds

Shamrock Chandlery

What ever your budget, we've got it covered!

seago SP GOTOP BALTIC LIFEJACKETS SWEDEN XM
spinlock SEBAGO
WEST SYSTEM ECHOMAX Barton MARINE ADMIRALTY LEISURE
PLASTIMO SHURHOLD BLAKES Paints LALIZAS International

To buy these and many other brands visit our new on-line shop

www.shamrock.co.uk

Then click on GO SHOPPING

2009/MG128/e

Our extensively stocked Chandlery is open 7 days a week Winter and Summer
Shamrock Quay William Street
Southampton SO14 5QL

VISA Maestro MasterCard

Tel: 023 8063 2725

HOLYHEAD MARINA
GATEWAY TO NORTH WALES

24 hour todal access

Improved facilities from 2007:

• Private shower rooms
• Washing machines & tumble dryers
• General store
• Yacht brokerage and chandlery

Fully equipped boat yard

Tel: 01407 764 242
Fax: 01407 769 152
VHF: CH37 or M1

info@holyheadmarina.co.uk
www.holyheadmarina.co.uk

2009/MG92/z

YACHTSHOP
HOLYHEAD MARINA

Exclusive dealers for wales and the North West for

DUFOUR
YACHTS

CHANDLERY - BROKERAGE - NEW BOAT SALES - ENGINES - ELECTRONICS - CLOTHING

01407 760031 / 769536

sales@yachtshop.co.uk / www.yachtshop.co.uk

2009/MG160/z

PWLLHELI MARINA

Pwllheli Marina
Glan Don, Pwllheli, North Wales, LL53 5YT
Tel: 01758 701219 Fax: 01758 701443
Email: hafanpwllheli@hafanpwllheli.co.uk

| VHF | Ch 80 |
| ACCESS | H24 |

Pwllheli is an old Welsh market town providing the gateway to the Llyn Peninsula, which stretches out as far as Bardsey Island to form an 'Area of Outstanding Natural Beauty'. Enjoying the spectacular backdrop of the Snowdonia Mountains, Pwllheli's numerous attractions include an open-air market every Wednesday, 'Neuadd Dwyfor', offering a mix of live theatre and latest films, and beautiful beaches.

Pwllheli Marina is situated on the south side of the Llyn Peninsula. One of Wales' finest marinas and sailing centres, it has over 400 pontoon berths and excellent onshore facilities.

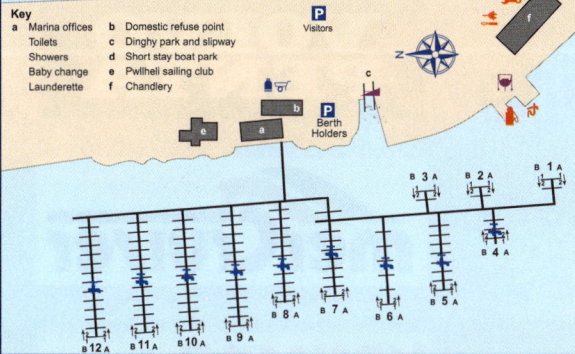

FACILITIES AT A GLANCE

Key
a Marina offices
   Toilets
   Showers
   Baby change
   Launderette
b Domestic refuse point
c Dinghy park and slipway
d Short stay boat park
e Pwllheli sailing club
f Chandlery

Offshore Sea School

Based at Pwllheli Marina, North Wales

RYA Children's Powerboat Courses (age 8+)
RYA PWC and Powerboat Courses
Own Boat / Individual Tuition
All RYA Shorebased Courses

RYA Training Centre

RYA Motor Cruising Courses
International Certificate of Competence
Boat Delivery by Commercial Skippers
Gift Vouchers available

Have a fabulous day out on our luxury Motor Cruiser for a special event or corporate day

For friendly advice and information come and see us, visit our website, call or email

1st Floor, Unit 6, Marina Workshops
Pwllheli, Gwynedd, LL53 5YT
www.offshoreseaschool.com   mail@offshoreseaschool.com
Telephone: 01758 701379 LL53 5YT   Mobile: 07860 458260

2009/MG34/e

When responding to adverts please mention the **2009 Marina Guide** →

REEDS
MARINA GUIDE 2009

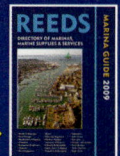

FIRMHELM Ltd
PWLLHELI BOATYARD

- Boatbuilders
- Maintenance
- Repairs, Refits
- Insurance Work
- Mast and Wire Work
- Rigging and Splicing
- Blakes Osmosis Centre
- Hot Vac Hull Cure Systems
- Spray Centre
- Boat Hoists up to 40 Ton
- Secure Storage
- 25 Ton Mobile Crane Hire
- Chandlery
- Marine Leisurewire

We pride ourselves in providing the most professional and extensive Boatyard Services in the area together with the areas leading chandlery and leisurewear retail outlet stocking all the major brands. e.g. Musto, Henri Lloyd, Gill, Kikoy, Dubarry, Chatham, Quayside, Wombat, International & Blakes Paints, Harken, Lewmar, Spinlock, Holt, Plastimom Wichard, Liros Ropes, XM Yachting etc

Pwllheli Marine Centre
Hafan Pwllheli LL53 5YQ
TEL: 01758 612251
FAX: 01758 613356

FIRMHELM Ltd
Visit our online shop at
www.firmhelm-marine.co.uk
E-MAIL: enquiries@firmhelm.com

Outer Harbour
Pwllheli LL53 5AY
TEL: 01758 612244
FAX: 01758 614790

2009/MG37/sZ

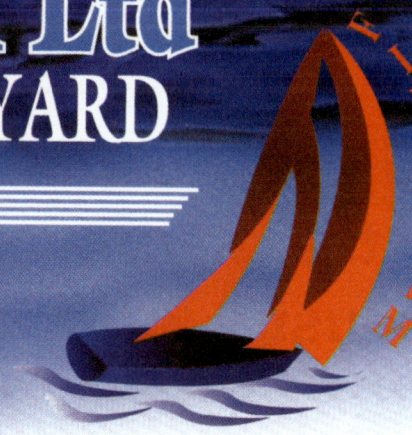

10

Advance Marine

Marine Engineering

VOLVO PENTA

- **Extensive Chandlery**

merCruiser

- **Rigging wire & swaging**

YANMAR marine

- **Mobile repair service**

nanni diesel

- **25 years experience in the marine industry**

MERCURY

HONDA

SUZUKI MARINE

Portishead, Bristol

Tel: 01275 815910

www.advancemarine.co.uk

2009/MG100/z

SOUTH WALES & BRISTOL CHANNEL - Bardsey Island to Land's End

ADLARD COLES NAUTICAL
WEATHER FORECASTS
BY FAX & TELEPHONE

Coastal/Inshore	2-day by Fax	5-day by Phone
North West	09065 222 351	09068 969 651
Wales	09065 222 350	09068 969 650
Bristol	09065 222 349	09068 969 649
South West	09065 222 348	09068 969 648
National (3-5 day)	09065 222 340	09068 969 640

Offshore	2-5 day by Fax	2-5 day by Phone
Irish Sea	09065 222 359	09068 969 659
English Channel	09065 222 357	09068 969 657
Biscay	09065 222 360	09068 969 660
North West Scotland	09065 222 361	09068 969 661

09068 CALLS COST 60P PER MIN. 09065 CALLS COST £1.50 PER MIN.

Key to Marina Plans symbols

- Bottled gas
- Chandler
- Disabled facilities
- Electrical supply
- Electrical repairs
- Engine repairs
- First Aid
- Fresh Water
- Fuel - Diesel
- Fuel - Petrol
- Hardstanding/boatyard
- Internet Café
- Laundry facilities
- Lift-out facilities
- P Parking
- Pub/Restaurant
- Pump out
- Rigging service
- Sail repairs
- Shipwright
- Shop/Supermarket
- Showers
- Slipway
- WC Toilets
- Telephone
- Trolleys
- V Visitors berths
- Wi-Fi

Area 11 - South Wales & Bristol Channel

MARINAS
Telephone Numbers
VHF Channel
Access Times

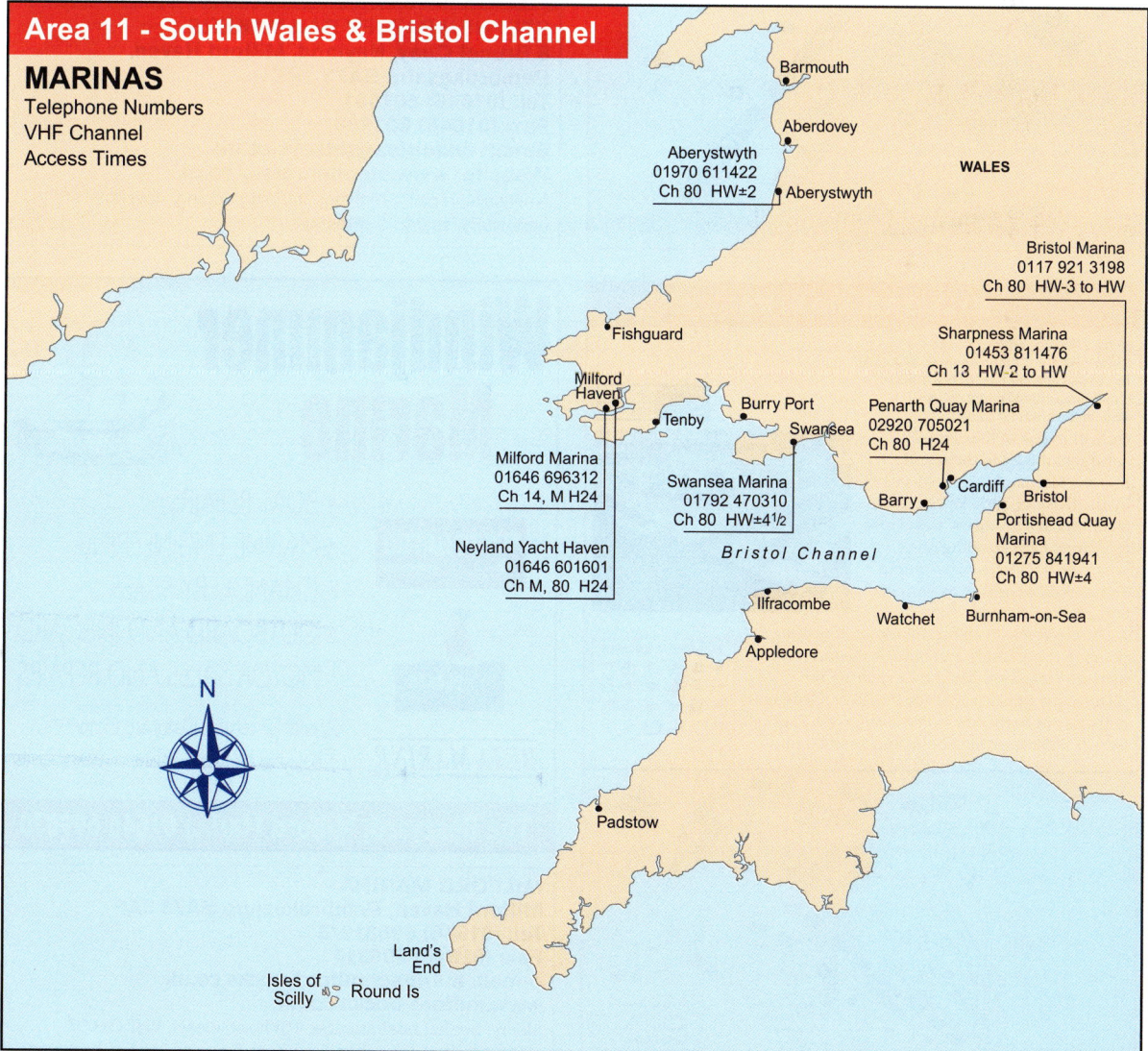

WALES

Barmouth
Aberdovey
Aberystwyth 01970 611422 Ch 80 HW±2
Fishguard
Bristol Marina 0117 921 3198 Ch 80 HW-3 to HW
Sharpness Marina 01453 811476 Ch 13 HW 2 to HW
Milford Haven
Tenby
Burry Port
Swansea
Penarth Quay Marina 02920 705021 Ch 80 H24
Milford Marina 01646 696312 Ch 14, M H24
Swansea Marina 01792 470310 Ch 80 HW±4½
Barry
Cardiff
Bristol
Neyland Yacht Haven 01646 601601 Ch M, 80 H24
Bristol Channel
Portishead Quay Marina 01275 841941 Ch 80 HW±4
Ilfracombe
Watchet
Burnham-on-Sea
Appledore
N
Padstow
Land's End
Isles of Scilly Round Is

ABERYSTWYTH MARINA

Aberystwyth Marina, IMP Developments
Trefechan, Aberystwyth, Ceredigion, SY23 1AS
Tel: 01970 611422 Fax: 01970 624122
Email: enquiries@aberystwythmarina.com

VHF	Ch 80
ACCESS	HW±2

Aberystwyth is a picturesque university seaside town on the west coast of Wales. Its £9 million marina provides over 150 permanent pontoon berths and welcomes on average between 1,500 and 2,000 visiting yachts per year. Accessible two hours either side of high water, its facilities incorporate the usual marine services as well as an on-site pub and restaurant.

A short distance away are several pretty Welsh harbours, including Fishguard, Cardigan, Porthmadog and Abersoch, while the east coast of Ireland can be reached within a day's sail.

FACILITIES AT A GLANCE

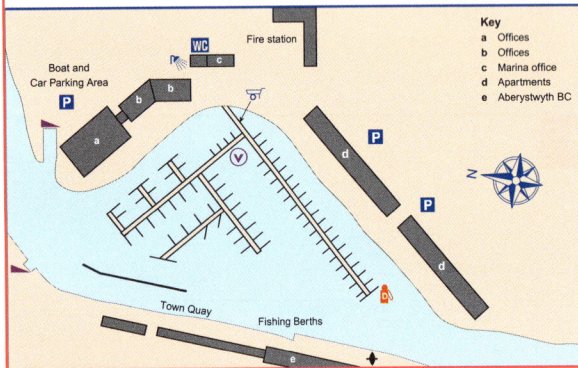

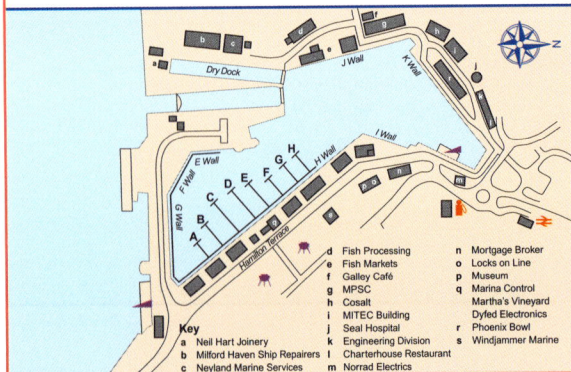

Key
- a Offices
- b Offices
- c Marina office
- d Apartments
- e Aberystwyth BC

Fire station

Boat and Car Parking Area

Town Quay

Fishing Berths

ABERYSTWYTH MARINA - IMP DEVELOPMENTS

Y Lanfa-Aberystwyth Marina, Trefechan, Aberystwyth SY23 1AS
Tel: (01970) 611422
Fax: (01970) 624122
www.abermarina.com

Fully serviced marina. Diesel, gas, water, toilets and hot showers.

2009/L4/v

NEYLAND MARINE SERVICES

Tel: 01646 698968
Fax: 01646 695303
e-mail: neylandmarine@aol.com
www.neylandmarine.co.uk

We provide unequalled sales and service to the pleasure boating, fishing and shipping industry. Your complete repair and supply service for electrical and electronic equipment, engineering installations and components. Supply, service dealers for most manufacturers.

2009/L7/e

STEPHEN RATSEY SAILMAKERS

8 Brunel Quay, Neyland, Milford Haven, Pembrokeshire SA73 1PY
Tel: (01646) 601561
Fax: (01646) 601968
Email: enquiries@ratseys.co.uk
Website: www.stephenratsey.co.uk

New sails, repairs, running, standing rigging, covers, upholstery, seldon & rotostay.

2009/L15/k

MILFORD MARINA

Milford Marina, Milford Docks
Milford Haven, Pembrokeshire SA73 3AF
Tel: 01646 696312 Fax: 01646 696314
Email: enquiries@mhpa.co.uk
www.milford-docks.co.uk

VHF	Ch 14, M
ACCESS	H24

Set within one of the deepest natural harbours in the world, Milford Marina was opened in 1991 by the Duke of York. Since then its facilities have gradually developed to include hard standing areas, secure boat yards, a diesel pump and chandlery as well as various bars and restaurants.

Accessed via an entrance lock (with waiting pontoons both inside and outside the lock), the marina is ideally situated for exploring the picturesque upper reaches of the River Cleddau or cruising out beyond St Ann's Head to the unspoilt islands of Skomer, Skokholm and Grassholm.

FACILITIES AT A GLANCE

Dry Dock
J Wall
K Wall
I Wall
E Wall
F Wall
G Wall
H Wall
Hamilton Terrace

- d Fish Processing
- e Fish Markets
- f Galley Café
- g MPSC
- h Cosalt
- i MITEC Building
- j Seal Hospital
- k Engineering Division
- l Charterhouse Restaurant
- m Norrad Electrics
- n Mortgage Broker
- o Locks on Line
- p Museum
- q Marina Control
- Martha's Vineyard
- Dyfed Electronics
- r Phoenix Bowl
- s Windjammer Marine

Key
- a Neil Hart Joinery
- b Milford Haven Ship Repairers
- c Neyland Marine Services

2009/MG132/d

Windjammer Marine

TOHATSU Outboards

BLAKES Paints

BETA MARINE

- BOAT REPAIRS
- MARINE ENGINEERING
- CHANDLERY SALES
- OUTBOARD AND INBOARD MOTOR SALES AND REPAIRS

Agents for Tohatsu Outboard Motors
• Beta Marine Diesel Engines • Blakes Paints

The Boatyard, Milford Marina 01646 699070

MILFORD MARINA

Milford Haven, Pembrokeshire SA73 3AF
Tel: (01646) 696312/3
Fax: (01646) 696314
e-mail: marina@milford-docks.co.uk
www.milford-docks.co.uk

Marina berths, boat storage, 16t hoist, diesel, VHF.CH.37, electricity, laundery, chandlery, boat & engine repairs, brokerage, engine sale, restaurants, retail park on site, 24 hour staff, 22 miles of sheltered estuary for all year round sailing.

2009/L16/e

NEYLAND YACHT HAVEN

Neyland Yacht Haven Ltd
Brunel Quay, Neyland, Pembrokeshire, SA73 1PY
Tel: 01646 601601 Fax: 01646 600713
Email: neyland@yachthavens.com

VHF Ch M, 80
ACCESS H24

Approximately 10 miles from the entrance to Milford Haven lies Neyland Yacht Haven. Tucked away in a well protected inlet just before the Cleddau Bridge, this marina has around 380 berths and can accommodate yachts up to 25m LOA with draughts of up to 2.5m. The marina is divided into two basins, with the lower one enjoying full tidal access, while entry to the upper one is restricted by a tidal sill.

Offering a comprehensive range of services, Neyland Yacht Haven is within a five minute walk of the town centre where the various shops and takeaways cater for most everyday needs.

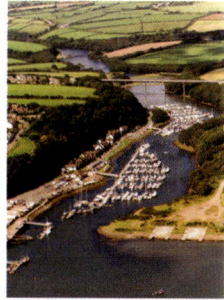

FACILITIES AT A GLANCE

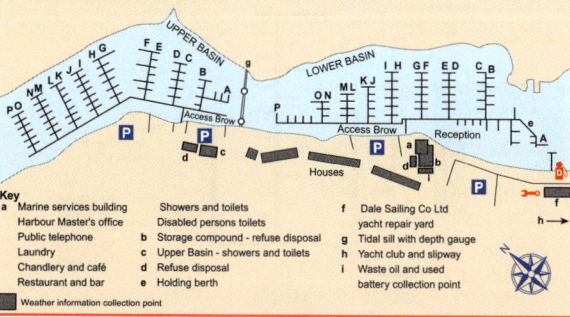

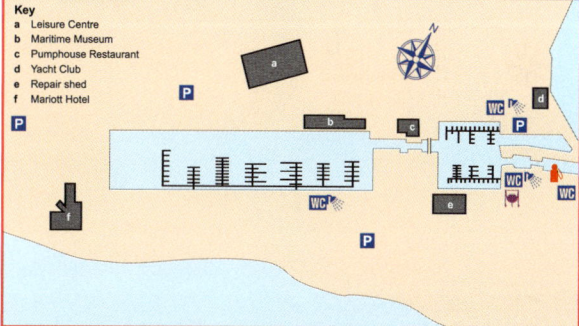

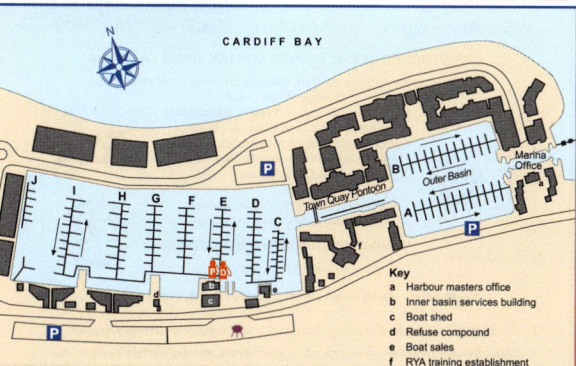

Key
a Marine services building
   Harbour Master's office
   Public telephone
   Laundry
   Chandlery and café
   Restaurant and bar
   Showers and toilets
   Disabled persons toilets
b Storage compound - refuse disposal
c Upper Basin - showers and toilets
d Refuse disposal
e Holding berth
f Dale Sailing Co Ltd
   yacht repair yard
g Tidal sill with depth gauge
h Yacht club and slipway
i Waste oil and used
   battery collection point
■ Weather information collection point

SWANSEA MARINA

Swansea Marina
Lockside, Maritime Quarter, Swansea, SA1 1WG
Tel: 01792 470310 Fax: 01792 463948
www.swansea.gov.uk/swanseamarina
Email: swanmar@swansea.gov.uk

VHF Ch 80
ACCESS HW±4.5

At the hub of the city's recently redeveloped and award winning Maritime Quarter, Swansea Marina can be accessed HW±4½ hrs via a lock. Surrounded by a plethora of shops, restaurants and marine businesses to cater for most yachtsmen's needs, the marina is in close proximity to the picturesque Gower coast, where there is no shortage of quiet sandy beaches off which to anchor. It also provides the perfect starting point for cruising to Ilfracombe, Lundy Island, the North Cornish coast or West Wales.

Within easy walking distance of the marina is the city centre, boasting a covered shopping centre and market. For those who prefer walking or cycling, take the long promenade to the Mumbles fishing village from where there are plenty of coastal walks.

FACILITIES AT A GLANCE

Key
a Leisure Centre
b Maritime Museum
c Pumphouse Restaurant
d Yacht Club
e Repair shed
f Mariott Hotel

PENARTH QUAYS MARINA

Penarth Quays Marina
Penarth, Vale of Glamorgan, CF64 1TQ
Tel: 02920 705021 Fax: 02920 712170
www.quaymarinas.com
Email: sjones@quaymarinas.com

VHF Ch 80
ACCESS H24

Penarth Quays Marina has been established in the historic basins of Penarth Docks for over 20 years and is the premier boating facility in the region. The marina is Cardiff Bay's only 5 Gold Anchor marina and provides an ideal base for those using the Bay and the Bristol Channel. With 24hr access there is always water available for boating. Penarth and Cardiff boast an extensive range of leisure facilities, shops and restaurants making this marina an ideal base or destination.

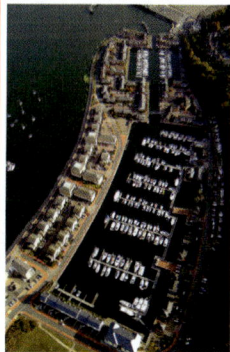

FACILITIES AT A GLANCE

Key
a Harbour masters office
b Inner basin services building
c Boat shed
d Refuse compound
e Boat sales
f RYA training establishment

PENARTH MARINA & CARDIFF BAY ONE STOP MARINE CENTRE

The Area leaders in Marine Engineering, Electrical & Electronic Installations and Repairs. All aspects of boat repairs, GRP a speciality.
Large well stocked Chandlery supplying most well known brands of Marine Leisure Equipment

VOLVO PENTA   WIGMORE WRIGHT MARINE SERVICES   YANMAR marine
CM   YAMAHA   COMBALTY   ZF MARINE
BLAKES Paint   Authorised Dealers   vetus   MARINER

2008/MG55/v

THE BOATYARD, PENARTH MARINA, PENARTH CF64 1TT
TEL: (029) 2070 9983 / FAX: (029) 2070 7771

QUAY MARINAS LTD
A & W Building, The Docks, Portishead, N. Somerset BS20 7DF
Tel: (01275) 841188
Fax: (01275) 841189
e-mail: sriggs@quaymarinas.com
A wholly owned subsidiary of Quay Marinas, operate comprehensive yachting facilities at 5 locations in the UK and are marketing agents for Malahide Marina in Dublin Bay.

2009/EXT3/e

When responding to adverts please mention the 2009 Marina Guide →

REEDS

11

SHARPNESS MARINA

Sharpness Marina, Sharpness
Berkeley, Gloucestershire GR13 9UN
Tel: 01453 811476
Email: sharpnessmarina@ukonline.co.uk

VHF Ch 13
ACCESS HW-2

Sharpness is a small port on the River Severn lying at the entrance to the Gloucester and Sharpness Canal. At the time of its completion in 1827, the canal was the largest and deepest ship canal in the world. However, although once an important commercial waterway, it is now primarily used by pleasure boats. Yachts approaching the marina from seaward can do so via a lock two hours before high water, but note that the final arrival should be timed as late as possible to avoid strong tides in the entrance. From the lock, a passage under two swing bridges and a turn to port brings you to the marina, where pontoon berths are equipped

FACILITIES AT A GLANCE

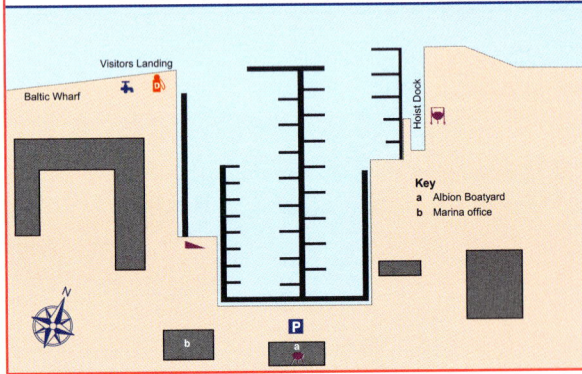

BRISTOL MARINA

Bristol Marina Ltd
Hanover Place, Bristol, BS1 6TZ
Tel: 0117 921 3198 Fax: 0117 929 7672
Email: info@bristolmarina.co.uk

VHF Ch 80
ACCESS HW-3 to HW

Situated in the heart of the city, Bristol is a fully serviced marina providing over 100 pontoon berths for vessels up to 20m LOA. Among the facilities are a new fuelling berth and pump out station as well as an on site chandler and sailmaker. It is situated on the south side of the Floating Harbour, about eight miles from the mouth of the River Avon. Accessible from seaward via the Cumberland Basin, passing through both Entrance Lock and Junction Lock, it can be reached approximately three hours before HW.

Shops, restaurants, theatres and cinemas are all within easy reach of the marina, while local attractions include the SS *Great Britain*, designed by Isambard Kingdom Brunel, and the famous Clifton Suspension Bridge, which has an excellent visitors' centre depicting its fascinating story.

FACILITIES AT A GLANCE

Key
a Albion Boatyard
b Marina office

PORTISHEAD QUAYS MARINA

Portishead Quays Marina
The Docks, Portishead, Bristol BS20 7DF
Tel: 01275 841941 Fax: 01275 841942
Email: portisheadmarina@quaymarinas.com
www.quaymarinas.com

VHF Ch 80
ACCESS HW±4

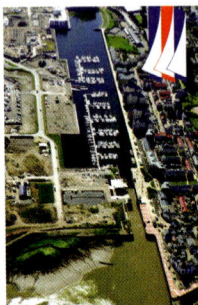

Opened in May 2001, Portishead Quays Marina, with its excellent facilities and 24 hour security, is becoming increasingly popular with locals and visitors alike. However, visiting yachtsmen should be aware of the large tidal ranges and strong tidal flows that they are likely to encounter in this part of the Bristol Channel as well as shipping plying to and from the Avonmouth and Portbury Docks. The entrance to the marina is via a lock, with access for a 1.5m yacht being at HW±4½ hrs on neaps and HW±3¾ hrs on springs – contact the marina on VHF Ch 80 ahead of time for the next available lock.

FACILITIES AT A GLANCE

Key
a Control building (reception, showers, laundry)
b Advance Marine Services & Chandlery
c A&W Building + Coastguard
d Berth holder facilities, boat sales & café
e Ray Williams Marine

A.W. HAYNES
Marine Surveyor   Y.B.D.S.A.
Weighbridge Yard, Lawrenny, Pembrokeshire SA68 0PN
Tel: 01646 651561 Mobile: 07786 890882
Email: alan.haynes@talk21.com

Christopher Berry Marine Surveyor
Stable Cottage, Lower Morton, Thornbury, Bristol. BS35 1LF.
Telephone: Office – 01454 413556   Mobile – 07710 175871.
CHRISTOPHER BERRY MARINE SURVEY. MIIMS - AMYDSA
Pre-Purchase/Insurance Surveys, Osmosis Examinations/Consultancy
Damage Assessment
Sailing Vessel Code of Practice Examination
Recreational Craft Directive (RCD)
British Ships Registration Measurements
Non-destructive Testing of Steel Hulls
All Constructions
Bespoke Build Project Management
Full Professional Indemnity Insurance
www.marinesurveyor.org.uk
chrisberry.marinesurvey@virgin.net
South West - South Coast - West Country - South Wales - Abroad
Underwritten by Lloyds of London.   www.marinesurveyor.org.uk
enquiries@marinesurveyor.org.uk   chrisberry.marinesurvey@virgin.net

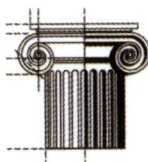

THE WELSH COLLECTION
Y Casgliad Cymraeg

YOU CAN LIVE HERE

If you yearn for a beautiful home by the sea, here's an opportunity you won't want to miss. New developments of outstanding quality, in modern and traditional styles, offering tranquillity, breathtaking natural beauty and captivating views.

The Thornsett Group offer this and so much more with its Welsh Collection. What more could you want?

For further information about all of Thornsett's Welsh developments, call or visit www.welshcollection.co.uk

01834 869 142

THORNSETT GROUP
REALISING THE POTENTIAL

www.thornsettgroup.com

2009/mgd/v

11

IRELAND'S LARGEST MARINA

1D2O0018 Photo: © Peter Barrow 14th July 2007. Tel: 0872-559638

Dun Laoghaire Marina

- 820 berth fully serviced marina
- Located in Dublin's major sailing centre
- Awarded ISO 14001 – Environment Management System
- Visitor berths available from €4 per metre per night
- 24 hour access
- Friendly, knowledgably and welcoming staff 24/7
- All visitor berths fully serviced, shore power supply metered.
- Petrol, diesel and holding tank pump out
- Laundry facilities onsite
- Oceanwave WiFi
- Full disabled access and facilities
- Direct access to UK with Stena HSS ferry and airport coach transfer
- Volvo Dun Laoghaire Regatta 9-12 July 2009

www.dlmarina.com
Contact: info@dlmarina.com

mmm
mm+m.
mmm
Marina Marketing & Management Ltd.

2009/MG168/z

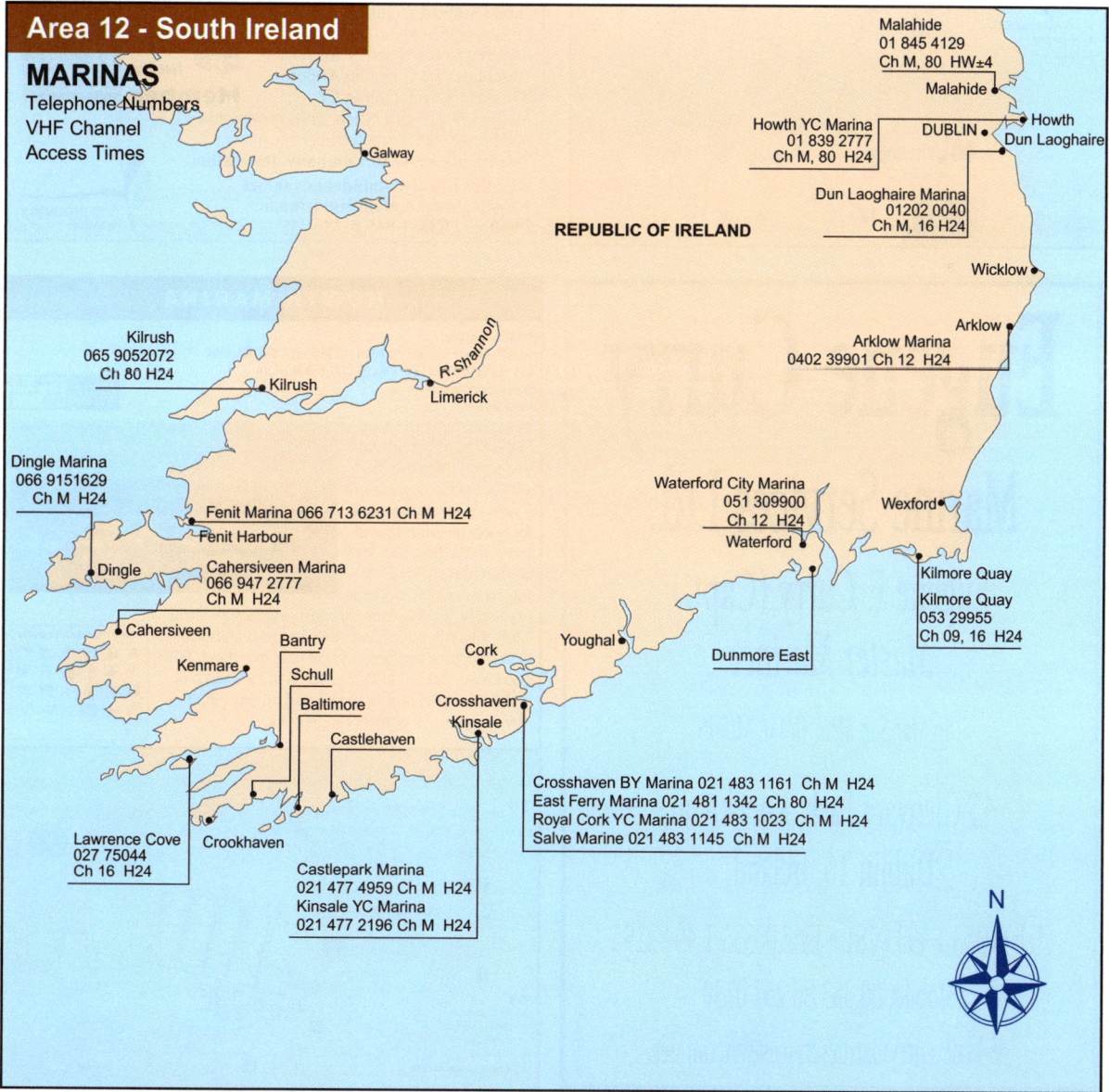

SOUTH IRELAND - Malahide, south to Liscanor Bay

ADLARD COLES NAUTICAL
WEATHER FORECASTS
BY FAX & TELEPHONE

Coastal/Inshore	2-day by Fax	5-day by Phone
Northern Ireland	09065 222 355	09068 969 655
Wales	09065 222 350	09068 969 650
Bristol	09065 222 349	09068 969 649
South West	09065 222 348	09068 969 648
National (3-5 day)	09065 222 340	09068 969 640

Offshore	2-5 day by Fax	2-5 day by Phone
Irish Sea	09065 222 359	09068 969 659
English Channel	09065 222 357	09068 969 657
Biscay	09065 222 360	09068 969 660
North West Scotland	09065 222 361	09068 969 661

09068 CALLS COST 60P PER MIN. 09065 CALLS COST £1.50 PER MIN.

Key to Marina Plans symbols

Bottled gas, Chandler, Disabled facilities, Electrical supply, Electrical repairs, Engine repairs, First Aid, Fresh Water, Fuel - Diesel, Fuel - Petrol, Hardstanding/boatyard, Internet Café, Laundry facilities, Lift-out facilities

Parking, Pub/Restaurant, Pump out, Rigging service, Sail repairs, Shipwright, Shop/Supermarket, Showers, Slipway, Toilets, Telephone, Trolleys, Visitors berths, Wi-Fi

Area 12 - South Ireland

MARINAS
Telephone Numbers
VHF Channel
Access Times

Malahide 01 845 4129 Ch M, 80 HW±4
Howth YC Marina 01 839 2777 Ch M, 80 H24
Dun Laoghaire Marina 01202 0040 Ch M, 16 H24
Arklow Marina 0402 39901 Ch 12 H24
Kilrush 065 9052072 Ch 80 H24
REPUBLIC OF IRELAND
Dingle Marina 066 9151629 Ch M H24
Fenit Marina 066 713 6231 Ch M H24
Cahersiveen Marina 066 947 2777 Ch M H24
Waterford City Marina 051 309900 Ch 12 H24
Kilmore Quay 053 29955 Ch 09, 16 H24
Lawrence Cove 027 75044 Ch 16 H24
Crosshaven BY Marina 021 483 1161 Ch M H24
East Ferry Marina 021 481 1342 Ch 80 H24
Royal Cork YC Marina 021 483 1023 Ch M H24
Salve Marine 021 483 1145 Ch M H24
Castlepark Marina 021 477 4959 Ch M H24
Kinsale YC Marina 021 477 2196 Ch M H24

Galway, Limerick, Wicklow, Arklow, Wexford, Waterford, Youghal, Dunmore East, Cork, Crosshaven, Kinsale, Bantry, Schull, Baltimore, Castlehaven, Kenmare, Crookhaven, Dingle, Cahersiveen, Fenit Harbour, Kilrush, DUBLIN, Malahide, Howth, Dun Laoghaire, Kilmore Quay

N

MALAHIDE MARINA

Malahide Marina
Malahide, Co. Dublin
Tel: +353 1 845 4129 Fax: +353 1 845 4255
Email: info@malahidemarina.net
www.malahidemarina.net

VHF	Ch M, 80
ACCESS	HW±4

Malahide Marina, situated just 10 minutes from Dublin Airport and 20 minutes north of Dublin's city centre, is a fully serviced marina accommodating up to 350 yachts. Capable of taking vessels of up to 75m in length, its first class facilities include a boatyard with hard standing for approximately 170 boats and a 30-ton mobile hoist. Its on site restaurant, Cruzzo, provides a large seating area in convivial surroundings. The village of Malahide has plenty to offer the visiting yachtsmen, with a wide variety of eating places, nearby golf courses and tennis courts as well as a historic castle and botanical gardens.

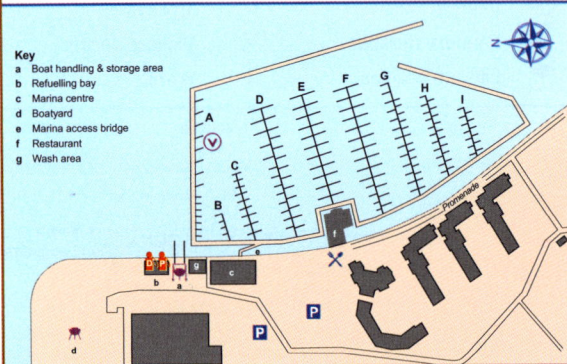

FACILITIES AT A GLANCE

Key
a   Boat handling & storage area
b   Refuelling bay
c   Marina centre
d   Boatyard
e   Marina access bridge
f   Restaurant
g   Wash area

2009/MG44/s

docklands

Dublin City Moorings

Custom House Quay, Docklands, Dublin 1

**the only mooring in the
Centre of Dublin City**

Beside the Custom House and IFSC.
Electricity/water. Showers/toilets. 24 hour security.
Swipe card access.
Telephone +353 1 8183300 Fax: +353 1 8183399

Email: info@dublindocklands.ie   Website: http://www.dublindocklands.ie

2009/MG5/e

MALAHIDE MARINA

**Marina Centre, Malahide Marina Village,
Malahide, Co. Dublin**
350 Berths in fully serviced marina.
On-shore facilities include showers/bath, laundry
and Disabled facilities.
Full service boatyard
Covered Repair Facility for re-fits.
10 minutes from Dublin Airport
25 minutes from Dublin City
Idyllic setting with beach, golf, restaurants
and many other amenities.
The Ideal Cruise in Company destination.
e-mail: info@malahidemarina.net
website: www.malahidemarina.net
Phone: 003531 845 4129

Irish
Marine
Federation
Member

British Marine
Federation

2009/MG44/s

Eugene Curry

Marine Services Ltd.

Eugene F. Curry (Capt.)

Master Mariner

Dip Mar Sur, MNI, IIMM, MIIMS

45 Glenvara Park, Knocklyon,
Dublin 16, Ireland.

Tel: 00353 1 493 9781 • Fax: 00353 1 494 2195

Mobile: 00 353 86 257 0730

E-Mail: currymarineservices@eircom.net

2009/MG167/s

HOWTH MARINA

Howth Marina
Howth Marina, Harbour Road, Howth, Co. Dublin
Tel: +353 1 8392777 Fax: +353 1 8392430
Email: marina@hyc.ie
www.hyc.ie

VHF	Ch M, 80
ACCESS	H24

Based on the north coast of the rugged peninsula that forms the northern side of Dublin Bay, Howth Marina is ideally situated for north or south-bound traffic in the Irish Sea. Well sheltered in all winds, it can be entered at any state of the tide. Overlooking the marina is Howth Yacht Club, which has in recent years been expanded and is now said to be the largest yacht club in Ireland. With good road and rail links, Howth is in easy reach of Dublin's airport and ferry terminal, making it an obvious choice for crew changeovers.

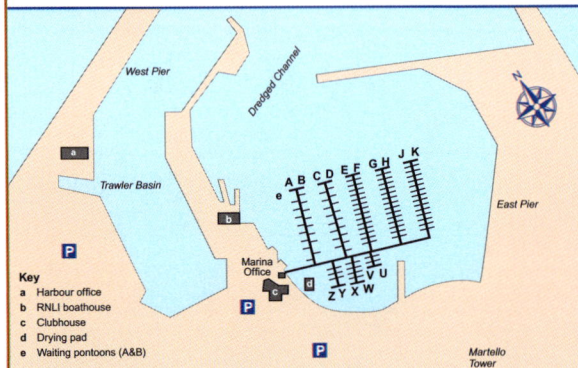

FACILITIES AT A GLANCE

Key
a   Harbour office
b   RNLI boathouse
c   Clubhouse
d   Drying pad
e   Waiting pontoons (A&B)

YPP

YACHT PARTS PLYMOUTH

QUEEN ANNE'S BATTERY MARINA
PLYMOUTH
PL4 0LP

01752 252489
www.yachtparts.co.uk
sales@yachtparts.co.uk

2 SHOPS - 1 AIM
TO GET YOU & KEEP YOU ON THE WATER

YAMAHA

AVON
ZODIAC
TERHI

The DINGHY & RIB Warehouse

DISTRIBUTORS FOR YAMAHA - AVON - ZODIAC - TERHI

QUEEN ANNE'S BATTERY MARINA, PLYMOUTH, PL4 0LP
01752 222265   www.dinghyandrib.co.uk   sales@dinghyandrib.co.uk

2009/MG170/z

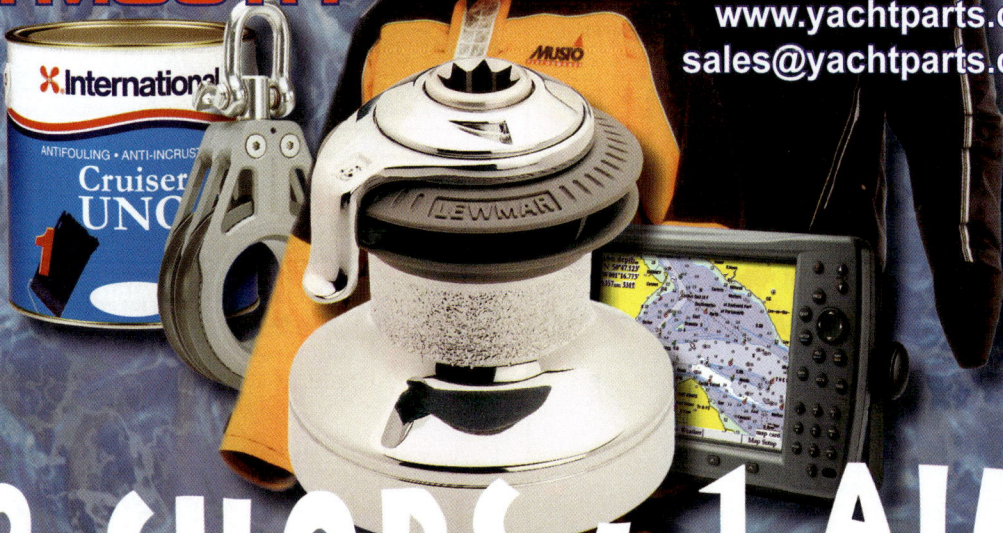

12

DUN LAOGHAIRE MARINA

Dun Laoghaire Marina
Harbour Road, Dun Laoghaire, Co Dublin, Eire
Tel: +353 1 202 0040 Fax: +353 1 202 0043
Email: info@dlmarina.com   www.dlmarina.com

VHF	Ch M, 16
ACCESS	H24

With over 800 berths Dun Laoghaire Marina is the largest in Ireland. The town centre is within 400m and with plenty of shops, supermarkets, restaurants, and chandlers. Berthing is available for yachts from 8 to 23m and linear berthing is available for yachts up to 35m. The minimum draught is 3.6m LWS. Dublin City centre is 12 kms away with frequent rail service. Dublin Airport is 22 km. Dun Laoghaire Marina is an ideal location for crew change or cruise rest. Berths are identified by access route, bay identification and number – ascending from bay entrance – odd numbers to port, even to starboard, eg SD10 indicates South Fairway, Bay D 5th berth on starboard hand. Visitor berths mainly located on

FACILITIES AT A GLANCE

Key
a Royal Irish Yacht Club
b Marina office
c WC
d Royal St George Yacht Club

WESTERN MARINE

PH: (01) 2800321

... ALL within ROWING DISTANCE of DUNLAOGHAIRE MARINA ...

Shamrock Chandlery — What ever your budget, we've got it covered!

seaGo SP GOTOP BALTIC LIFEJACKETS SWEDEN XM
spinlock SEBAGO
WES.SYSTEM ECHOMAX Barton MARINE ADMIRALTY LEISURE
PLASTIMO SHURHOLD BLAKES Paints BLUE GEE LALIZAS International

To buy these and many other brands visit our new on-line shop

www.shamrock.co.uk - then click on GO SHOPPING

Tel: 023 8063 2725

Ireland's Largest Marina

DunLaoghaire Marina: 820 berths
• Visitor berths on hammerheads
• Location 12km from Dublin City Centre
• 100 metres from Dun Laoghaire Town Centre
• Supermarkets, Restaurants, Cinema, Theatre and Pubs all local
• Ferry terminal and rail station 50 metres
• Dublin Airport 25 km

Visitor Berths Available - €4 per metre per night
• Charges include unlimited access to showers etc.
• Shore power supply metered
• Petrol, diesel and holding tank pump out
• Oceanwave Wi-Fi available
• Full disabled access and facilities including hoist
• 24 Hour Access

ARKLOW MARINA

Arklow Marina
North Quay, Arklow, Co. Wicklow, Eire
Tel: +353 402 39901 Fax: +353 402 39902
Mobiles: 087 2375189 or 087 2515699
Email: technical@asl.ie
www.arklowmarina.com

| VHF | Ch12 |
| ACCESS | H24 |

Arklow is a popular fishing port and seaside town situated at the mouth of the River Avoca, just 16 miles south of Wicklow and 11 miles north east of Gorey. Historically noted for building wooden boats, the town is ideally placed for visiting the many beauty spots of County Wicklow including Glenmalure, Glendalough and Clara Lara, Avoca (Ballykissangel).

Lying on the north bank of the river, just upstream of the commercial quays, is Arklow Marina, which provides 42 berths in an inner harbour and 30 berths on pontoons outside the marina entrance. Note that vessels over 14m LOA should moor on the river pontoons. Just a five-minute walk from the town, the marina is within easy reach of as many as 19 pubs and several restaurants.

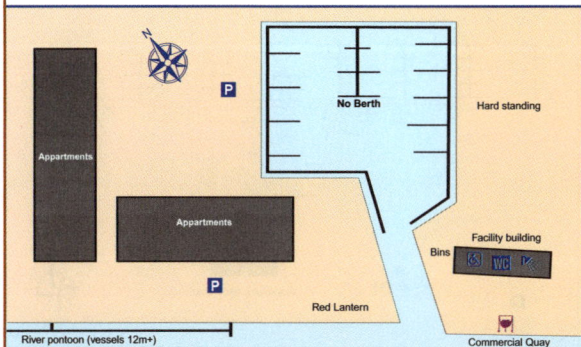

FACILITIES AT A GLANCE

KILMORE QUAY

Kilmore Quay
Wexford, Ireland
Tel: +353 53 9129955 Fax: +353 53 9129915
Email: hmkilmorequay@eircom.net

| VHF | Ch 09, 16 |
| ACCESS | H24 |

Located in the SE corner of Ireland, Kilmore Quay is a small rural fishing village situated approximately 14 miles from the town of Wexford and 12 miles from Rosslare ferry port.

Its 55-berthed marina, offering shelter from the elements as well as various on shore facilities, has become a regular port of call for many cruising yachtsmen. Kilmore's fishing industry dates back over the last hundred years and among the species of fresh fish available are bass, shark, skate and whiting. With several nearby areas of either historical or natural significance, Kilmore is renowned for its 'green' approach to the environment.

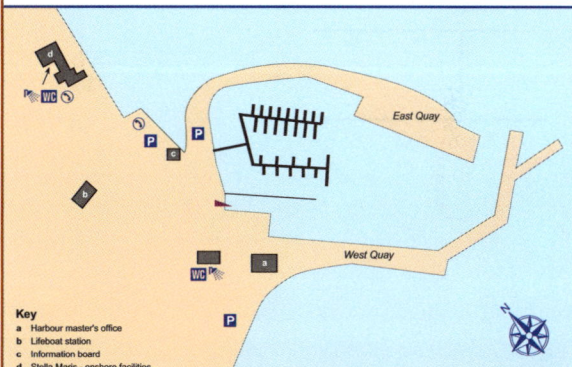

FACILITIES AT A GLANCE

Key
a Harbour master's office
b Lifeboat station
c Information board
d Stella Maris - onshore facilities

WATERFORD CITY MARINA

Waterford City Marina
Waterford, Ireland
Tel: +353 51 309900 Fax: +353 51 870813

| VHF | Ch 12 |
| ACCESS | H24 |

Famous for its connections with Waterford Crystal, now manufactured on the outskirts of the city, Waterford is the capital of the south east region of Ireland. As a major city, it benefits from good rail links with Dublin, Limerick and Rosslare, a regional airport with daily flights to Britain and an extensive bus service to surrounding towns and villages. The marina can be located on the banks of the River Suir, in the heart of this historic Viking city dating back to the ninth century. Yachtsmen can therefore make the most of Waterford's wide range of shops, restaurants and bars without having to walk too far from their boats. With 150 fully serviced berths and first rate security, Waterford City Marina now provides shower, toilet and laundry facilities in its new reception building.

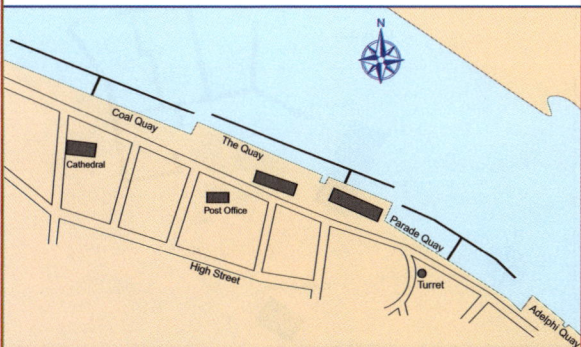

FACILITIES AT A GLANCE

CROSSHAVEN BOATYARD MARINA

Crosshaven Boatyard Marina
Crosshaven, Co Cork, Ireland
Tel: +353 214 831161 Fax: +353 214 831603
Email: cby@eircom.net

| VHF | Ch M |
| ACCESS | H24 |

One of three marinas at Crosshaven, Crosshaven Boatyard was founded in 1950 and originally made its name from the construction of some of the most world-renowned yachts, including *Gypsy Moth* and Denis Doyle's *Moonduster*. Nowadays, however, the yard has diversified to provide a wide range of services to both the marine leisure and professional industries. Situated on a safe and sheltered river only 12 miles from Cork City Centre, the marina boasts 100 fully-serviced berths along with the capacity to accommodate yachts up to 35m LOA with a 4m draught. In addition, it is ideally situated for cruising the stunning south west coast of Ireland.

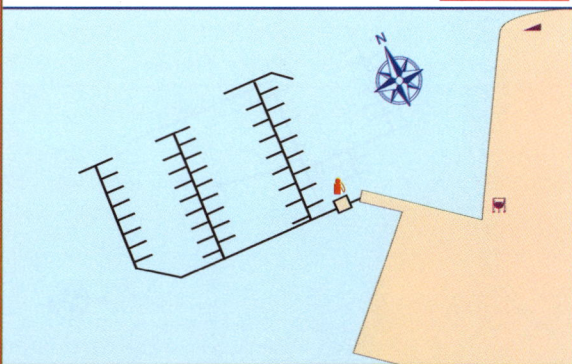

FACILITIES AT A GLANCE

12

SALVE MARINE

Salve Marine
Crosshaven, Co Cork, Ireland
Tel: +353 214 831 145 Fax: +353 214 831 747
Email: salvemarine@eircom.net

VHF | Ch M
ACCESS | H24

Crosshaven is a picturesque seaside resort providing a gateway to Ireland's south and south west coasts. Offering a variety of activities to suit all types, its rocky coves and quiet sandy beaches stretch from Graball to Church Bay and from Fennell's Bay to nearby Myrtleville. Besides a selection of craft shops selling locally produced arts and crafts, there are plenty of pubs, restaurants and takeaways to suit even the most discerning of tastes. Lying within a few hundred metres of the village centre is Salve Marine, accommodating yachts up to 43m LOA with draughts of up to 4m. Its comprehensive services range from engineering and welding facilities to hull and rigging repairs.

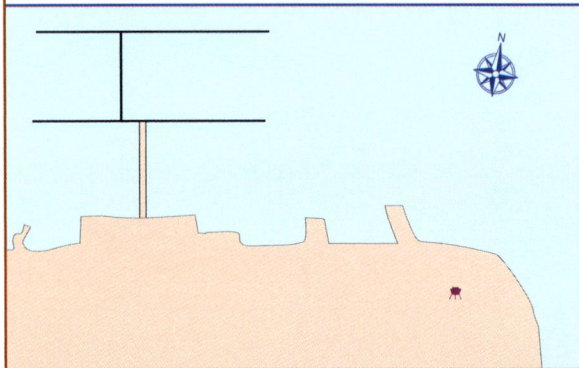

FACILITIES AT A GLANCE

ROYAL CORK YACHT CLUB

Royal Cork Yacht Club Marina
Crosshaven, Co Cork, Ireland
Tel: +353 21 483 1023 Fax: +353 21 483 1586
Email: office@royalcork.com   www.royalcork.com

VHF | Ch M
ACCESS | H24

Founded in 1720, the Royal Cork Yacht Club is one of the oldest and most prominent yacht clubs in the world. Organising, among many other events, the prestigious biennial Ford Cork Week, it boasts a number of World, European and National sailors among its membership.

The Yacht Club's marina is situated at Crosshaven, which nestles on the hillside at the mouth of the Owenabue River just inside the entrance to Cork Harbour. The harbour is popular with yachtsmen as it is accessible and well sheltered in all weather conditions. It also benefits from the Gulf Stream producing a temperate climate practically all year round.

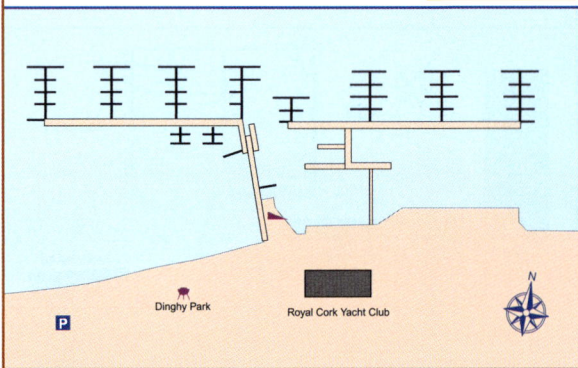

FACILITIES AT A GLANCE

Dinghy Park   Royal Cork Yacht Club

EAST FERRY MARINA

East Ferry Marina
Cobh, Co Cork, Ireland
Tel: +353 21 481 1342 Fax: +353 21 481 1342

VHF | Ch 80
ACCESS | H24

East Ferry Marina lies on the east side of Great Island, one of three large islands in Cork Harbour which are now all joined by roads and bridges. Despite its remote, tranquil setting, it offers all the fundamental facilities including showers, water, fuel, electricity and that all important pub. The nearest town is Cobh, which is a good five mile walk away, albeit a pleasant one.

Formerly known as Queenstown, Cobh (pronounced 'cove') reverted back to its original Irish name in 1922 and is renowned for being the place from where thousands of Irish men and women set off to America to build a new life for themselves, particularly during the famine years of 1844–48.

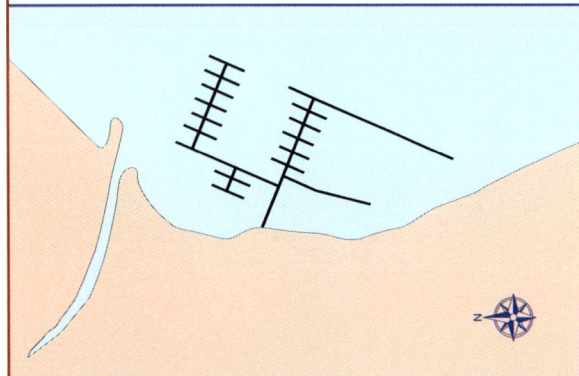

FACILITIES AT A GLANCE

KINSALE YACHT CLUB MARINA

Kinsale Yacht Club Marina
Kinsale, Co Cork, Ireland
Tel: +353 21 4772196 Fax: +353 21 4774455
Email: kyc@iol.ie

VHF | Ch M
ACCESS | H24

Kinsale is a natural, virtually land-locked harbour on the estuary of the Bandon River, approximately 12 miles south west of Cork harbour entrance. Home to a thriving fishing fleet as well as frequented by commercial shipping, it boasts two fully serviced marinas, with the Kinsale Yacht Club & Marina being the closest to the town. Visitors to this marina automatically become temporary members of the club and are therefore entitled to make full use of the facilities, which include a fully licensed bar and restaurant serving evening meals on Wednesdays, Thursdays and Saturdays. Fuel, water and repairs services are also readily available.

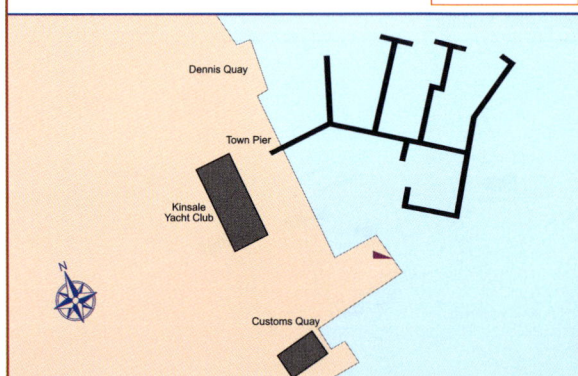

FACILITIES AT A GLANCE

Dennis Quay

Town Pier

Kinsale Yacht Club

Customs Quay

CASTLEPARK MARINA

Castlepark Marina Centre
Kinsale, Co Cork, Ireland
Tel: +353 21 4774959 Fax: +353 21 4774595
Email: maritime@indigo.ie

VHF Ch M
ACCESS H24

Situated on the south side of Kinsale Harbour, Castlepark is a small marina with deep water pontoon berths that are accessible at all states of the tide. Surrounded by rolling hills, it boasts its own beach as well as being in close proximity to the parklands of James Fort and a traditional Irish pub. The attractive town of Kinsale, with its narrow streets and slate-clad houses, lies just 1.5 miles away by road or five minutes away by ferry. Known as Ireland's 'fine food centre', it incorporates a number of gourmet food shops and high quality restaurants as well as a wine museum.

FACILITIES AT A GLANCE

LAWRENCE COVE MARINA

Lawrence Cove Marina
Lawrence Cove, Bere Island, Co Cork, Ireland
Tel: +353 27 75044 Fax: +353 27 75044
Email: lcm@iol.ie
www.lawrencecovemarina.com

VHF Ch 16
ACCESS H24

Lawrence Cove enjoys a peaceful location on an island at the entrance to Bantry Bay. Privately owned and run, it offers sheltered and secluded waters as well as excellent facilities and fully serviced pontoon berths. A few hundred yards from the marina you will find a shop, pub and restaurant, while the mainland, with its various attractions, can be easily reached by ferry. Lawrence Cove lies at the heart of the wonderful cruising grounds of Ireland's south west coast and, just two hours from Cork airport, is an ideal place to leave your boat for long or short periods.

FACILITIES AT A GLANCE

CAHERSIVEEN MARINA

Cahersiveen Marina
The Pier, Cahersiveen, Co. Kerry, Ireland
Tel: +353 66 9472777 Fax: +353 66 9472993
Email: info@cahersiveenmarina.ie
www.cahersiveenmarina.ie

VHF Ch M
ACCESS H24

Situated two miles up Valentia River from Valentia Harbour, Cahersiveen Marina is well protected in all wind directions and is convenient for sailing to Valentia Island and Dingle Bay as well as for visiting some of the spectacular uninhabited islands in the surrounding area. Boasting a host of sheltered sandy beaches, the region is renowned for salt and fresh water fishing as well as being good for scuba diving.

Within easy walking distance of the marina lies the historic town of Cahersiveen, incorporating an array of convivial pubs and restaurants.

FACILITIES AT A GLANCE

DINGLE MARINA

Dingle Marina
Strand Street, Dingle, Co Kerry, Ireland
Tel: +353 66 9151620 Fax: +353 69 5152546
Email:1dingle@eircom.net   www.dinglemarina.com

VHF Ch M
ACCESS H24

Dingle is Ireland's most westerly marina, lying at the heart of the sheltered Dingle Harbour, and is easily reached both day and night via a well buoyed approach channel. The surrounding area is an interesting and unfrequented cruising ground, with several islands, bays and beaches for the yachtsman to explore.

The marina lies in the heart of the old market town, renowned for its hospitality and traditional Irish pub music. Besides enjoying the excellent seafood restaurants and 52 pubs, other recreational pastimes include horse riding, golf, climbing and diving.

FACILITIES AT A GLANCE

Dingle Town Centre

Passenger Pontoons

5m

2·6m

Ice plant

Key
a Marina centre building - cafe, dive centre, sailing and rowing centre, chandlery and showers
b Sea Life Centre

12

FENIT HARBOUR MARINA

Fenit Harbour
Fenit, Tralee, Co. Kerry, Republic of Ireland
Tel: +353 66 7136231 Fax: +353 66 7136473
Email: fenitmarina@eircom.net

VHF Ch M
ACCESS H24

Fenit Harbour Marina is tucked away in Tralee Bay, not far south of the Shannon Estuary. Besides offering a superb cruising ground, being within a day's sail of Dingle and Kilrush, the marina also provides a convenient base from which to visit inland attractions such as the picturesque tourist towns of Tralee and Killarney. This 120-berth marina accommodates boats up to 15m LOA and benefits from deep water at all states of the tide.

The small village of Fenit incorporates a grocery shop as well a several pubs and restaurants, while among the local activities are horse riding, swimming from one of the nearby sandy beaches and golfing.

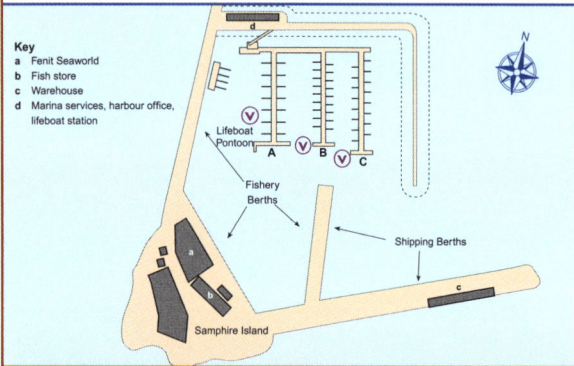

Key
a Fenit Seaworld
b Fish store
c Warehouse
d Marina services, harbour office, lifeboat station

KILRUSH MARINA

Kilrush Creek Marina Ltd
Kilrush, Co. Clare, Ireland
Tel: +353 65 9052072 Fax: +353 65 9051692
Email: hehir@shannon.dev.ie

VHF Ch 80
ACCESS H24

Kilrush Marina and boatyard is strategically placed for exploring the unspoilt west coast of Ireland, including Galway Bay, Dingle, West Cork and Kerry. It also provides a gateway to over 150 miles of cruising on Lough Derg, the River Shannon and the Irish canal system. Accessed via lock gates, the marina lies at one end of the main street in Kilrush, a vibrant market town with a long maritime history. A 15-minute ferry ride from the marina takes you to Scattery Island, once a sixth century monastic settlement but now uninhabited except by wildlife. The Shannon Estuary is reputed for being the country's first marine Special Area of Conservation (SAC) and is home to Ireland's only

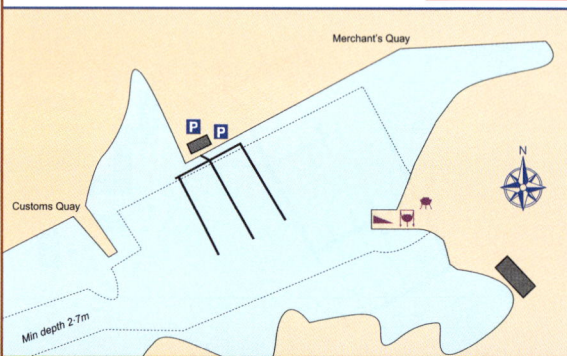

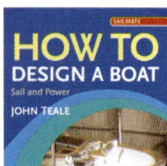

Adlard Coles Nautical
THE BEST SAILING BOOKS

How to Design a Boat
John Teale
978 0 7136 7572 6
£11.99

How to Choose the Right Yacht
J Muhs
978 0 7136 7581 8
£11.99

How to Paint Your Boat
Nigel Clegg
978 0 7136 7571 9
£11.99

How to Cope with Storms
D von Haeften
978 0 7136 7582 5
£11.99

How to Trim Sails
Peter Schweer
978 0 7136 7570 2
£11.99

How to Install a New Diesel Engine
Peter Cumberlidge
978 0 7136 7580 1
£11.99

TO ORDER MDL, Brunel Road, Houndmills, Basingstoke RG21 6XS
Tel: 01256 302699 email: direct@macmillan.co.uk or www.adlardcoles.com

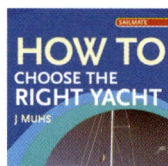

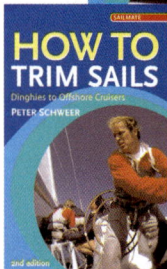

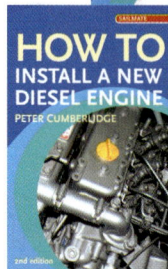

in2sail

Experience the fine art of sailing with In2Sail

"Seriously Good Sail Training On-Board Quality Yachts with Friendly Professional Skippers, Served with Good Food and Fun."

RYA Training Courses

- ☐ Practical Sailing Courses in the Solent.
- ☐ Theory Courses in Central London.
- ☐ Solent Combined Theory & Practical.
- ☐ Patient and Personable Instructors to help you Learn Skills & Improve Existing Knowledge.
- ☐ Personalised for Families & Couples.

Blue Water & Long Distance

- ☐ Fun Long Weekend Trips to Cherbourg & St Vaast.
- ☐ Discover UK & Irish Sailing Waters.
- ☐ Normandy & Brittany Coastlines.
- ☐ Adventure Sailing to Spain & Portugal.
- ☐ Customised Skippered Charter to Locations of your Choice.

Specialist Courses

- ☐ Racing Yacht Training and Race Participation.
- ☐ Specialised Boat Handling and Technical Sailing Courses.
- ☐ Yacht Maintenance Programme.
- ☐ Fast Track Yachtmaster.

Racing Events

- ☐ Fastnet Yacht Race 2009.
- ☐ Round the Island 2008.
- ☐ Cowes Week 2008.
- ☐ Cork Week.
- ☐ Spring and Winter Series.

"New or Experienced - In2Sail Welcomes You."

RYA Training Centre

+44 (0) 1983 615557 | INFO@IN2SAIL.COM | WWW.IN2SAIL.COM

ONLINE BOOKING | SUBSCRIBE TO E- NEWSLETTER TO HEAR ABOUT SPECIAL OFFERS

2009/mg171/v

12

MAILSPEED Marine

The World's Local Chandler!

The UK's Largest Mail Order Chandler

Fast Efficient Delivery Service

Stores Open 7 Days a Week

Call Now for your Copy of the Marine Equipment Bible

MAILSPEED Marine 2009
International Discount Mail Order Catalogue

Mail Order Hotline:
0870 118 2628

Order Online:
www.mailspeedmarine.com

e-mail
sales@mailspeedmarine.com

Mail Order International Hotline:
+44 870 118 2628

Mail Order Hotline: 0870 118 2628
Online: www.mailspeedmarine.com
Email: sales@mailspeedmarine.com

2009/MG165/z

Unit 16 Greys Court	The Squash Courts	Essex Marina	Local 15
Kingsland Grange	Belvedere Road	Wallasea Island	Paseo Maritimo 1
Warrington	Burnham-On-Crouch	Essex	Alcudiamar 07410
Cheshire	Essex	SS4 2HF	Port Alcudia
WA1 4SH	CM0 8AX		Mallorca, SPAIN

NORTH IRELAND - Lambay Island, north to Liscanor Bay

13

ADLARD COLES NAUTICAL
WEATHER FORECASTS
BY FAX & TELEPHONE

Coastal/Inshore	2-day by Fax	5-day by Phone
Caledonia	09065 222 353	09068 969 653
Northern Ireland	09065 222 355	09068 969 655
Clyde	09065 222 352	09068 969 652
North West	09065 222 341	09068 969 641
National (3-5 day)	09065 222 340	09068 969 640

Offshore	2-5 day by Fax	2-5 day by Phone
Irish Sea	09065 222 359	09068 969 659
English Channel	09065 222 357	09068 969 657
Biscay	09065 222 360	09068 969 660
North West Scotland	09065 222 361	09068 969 661

09068 CALLS COST 60P PER MIN. 09065 CALLS COST £1.50 PER MIN.

Key to Marina Plans symbols

Bottled gas		P	Parking
Chandler			Pub/Restaurant
Disabled facilities			Pump out
Electrical supply			Rigging service
Electrical repairs			Sail repairs
Engine repairs			Shipwright
First Aid			Shop/Supermarket
Fresh Water			Showers
Fuel - Diesel			Slipway
Fuel - Petrol		WC	Toilets
Hardstanding/boatyard			Telephone
@ Internet Café			Trolleys
Laundry facilities		V	Visitors berths
Lift-out facilities			Wi-Fi

Area 13 - North Ireland

MARINAS
Telephone Numbers
VHF Channel
Access Times

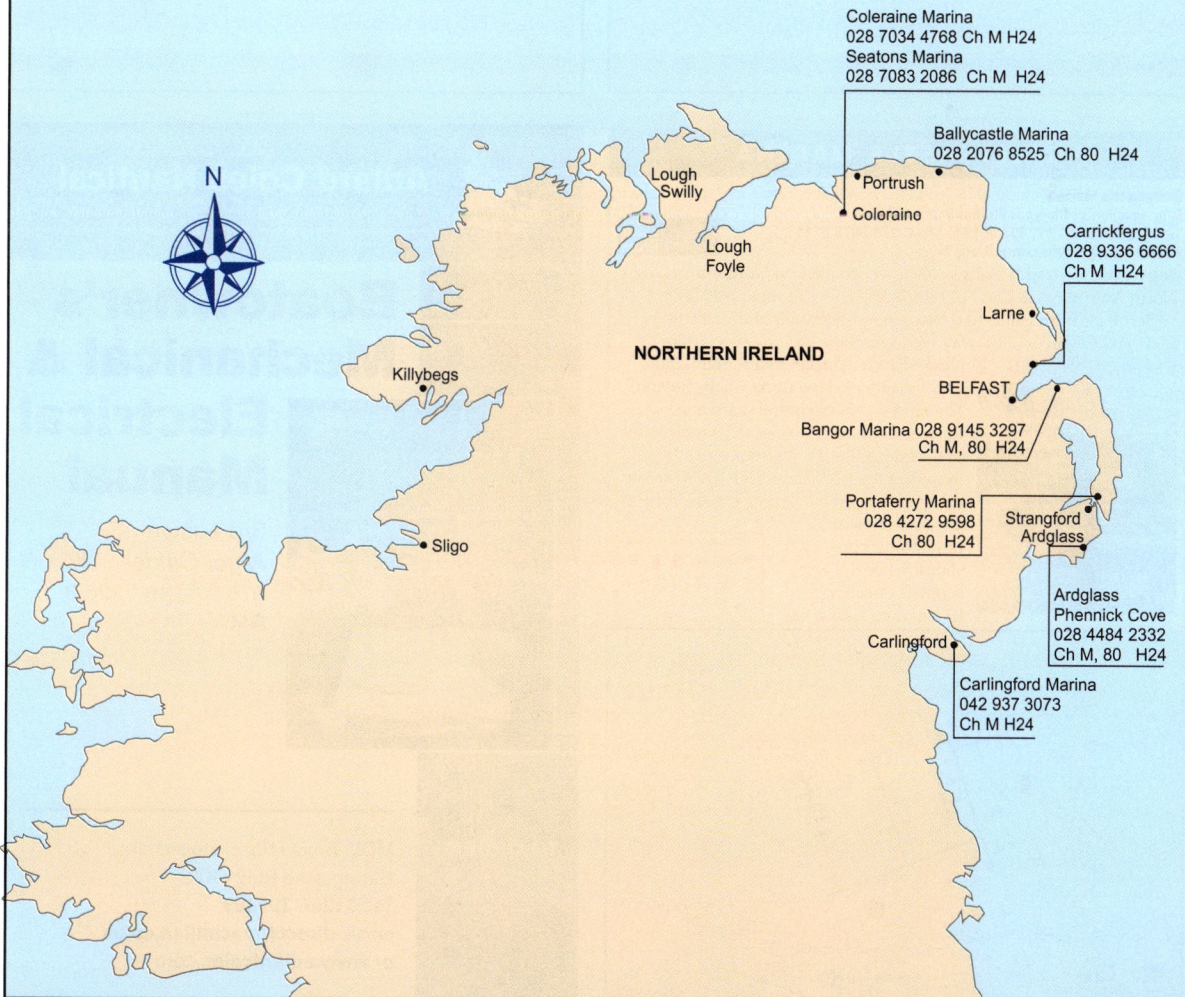

N

Coleraine Marina
028 7034 4768 Ch M H24
Seatons Marina
028 7083 2086 Ch M H24

Ballycastle Marina
028 2076 8525 Ch 80 H24

Lough
Swilly

• Portrush

• Coloraino

Carrickfergus
028 9336 6666
Ch M H24

Lough
Foyle

Larne •

NORTHERN IRELAND

Killybegs

BELFAST

Bangor Marina 028 9145 3297
Ch M, 80 H24

Portaferry Marina
028 4272 9598
Ch 80 H24

Strangford
Ardglass

Ardglass
Phennick Cove
028 4484 2332
Ch M, 80 H24

• Sligo

Carlingford

Carlingford Marina
042 937 3073
Ch M H24

COLERAINE MARINA

Coleraine Marina
64 Portstewart Road, Coleraine,
Co Londonderry, BT52 1RS
Tel: 028 7034 4768

VHF	Ch M,16
ACCESS	H24

Coleraine Marina complex enjoys a superb location in sheltered waters just one mile north of the town of Coleraine and four and a half miles south of the River Bann Estuary and the open sea. Besides accommodating vessels up to 18m LOA, this modern marina with 105 berths offers hard standing, fuel, a chandlery and shower facilities.

Among one of the oldest known settlements in Ireland, Coleraine is renowned for its linen, whiskey and salmon. Its thriving commercial centre includes numerous shops, a four-screen cinema and ice rink as well as a state-of-the-art leisure complex.

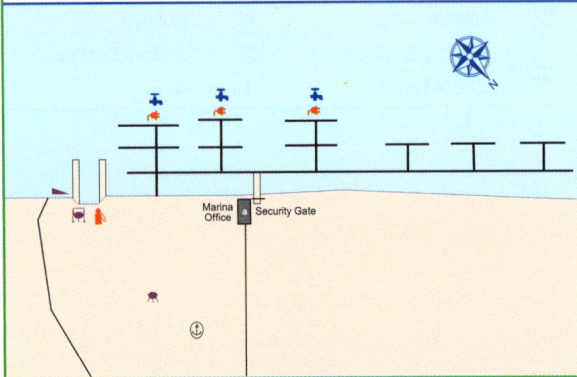

FACILITIES AT A GLANCE

SEATONS MARINA

Seatons Marina
Drumslade Rd, Coleraine, Londonderry, BT52 1SE
Tel: 028 7083 2086
Email: ssp@seatonsmarina.co.uk   www.seatonsmarina.co.uk

VHF	Ch M
ACCESS	H24

Seatons Marina is a privately owned business on the north coast of Ireland, which was established by Eric Seaton in 1962. It lies on the east bank of the River Bann, approximately two miles downstream from Coleraine and three miles from the sea. Although facilities are currently rather limited, plans are underway to improve the services available to yachtsmen. The pontoon berths are suitable for yachts up to 13.5m, with a minimum depth of 2.4m on the outer berths, although some of the inner berths do occasionally dry out. Seatons is also able to provide swinging moorings, all of which come with a galvanised chain riser passed over the stem roller.

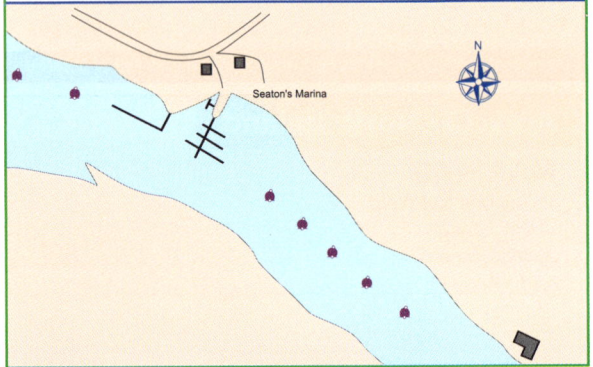

FACILITIES AT A GLANCE

Seaton's Marina

BALLYCASTLE MARINA

Ballycastle Marina
Bayview Road, Ballycastle, Northern Ireland
Tel: 028 2076 8525/07803 505084   Fax: 028 2076 6215
Email: info@moyle-council.org

VHF	Ch 80
ACCESS	H24

Ballycastle is a traditional seaside town situated on Northern Ireland's North Antrim coast. The 74-berthed, sheltered marina provides a perfect base from which to explore the well known local attractions such as the Giant's Causeway world heritage site, the spectacular Nine Glens of Antrim, and Rathlin, the only inhabited island in Northern Ireland. The most northern coastal marina in Ireland, Ballycastle is accessible at all states of the tide, although yachts are required to contact the marina on VHF Ch 80 before entering the harbour. Along the seafront are a selection of restaurants, bars and shops, while the town centre is only about a five-minute walk away.

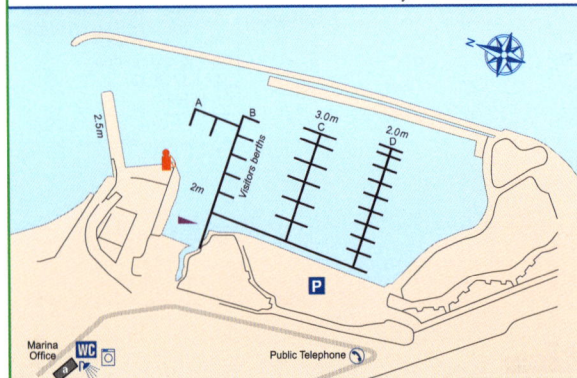

FACILITIES AT A GLANCE

Adlard Coles Nautical
THE BEST SAILING BOOKS

Maintenance

Boatowner's Mechanical & Electrical Manual

Third Edition
BOATOWNER'S Mechanical AND Electrical Manual
How to Maintain, Repair, and Improve Your Boat's Essential Systems
Nigel Calder

3rd edition
Nigel Calder
978 0 7136 7226 8
£45

TO ORDER

MDL, Brunel Road, Houndmills,
Basingstoke RG21 6XS
Tel: **01256 302699**
email: **direct@macmillan.co.uk**
or **www.adlardcoles.com**

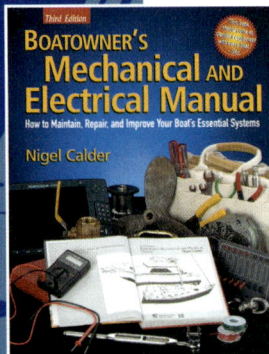

13

CARRICKFERGUS MARINA

Carrickferus Marina
3 Quayside, Carrickfergus, Co. Antrim, BT38 8BJ
Tel: 028 9336 6666 Fax: 028 9335 0505
Email: bwithers.marina@carrickfergus.org
www.carrickfergus.org

VHF Ch M
ACCESS H24

Located on the north shore of Belfast Lough, Carrickfergus Marina and harbour incorporates two sheltered areas suitable for leisure craft. The harbour is dominated by a magnificent 12th century Norman Castle which, recently renovated, includes a film theatre, banqueting room and outdoor models depicting the castle's chequered history.

The marina is located 250 metres west of the harbour and has become increasingly popular since its opening in 1985. A range of shops and restaurants along the waterfront caters for most yachtsmen's needs.

FACILITIES AT A GLANCE

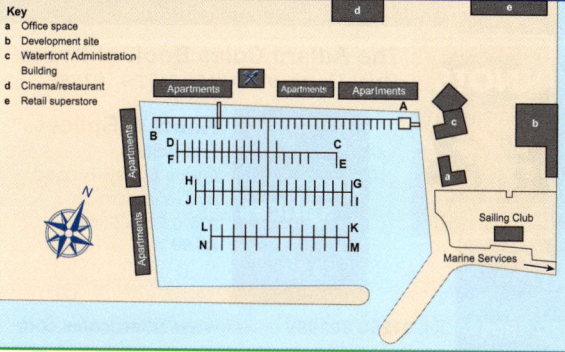

Key
a Office space
b Development site
c Waterfront Administration Building
d Cinema/restaurant
e Retail superstore

BANGOR MARINA

Quay Marinas Limited
Bangor Marina, Bangor, Co. Down, BT20 5ED
Tel: 028 9145 3297 Fax: 028 9145 3450
Email: ajaggers@quaymarinas.com
www.quaymarinas.com

VHF Ch 80
ACCESS H24

Situated on the south shore of Belfast Lough, Bangor is located close to the Irish Sea cruising routes. The Marina is right at the town's centre, within walking distance of shops, restaurants, hotels and bars. The Tourist information centre is across the road from marina reception and there are numerous visitors' attractions in the Borough. The Royal Ulster Yacht Club and the Ballyholme Yacht Club are both nearby and welcome visitors.

FACILITIES AT A GLANCE

Key
a Boat hoist - BJ Marine
b Boat yard - BJ Marine
c Bregenz House
d Chandlery/brokerage BJ Marine
e Dinghy berths
f Access bridge
g Lifeboat slipway
h Domestic waste facilities
i Waste oil tank
j Disabled berthing
k Flare disposal

Carrickfergus Borough

Carrickfergus Marina
3 Quayside, Carrickfergus BT38 8BJ
T: +44 (0) 28 9336 6666   F: +44 (0) 28 9335 0505
E: marinarec@carrickfergus.org

SPECIAL OFFER
Upon presentation of this publication, you will receive a second night's accomodation free, subject to the first night being paid in advance.

Shamrock Chandlery — What ever your budget, we've got it covered!

seago · SP · GOTOP · BALTIC · XM · spinlock · SEBAGO · WEST SYSTEM · ECHOMAX · Barton · ADMIRALTY · PLASTIMO · SHURHOLD · BLAKES Paints · LALIZAS · International

To buy these and many other brands visit our new on-line shop
www.shamrock.co.uk - then click on GO SHOPPING
Tel: 023 8063 2725

CHMARINE Ltd

Ireland's Largest Chandler - 14,000 Items in Stock
Excellent Spare Parts & Procurement Service
Scrabo Business Park, Jubilee Rd., Newtownards,
Co. Down, BT23 4YH, Northern Ireland
Tel: +44 (0)28 91 828405 Fax: +44 (0)28 91 828410
e-mail: sales@chmarine.co.uk

IRELAND'S PREMIER MARINE SUPPLIER

QUAY MARINAS LTD
A & W Building, The Docks, Portishead, N. Somerset BS20 7DF
Tel: (01275) 841188
Fax: (01275) 841189
e-mail: sriggs@quaymarinas.com
A wholly owned subsidiary of Quay Marinas, operate comprehensive yachting facilities at 5 locations in the UK and are marketing agents for Malahide Marina in Dublin Bay.
2009/EXT3/e

When responding to adverts please mention the 2009 Marina Guide REEDS

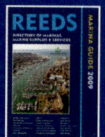

CARLINGFORD MARINA

Carlingford Marina
Co. Louth, Ireland
Tel: +353 (0)42 937 3073 Fax: +353 (0)42 937 3075
Email: cmarina@iol.ie
www.carlingfordmarina.ie

VHF Ch M
ACCESS H24

Carlingford Lough is an eight-mile sheltered haven between the Cooley Mountains to the south and the Mourne Mountains to the north. The marina is situated on the southern shore, about four miles from Haulbowline Lighthouse, and can be easily reached via a deep water shipping channel. Among the most attractive destinations in the Irish Sea, Carlingford is only 60 miles from the Isle of Man and within a day's sail from Strangford Lough and Ardglass. Full facilities in the marina include a first class bar and restaurant offering superb views across the water.

FACILITIES AT A GLANCE

Key
a Bar and restaurant
b Toilets, showers and laundry
c Refuse
d Office
e Chandlery
f Marina office
g Waiting pontoon

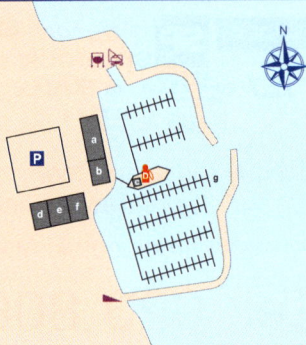

2009/MG68b/v

CHMARINE Ltd

Loughway Business Park, Unit 7C,
Greenbank Industrial Estate, Newry, Co. Down.
Northern Island BT34 2TH
email: newry@chmarine.co.uk
Tel +44 (0)2830 835770 Fax: +44(0)2830 835572

Part of CH Marine Ltd. Company

- APPROVED Liferaft Service Station
- Marine Safety Equipment
- Expert Sales & Service

Adlard Coles Nautical
THE BEST SAILING BOOKS

The Adlard Coles Book of Knots
Peter Owen 978 0 7136 8152 9 £7.99

Knots & Splices
2nd edition
Cyrus L Day, revised by Colin Jarman
978 0 7136 7748 5
£3.99

TO ORDER Tel: 01256 302699 or visit www.adlardcoles.com

Carlingford Marina
North commons
Carlingford
Co. Louth
Ireland

Tel: +00353 (0)42 9373073
Fax: +00353 (0)42 9373075
Email: cmarina@iol.ie
Web: www.carlingfordmarina.ie
VHF Channel 37 or 16
Helipad Co-Ordinates
54°03'00.7"N/6°11'28.3"W

Carlingford Marina... where the world is your Oyster

Carlingford Marina is situated on the South Western side of Carlingford Lough.
Boasting a host of facilities to include;

- Over 200 berths most with power and water. Max LOA 30 metres.
- Diesel available on fuel quay
- Showers, toilets and laundry facilities
- 50T travel lift, winter storage and slipway
- Bar & Restaurant with food served all day
- Luxury 4 star Fàilte Ireland Approved Accommodation
- Easy access from land, air or sea with the addition of a newly constructed Helipad

2009/MG161/Z

PORTAFERRY MARINA

Portaferry Marina
11 The Strand, Portaferry, BT22 1PF
Tel: 028 4272 9598 Mobile: 07703 209 780 Fax: 028 4272 9784
Email: barholm.portaferry@virgin.net

VHF	Ch 80
ACCESS	H24

Portaferry Marina lies on the east shore of the Narrows, the gateway to Strangford Lough on the north east coast of Ireland. A marine nature reserve of outstanding natural beauty, the Lough offers plenty of recreational activities. The marina, which caters for draughts of up to 2.5m, is fairly small, accommodating around 30 yachts. The office is situated about 200m from the marina itself, where you will find ablution facilities along with a launderette.

Portaferry incorporates several pubs and restaurants as well as a few convenience stores, while one of its prime attractions is the Exploris Aquarium. Places of historic interest in the vicinity include Castleward, an 18th century mansion in Strangford, and Mount Stewart House & Garden in Newtownards.

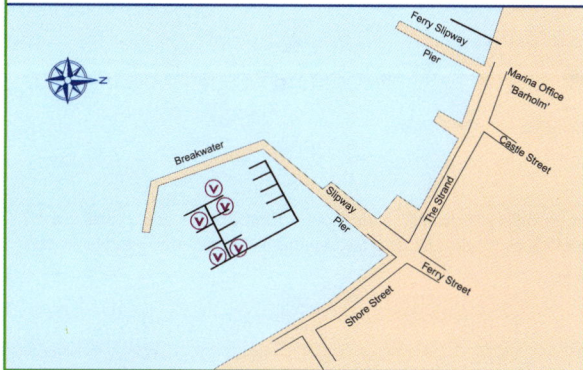

FACILITIES AT A GLANCE

ARDGLASS MARINA

Ardglass Marina
19 Quay Street, Ardglass, BT30 7SA
Tel: 028 4484 2332 Fax: 028 4484 2332
Email: ardglassmarina@tiscali.co.uk
www.ardglassmarina.co.uk

VHF	Ch M, 80
ACCESS	H24

Situated just south of Strangford, Ardglass has the capacity to accommodate up to 33 yachts as well as space for small craft. Despite being relatively small in size, the marina boasts an extensive array of facilities, either on site or close at hand. Most of the necessary shops, including grocery stores, a post office, chemist and off-licence, are all within a five-minute walk from the marina. Among the local onshore activities are golf, mountain climbing in Newcastle, which is 18 miles south, as well as scenic walks at Ardglass and Delamont Park.

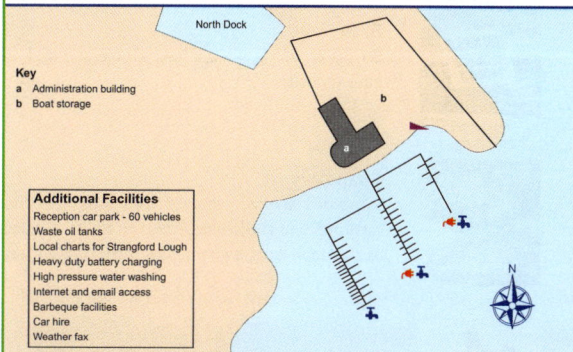

FACILITIES AT A GLANCE

Ferry Slipway
Pier
Marina Office 'Barholm'
Castle Street
The Strand
Breakwater
Slipway
Pier
Ferry Street
Shore Street

North Dock

Key
a Administration building
b Boat storage

Additional Facilities
Reception car park - 60 vehicles
Waste oil tanks
Local charts for Strangford Lough
Heavy duty battery charging
High pressure water washing
Internet and email access
Barbeque facilities
Car hire
Weather fax

N

Shamrock Chandlery

What ever your budget, we've got it covered!

seaGo · SP · GOTOP · BALTIC LIFEJACKETS SWEDEN · XM
WEST SYSTEM · spinlock · SEBAGO · Barton MARINE
PLASTIMO · SHURHOLD · BLAKES Paints · BLUE GEE G · LALIZAS · ADMIRALTY LEISURE · International

To buy these and many other brands visit our new on-line shop

www.shamrock.co.uk - then click on GO SHOPPING

Tel: 023 8063 2725

2009/MG128/e

Adlard Coles Nautical
THE BEST SAILING BOOKS

New

Reeds **Astro Navigation Tables** 2009

REEDS 2009 · ASTRO NAVIGATION TABLES · LT CDR HARRY J BAKER

Lt Cdr Harry Baker

An established book of annual astro-navigation tables for yachtsmen.
978 0 7136 8996 9
£17.99

Reeds Astro Navigation Tables 2009 can be obtained from your normal supplier - or please contact www.adlardcoles.com.

Adlard Coles Nautical
THE BEST SAILING BOOKS

Safety

Sail safely with **Adlard Coles Nautical**
First Aid at Sea

5th edition
Colin Berry and Douglas Justins
978 1 4081 0599 3
£9.99

FIRST AID AT SEA
DOUGLAS JUSTINS AND COLIN BERRY

TO ORDER Tel: 01256 302699 or visit www.adlardcoles.com

JACKSON YACHT SERVICES

Established for over 30 years, a traditional boatyard owned by Mike and Kay Jackson

Contact Mike about all aspects of yacht management, and Kay to discuss the sale of your vessel and for assistance in your search for the ideal yacht from the largest sailing vessel to the smallest dinghy. Also contact us for boat surveys.

ZODIAC Zodiac Boat Sales and Service

What we do
Liferaft, Lifejacket, Sales, Hire and Service Jersey's only British Marine and Coastguard Agency (MCA) approved service station qualifying us to service commercial and yachting liferafts to the most stringent specifications. We pride ourselves on meticulous care and attention with your safety equipment and regularly attend manufacturers premises in order to keep abreast of the various liferaft packing methods so that your lifesaving apparatus will operate efficiently when required. We are sales agents and have been awarded servicing certificates for the following manufacturers: - Zodiac, Bombard, RFD, ML Lifeguard, BFA (XM), Plastimo, and Crewsaver. Owners of rafts are advised to have them serviced by a properly certificated service station as recommended by their manufacturer to ensure validity of guarantees.

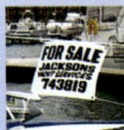

Brokerage
Buying or selling, we can help. Come and look through our listings or visit our website for further details of the vessels we have for sale.

Chandlery
We stock a large range of traditional and modern chandlery including nautical publications, books and charts, paints, varnishes and antifouling. A complrehensive selection of ropes, blocks and shackles together with boat fishing tackle enables us to supply boat owners with most of their needs.

Clothing
Fashionable and conventional yachting clothing for adults and children by Le Glazic, Coude Maille, and St. James. Extensive leather deck shoe range by TBS and Sebago, as well as boots, offshore foul weather gear and equipment.

Boat Repairs and Maintenance
Motor & Sailing yacht repairs in GRP and timber, lifting out up to 65 Ton, cleaning and antifouling undertaken. All types of moorings made up and laid from deep water to marina berth.

Rigging Loft
Have your rigging checked, repaired or renewed by experienced staff. Masts, spars and furling gear supplied and fitted. Wire swageing machinery in workshop. Specialists in architectural rigging and wire work.

Sail Loft
All types of sails and covers supplied, valeted and repaired. Embroidery service for crew & team wear.

Yacht Management
Comprehensive management service ensuring smooth and cost effective running of your vessel. Marine consultancy and guardiennage service for non resident owners. We are a small, owner operated business and pride ourselves in the attention to detail commonly missing in large enterprises to-day. We look forward to meeting you and pledge our commitment to fulfil your boating requirements in connection with the smallest dinghy to the largest yacht.

Le Boulevard, St Aubin, Jersey, Channel Islands JE3 8AB
+44 (0) 1534 743819   **+44 (0) 1534 745952**
sales@jacksonyacht.com • www.jacksonyacht.com

14

ADLARD COLES NAUTICAL
WEATHER FORECASTS
BY FAX & TELEPHONE

Coastal/Inshore	2-day by Fax	5-day by Phone
South West	09065 222 348	09068 969 648
Mid Channel	09065 222 347	09068 969 647
N France	09065 501 612	09064 700 422
N Brittany	09065 501 613	09064 700 423
National (3-5 day)	09065 222 340	09068 969 640

Offshore	2-5 day by Fax	2-5 day by Phone
English Channel	09065 222 357	09068 969 657
Southern North Sea	09065 222 358	09068 969 658
Irish Sea	09065 222 359	09068 969 659
Biscay	09065 222 360	09068 969 660

09064/68 CALLS COST 60P PER MIN. 09065 CALLS COST £1.50 PER MIN.

Key to Marina Plans symbols

Bottled gas		Parking	
Chandler		Pub/Restaurant	
Disabled facilities		Pump out	
Electrical supply		Rigging service	
Electrical repairs		Sail repairs	
Engine repairs		Shipwright	
First Aid		Shop/Supermarket	
Fresh Water		Showers	
Fuel - Diesel		Slipway	
Fuel - Petrol		Toilets	
Hardstanding/boatyard		Telephone	
Internet Café		Trolleys	
Laundry facilities		Visitors berths	
Lift-out facilities		Wi-Fi	

Area 14 - Channel Islands

MARINAS
Telephone Numbers
VHF Channel
Access Times

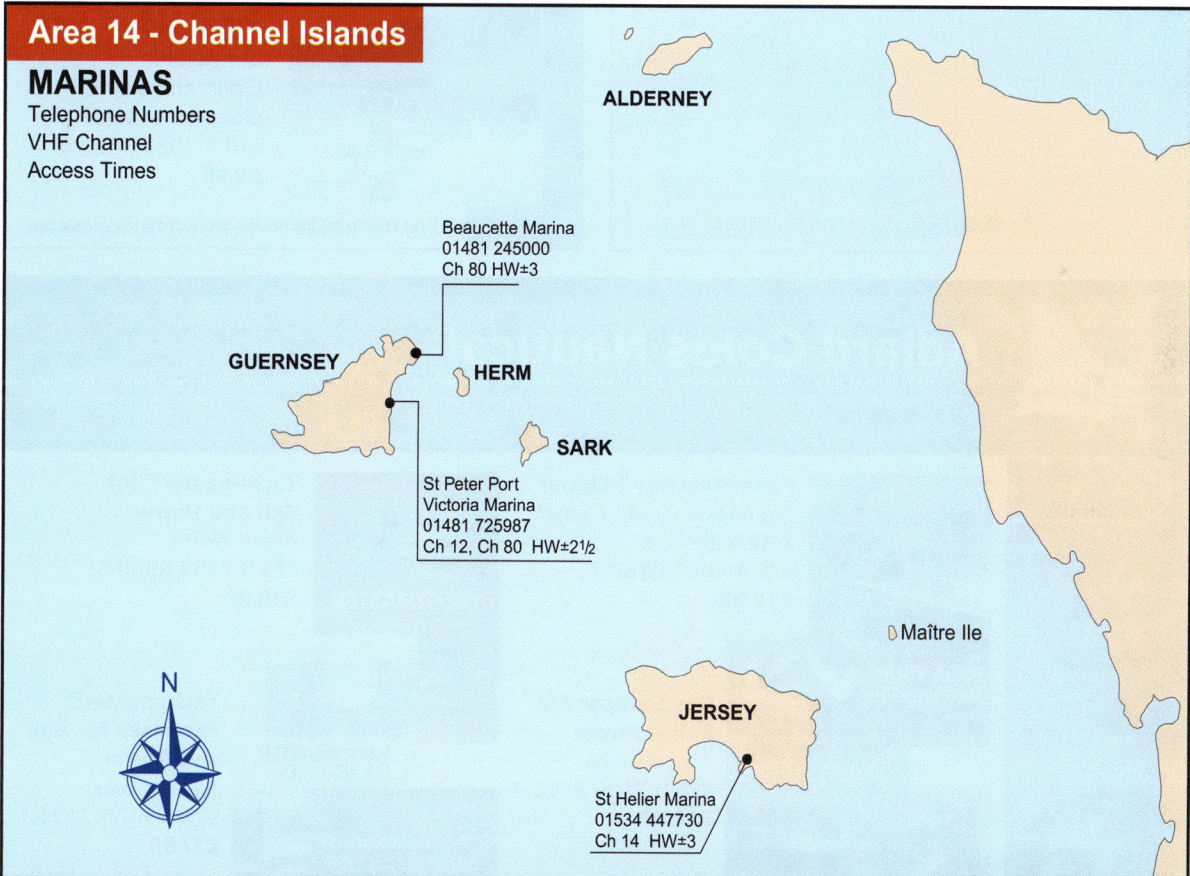

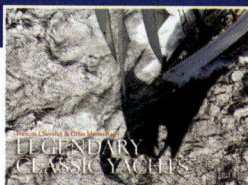

ALDERNEY

Beaucette Marina
01481 245000
Ch 80 HW±3

GUERNSEY HERM

SARK

St Peter Port
Victoria Marina
01481 725987
Ch 12, Ch 80 HW±2½

Maître Ile

JERSEY

St Helier Marina
01534 447730
Ch 14 HW±3

Adlard Coles Nautical THE BEST SAILING BOOKS

Legendary Classic Yachts
Gilles Martin-Raget & Francois Chevalier
978 1 4081 0518 4 **£50**

TO ORDER Tel: **01256 302699** email: **direct@macmillan.co.uk** or **www.adlardcoles.com**

BEAUCETTE MARINA

Beaucette Marina
Vale, Guernsey, GY3 5BQ
Tel: 01481 245000 Fax: 01481 247071
Mobile: 07781 102302
Email: info@beaucettemarina.com

VHF Ch 80
ACCESS HW±3

Situated on the north east tip of Guernsey, Beaucette enjoys a peaceful, rural setting in contrast to the more vibrant atmosphere of Victoria Marina. Now owned by a private individual and offering a high standard of service, the site was originally formed from an old quarry.

There is a general store close by, while the bustling town of St Peter Port is only 20 minutes away by bus.

FACILITIES AT A GLANCE

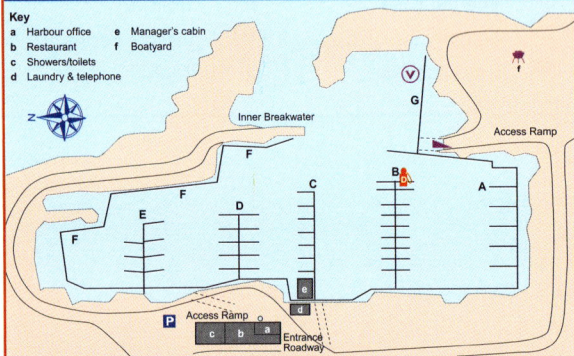

Key
a Harbour office
b Restaurant
c Showers/toilets
d Laundry & telephone
e Manager's cabin
f Boatyard

Visit Guernsey's Northern Marine & Leisure Store

QUAYSIDE MARINE & LEISURE

at St. Sampson's Harbour

Tel: 01481 245881

Chandlery • Electronics • Fishing Tackle
Protective & Leisure Clothing & Shoes
VAT - FREE PRICES

2009/MG47/S

Adlard Coles Nautical
THE BEST SAILING BOOKS

Safety

Sail safely with
Adlard Coles Nautical
First Aid at Sea
5th edition
Colin Berry and Douglas Justins
978 1 4081 0599 3
£9.99

TO ORDER Tel: **01256 302699** or visit **www.adlardcoles.com**

Adlard Coles Nautical
THE BEST SAILING BOOKS

Courses

Pass Your Day Skipper
3rd edition *David Fairhall & Mike Peyton*
978 1 4081 0380 7
£12.99

Day Skipper for Sail & Power
Alison Noice
978 0 7136 8272 4
£19.99

Day Skipper Exercises for Sail and Power
Alison Noice
978 0 7136 8271 7
£19.99

Yachtmaster™ for Sail and Power
Alison Noice
978 0 7136 6988 6
£19.99

Yachtmaster™ Exercises for Sail and Power
Alison Noice
978 0 7136 7126 1
£17.99

The Complete Yachtmaster™
6th edition *Tom Cunliffe*
978 0 7136 8948 8
£24.99

TO ORDER MDL, Brunel Road, Houndmills, Basingstoke RG21 6XS
Tel: **01256 302699** email: **direct@macmillan.co.uk** or **www.adlardcoles.com**

ST PETER PORT

Harbour Authority
PO Box 631, St Julian's Emplacement, St Peter Port
Tel: 01481 720229 Fax: 01481 714177
Email: guernsey.harbour@gov.gg

VHF	Ch 12, 80
ACCESS	HW±2.5

The harbour of St Peter Port comprises the Queen Elizabeth II Marina to the N and Victoria and Albert Marinas to the S, with visiting yachtsmen usually accommodated in Victoria Marina.

Renowned for being an international financial centre and tax haven, St Peter Port is the capital of Guernsey. Its regency architecture and picturesque cobbled streets filled with restaurants and boutiques help to make it one of the most attractive harbours in Europe. Among the places of interest are Hauteville House, home of the writer Victor Hugo, and Castle Cornet.

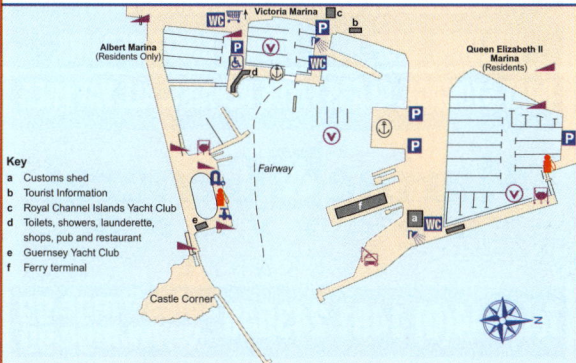

FACILITIES AT A GLANCE

Key
a Customs shed
b Tourist Information
c Royal Channel Islands Yacht Club
d Toilets, showers, launderette, shops, pub and restaurant
e Guernsey Yacht Club
f Ferry terminal

SEAQUEST MARINE LIMITED

YACHT CHANDLERS
NORTH PLANTATION, ST. PETER PORT, GUERNSEY
TEL: (01481) 721773 FAX: (01481) 716738
Email: seaquestmarine@cwgsy.net web: seaquestgsy.com

A GLAZE   COBRA   **GARMIN**

All general Chandlery stocked. Large range of Marine Electronics. Admiralty charts and books, water sports equipment, Hanson Fleming flares. We are well stocked for all your boating needs. Oregon weather stations. Yacht brokerage.

NO CHARGE FOR FRIENDLY ADVICE, LOWEST PRICES ON THE ISLAND, GPS SPECIALISTS.

QUBA SAILS CLOTHING   QUAYSIDE SHOES

CAR HIRE   XM CLOTHING   PEN-DUICK CLOTHING

2009/MGM5/er

Agents for Bukh Marine Engines.
We specialise in safety and survival equipment, MCA approved service station for liferafts, including RFD, Beaufort/Dunlop, Zodiac, Avon, Plastimo and Lifeguard. Full range of liferafts, dinghies and lifejackets and distress flares.
Telephone: 01481 722378
A B Marine Limited
Castle Walk, St Peter Port, Guernsey, Channel Islands
2009/MD2/e

When responding to adverts please mention the 2009 Marina Guide →
REEDS

FOR ALL MARINE SERVICES
STS
TEL: 249090

Guernsey Sailing Ships
+ SAILING & TECHNICAL SERVICES

John Cluett
Marine Manager

Whatever your needs, we'll try harder to meet them

FOR COMPLETE & FRIENDLY SERVICE ON:

NEW & USED: CHANDLERY MOTORS, HULLS TO COMPLETE BOATS, ELECTRONICS, INSTRUMENTS, ETC. BUILDING & REPAIRS, GENERAL ENGINEERING, HYDRAULICS, ELECTRIC'S. RIGGING, SAILS, ETC.

LOCAL PILOTAGE & TUITION, DELIVERIES, SKIPPERING, SURVEYS, BROKERAGE & GUARDIENNAGE, ETC. ENGLISH-FRENCH TRANSLATOR INTERPRETER, TECHNICAL ADVICE & 24HR COVER AVAILABLE.

CI Agents for FOB Anchors   WOODEN BOAT REPAIRS & CONSTRUCTION ARE OUR SPECIALITY

Northside, St. Sampson, Guernsey, C.I.
Tel: 01481 249090 fax: 01481 241079
Emergency: 01481 264630

2009/MG138/z

ST PETER PORT VICTORIA MARINA

Harbour Authority
PO Box 631, St Julian's Emplacement, St Peter Port
Tel: 01481 725987 Fax: 01481 714177
Email: guernsey.harbour@gov.gg

VHF	Ch 80
ACCESS	HW±2.5

Victoria Marina in St Peter Port accommodates approximately 300 visiting yachts. In the height of the season it gets extremely busy, but when full visitors can berth on 5 other pontoons in the Pool or pre-arrange a berth in the QE II or Albert marinas. There are no visitor moorings in the Pool. Depending on draught, the marina is accessible approximately two and a half hours either side of HW, with yachts crossing over a sill drying to 4.2m. The marina dory will direct you to a berth on arrival or else will instruct you to moor on one of the waiting pontoons just outside.

Once in the marina, you can benefit from its superb facilities as well as from its central location to St Peter Port's shops and restaurants.

Guernsey is well placed for exploring the rest of the Channel Islands, including the quiet anchorages off Herm and Sark, or making a short hop to one of the French ports such as St Malo,

FACILITIES AT A GLANCE

Key
a   Toilets, showers, launderette and shops
b   Royal Channel Islands Yacht Club
c   Refuse skip
d   Marina control, port office
e   Dinghy/tender landing pontoon
f   Pub/restaurant

75 TON HOIST

VOLVO PENTA

CATERPILLAR®

nanni diesel

energy in blue

2009/MG67/e

FULL ENGINE WORKSHOP, MACHINE SHOP, WELDING SHOP, HULL, PROP & SHAFT REPAIRS, BOAT STORAGE, GLASS FIBRE REPAIRS, ALL VAT FREE

Marine & General BOATYARD
GUERNSEY

Tel: +44(0) 1481 243048   sales@mge.gg   www.mge.gg

we like to say... **Yes!**

MUSTO

GORE-TEX

FOUNTAIN ST.
ARCADE
CHURCH
HIGH STREET
LA PERLA RESTAURANT
BUS TERMINUS
SOUTH ESPLANADE
QUAY
HAVELET BAY
MARINA
ALBERT PIER
VISITORS MARINA
CROWN PIER
WE ARE HERE
MODEL YACHT POND
CASTLE CORNET
BOATWORKS+ GUERNSEY

2009/Mg23/v

BOATWORKS+ GUERNSEY

✓ ADMIRALTY PUBLICATIONS
✓ BOATYARD SERVICES
✓ BOAT LIFTING
✓ CHANDLERY
✓ DIESEL
✓ FISHING TACKLE
✓ GAS
✓ LEISURE CLOTHING
✓ NAUTICAL PUBLICATIONS
✓ OSMOSIS TREATMENT
✓ PETROL
✓ PROVISIONS
✓ RIGGING
✓ SLIPPING
✓ TECHNICAL CLOTHING

Boatworks+, Castle Emplacement, St Peter Port, Guernsey GY1 1AU. Channel Islands
Telephone:+44 (0)1481 726071   Facsimile:+44 (0)1481 714224   Email: boatworks@cwgsy.net

ST HELIER HARBOUR

St Helier Harbour
Maritime House, La Route du Port Elizabeth
St Helier, Jersey, JE1 1HB
Tel: 01534 447730
www.jersey-harbours.com Email: s.marina@gov.je

VHF
ACCESS HW±3

Jersey is the largest of the Channel Islands, attracting the most number of tourists per year. Although St Helier can get very crowded in the height of the summer, if you hire a car and head out to the north coast in particular you will soon find isolated bays and pretty little fishing villages.

All visiting craft are directed to St Helier Marina, which may be entered three hours either side of HW via a sill. There is a long holding pontoon to port of the entrance accessible at any state of the tide. La Collette Yacht Basin is not for visitors but Elizabeth Marina may accept larger craft by prior arrangement.

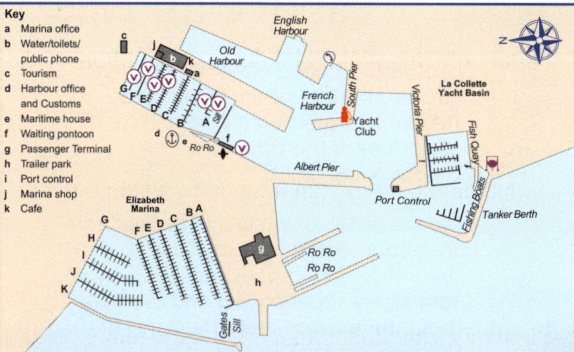

FACILITIES AT A GLANCE

Key
a Marina office
b Water/toilets/public phone
c Tourism
d Harbour office and Customs
e Maritime house
f Waiting pontoon
g Passenger Terminal
h Trailer park
i Port control
j Marina shop
k Cafe

English Harbour
Old Harbour
French Harbour
Yacht Club
South Pier
Victoria Pier
La Collette Yacht Basin
Albert Pier
Fishing Boats
Port Control
Elizabeth Marina
Tanker Berth
Ro Ro
Ro Ro
Gates Sill

YOUR MARINE & LEISURE CONVENIENCE STORE

Whatever baits your hook, we've got what you're looking for!

Ocean Kayak
Don't miss out on the fun

Fishing equipment
Rods, reels and tackle by Shakespeare, Fladen, Flashmer, Pen and Rapala

Boat care
Official suppliers of Blakes paints

Gift ideas
Birthday, Anniversary, Christmas or just to say thank you

Apparel & accessories
By Crewsaver

Shoes by
Quayside and
Sebago Dockside

Clothing by
Helly Hansen, Gill
Splashdown, Weird Fish

Wetsuits & diving equipment by
Marlin
Typhoon
Beuchat

Family Fun
Ocean Kayaks
Bic Kayaks
SportStuff inflatables
Waterskis

Fishing equipment by
Shakespeare
Penn
Rapala

Life saving equipment by
Crewsaver, Typhoon
Eletronics
Navman, Lowrance
General chandlery
Marlow ropes
Charts
Blakes paints
Trailer parts
Boat care products
Inflatable Dinghies

Mg69/2009/v

15-16 Commercial Buildings St. Helier.
Telephone: 01534 850090
Facsimile: 01534 850099

Iron Stores

incorporating I.S. Marine

Adlard Coles Nautical
THE BEST SAILING BOOKS

Sailmate

How to Design a Boat
John Teale
978 0 7136 7572 6
£11.99

How to Choose the Right Yacht
J Muhs
978 0 7136 7581 8
£11.99

How to Paint Your Boat
Nigel Clegg
978 0 7136 7571 9
£11.99

How to Cope with Storms
D von Haeften
978 0 7136 7582 5
£11.99

How to Trim Sails
Peter Schweer
978 0 7136 7570 2
£11.99

How to Install a New Diesel Engine
Peter Cumberlidge
978 0 7136 7580 1
£11.99

TO ORDER
MDL, Brunel Road, Houndmills, Basingstoke RG21 6XS
Tel: **01256 302699** email: **direct@macmillan.co.uk** or **www.adlardcoles.com**

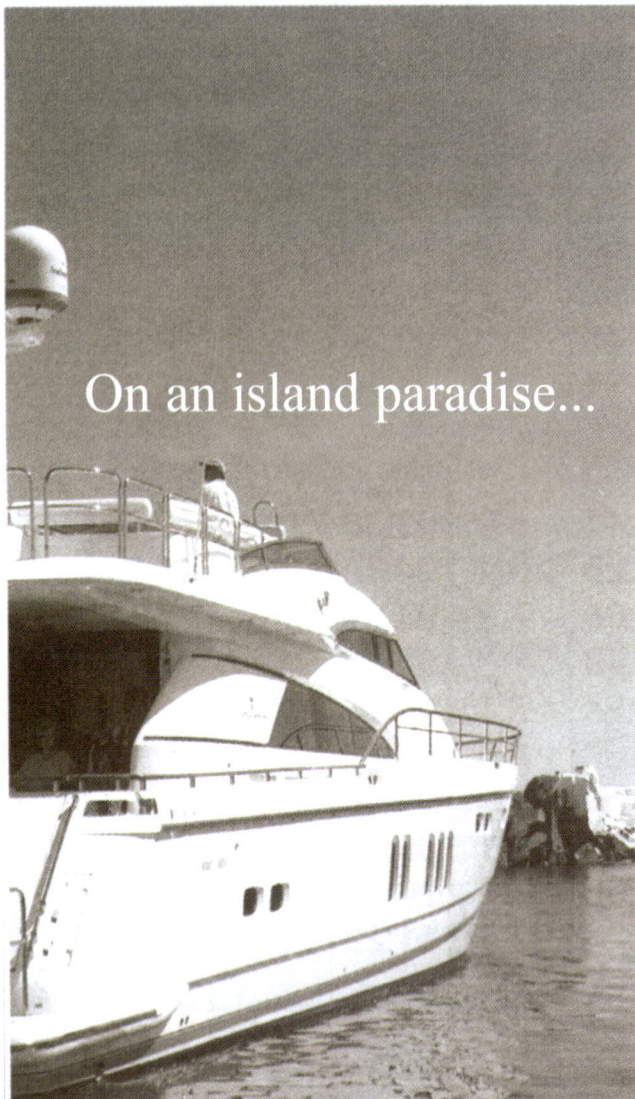

On an island paradise...

BEAUCETTE
MARINA

... one gem shines above all else

Accesible 3 hours either side of high water at St Peter Port, Beaucette Marina, situated on the North East of Guernsey, is the perfect base to discover the island.

All the services you would expect from a modern facility are on-hand to make your stay easy and ejoyable. Our staff are highly experienced and ready to help, so you can feel safe in the knowledge that your boat and your crew are in good hands.

Contact us by using the details below or call us on VHF 80 - call sign 'Beaucette Marina'. If you are unsure of the buoyed channel or the entrance to Beaucette, please call on VHF 80 and we will send a boat out to assist you.

For more information, please visit our website at: www.beaucettemarina.com

We look forward to welcoming you.

**BEAUCETTE MARINA LTD,
VALE, GUERNSEY,
CHANNEL ISLANDS GY3 5BQ
T: +44 (0)1481 245000
F: +44 (0)1481 247071
E: INFO@BEAUCETTEMARINA.COM
M: +44 (0)7781 102302
W: WWW.BEAUCETTEMARINA.COM
VHF CHANNEL 80**

**VISITING & ANNUAL BERTHS | WATER
& ELECTRICITY ON ALL BERTHS |
FUEL & GAS | LAUNDERETTE
RESTAURANT | SHOWERS & TOILETS |
WEATHER FORECAST | FREE WIFI
ACCESS | CAR HIRE**

SECTION 2
MARINE SUPPLIES AND SERVICES GUIDE

NFR
COOLING SOLUTIONS

Specialist in Marine Refrigeration,
Air Conditioning and Electrical work.

Call Us Now 01489 782277   info@nf-ref.co.uk

www.nf-ref.co.uk

2009/MG79's

ADHESIVES

Adtech Ltd
Braintree   01376 346511

Bettabond Adhesives
Leeds   0113 278 5088

Casco Products Industrial Adhesives
St Neots   01480 476777

CC Marine Services Ltd
West Mersea   01206 381801

Industrial Self Adhesives Ltd
Nottingham   0115 9681895

Sika Ltd Garden City   01707 394444

Technix Rubber & Plastics Ltd
Southampton   01489 789944

Tiflex Liskeard   01579 320808

Trade Grade Products Ltd
Poole   01202 820177

UK Epoxy Resins
Burscough   01704 892364

Wessex Resins & Adhesives Ltd
Romsey   01794 521111

3M United Kingdom plc
Bracknell   01344 858315

ASSOCIATIONS/ AGENCIES

Cruising Association
London   020 7537 2828

Fishermans Mutual Association (Eyemouth) Ltd
Eyemouth   01890 750373

Maritime and Coastguard Agency
Southampton   0870 6006505

Royal Institute of Navigation
London   020 7591 3130

Royal National Lifeboat Institution
Poole   01202 663000

Royal Yachting Association (RYA)
Southampton   0845 345 0400

BERTHS & MOORINGS

ABC Powermarine
Beaumaris   01248 811413

Aqua Bell Ltd Norwich   01603 713013

Ardfern Yacht Centre
Lochgilphead   01852 500247/500636

Ardmair Boat Centre
Ullapool   01854 612054

Arisaig Marine Ltd
Inverness-shire   01687 450224

Bristol Boat Ltd Bristol 01225 872032

British Waterways Argyll
                             01546 603210

Burgh Castle Marine
Norfolk   01493 780331

Cambrian Marine Services Ltd
Cardiff   029 2034 3459

Chelsea Harbour Ltd
London   020 7225 9108

Clapson & Son (Shipbuilders) Ltd
Barton-on-Humber   01652 635620

Crinan Boatyard
Crinan   01546 830232

Dartside Quay Brixham 01803 845445

Douglas Marine Preston
                             01772 812462

Dublin City Moorings
Dublin   +353 1 8183300

Emsworth Yacht Harbour
Emsworth   01243 377727

Exeter Ship Canal   01392 274306

HAFAN PWLLHELI
Glan Don, Pwllheli, Gwynedd LL53 5YT
Tel: (01758) 701219
Fax: (01758) 701443 VHF Ch80
Hafan Pwllheli has over 400 pontoon berths and offers access at virtually all states of the tide. Ashore, its modern purpose-built facilities include luxury toilets, showers, launderette, a secure boat park for winter storage, 40-ton travel hoist, mobile crane and plenty of space for car parking. Open 24-hours a day, 7 days a week.   L14

Highway Marine
Sandwich   01304 613925

Iron Wharf Boatyard
Faversham   01795 537122

Jalsea Marine Services Ltd
Northwich   01606 77870

Jersey Harbours
St Helier   01534 885588

Jones (Boatbuilders), David
Chester   01244 390363

Lawrenny Yacht Station
Kilgetty   01646 651212

MacFarlane & Son
Glasgow   01360 870214

Maramarine
Helensburgh   01436 810971

MELFORT PIER & HARBOUR
Tel: 01852 200333
www.mellowmelfort.com
Swinging moorings on stunning Loch Melfort. Restaurant on site.   2009/L18/z

NEPTUNE MARINA LTD
Neptune Quay, Ipswich, Suffolk IP4 1AX
Tel: (01473) 215204
Fax: (01473) 215206
e-mail:
enquiries@neptune-marina.com
www.neptune-marina.com
Accessible through continuously operating lockgates (VHF Channel 68) Neptune Marina (VHF Channels 80 or 37) is located on the north side of Ipswich wet dock immediately adjacent to the town centre and part of the rapidly regenerating northern quays area.   2009/L8/e

Orkney Marinas Ltd
Kirkwall   07810 465835

PADSTOW HARBOUR COMMISSIONERS
Harbour Office, Padstow, Cornwall PL28 8AQ
Tel: (01841) 532239
Fax: (01841) 533346
e-mail:
padstowharbour@btconnect.com
www.padstow-harbour.co.uk
Inner harbour controlled by tidal gate - opens HW±2 hours. Minimum depth 3 metres at all times. Yachtsmen must be friendly as vessels raft together. Services include showers, toilets, diesel, water and ice. Wi-fi internet access. Security by CCTV.   2009/Ext1/ez

Surry Boatyard
Shoreham-by-Sea   01273 461491

Sutton Harbour Marina Plymouth
                             01752 204186

Wicor Marine Fareham   01329 237112

Winters Marine Ltd
Salcombe   01548 843580

Yarmouth Marine Service
Yarmouth   01983 760521

Youngboats Faversham   01795 536176

BOAT BUILDERS & REPAIRS

ABC Powermarine
Beaumaris   01248 811413

Aqua-Star Ltd
St Sampsons   01481 244550

Ardoran Marine
Oban   01631 566123

Baumbach Bros Boatbuilders
Hayle   01736 753228

BB Marine Restoration Services Ltd
Southampton   023 8045 4145

Beacon Boatyard
Rochester   01634 841320

Bedwell & Co
Walton on the Naze   01255 675873

Black Dog
Falmouth   01326 318058

Blackwell, Craig
Co Meath   +353 87 677 9605

Bluewater Horizons
Weymouth   01305 782080

Bowman Yachts Penryn 01326 376107

Brennan, John
Dun Laoghaire   +353 1 280 5308

Burghead Boat Centre
Findhorn   01309 690099

Camper & Nicholsons Yachting
Portsmouth   023 9258 0221

Carrick Marine Projects
Co Antrim   02893 355884

Chicks Marine Ltd
Guernsey   01481 724536

Cooks Maritime Craftsmen - Poliglow
Lymington   01590 675521

Creekside Boatyard (Old Mill Creek)
Dartmouth   01803 832649

CTC Marine & Leisure
Middlesbrough 01642 372600

Davies Marine Services
Ramsgate 01843 586172

Dickie & Sons Ltd, AM
Bangor 01248 363400

Dickie & Sons Ltd, AM
Pwllheli 01758 701828

East & Co, Robin - Frogmore BY
Kingsbridge 01548 531257

East Llanion Marine Ltd
Pembroke Dock 01646 686866

Emblem Enterprises
East Cowes 01983 294243

Exe Leisure Exeter 01392 879055

Fairlie Quay Fairlie 01475 568267

Fairweather Marine
Fareham 01329 283500

Fast Tack Plymouth 01752 255171

Fergulsea Engineering
Ayr 01292 262978

Ferrypoint Boat Co
Youghal +353 24 94232

Floetree Ltd (Loch Lomond Marina)
Balloch 01389 752069

Freshwater Boatyard
Truro 01326 270443

Furniss Boat Building
Falmouth 01326 311766

Gallichan Marine Ltd
Jersey 01534 746387

Goodchild Marine Services
Great Yarmouth 01493 782301

Gosport Boatyard
Gosport 023 9252 6534

Gweek Quay Boatyard
Helston 01326 221657

Halls
Walton on the Naze 01255 675596

Hardway Marine
Gosport 023 9258 0420

Harris Marine (1984) Ltd, Ray
Barry 01446 740924

Haven Boatyard
Lymington 01590 677073

Hayling Yacht Company
Hayling Island 023 9246 3592

Hoare Ltd, Bob
Poole 01202 736704

Holyhead Marine Services Ltd
Holyhead 01407 760111

International Marine Designs
Aberdyfi 01654 767572

Jackson Marine
Whitehaven 01946 699332

Jackson Yacht Services
Jersey 01534 743819

JEP Marine
Canterbury 01227 710102

Jones (Boatbuilders), David
Chester 01244 390363

JWS Marine Services
Southsea 023 9275 5155

KG McColl Oban 01852 200248

Kimelford Yacht Haven
Oban 01852 200248

Kingfisher Marine
Weymouth 01305 766595

Kingfisher Ultraclean UK Ltd
Tarporley 0800 085 7039

Kippford Slipway Ltd
Dalbeattie 01556 620249

Langley Marine Services Ltd
Eastbourne 01323 470244

Lavis & Son, CH
Exmouth 01395 263095

Lawrenny Yacht Station
Lawrenny 01646 651212

Lencraft Boats Ltd
Dungarvan +353 58 682220

Lifeline Marine Services
Poole 01202 669676

Mackay Boatbuilders
Arbroath 01241 872879

Marine Services
Norwich 01692 582239

Mashford Brothers
Torpoint 01752 822232

Mayor & Co Ltd, J
Preston 01772 812250

McKellar's Slipway Ltd
Helensburgh 01436 842334

Mears, HJ Axmouth 01297 23344

Medusa Marina
Woolverstone 01473 780090

Moody Yachts International Ltd
Swanwick 01489 885000

Morrison, A Killyleagh 028 44828215

Moss (Boatbuilders), David
Thornton-Cleveleys 01253 893830

Multi Marine Composites Ltd
Torpoint 01752 823513

Newing, Roy E
Canterbury 01227 860345

Noble and Sons, Alexander
Girvan 01465 712223

Northney Marine Services
Hayling Island 023 9246 9246

Northshore Sport & Leisure
King's Lynn 01485 210236

O'Sullivans Marine Ltd
Tralee +353 66 7124524

Oulton Manufacturing Ltd
Lowestoft 01502 585631

Oyster Marine Ltd
Ipswich 01473 688888

Pachol, Terry Brighton 01273 682724

Partington Marine Ltd, William
Pwllheli 01758 612808

Pasco's Boatyard
Truro 01326 270269

Penrhos Marine
Aberdovey 01654 767478

Penzance Marine Services
Penzance 01736 361081

Pepe Boatyard
Hayling Island 023 9246 1968

PJ Bespoke Boat Fitters Ltd
Crewe 01270 812244

Preston Marine Services Ltd
Preston 01772 733595

Rampart Yachts
Southampton 023 8023 4777

Red Bay Boats Ltd
Cushendall 028 2177 1331

Reliance Marine
Wirral 0151 625 5219

Retreat Boatyard Ltd
Exeter 01392 874720/875934

Richards, Eddie
East Cowes 01983 299740

Richardson Boatbuilders, Ian
Stromness 01856 850321

Richardson Yacht Services Ltd
Newport 01983 821095

River Tees Engineering & Welding Ltd
Middlesbrough 01642 226226

Roberts Marine Ltd, S
Liverpool 0151 707 8300

Rustler Yachts Penryn 01326 310120

Salterns Boatyard
Poole 01202 707391

Sea & Shore Ship Chandler
Dundee 01382 450666

Seamark-Nunn & Co
Felixstowe 01394 275327

Seaquest Yachts
Southampton 023 8045 4549

Searanger Yachts
Peterborough 01832 274199

Shipways Yard
North Street, Maldon, Essex
www.marinestore.co.uk

Small, friendly yard with economical half-tide mud berths, covered storage, hard standing and pontoons. On site shipwrights specialising in traditional wooden craft. Excellent traditional chandlers also on site

2009/MG30b/e

TEL: 01621 854280   EMAIL: chandlery@marinestore.co.uk

SEAWARD MARINE LTD
Prospect Road, Cowes,
Isle of Wight PO31 7AD
Tel: 01983 280333
Fax: 01983 295095
e-mail: sales@seawardboat.com
www.seawardboat.com
Builders of the Seaward brand of Nelson
semi-displacement motor cruisers,
renowned for their good seakeeping and
traditional style. Custom building and
repairs. Used Seaward craft also
available.   2009/L6/v

Slipway Cooperative Ltd
Bristol   0117 907 9938

Spencer Sailing Services, Jim
Brightlingsea   01206 302911

Spicer Boatbuilder, Nick
Weymouth Marina   01305 767118

Starlight Yachts Penryn 01326 310120

Storrar Marine Store
Newcastle upon Tyne   0191 266 1037

Tarquin Boat Co
Emsworth   01243 375211

Trio Mouldings Marine
Southampton   01489 787887

Troon Marine Services
Troon   01292 316180

TT Marine Ashwell   01462 742449

WA Simpson Marine Ltd
Dundee   01382 566670

Waterfront Marine
Bangor   01248 352513

WestCoast Marine
Troon   01292 318121

Western Marine
Dublin   +353 1 280 0321

Wigmore Wright Marine Services
Penarth   029 2070 9983

Williams, Peter
Fowey   01726 870987

Woodwind Composite Marine
Southampton   023 8033 7722

WQI Ltd
Bournemouth   01202 771292

Yarmouth Marine Service
                      01983 760521

Youngboats Faversham 01795 536176

BOATYARD SERVICES & SUPPLIES

A & P Ship Care
Ramsgate   01843 593140

Abersoch Boatyard Services Ltd
Abersoch   01758 713900

Amble Boat Co Ltd
Amble   01665 710267

Amsbrisbeg Ltd
Port Bannatyne   01700 502719

Ardmair Boat Centre
Ullapool   01854 612054

Ardmaleish Boat Building Co
Rothesay   01700 502007
www.ardoran.co.uk
West coast Scotland. All marine facilities.

Ardrishaig Boatyard
Lochgilphead   01546 603280

Arklow Slipway
Arklow   +353 402 33233

Baltic Wharf Boatyard
Totnes   01803 867922

Baltimore Boatyard
Baltimore   +353 28 20444

Battricks Boatyard
St Aubin   01534 743412

Bedwell and Co
Walton-on-the-Naze   01255 675873

Berthon Boat Co
Lymington   01590 673312

Birch Boatbuilders, ER 01268 696094

Birdham Shipyard
Chichester   01243 512310

BJ Marine Ltd Bangor   028 91271434

Blagdon, A Plymouth   01752 561830

Boatworks + Ltd
St Peter Port   01481 726071

Booth W Kelly Ltd
Ramsey   01624 812322

Brennan, John
Dun Laoghaire   +353 1 280 5308

Brightlingsea Boatyard
Brightlingsea   01206 302003/8

Brighton Marina Boatyard
Brighton   01273 819919

Bristol Marina (Yard)
Bristol   0117 921 3198

Buchan & Son Ltd, J
Peterhead   01779 475395

Buckie Shipyard Ltd
Buckie   01542 831245

Bucklers Hard Boat Builders Ltd
Brockenhurst   01590 616214

Bure Marine Ltd
Great Yarmouth   01493 656996

C & J Marine Services
Newcastle Upon Tyne   0191 295 0072

Caley Marina Inverness 01463 236539

Cambrian Boat Centre
Swansea   01792 467263

Cambrian Marine Services Ltd
Cardiff   029 2034 3459

Cantell and Son Ltd
Newhaven   01273 514118

Carroll's Ballyhack Boatyard
New Ross   +353 51 389164

Castlepoint Boatyard
Crosshaven   +353 21 4832154

Chabot, Gary Newhaven 01273 611076

Chapman & Hewitt Boatbuilders
Wadebridge   01208 813487

Chippendale Craft Rye 01797 227707

Clapson & Son (Shipbuilders) Ltd
Barton on Humber   01652 635620

Coastal Marine Boatbuilders
(Berwick upon Tweed)
Eyemouth   01890 750328

Coastcraft Ltd
Cockenzie   01875 812150

Coates Marine Ltd
Whitby   01947 604486

Coombes, AA
Bembridge   01983 872296

Corpach Boatbuilding Company
Fort William   01397 772861

Craobh Marina
By Lochgilphead   01852 500222

Creekside Boatyard (Old Mill Creek)
Dartmouth   01803 832649

Crinan Boatyard
By Lochgilphead   01546 830232

Crosshaven Boatyard Co Ltd
Crosshaven   +353 21 831161

Dale Sailing Co Ltd
Neyland   01646 603110

Darthaven Marina
Kingswear   01803 752242

Dartside Quay Brixham 01803 845445

Dauntless Boatyard Ltd
Canvey Island   01268 793782

Davis's Boatyard Poole 01202 674349

Dinas Boat Yard Ltd
Y Felinheli   01248 671642

Dorset Yachts Poole   01202 674531

Douglas Boatyard
Preston   01772 812462

Dover Yacht Co Dover   01304 201073

Dun Laoghaire Marina
Dun Laoghaire   +353 1 2020040

Elephant Boatyard
Southampton   023 8040 3268

Elton Boatbuilding Ltd
Kirkcudbright   01557 330177

Farrow & Chambers Yacht Builders
Humberston   01472 632424

Felixstowe Ferry Boatyard
Felixstowe   01394 282173

Ferguson Engineering
Wexford   +353 6568 66822133

Ferry Marine South
Queensferry   0131 331 1233

Ferrybridge Marine Services Ltd
Weymouth   01305 781518

Findhorn Boatyard
Findhorn   01309 690099

Firmhelm Ltd Pwllheli 01758 612251

Fishbourne Quay Boatyard
Ryde   01983 882200

Fleming Engineering, J
Stornoway   01851 703488

Forrest Marine Ltd
Exeter   08452 308335

Fowey Boatyard Fowey   01726 832194

Fox's Marina Ipswich   01473 689111

Frank Halls & Son
Walton on the Naze   01255 675596

Freeport Marine Jersey 01534 888100

Furniss Boat Building
Falmouth   01326 311766

Goodchild Marine Services
Great Yarmouth   01493 782301

Gosport Boatyard
Gosport   023 9252 6534

Gweek Quay Boatyard
Helston   01326 221657

Haines Boatyard
Chichester   01243 512228

Harbour Marine
Plymouth   01752 204690/1

Harbour Marine Services Ltd
Southwold   01502 724721

Harris Marine Barry   01446 740924

Hartlepool Marine Engineering
Hartlepool   01429 867883

Hayles, Harold Yarmouth 01983 760373

Henderson, J Shiskine   01770 860259

Heron Marine
Whitstable   01227 361255

Hewitt, George Binham   01328 830078

Hillyard, David
Littlehampton   01903 713327

Holyhead Marina & Trinity Marine Ltd
Holyhead   01407 764242

Instow Marine Services
Bideford   01271 861081

Ipswich Haven Marina
Ipswich   01473 236644

Iron Wharf Boatyard
Faversham   01795 537122

Island Boat Services
Port of St Mary   01624 832073

Isle of Skye Yachts
Ardvasar   01471 844216

Jalsea Marine Services Ltd Weaver
Shipyard, Northwich   01606 77870

J B Timber Ltd
North Ferriby   01482 631765

Jersey Harbours Dept
St Helier   01534 885588

Kilnsale Boatyard
Kinsale   +353 21 4774774

Kilrush Marina & Boatyard – Ireland
                         +353 65 9052072

Kingfisher Ultraclean UK Ltd
Tarporley   0800 085 7039

Lake Yard Poole   01202 674531
Lallow, C Isle of Wight 01983 292112

Latham's Boatyard
Poole   01202 748029

Leonard Marine, Peter
Newhaven   01273 515987

Lincombe Marine
Salcombe   01548 843580

Lomax Boatbuilders
Cliffony   +353 71 66124

Lymington Yacht Haven
Lymington   01590 677071

MacDougalls Marine Services
Isle of Mull   01681 700294

Macduff Shipyard Ltd
Macduff   01261 832234

Madog Boatyard
Porthmadog   01766 514205/513435

Mainbrayce Marine
Alderney   01481 822772

Malakoff and Moore
Lerwick   01595 695544

**Mallaig Boat Building and
Engineering** Mallaig   01687 462304

Maramarine
Helensburgh   01436 810971

Marindus Engineering
Kilmore Quay   +353 53 29794

Marine Gleam
Lymington   0800 074 4672

Mariners Farm Boatyard
Gillingham   01634 233179

McCallum & Co Boat Builders, A
Tarbert   01880 820209

McCaughty (Boatbuilders), J
Wick   01955 602858

McGruar and Co Ltd
Helensburgh   01436 831313

Mitchell's Boatyard
Poole   01202 747857

Mooney Boats
Killybegs   +353 73 31152/31388

Moore & Son, J
St Austell   01726 842964

Morrison, A Killyleagh   028 44828215

Moss (Boatbuilders), David
Thornton-Cleveleys   01253 893830

New Horizons Rhu   01436 821555

Noble and Sons, Alexander
Girvan   01465 712223

North Pier (Oban) Oban 01631 562892

North Wales Boat Centre
Conwy   01492 580740

Northshore Yacht Yard
Chichester   01243 512611

Oban Yachts and Marine Services
By Oban   01631 565333

Oulton Manufacturing Ltd
Lowestoft   01502 585631

Parker Yachts and Dinghys Ltd
Nr Boston   01205 722697

Pearn and Co, Norman
Looe   01503 262244

Penrhos Marine
Aberdovey   01654 767478

**Penzance Dry Dock and Engineering
Co Ltd** Penzance   01736 363838

Pepe Boatyard
Hayling Island   023 9246 1968

Philip & Son Dartmouth 01803 833351

Phillips, HJ Rye   01797 223234

Ponsharden Boatyard
Penryn   01326 372215

Powersail and Island Chandlers Ltd
East Cowes Marina   01983 299800

Pratt and Son, VJ
King's Lynn   01553 764058

Priors Boatyard
Burnham-on-Crouch   01621 782160

R K Marine Ltd
Swanwick   01489 583572

Rat Island Sailboat Company (Yard)
St Mary's   01720 423399

Retreat Boatyard Ltd
Exeter   01392 874720/875934

Rice and Cole Ltd
Burnham-on-Crouch   01621 782063

Richardson Boatbuilders, Ian
Stromness   01856 850321

Richardsons Boatbuilders
Binfield   01983 821095

Riverside Yard
Shoreham Beach   01273 592456

RJ Prior (Burnham) Ltd
Burnham-on-Crouch   01621 782160

Robertsons Boatyard
Woodbridge   01394 382305

Rossbrin Boatyard
Schull   +353 28 37352

Rossiter Yachts Ltd
Christchurch   01202 483250

Rossreagh Boatyard
Rathmullan   +353 74 51082

Rudders Boatyard & Moorings
Milford Haven   01646 600288

Ryan & Roberts Marine Services
Askeaton   +353 61 392198

Rye Harbour Marina Rye
                         01797 227667

Rynn Engineering, Pat
Galway   +353 91 562568

Salterns Boatyard
Poole   01202 707391

Sandbanks Yacht Company
Poole   01202 707500

Sandy Morrison Engineering
Uig   01470 542300

Scarborough Marine Engineering Ltd
Scarborough   01723 375199

Severn Valley Cruisers Ltd (Boatyard)
Stourport-on-Severn   01299 871165

Shepards Wharf Boatyard Ltd
Cowes   01983 297821

MARINE ENGINEERING
STAINLESS STEEL & ALUMINIUM FABRICATION
STORAGE   REPAIRS   OSMOSIS TREATMENT
SPRAY PAINTING   RIGGING

SILVERS MARINE

SILVERHILLS ROSNEATH
HELENSBURGH G84 0RW

**NAUTOR'S
SWAN
AUTHORISED
SERVICE CENTRE**

Tel (01436) 831222
Fax (01436) 831879

email: enquiries@silversmarine.co.uk www.silversmarine.co.uk

2009/MGM7/e

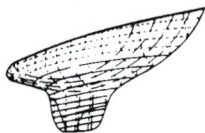

Shotley Marina Ltd	
Ipswich	01473 788982
Shotley Marine Services Ltd	
Ipswich	01473 788913
Silvers Marina Ltd	
Helensburgh	01436 831222
Skinners Boat Yard	
Baltimore	+353 28 20114
Smith & Gibbs	
Eastbourne	01323 833830
South Dock (Seaham Harbour Dock Co) Seaham	0191 581 3877
Sparkes Boatyard	
Hayling Island	023 92463572
Spencer Sailing Services, Jim	
Brightlingsea	01206 302911
Standard House Boatyard	
Wells-next-the-Sea	01328 710593
Storrar Marine Store	
Newcastle upon Tyne	0191 266 1037
Strand Shipyard Rye	01797 222070
Stratton Boatyard, Ken	
Bembridge	01983 873185
Surry Boatyard	
Shoreham-by-Sea	01273 461491
Titchmarsh Marina	
Walton-on-the-Naze	01255 672185
Tollesbury Marina	
Tollesbury	01621 869202
T J Rigging Conwy	07780 972411
Toms and Son Ltd, C	
Fowey	01726 870232
Tony's Marine Service	
Coleraine	028 7035 6422
Torquay Marina	
Torquay	01803 200210
Trinity Marine & Holyhead Marina	
Holyhead	01407 763855
Trouts Boatyard (River Exe)	
Topsham	01392 873044
Upson and Co, RF	
Aldeburgh	01728 453047
Versatility Workboats	
Rye	01797 224422
Weir Quay Boatyard	
Bere Alston	01822 840474
West Solent Boatbuilders	
Lymington	01590 642080
Wicor Marine Fareham	01329 237112
Woodrolfe Boatyard	
Maldon	01621 869202

BOAT DELIVERIES & STORAGE

Abersoch Boatyard Services Ltd	
Pwllheli	01758 713900
Ambrisbeg Ltd	
Port Bannatyne	01700 502719
Arisaig Marine	
Inverness-shire	01687 450224
Bedwell and Co	
Walton-on-the-Naze	01255 675873
Bembridge Boatyard Marine Works	
Bembridge	01983 872911

Berthon Boat Company	
Lymington	01590 673312
Bluewater Horizons	
Weymouth	01305 782080
Bure Marine Ltd	
Great Yarmouth	01493 656996
C & J Marine Services	
Newcastle upon Tyne	0191 295 0072
Caley Marine	
Inverness	01463 233437
Carrick Marine Projects	
Co Antrim	02893 355884
Challenger Marine	
Penryn	01326 377222
Coates Marine Ltd	
Whitby	01947 604486
Creekside Boatyard (Old Mill Creek)	
Dartmouth	01803 832649
Crinan Boatyard Ltd	
Crinan	01546 830232
Dale Sailing Co Ltd	
Neyland	01646 603110
Dartside Quay	
Brixham	01803 845445
Dauntless Boatyard Ltd	
Canvey Island	01268 793782
Debbage Yachting	
Ipswich	01473 601169
Douglas Marine Preston	01772 812462
East & Co, Robin	
Kingsbridge	01548 531257
Emsworth Yacht Harbour	
Emsworth	01243 377727
Exeter Ship Canal	01392 274306
Exmouth Marina	01395 2693146

Fairlie QUAY marina

Main Road
Fairlie
North Ayrshire
KA29 0AS

A prime facility just south of the town of Largs
• 80 ton hoist • 64,000sq.ft undercover storage
• 240v power available throughout shed • on-site contractors for all your maintenance needs •
clean concrete outside storage yard
• call VHF 80 call sign Fairlie Quay.

Visitors are welcome at this developing facility.

Tel: 01475 568267 Fax: 01475 568410
info@fairliequay.co.uk

website: www.fairliequay.co.uk

2009/MD6c/z

Firmhelm Ltd Pwllheli	01758 612244
Fowey Boatyard Fowey	01726 832194
Freshwater Boatyard	
Truro	01326 270443
Hafan Pwllheli Pwllheli	01758 701219
Gweek Quay Boatyard	
Helston	01326 221657
Iron Wharf Boatyard	
Faversham	01795 537122
Jalsea Marine Services Ltd	
Northwich	01606 77870
KG McColl Oban	01852 200248
Latham's Boatyard	
Poole	01202 748029
Lavis & Son, CH	
Exmouth	01395 263095

Lincombe Boat Yard	
Salcombe	01548 843580
Marine Resource Centre Ltd	
Oban	01631 720291
Marine & General Engineers	
Guernsey	01481 245808
Milford Marina	
Milford Haven	01646 696312/3
Northshore Yachts	
Chichester	01243 512611
Oulton Manufacturing Ltd	
Lowestoft	01502 585631
Pasco's Boatyard	
Truro	01326 270269
Pearn and Co, Norman	
Looe	01503 262244
Pepe Boatyard	
Hayling Island	023 9246 1968
Philip Leisure Group	
Dartmouth	01803 833351
Ponsharden Boatyard	
Penryn	01326 372215
Portsmouth Marine Engineering	
Fareham	01329 232854
Priors Boatyard	
Burnham-on-Crouch	01621 782160
Rossiter Yachts	
Christchurch	01202 483250
Shepards Wharf Boatyard Ltd	
Cowes	01983 297821
Silvers Marina Ltd	
Helensburgh	01436 831222
Waterfront Marine	
Bangor	01248 352513
Wicor Marine Fareham	01329 237112
Winters Marine Ltd	
Salcombe	01548 843580
Yacht Solutions Ltd	
Portsmouth	023 9220 0670
Yarmouth Marine Service	
Yarmouth	01983 760521
Youngboats Faversham	01795 536176

BOOKS, CHARTS & PUBLISHERS

Adlard Coles Nautical	
London	0207 7580200
Brown Son & Ferguson Ltd	
Glasgow	0141 429 1234
Chattan Security Ltd	
Edinburgh	0131 555 3155
Cooke & Son Ltd, B Hull	01482 223454
Dubois Phillips & McCallum Ltd	
Liverpool	0151 236 2776
Imray, Laurie, Norie & Wilson	
Huntingdon	01480 462114
Kelvin Hughes	
Southampton	023 8063 4911
Lilley & Gillie Ltd, John	0191 257 2217
Marine Chart Services	
Wellingborough	01933 441629
Nautical Data	
Emsworth	01243 389352
Price & Co Ltd, WF	
Bristol	0117 929 2229

Warsash Nautical Bookshop

Books, Charts, Shipping, Yachting.
Callers & Mail Order. Credit cards accepted.
New and Secondhand book catalogues free.

Also on Internet: *http://www.nauticalbooks.co.uk*

6 Dibles Road, Warsash, Southampton SO31 9HZ
Tel: 01489 572384   Fax: 01489 885756

e-mail: *orders@nauticalbooks.co.uk*

2009/MG46/s

QPC
Fareham · 01329 287880

SEA CHEST, THE
Admiralty Chart Agent
Queen Anne's Battery Marina,
Plymouth PL4 0LP
Tel: 01752 222012
Fax: 01752 252679
www.seachest.co.uk
Admiralty and Imray Chart Agent, Huge
stocks of Books and Charts, Rapid
dispatch. 2009/15/v

Stanford Charts
Bristol · 0117 929 9966

Stanford Charts
London · 020 7836 1321

Stanford Charts
Manchester · 0870 890 3730

Wiley Nautical
Chichester · 01243 779777

BOW THRUSTERS

ARS Anglian Diesels Ltd
Norfolk · 01508 520555

Buckler's Hard Boat Builders Ltd
Beaulieu · 01590 616214

JS Mouldings International
Bursledon · 023 8063 4400

BREAKDOWN

BJ Marine Ltd
Bangor, Ireland · 028 9127 1434

Seafit Marine Services
Falmouth · 01326 313713

CHANDLERS

ABC Powermarine
Beaumaris · 01248 811413

Acamar Marine Services/Sirius Yacht Training Christchurch · 01202 488030

Admiral Marine Supplies
Bootle · 01469 575909

Aladdin's Cave Chandlery Ltd
(Deacons) Bursledon · 023 8040 2182

Aladdin's Cave Chandlery Ltd
Chichester · 01243 773788

Aladdin's Cave Chandlery Ltd (Hamble Point) Southampton · 023 80455 058

Aladdin's Cave Chandlery Ltd
(Mercury) Southampton · 023 8045 4849

Aladdin's Cave Chandlery Ltd (Port Hamble) Southampton · 023 8045 4858

Aladdin's Cave Chandlery Ltd
(Swanwick) Swanwick · 01489 555999

Alderney Boating Centre
Alderney · 01481 823725

Allgadgets.co.uk
Basingstoke · 01256 478000

Alpine Room & Yacht Equipment
Chemsford · 01245 223563

Aquatogs Cowes · 01893 247890

Arbroath Fishermen's Association
Arbroath · 01241 873132

Ardfern Yacht Centre Ltd
Argyll · 01852 500247

Ardoran Marine Oban · 01631 566123

Arthurs Chandlery
Gosport · 023 9252 6522

Arun Aquasports
Littlehampton · 01903 713553

Arun Canvas and Rigging Ltd
Littlehampton · 01903 732561

Arun Nautique
Littlehampton · 01903 730558

Aruncraft Chandlers
Littlehampton · 01903 713327

ASAP Supplies – Equipment & Spares Worldwide
Beccles · 0845 1300870

Auto Marine Sales
Southsea · 023 9281 2263

Bayside Marine
Brixham · 01803 856771

Bedwell and Co
Walton on the Naze · 01255 675873

BJ Marine Ltd Bangor · 028 9127 1434

Bluecastle Chandlers
Portland · 01305 822298

Bluewater Horizons
Weymouth · 01305 782080

Blue Water Marine Ltd
Pwllheli · 01758 614600

Boatshop Chandlery
Brixham · 01803 882055

Boatacs
Westcliffe on Sea · 01702 475057

Boathouse, The Penryn · 01326 374177

Boston Marina · 01205 364420

Bosun's Locker, The
Falmouth · 01326 312212

Bosun's Locker, The
Milford Haven · 01646 697834

Bosun's Locker, The
Ramsgate · 01843 597158

Bosuns Locker, The
South Queensferry · 0131 331 3875/4496

Brancaster Sailing and Sailboard Centre Kings Lynn · 01485 210236

Bridger Marine, John
Exeter · 01392 216420

Brigantine Teignmouth · 01626 872400

Brighton Chandlery
Brighton · 01273 612612

Bristol Boat Ltd Bristol · 01225 872032

Brixham Chandlers
Brixham · 01803 882055

Brixham Yacht Supplies Ltd
Brixham · 01803 882290

Brundall Angling Centre
Norwich · 01603 715289

Brunel Chandlery Ltd
Neyland · 01646 601667

Bucklers Hard Boat Builders
Beaulieu · 01590 616214

Burghead Boat Centre
Findhorn · 01309 690099

Bussell & Co, WL
Weymouth · 01305 785633

Buzzard Marine
Yarmouth · 01983 760707

C & M Marine
Bridlington · 01262 672212

Cabin Yacht Stores
Rochester · 01634 718020

Caley Marina Inverness · 01463 236539

Cambrian Boat Centre
Swansea · 01792 467263

Cantell & Son Ltd
Newhaven · 01273 514118

Carne (Sales) Ltd, David
Falmouth · 01326 318314

Carne (Sales) Ltd, David
Penryn · 01326 374177

Carrickcraft
Malahide · +353 1 845 5438

Caters Carrick Ltd
Carrickfergus · 028 93351919

CH Marine (Cork)
Cork · +353 21 4315700

CH Marine Skibbereen · +353 28 23190

Charity & Taylor Ltd
Lowestoft · 01502 581529

Chertsey Marine Ltd
Penton Hook Marina · 01932 565195

Chicks Marine Ltd
Guernsey · 01481 724536

Christchurch Boat Shop
Christchurch · 01202 482751

Churcher Marine
Worthing · 01903 230523

Clapson & Son (Shipbuilders) Ltd
South Ferriby Marina · 01652 635620

Clarke, Albert
Newtownards · 01247 872325

Coastal Marine Boatbuilders Ltd
(Dunbar) Eyemouth · 01890 750328

Coates Marine Ltd
Whitby · 01947 604486

Collins Marine St Helier · 01534 732415

Compass Marine
Lancing · 01903 761773

Also on the same line (Smith AM (Marine) Ltd):

Smith AM (Marine) Ltd
London · 020 8529 6988

Cosalt International Ltd Aberdeen 01224 588327	**Eccles Marine Co** Middlesbrough 01642 372600	**Green Marine, Jimmy** Fore St Beer 01297 20744
Cosalt International Ltd Southampton 023 8063 2824	**Ely Boat Chandlers** Hayling Island 023 9246 1968	**Greenham Marine** Emsworth 01243 378314
Cotter, Kieran Baltimore +353 28 20106	**Emsworth Chandlery** Emsworth 01243 375500	**Gunn Navigation Services, Thomas** Aberdeen 01224 595045
Cox Yacht Charter Ltd, Nick Lymington 01590 673489	**Exe Leisure** Exeter 01392 879055	**Hale Marine, Ron** Portsmouth 023 92732985
C Q Chandlers Ltd Poole 01202 682095	**Express Marine Services** Chichester 01243 773788	**Harbour Marine Services Ltd (HMS)** Southwold 01502 724721
Crinan Boats Ltd Lochgilphead 01546 830232	**Fairways Chandlery** Burnham-on-Crouch 01621 782659	**Hardware & Marine Supplies** Wexford +353 53 29791
CTC Marine & Leisure Middlesbrough 01642 230123	**Fairweather Marine** Fareham 01329 283500	**Hardway Marine** Gosport 023 9258 0420
Dale Sailing Co Ltd Milford Haven 01646 603110	**Fal Chandlers** Falmouth Marina 01326 212411	**Harris Marine (1984) Ltd, Ray** Barry 01446 740924
Danson Marine Sidcup 0208 304 5678	**Ferrypoint Boat Co** Youghal +353 24 94232	**Hartlepool Marine Supplies** Hartlepool 01429 862932
Dartside Quay Brixham 01803 845445	**Findhorn Marina & Boatyard** Findhorn 01309 690099	**Harwich Chandlers Ltd** Harwich 01255 504061
Dauntless Boatyard Ltd Canvey Island 01268 793782	**Firmhelm Ltd** Pwllheli 01758 612244	**Harwoods** Yarmouth 01983 760258
Davis's Yacht Chandler Littlehampton 01903 722778	**Fisherman's Mutual Asssociation (Eyemouth) Ltd** Eyemouth 01890 750373	**Hawkins Marine Shipstores, John** Rochester 01634 840812
Denholm Fishselling Scrabster 01847 896968	**Fleetwood Trawlers' Supply Co Ltd, The** Fleetwood 01253 873476	**Hayles, Harold** Yarmouth 01983 760373
Denney & Son, EL Redcar 01642 483507	**Floetree Ltd (Loch Lomond Marina)** Balloch 01389 752069	**Herm Seaway Marine Ltd** St Peter Port 01481 726829
Deva Marine Conwy 01492 572777	**Foc'sle, The** Exeter 01392 874105	**Highway Marine** Sandwich 01304 613925
Dickie & Sons Ltd, AM Bangor 01248 363400	**Freeport Marine** Jersey 01534 888100	**Hill Head Chandlers** Hill Head 01329 664621
Dickie & Sons Ltd, AM Pwllheli 01758 701828	**French Marine Motors Ltd** Brightlingsea 01206 302133	**Hoare Ltd, Bob** Poole 01202 736704
Dinghy Supplies Ltd/Sutton Marine Ltd Sutton +353 1 832 2312	**Furneaux Riddall & Co Ltd** Portsmouth 023 9266 8621	**Hornsey (Chandlery) Ltd, Chris** Southsea 023 9273 4728
Diverse Yacht Services Hamble 023 80453399	**Gallichan Marine Ltd** Jersey 01534 746387	**Hunter & Combes** Cowes 01983 299599
Dixon Chandlery, Peter Exmouth 01395 273248	**Galway Marine Chandlers Ltd** Galway +353 91 566568	**Iron Stores Marine** St Helier 01534 877755
Doling & Son, GW Barrow In Furness 01229 823708	**GB Attfield & Company** Dursley 01453 547185	**Isles of Scilly Steamship Co** St Mary's 01720 422710
Dovey Marine Aberdovey 01654 767581	**Gibbons Ship Chandlers Ltd** Sunderland 0191 567 2101	**Jackson Yacht Services** Jersey 01534 743819
Down Marine Co Ltd Belfast 028 9048 0247	**Gibbs Chandlery** Shepperton 01932 242977	**Jamison and Green Ltd** Belfast 028 9032 2444
Douglas Marine Preston 01772 812462	**Glaslyn Marine Supplies Ltd** Porthmadog 01766 513545	**Jeckells and Son Ltd** Lowestoft 01502 565007
Dubois Phillips & McCallum Ltd Liverpool 0151 236 2776	**Goodwick Marine** Fishguard 01348 873955	**JF Marine Chandlery** Rhu 01436 820584
Duncan Ltd, JS Wick 01955 602689	**Gorleston Marine Ltd** Great Yarmouth 01493 661883	**JNW Services** Aberdoon 01224 594050
Duncan Yacht Chandlers Ely 01353 663095	**GP Barnes Ltd** Shoreham 01273 591705/596680	**JNW Services** Peterhead 01779 477346
East Anglian Sea School Ipswich 01473 659992		**Johnston Brothers** Mallaig 01687 462215

Findhorn Marina & Boatyard

Findhorn, Morayshire IV36 3YE
Tel: 01309 690099
www.findmar.com

Open 7 days a week

- Boat Storage
- Chandlery & Cafe
- Slipway
- Moorings
- Safety Equipment
- Books & Charts
- Mercury, Yamaha Dealers

2009/MG39/s

Johnstons Marine Stores Lamlash 01770 600333
Kearon Ltd, George Arklow +353 402 32319
Kelpie Boats Pembroke Dock 01646 683661
Kelvin Hughes Ltd Southampton 023 80634911
Kildale Marine Hull 01482 227464
Kingfisher Marine Weymouth 01305 766595
Kings Lock Chandlery Middlewich 01606 737564
Kip Chandlery Inverkip Greenock 01475 521485

kip marina

www.kipmarina.co.uk
e-mail: dduffield@kipmarina.co.uk

Huge variety of stock covering virtually every aspect of boat maintenance. Yanmar dealers for Scotland with extensive range of maintenance parts and spares available. Open 7 days a week.
Tel: 01475 521485

The Yacht Harbour, Inverkip, Renfrewshire PA16 0AS

2009/MG82/zz

Kirkcudbright Scallop Gear Ltd
Kirkcudbright   01557 330399
Kyle Chandlers Troon   01292 311880
Landon Marine, Reg
Truro   01872 272668
Largs Chandlers Largs   01475 686026
Lencraft Boats Ltd
Dungarvan   +353 58 68220
Lincoln Marina Lincoln   01522 526896
Looe Chandlery
West Looe   01503 264355
Lynch Ltd, PA Morpeth   01670 512291
Mackay Boatbuilders (Arbroath) Ltd
Aberdeen   01241 872879
Mackay Marine Services
Aberdeen   01224 575772
Mailspeed Marine
Burnham-on-Crouch   01621 781120
Mailspeed Marine
Southsea Marina   023 9275 5450
Mailspeed Marine
Warrington   01925 838858
Manx Marine Ltd
Douglas   01624 674842
Marine & Leisure Europe Ltd
Plymouth   01752 268826
Marine Instruments
Falmouth   01326 312414
Marine Scene Cardiff   029 2070 5780
Marine Services Jersey   01534 626930
Marine Store Wyatts
West Mersea   01206 384745
Marine Store Maldon   01621 854380
Marine Store
Walton on the Naze   01255 679028
Marine Superstore Port Solent
Chandlery Portsmouth   023 9221 9843
MarineCo Looe   01503 265444
Maryport Harbour and Marina
Maryport   01900 814431
Matchett Ltd, HC
Widnes   0151 423 4420
Matthews Ltd, D
Cork   +353 214 277633
Mayflower Chandlery
Plymouth   01752 500121
McCready Sailboats Ltd
Holywood   028 9042 1821
Moore & Son, J
Mevagissey   01726 842964
Morgan & Sons Marine, LH
Brightlingsea   01206 302003

Mount Batten Boathouse
Plymouth   01752 482666
MR Marine Ltd Brighton   01273 668900
Murphy, Nicholas
Dunmore East   +353 51 383259
Mylor Chandlery & Rigging
Falmouth   01326 375482
Nancy Black Oban   01631 562550
Nautical World Bangor   028 91460330
New World Yacht Care
Helensburgh   01436 820586
Newhaven Chandlery
Newhaven   01273 612612
Nifpo Ardglass   028 4484 2144
Norfolk Marine
Great Yarmouth   01692 670272
Norfolk Marine Chandlery Shop
Norwich   01603 783150
Northshore Sport & Leisure
Brancaster Staithe   01485 210236
Ocean Leisure Ltd
London   020 7930 5050
One Stop Chandlery
Maldon   01621 853558
Partington Marine Ltd, William
Pwllheli   01758 612808
Pascall Atkey & Sons Ltd
Isle of Wight   01983 292381
Peculiar's Chandlery
Gosport   023 9258 9953
Pennine Marine Ltd
Skipton   01756 792335
Penrhos Marine
Aberdovey   01654 767478

Penzance Marine Services
Penzance   01736 361081
Perry Marine, Rob
Axminster   01297 631314
Pepe Boatyard
Hayling Island   023 9246 1968
Peters PLC Chichester   01243 511033
Pinnell & Bax
Northampton   01604 592808
Piplers of Poole Poole   01202 673056
Pirate's Cave, The
Rochester   01634 295233
Powersail Island Chandlers Ltd
East Cowes Marina   01983 299800
Preston Marine Services Ltd
Preston   01772 733595
Price & Co Ltd, WF
Bristol   0117 929 2229
PSM Ltd Alderney   01481 824968
Purple Sails & Marine
Walsall   01922 614787
Quay West Chandlers
Poole   01202 742488
Quayside Marine
Salcombe   01548 844300
Racecourse Yacht Basin (Windsor)
Ltd Windsor   01753 851501
Rat Rigs Water Sports
Cardiff   029 2062 1309
Reliance Marine Wirral   0151 625 5219
RHP Marine Cowes   01983 290421
Rhu Chandlery Rhu   01436 820584
RNS Marine Northam   01237 474167
Sail Loft Bideford   01271 860001
Sailaway St Anthony   01326 231357
Salcombe Boatstore
Salcombe   01548 843708
Salterns Chandlery
Poole   01202 701556
Sand & Surf Chandlery
Salcombe   01548 844555
Sandrock Marine Rye   01797 222679
Schull Watersports Centre
Schull   +353 28 28554
Sea & Shore Ship Chandler
Dundee   01382 450666
Sea Cruisers of Rye Rye   01797 222070
Sea Span Edinburgh   0131 552 2224
Sea Teach Ltd Emsworth   01243 375774
Seafare Tobermory   01688 302277

manx marine
Limited   Yacht Chandlers

Yacht Chandlers
The Tongue Building, The Tongue, Douglas Harbour, Douglas IM1 5AO
The Islands leading and most established Yacht Chandlery. Stockists of quality foul weather clothing and thermal wear. Large stock holding of s/steel fixtures and fittings and a comprehensive range of general chandlery including rigging facilities

Telephone: 01624 674842
Web: www.manxmarine.com
E-mail: manxmarine@mcb.net

2009/MG33/v

MARINE SUPPLIES AND SERVICES GUIDE

CHANDLERS

Seahog Boats Preston 01772 633016
Seamark-Nunn & Co
Felixstowe 01394 451000
Seaquest Marine Ltd
St Peter Port 01481 721773
Seaware Ltd Penryn 01326 377948
Seaway Marine Macduff 01261 832877
Severn Valley Boat Centre
Stourport-on-Severn 01299 871165
Shamrock Chandlery
Southampton 023 8063 2725
Sharp & Enright Dover 01304 206295
Shearwater Engineering Services Ltd
Dunoon 01369 706666
Shipmates Chandlery
Dartmouth 01803 839292
Shipshape Marine
King's Lynn 01553 764058
Ship Shape
Ramsgate 01843 597000
Shipsides Marine Ltd
Preston 01772 797079
Shorewater Sports
Chichester 01243 672315
Simpson Marine Ltd
Newhaven 01273 612612
Simpson Marine Ltd, WA
Dundee 01382 566670
Sketrick Marine Centre
Killinchy 028 9754 1400
Smith & Gibbs
Eastbourne 01323 723824
Smith AM (Marine) Ltd
London 020 8529 6988
Solent Marine Chandlery Ltd
Gosport 023 9258 4622
South Coast Marine
Christchurch 01202 482695
South Pier Shipyard
St Helier 01534 711000
Southampton Yacht Services Ltd
Southampton 023 803 35266
Southern Masts & Rigging
Brighton 01273 818189
S Roberts Marine Ltd
Liverpool 0151 707 8300
Standard House Chandlery
Wells-next-the-Sea 01328 710593
Stornoway Fishermen's Co-op
Stornoway 01851 702563
Sunset Marine & Watersports
Sligo +353 71 9162792
Sussex Marine
St Leonards on Sea 01424 425882
Sussex Marine Centre
Shoreham 01273 454737
Sutton Marine (Dublin)
Sutton +353 1 832 2312
SW Nets Newlyn 01736 360254
Tarbert Ltd, JSB Tarbert 01880 820180
TCS Chandlery Grays 01375 374702
TCS Chandlery
Southend 01702 444423
Thulecraft Ltd Lerwick 01595 693192
The Monkeys Fist
Hayling Island 023 9246 1610
Torbay Boating Centre
Paignton 01803 558760

Torquay Chandlers
Torquay 01803 211854
Trafalgar Yacht Services
Fareham 01329 822445
Trident UK N Shields 0191 490 1736
Union Chandlery
Cork +353 21 4554334
Uphill Boat Services
Weston-Super-Mare 01934 418617
Upper Deck Marine and Outriggers
Fowey 01726 832287
V Ships (Isle of Man)
Douglas 01624 688886
V F Marine Rhu 01436 820584
Viking Marine Ltd
Dun Laoghaire +353 1 280 6654
Waterfront Marine
Bangor 01248 352513
Wayne Maddox Marine
Margate 01843 297157
Western Marine
Dalkey +353 1280 0321
Whitstable Marine
Whitstable 01227 274168
Williams Ltd, TJ Cardiff 029 20 487676
Work & Leisure
Arbroath 01241 431134
XM Yachting
Southampton 0870 751 4666
Yacht & Boat Chandlery
Faversham 01795 531777
Yacht Parts Plymouth 01752 252489
Yacht Shop, The
Fleetwood 01253 879238
Yachtmail Ltd Lymington 01590 672784

CHART AGENTS

Brown Son & Ferguson Ltd
Glasgow 0141 429 1234
Chattan Security Ltd
Edinburgh 0131 554 7527
Cooke & Son Ltd, B
Hull 01482 223454
Dubois Phillips & McCallum Ltd
Liverpool 0151 236 2776
Imray Laurie Norie and Wilson Ltd
Huntingdon 01480 462114
Kelvin Hughes
Southampton 023 8063 4911
Lilley & Gillie Ltd, John
North Shields 0191 257 2217

Marine Chart Services
Wellingborough 01933 441629
Morgan Mapping
Exeter 01392 255788
Price & Co, WF Bristol 0117 929 2229
Sea Chest Nautical Bookshop
Plymouth 01752 222012
Seath Instruments (1992) Ltd
Lowestoft 01502 573811
Small Craft Deliveries
Woodbridge 01394 382655
Smith (Marine) Ltd, AM
London 020 8529 6988
South Bank Marine Charts Ltd
Grimsby 01472 361137
Stanford Charts
Bristol 0117 929 9966
Stanford Charts
London 020 7836 1321
Stanford Charts
Manchester 0161 831 0250
Todd Chart Agency Ltd
County Down 028 9146 6640
UK Hydrographics Office
Taunton 01823 337900
Warsash Nautical Bookshop
Warsash 01489 572384

CLOTHING

Absolute
Gorleston on Sea 01493 442259
Aquatogs Cowes 01493 247890
Crew Clothing London 020 8875 2300
Crewsaver Gosport 023 9252 8621
Douglas Gill Nottingham 0115 9460844
Fat Face fatface.com
Gul International Ltd
Bodmin 01208 262400
Guy Cotten UK Ltd
Liskeard 01579 347115
Harwoods Yarmouth 01983 760258
Helly Hansen
Nottingham 0115 9608797
Henri Lloyd Manchester 0161 799 1212
Joules
Market Harborough 01858 461156
Mad Cowes Clothing Co
Cowes 0845 456 5158
Matthews Ltd, D
Cork +353 214 277633

SMALL CRAFT DELIVERIES
LTD
Est. 1959
International Admiralty Charts Agents & Marine Suppliers
Worldwide stocks of Admiralty Charts and Publications
ARCS & C-Map Electronic Chart Service
Wide Range of: Imray Charts & Publications, Stanford Charts, Instructional Books, RYA Publications, Chart-Instruments, Safety Equipment, Flags, Binoculars, Bells, GPS, VHF etc.
Navigation House, 4 Wilford Bridge Spur, Melton, Woodbridge, Suffolk IP12 1RJ
Tel: 01394 382600 Fax: 01394 387672
E-mail: sale@scd-charts.co.uk www.scd-charts.co.uk

Mountain & Marine
Stockport 0800 093 5793
Musto Ltd Laindon 01268 491555
Ocean World Ltd Cowes 01983 291744
Purple Sails & Marine Walsall
01922 614787
Quba Sails Cowes 01983 299004
Quba Sails Lymington 01590 689362
Quba Sails Salcombe 01548 844599
Ravenspring Ltd Totnes 01803 867092
Shorewater Sports
Chichester 01243 672315
Splashdown Leeds 0113 270 7000
Yacht Parts
Plymouth 01752 252489

CODE OF PRACTICE EXAMINERS

Booth Marine Surveys, Graham
Birchington-on-Sea 01843 843793
Cannell & Associates, David M
Wivenhoe 01206 823337

COMPUTERS & SOFTWARE

C-map Ltd Fareham 01329 517777
Dolphin Maritime Software
White Cross 01524 841946
Forum Software Ltd
Nr Haverfordwest 01646 636363
Kelvin Hughes Ltd
Southampton 023 8063 4911
Maptech-Marine
Aldermaston 0870 740 9040
PC Maritime Plymouth 01752 254205
Sea Information Systems Ltd
Aberdeen 01224 621326
Square Mile Marlow 0870 1202536

DECK EQUIPMENT

Aries Van Gear Spares
Penryn 01326 377467
Frederiksen Boat Fittings (UK) Ltd
Gosport 023 9252 5377
Harken UK Lymington 01590 689122
Kearon Ltd George +353 402 32319
Marine Maintenance
Tollesbury 01621 860441
Nauquip Warsash 01489 885336
Pro-Boat Ltd
Burnham-on-Crouch 01621 785455
Ryland, Kenneth
Stanton 01386 584270
Smith, EC & Son Ltd
Luton 01582 729721
Timage & Co Ltd
Braintree 01376 343087

DIESEL MARINE/ FUEL ADDITIVES

Corralls Poole 01202 674551
Cotters Marine & General Supplies
Baltimore +353 28 20106
Diesel Dialysis
St Austelll 0800 389 7874
Expresslube Henfield 01444 881883

Gorey Marine Fuel Supplies
Gorey 07797 742384
Hammond, George
Dover 01304 206809
Iron Wharf Boatyard
Faversham 01795 536296
Lallow, Clare Cowes 01983 760707
Marine Support & Towage
Cowes 01983 200716/07860 297633
Quayside Fuel
Weymouth 07747 182181
Rossiter Yachts
Christchurch 01202 483250
Sleeman & Hawken
Shaldon 01626 872750

DIVERS

Abco Divers Belfast 028 90610492
Andark Diving So'ton 01489 581755
Argonaut Marine
Aberdeen 01224 706526
**Baltimore Diving and Watersports
Centre** West Cork +353 28 20300
C & C Marine Services
Largs 01475 687180
**Cardiff Commercial Boat Operators
Ltd** Cardiff 029 2037 7872
C I Diving Services Ltd
Invergordon 01349 852500
Clyde Diving Centre
Inverkip 01475 521281
Divesafe Sunderland 0191 567 8423
Divetech UK King's Lynn 01485 572323
Diving & Marine Engineering
Barry 01446 721553
Donnelly, R South Shields 07973 119455
DV Diving 028 9146 4671
Falmouth Divers Ltd
Penryn 01326 374736
Fathom Diving (Chislehurst)
Chislehurst 020 8289 8237
Fathoms Ltd Wick 01955 605956
Felixarc Marine Ltd
Felixstowe 01394 676497
Grampian Diving Services
New Deer 01771 644206
Higgins, Noel +353 872027650
Hudson, Dave
Trearddur Bay 01407 860628
Hunt, Kevin Tralee +353 6671 25979
Kaymac Diving Services
Swansea 01792 301818
Keller, Hilary
Buncrana +353 77 62146
Kilkee Diving Centre
Kilkee +353 6590 56707
Leask Marine Kirkwall 01856 874725
Looe Divers Hannafore 01503 262727
MacDonald, D Nairn 01667 455661
Medway Diving Contractors Ltd
Gillingham 01634 851902
Mojo Maritime Penzance 01736 762771

Murray, Alex Stornoway 01851 704978
New Dawn Dive Centre
Lymington 01590 675656
New Tec Diving Services
Blackpool 01253 691665
Northern Divers (Engineering) Ltd
Hull 01482 227276
Offshore Marine Services Ltd
Bembridge 01983 873125
**Parkinson (Sinbad Marine Services),
J** Killybegs +353 73 31417
Port of London Authority
Gravesend 01474 560311
Purcell, D – Crouch Sailing School
Burnham 01621 784140/0585 33
Salvesen UK Ltd
Liverpool 0151 933 6038
Sea-Lift Diving Dover 01304 829956
Southern Cylinder Services
Fareham 01329 221125
Sub Aqua Services
North Ormesby 01642 230209
Teign Diving Centre
Teignmouth 01626 773965
Thorpe, Norman Portree 01478 612274
Tuskar Rock Marine
Rosslare +353 53 33376
Underwater Services
Dyffryn Arbwy 01341 247702
Wilson Alan c/o Portrush Yacht Club
Portrush 028 2076 2225
Woolford, William
Bridlington 01262 671710

ELECTRICAL AND ELECTRONIC ENGINEERS

Allworth Riverside Services, Adrian
Chelsea Harbour Marina 07831 574774
Belson Design Ltd, Nick
Southampton 077 6835 1330
Biggs, John Weymouth Marina,
Weymouth 01305 778445
BJ Marine Ltd Bangor 028 9127 1434
Calibra Marine
Dartmouth 01803 833094
Campbell & McHardy Lossiemouth
Marina, Lossiemouth 01343 812137
CES Sandown Sparkes Marina,
Hayling Island 023 9246 6005
Colin Coady Marine
Malahide +353 87 265 6496
Contact Electrical
Arbroath 01241 874528
DDZ Marine Ardossan 01294 607077
EC Leisure Craft
North Fambridge 01621 744424
Energy Solutions
Rochester 01634 290772
**Enterprise Marine Electronic &
Technical Services Ltd**
Aberdeen 01224 593281

Eurotex Brighton   01273 818990

Floetree Ltd (Loch Lomond Marina)
Balloch   01389 752069

HNP Engineers (Lerwick) Ltd
Lerwick   01595 692493

Index Marine
Bournemouth   01202 470149

Jackson Yacht Services
Jersey   01534 743819

Jedynak, A Salcombe   01548 843321

Kippford Slipway Ltd
Dalbeattie   01556 620249

Land & Sea Electronics
Aberdeen   01224 593281

Lifeline Marine Services
Dolphin Haven, Poole   01202 669676

Lynch Ltd, PA Morpeth   01670 512291

Mackay Boatbuilders (Arbroath) Ltd
Aberdeen   01241 872879

Marine, AW Gosport   023 9250 1207

Marine Electrical Repair Service
London   020 7228 1336

MES Falmouth Marina,
Falmouth   01326 378497

Mount Batten Boathouse
Plymouth   01752 482666

New World Yacht Care
Rhu   01436 820586

Neyland Marine Services Ltd
Milford Haven   01646 698968

Powell, Martin Shamrock Quay,
Southampton   023 8033 2123

R & J Marine Electricians Suffolk Yacht
Harbour Ltd, Ipswich   01473 659737

Radio & Electronic Services Beaucette
Marina, Guernsey   01481 728837

Redcar Fish Company
Stockton-on-Tees   01642 633638

RHP Marine Cowes   01983 290421

Rothwell, Chris
Torquay Marina   01803 850960

Rutherford, Jeff Largs   01475 568026

Sea Electric Hamble   023 8045 6255

SM International
Plymouth   01752 662129

Sussex Fishing Services
Rye   01797 223895

Ultra Marine Systems
Mayflower International Marina, Plymouth
   07989 941020

WESTERN MARINE POWER LTD
Eastern Hangar, Shaw Way,
Mount Batten, Plymouth, PL9 9XH
TEL: (01752) 408804 FAX: (01752) 408807
e-mail: info@wmp.co.uk

Suppliers and installers of:-
Watermakers, Air Conditioning,
Generators, Electrical Systems,
Trim tabs, Electronic Engine Controls,
Bow and Stern Thrusters, Teak Decks,
Davits, Passarelles and Cranes,
Galley and Sanitation Equipment.
ISO 9001 Quality Assurance.
Website: www.wmp.co.uk/
2009/MD15/v

Upham, Roger
Chichester   01243 528299

Volspec Ipswich   01473 780144

Waypoint Marine
Plymouth   01752 661913

Weyland Marine Services
Milford Haven   01646 698968

Yoldings Marine
Eastbourne   01323 470882

ELECTRONIC DEVICES AND EQUIPMENT

Anchorwatch UK
Edinburgh   0131 447 5057

Aquascan International Ltd
Newport   01633 841117

Atlantis Marine Power Ltd
Plymouth   01752 225679

Autosound Marine
Bradford   01274 688990

AW Marine Gosport   023 9250 1207

Brookes & Gatehouse
Romsey   01794 518448

Boat Electrics & Electronics Ltd
Troon   01292 315355

Cactus Navigation & Communication
London   020 7833 3435

CDL Aberdeen   01224 706655

Charity & Taylor Ltd
Lowestoft   01502 581529

Diverse Yacht Services
Hamble   023 8045 3399

Dyfed Electronics Ltd
Milford Haven   01646 694572

Echopilot Marine Electronics Ltd
Ringwood   01425 476211

Euronav Ltd Portsmouth 023 9237 3855

Furuno (UK) Ltd
Denmead   023 9223 0303

Garmin (Europe) Ltd
Romsey   0870 850 1242

Golden Arrow Marine Ltd
Southampton   023 8071 0371

Greenham Regis Marine Electronics
Emsworth   01243 378314

Greenham Regis Marine Electronics
Lymington   01590 671144

Greenham Regis Marine Electronics
Poole   01202 676363

Greenham Regis Marine Electronics
Southampton   023 8063 6555

ICS Electronics Arundel 01903 731101

JG Technologies Ltd
Weymouth   0845 458 9616

KM Electronics
Lowestoft   01502 569079

Kongsberg Simrad Ltd
Aberdeen   01224 226500

Kongsberg Simrad Ltd
Wick   01955 603606

Landau UK Ltd Hamble 02380 454040

Land & Sea Electronics
Aberdeen   01224 593281

Marathon Leisure
Hayling Island   023 9263 7711

Marine Instruments
Falmouth   01326 375483

Maritek Ltd Glasgow   0141 571 9164

Microcustom Ltd Ipswich 01473 780724

Nasa Marine Instruments
Stevenage   01438 354033

Navcom Chichester   01243 776625

Navionics UK Plymouth   01752 204735

Ocean Leisure Ltd
London   020 7930 5050

Plymouth Marine Electronics
Plymouth   01752 227711

Radio & Electronic Services Ltd
St Peter Port   01481 728837

Raymarine Ltd
Portsmouth   023 9269 3611

Redfish Car Company
Stockton-on-Tees   01642 633638

Robertson, MK Oban   01631 563836

Satcom Distribution Ltd
Salisbury   01722 410800

Sea Information Systems Ltd
Aberdeen   01224 621326

Seaquest Marine Ltd
Guernsey   01481 721773

Seatronics Aberdeen   01224 853100

Selenia Communications
Aberdeen   01224 585334

Selenia Communications
Brixham   01803 851993

Selenia Communications
Fraserburgh   01346 518187

Selenia Communications
Lowestoft   01502 572365

Selenia Communications
Newlyn   01736 361320

Selenia Communications
Newcastle upon Tyne   0191 265 0374

Selenia Communications
Penryn   01326 378031

Selenia Communications
Southampton   023 8051 1868

Silva Ltd Livingston   01506 419555

SM International
Plymouth   01752 662129

Sperry Marine Ltd
Peterhead   01779 473475

Stenmar Ltd Aberdeen   01224 827288

STN Atlas Marine UK Ltd
Peterhead   01779 478233

Tacktick Ltd Emsworth   01243 379331

Transas Nautic
Portsmouth   023 9267 4016

Veripos Precise Navigation
Fraserburgh   01346 511411

Wema (UK) Bristol   01454 316103

Western Battery Service
Mallaig   01687 462044

Wilson & Co Ltd, DB
Glasgow   0141 647 0161

Woodsons of Aberdeen Ltd
Aberdeen   01224 722884

Yeoman Romsey   01794 521079

ENGINES AND ACCESSORIES

Airylea Motors
Aberdeen   01224 872891

Amble Boat Co Ltd
Amble   01665 710267

Anchor Marine Products
Benfleet   01268 566666

Aquafac Ltd Luton	01582 568700
Attfield & Company, GB Dursley	01453 547185
Barrus Ltd, EP Bicester	01869 363636
Brigantine Teignmouth	01626 872400
British Polar Engines Ltd Glasgow	0141 445 2455
Bukh Diesel UK Ltd Poole	01202 668840
Caledonian Marine Rhu	01436 821184
CJ Marine Mechanical Troon	01292 313400
Cleghorn Waring Ltd Letchworth	01462 480380
Cook's Diesel Service Ltd Faversham	01795 538553
Felton Marine Engineering Brighton	01273 601779
Felton Marine Engineering Eastbourne	01323 470211
Fender-Fix Maidstone	01622 751518
Fettes & Rankine Engineering Aberdeen	01224 573343
Fleetwood & Sons Ltd, Henry Lossiemouth	01343 813015
Gorleston Marine Ltd Great Yarmouth	01493 661883
Halyard Salisbury	01722 710922
Interseals (Guernsey) Ltd Guernsey	01481 246364
Kelpie Boats Pembroke Dock	01646 683661
Keypart Watford	01923 330570
Lancing Marine Brighton	01273 410025
Lencraft Boats Ltd Dungarvan	+353 58 68220
Lewmar Ltd Havant	023 9247 1841
Liverpool Power Boats Bootle	0151 944 1163
Lynch Ltd, PA Morpeth	01670 512291
MacDonald & Co Ltd, JN Glasgow	0141 334 6171
Marine Maintenance Tollesbury	01621 860441
Mariners Weigh Shaldon	01626 873698
Mooring Mate Ltd Bournemouth	01202 421199
Nauquip Warsash	01489 885336
Newens Marine, Chas Putney	020 8788 4587
Ocean Safety Southampton	023 8072 0800
Outboard Centre Fareham	01329 234277
Riley Marine Dover	01304 214544
RK Marine Ltd Hamble	01489 583585
RK Marine Ltd Swanwick	01489 583572
Rule – ITT Industries Hoddesdon	01992 450145
Sillette Sonic Ltd Sutton	020 8337 7543
Smith & Son Ltd, EC Luton	01582 729721

Sowester Simpson-Lawrence Ltd Poole	01202 667700
Timage & Co Ltd Braintree	01376 343087
Trident UK Gateshead	0191 259 6797
Vetus Den Ouden Ltd Totton	023 8086 1033
Western Marine Dublin	+353 1 280 0321
Whitstable Marine Whitstable	01227 262525
Yates Marine, Martin Galgate	01524 751750
Ynys Marine Cardigan	01239 613179

FOUL-WEATHER GEAR

Aquatogs Cowes	01983 295071
Century Finchampstead	0118 9731616
Crewsaver Gosport	023 9252 8621
Douglas Gill Nottingham	0115 9460844
Gul International Ltd Bodmin	01208 262400
Helly Hansen Nottingham	0115 9608797
Henri Lloyd Manchester	0161 799 1212
Musto Ltd Laindon	01268 491555
Pro Rainer Windsor	07752 903882
Splashdown Leeds	0113 270 7000

GENERAL MARINE EQUIPMENT & SPARES

Ampair Ringwood	01425 480780
Aries Vane Gear Spares Penryn	01326 377467
Arthurs Chandlery, R Gosport	023 9252 6522
Barden UK Ltd Fareham	01489 570770
Calibra Marine International Ltd Southampton	08702 400358
CH Marine (Cork) Cork	+353 21 4315700
Chris Hornsey (Chandlery) Ltd Southsea	023 9273 4728
Compass Marine (Dartmouth) Dartmouth	01803 835915
Cox Yacht Charter Ltd, Nick Lymington	01590 673489
CTC Marine & Leisure Middlesbrough	01642 372600
Docksafe Ltd Bangor	028 9147 0453
Frederiksen Boat Fittings (UK) Ltd Gosport	023 9252 5377
Furneaux Riddall & Co Ltd Portsmouth	023 9266 8621
Hardware & Marine Supplies Co Wexford	+353 (53) 29791
Index Marine Bournemouth	01202 470149
Kearon Ltd, George Arklow	+353 402 32319
Marathon Leisure Hayling Island	023 9263 7711
Pro-Boat Ltd Burnham-on-Crouch	01621 785455

Pump International Ltd Cornwall	01209 831937
Quay West Chandlers Poole	01202 742488
Rogers, Angie Bristol	0117 973 8276
Ryland, Kenneth Stanton	01386 584270
Tiflex Liskeard	01579 320808
Vetus Boating Equipment Southampton	023 8086 1033
Western Marine Power Ltd Plymouth	01752 408804
Whitstable Marine Whitstable	01227 262525
Yacht Parts Plymouth	01752 252489

HARBOUR MASTERS

Aberaeron	01545 571645
Aberdeen	01224 597000
Aberdovey	01654 767626
Aberystwyth	01970 611433
Alderney & Burhou	01481 822620
Amble	01665 710306
Anstruther	01333 310836
Appledore	01237 474569
Arbroath	01241 872166
Ardglass	028 4484 1291
Ardrossan Control Tower	01294 463972
Arinagour Piermaster	01879 230347
Arklow	+353 402 32466
Baltimore	+353 28 22145
Banff	01261 815544
Bantry Bay	+353 27 53277
Barmouth	01341 280671
Barry	01446 732665
Beaucette	01481 245000
Beaulieu River	01590 616200
Belfast Lough	028 90 553012
Belfast River Manager	028 90 328507
Bembridge	01983 872828
Berwick-upon-Tweed	01289 307404
Bideford	01237 346131
Blyth	01670 352678
Boston	01205 362328
Bridlington	01262 670148/9
Bridport	01308 423222
Brighton	01273 819919
Bristol	0117 926 4797
Brixham	01803 853321
Buckie	01542 831700
Bude	01288 353111
Burghead	01343 835337
Burnham-on-Crouch	01621 783602
Burnham-on-Sea	01278 782180
Burtonport	+353 075 42155
Caernarfon	01286 672118
Caernarfon	07786 730865
Camber Berthing Offices – Portsmouth	023 92297395
Campbeltown	01586 552552
Canal Off. (Inverness)	01463 233140
Cardiff	029 20400500
Carnlough Harbour	07703 606763
Castletown Bay	01624 823549

Charlestown	01726 67526
Chichester Harbour	01243 512301
Christchurch	01202 495061
Conwy	01492 596253
Cork	+353 21 4273125
Corpach Canal Sea Lock	01397 772249
Courtmacsherry	+353 23 46311/46600
Coverack	01326 380679
Cowes	01983 293952
Crail	01333 450820
Craobh Haven	01852 502222
Crinan Canal Office	01546 603210
Cromarty Firth	01381 600479
Cromarty Harbour	01381 600493
Crookhaven	+353 28 35319
Cullen	01261 842477
Dingle	+353 66 9151629
Douglas	01624 686628
Dover	01304 240400 Ext 4520
Dublin	+353 1 874871
Dun Laoghaire	+353 1 280 1130/8074
Dunbar	01368 863206
Dundee	01382 224121
Dunmore East	+353 51 383166
East Loch Tarbert	01859 502444
Eastbourne	01323 470099
Eigg Harbour	01687 482428
Elie	01333 330051
Estuary Control - Dumbarton	01389 726211
Exe	01392 274306
Eyemouth	01890 750223
Falmouth	01326 312285
Findochty	01542 831466 / 7900 920445
Fisherrow	0131 665 5900
Fishguard (Lower Hbr)	01348 874726
Fishguard	01348 404425
Fleetwood	01253 879060
Flotta	01856 701411
Folkestone	01303 715354
Fowey	01726 832471/2.
Fraserburgh	01346 515858
Galway Bay	+353 91 561874
Garlieston	01988 600274
Glasson Dock	01524 751724
Gorey	01534 447788
Gourdon	01569 762741
Great Yarmouth	01493 335501
Grimsby Dockmaster	01472 359181
Groomsport Bay	028 91 278040
Hamble River	01489 576387
Hayle	01736 754043
Helford River	01326 250749
Helmsdale	01431 821692
Holy Island	01289 389217
Holyhead	01407 763071
Hopeman	01343 835337
Howth	+353 1 832 2252
Ilfracombe	01271 862108
Inverness	01463 715715
Irvine	01294 487286
Johnshaven	01561 362262
Kettletoft Bay	01857 600227
Killybegs	+353 73 31032
Kilmore Quay	+353 53 912 9955
Kinlochbervie	01971 521235
Kinsale	+353 21 4772503
Kirkcudbright	01557 331135
Kirkwall	01856 872292
Langstone Harbour	023 9246 3419
Larne	02828 872100
Lerwick	01595 692991
Littlehampton	01903 721215
Liverpool	0151 949 6134/5
Loch Gairloch	01445 712140
Loch Inver	01571 844265
Looe	01503 262839 / 07918728955
Lossiemouth	01343 813066
Lough Foyle	028 7186 0555
Lowestoft	01502 572286
Lyme Regis	01297 442137
Lymington	01590 672014
Lyness	01856 791387
Macduff	01261 832236
Maryport	01900 814431
Menai Strait	01248 712312
Methil	01333 462725
Mevagissey	01726 843305
Milford Haven	01646 696100
Minehead	01643 702566
Montrose	01674 672302
Mousehole	01736 731511
Mullion Cove	01326 240222
Nairn	01667 454330
Newhaven	01273 612868
Newlyn	01736 362523
Newquay	01637 872809
Newport Harbour Office	01983 525994
Oban	01631 562892
Padstow	01841 532239
Par	01726 818337
Peel	01624 842338
Penrhyn Bangor	01248 352525
Penzance	01736 366113
Peterhead	01779 483630
Pierowall	01857 677216
Pittenweem	01333 312591
Plockton	01599 534589
Polperro	01503 272809
Poole	01202 440233
Port St Mary	01624 833205
Porth Dinllaen	01758 720276
Porthleven	01326 574207
Porthmadog	01766 512927
Portknockie	01542 840833
Portland	01305 824044
Portpatrick	01776 810355
Portree	01478 612926
Portrush	028 70822307
Portsmouth Harbour Commercial Docks	023 92297395
Portsmouth Harbour Control	023 92723694
Portsmouth Harbour	023 92723124
Preston	01772 726711
Pwllheli	01758 704081
Queenborough	01795 662051
Queens Gareloch/Rhu	01436 674321
Ramsey	01624 812245
Ramsgate	01843 572100
River Bann & Coleraine	028 7034 2012
River Blackwater	01621 856487
River Colne (Brightlingsea)	01206 302200
River Dart	01803 832337
River Deben	01394 270106
River Exe Dockmaster	01392 274306
River Humber	01482 327171
River Medway	01795 596593
River Orwell	01473 231010
River Roach	01621 783602
River Stour	01255 243000
River Tyne/North Shields	0191 257 2080
River Yealm	01752 872533
Rivers Alde & Ore	01473 450481
Rosslare Europort	+353 53 915 7921
Rothesay	01700 503842 / 07799 724225
Ryde	01983 613879
Salcombe	01548 843791
Sark	01481 832323
Scalloway	01595 880574
Scarborough	01723 373530
Scrabster	01847 892779
Seaham	0191 581 3246
Sharpness	01453 811862/64
Shoreham	01273 598100
Silloth	016973 31358
Sligo	+353 71 61197
Southampton	023 8033 9733
Southend-on-Sea	01702 611889
Southwold	01502 724712
St Helier	01534 447788
St Ives	01736 795018
St Margaret's Hope	01856 831454
St Mary's	01720 422768
St Michael's Mount	07870 400282
St Monans	01333 350055
St Peter Port	01481 720229
Stonehaven	01569 762741
Stornoway	01851 702688
Strangford Lough	028 44 881637
Stromness	01856 850744
Stronsay	01857 616317
Sullom Voe	01806 242551
Sunderland	0191 567 2626
Swale	01795 561234
Swansea	01792 653787
Tees & Hartlepool Port Authority	01429 277205
Teignmouth	01626 773165
Tenby	01834 842717
Thames Estuary	01474 562200
Tobermory Port Manager	01688 302017
Torquay	01803 292429
Troon	01292 281687
Truro	01872 272130
Ullapool	01854 612091

Walton-on-the-Naze	01255 851899
Watchet	01984 631264
Waterford	+353 51 874907
Wells-next-the-Sea	01328 711646
Wexford	+353 53 912 2039
Weymouth	01305 206423
Whitby	01947 602354
Whitehaven	01946 692435
Whitehills	01261 861291
Whitstable	01227 274086
Wick	01955 602030
Wicklow	+353 404 67455
Workington	01900 602301
Yarmouth	01983 760321
Youghal	+353 24 92626

For Expert, Helpful & Friendly Independent Marine Insurance Advice Call:
Porthcawl Insurance Consultants Ltd.
Open 7 days, Established 1967
Tel: 01656 784866   Fax: 01656 784872
Email: quotes@porthcawl-insurance.co.uk
or why not log for a quote on our website
www.porthcawl-insurance.co.uk
FSA. Member British Marine Federation
"P.I.C (UK) Ltd is authorised and regulated by the Financial Services Authority"
2009/MG21/v

HARBOURS

Bristol Harbour 0117 922 2000

Clyde Marina – Ardrossan 01294 607077

Jersey Harbours St Helier 01534 885588

Maryport Harbour and Marina Maryport 01900 818447/4431

QUAY MARINAS
A & W Building, The Docks, Portishead, N. Somerset BS20 7DF
Tel: (01275) 841188
Fax: (01275) 841189
e-mail: sriggs@quaymarinas.com
A wholly owned subsidary of Quay Marinas, operate comprehensive yachting facilities at 5 locations in the UK and are marketing agents for Malahide Marina in Dublin Bay. 2009/EXT3/e

PADSTOW HARBOUR COMMISSIONERS
Harbour Office, Padstow, Cornwall PL28 8AQ
Tel: (01841) 532239
Fax: (01841) 533346
e-mail: padstowharbour@btconnect.com
www.padstow-harbour.co.uk
Inner harbour controlled by tidal gate - opens HW±2 hours. Minimum depth 3 metres at all times. Yachtsmen must be friendly as vessels raft together. Services include showers, toilets, diesel, water and ice. Security by CCTV. 2009/Ext1/e

Peterhead Bay Authority Peterhead 01779 474020

Sark Moorings – Channel Islands 01481 832260

INSURANCE/FINANCE

Admiral Marine Ltd Salisbury 01722 416106

Bigfish London 020 8651 4096

Bishop Skinner Boat Insurance London 0800 7838057

Bristol Channel Marine Cardiff 029 2063 1163

Carter Boat Insurance, RA 0800 174061

Castlemain Ltd St Peter Port 01481 721319

Clark Insurance, Graham Tyneside 0191 455 8089

Craftinsure.com Orpington 01689 889507

Craven Hodgson Associates Leeds 0113 243 8443

Giles Insurance Brokers Irvine 01294 315481

GJW Direct Liverpool 0151 473 8000

Haven Knox-Johnston West Malling 01732 223600

Lombard Southampton 023 8024 2171

Mardon Insurance Shrewsbury 0800 515629

Marine & General Insurance Services Ltd Maidstone 01622 201106

Mercia Marine Malvern 01684 564457

Nautical Insurance Services Ltd Leigh-on-Sea 01702 470811

Navigators & General Brighton 01273 863400

Pantaenius UK Ltd Plymouth 01752 223656

Porthcawl Insurance Consultants Porthcawl 01656 784866

Saga Boat Insurance Folkestone 01303 771135

St Margarets Insurances London 020 8778 6161

Weysure Ltd Weymouth 07000 939787

LIFERAFTS & INFLATABLES

A B MARINE LTD
Castle Walk, St Peter Port, Guernsey, Channel Islands GY1 1AU.
Tel: (01481) 722378
Fax: (01481) 711080
We specialise in safety and survival equipment and are a M.C.A. approved service station for liferafts including R.F.D., Beaufort/Dunlop, Zodiac, Avon, Plastimo and Lifeguard. We also carry a full range of new liferafts, dinghies and lifejackets and distress flares. 2009/L1/e

Adec Marine Ltd Croydon 020 8686 9717

Avon Inflatables Llanelli 01554 882000

Cosalt International Ltd Aberdeen 01224 588327

Glaslyn Marine Supplies Ltd Porthmadog 01766 513545

Hale Marine, Ron Portsmouth 023 9273 2985

Herm Seaway Marine Ltd St Peter Port 01481 722838

IBS Boats South Woodham Ferrers 01245 323211/425551

KTS Seasafety Kilkeel 028 918 28405

Nationwide Marine Hire Warrington 01925 245788

Norwest Marine Ltd Liverpool 0151 207 2860

Ocean Safety Southampton 023 8072 0800

Polymarine Ltd Conwy 01492 583322

Premium Liferaft Services Burnham-on-Crouch 0800 243673

Ribeye Dartmouth 01803 832060

Secumar Swansea 01792 280545

South Eastern Marine Services Ltd Basildon 01268 534427

Suffolk Sailing Ipswich 01473 833010

Whitstable Marine Whitstable 01227 262525

MARINAS

Aberystwyth Marina	01970 611422
Amble Marina	01665 712168
Arbroath Harbour	01241 872166
Ardfern Yacht Centre Ltd	01852 500247
Ardglass Marina	028 44842332
Arklow Marina	+353 402 39901
Ballycastle Marina	028 2076 8525
Bangor Marina	028 91 453297
Beaucette Marina	01481 245000
Bembridge Harbour	01983 872828
Berthon Lymington Marina	01590 647405
Birdham Pool Marina	01243 512310
Blackwater Marina	01621 740264
Boston Marina	01205 364420
Bradwell Marina	01621 776235
Bray Marina	01628 623654
Brentford Dock Marina	020 8232 8941
Bridgemarsh Marine	01621 740414
Brighton Marina	01273 819919
Bristol Marina	0117 9213198

Brixham Marina	01803 882929
Bucklers Hard Marina	01590 616200
Burnham Yacht Harbour Marina Ltd	
	01621 782150
Cahersiveen Marina	
	+353 66 947 2777
Caley Marina	01463 236539
Carlingford Marina	+353 42 9373073
Carrickfergus Marina	028 9336 6666
Castlepark Marina	+353 21 477 4959
Chatham Maritime Marina	
	01634 899200
Chelsea Harbour Marina	
	020 7225 9157
Chichester Marina	01243 512731
Clyde Marina Ltd	01294 607077
Cobbs Quay Marina	01202 674299
Coleraine Marina	028 703 44768
Conwy Marina	01492 593000
Cowes Yacht Haven	01983 299975
Craobh Marina	01852 500222
Crosshaven Boatyard Marina	
	+353 21 483 1161
Dart Marina Yacht Harbour	
	01803 833351
Darthaven Marina	01803 752545
Dartside Quay	01803 845445
Deganwy Quay	01492 583984
Dingle Marina	+353 66 915 1629
Dover Marina	01304 241663
Dublin City Marina	
Dun Laoghaire Marina	
	+353 1 202 0040
Dunstaffnage Marina Ltd	
	01631 566555
East Cowes Marina	01983 293983
East Ferry Marina	+353 21 483 1342
Emsworth Yacht Harbour	
	01243 377727
Essex Marina	01702 258531
Falmouth Marina	01326 316620
Falmouth Visitors Yacht Haven	
	01326 310991
Fambridge Yacht Haven	
	01621 740370
Fenit Harbour Marina	
	+353 66 7136231
Fleetwood Harbour Village	
	01253 879062
Fox's Marina Ipswich Ltd	
	01473 689111
Gallions Point Marina	0207 476 7054
Gillingham Marina	01634 280022
Glasson Dock Marina	01524 751491
Gosport Marina	023 9252 4811
Gunwharf Quays	02392 836732
Hafan Pwllheli	01758 701219
Hamble Point Marina	023 8045 2464
Harbour of Rye	01797 225225
Hartlepool Marina	01429 865744
Haslar Marina	023 9260 1201
Heybridge Basin	01621 853506
Hillyards	01903 713327
Holy Loch Marina	01369 701800

Holyhead Marina	01407 764242
Hoo Marina	01634 250311
Howth Marina	+353 1839 2777
Hull Marina	01482 609960
Hythe Marina	023 8020 7073
Inverness Marina	07526 446348
Ipswich Haven Marina	01473 236644
Island Harbour Marina	01983 822999
Kemps Quay Marina	023 8063 2323
Kilmore Quay Marina	
	+353 5391 29955
Kilrush Creek Marina	
	+353 65 9052072
Kinsale Yacht Club Marina	
	+353 21 477 2196
Kip Marina	01475 521485
Kirkwall Marina	07810 465835
La Collette Yacht Basin	01534 885588
Lady Bee Marina	01273 593801
Lake Yard Marina	01202 674531
Largs Yacht Haven	01475 675333
Lawrence Cove Marina	
	+353 27 75044
Limehouse Marina	020 7308 9930
Littlehampton Marina	01903 713553
Liverpool Marina	0151 707 6777
Lossiemouth Marina	01343 813066
Lowestoft Haven Marina	
	01502 580300
Lymington Yacht Haven	01590 677071
Malahide Marina	+353 1 845 4129
Maryport Harbour and Marina	
	01900 814431
Mayflower International Marina	
	01752 556633
Melfort Pier & Harbour	01852 200333
Mercury Yacht Harbour	
	023 8045 5994
Meridian Quay Marina	01472 268424
Milford Marina	01646 696312
Multihull Centre	01752 823900
Mylor Yacht Harbour	01326 372121
Nairn Marina	01667 456008
Neptune Marina Ltd	01473 215204
Newhaven Marina	01273 513881
Neyland Yacht Haven	01646 601601
Northney Marina	023 9246 6321
Noss Marina	01803 839087

Ocean Village Marina	023 8022 9385
Parkstone Yacht Club Haven	
	01202 743610
Penarth Quays Marina	02920 705021
Penton Hook	01932 568681
Peterhead Bay Marina	01779 477868
Plymouth Yacht Haven	01752 404231
Poole Quay Boat Haven	
	01202 649488
Poplar Dock Marina	0207 308 9930
Port Edgar Marina & Sailing School	
	0131 331 3330
Port Ellen Marina	01496 300301
Port Falmouth Marina	01326 212100
Port Hamble Marina	023 8045 2741
Port Pendennis Marina	01326 211211
Port Solent Marina	02392 210765
Portaferry Marina	028 4272 9598
Portavadie Marina	01700 811075
Portishead Quays Marina	
	01275 841941
Portland Marina	08454 30 2012
Preston Marina	01772 733595
Queen Anne's Battery Marina	
	01752 671142
Rhu Marina Ltd	01436 820238
Ridge Wharf Yacht Centre	
	01929 552650
Royal Cork Yacht Club Marina	
	+353 21 483 1023
Royal Harbour Marina, Ramsgate	
	01843 572100
Royal Harwich Yacht Club Marina	
	01473 780319
Royal Norfolk and Suffolk Yacht Club	
	01502 566726
Royal Northumberland Yacht Club	
	01670 353636
Royal Quays Marina	0191 272 8282
Ryde Leisure Harbour	01983 613879
Salterns Marina Boatyard & Hotel	
	01202 709971
Salve Engineering Marina	
	+353 21 483 1145

QUAY
M·A·R·I·N·A·S

HEAD OFFICE:
A & W Building
The Docks
Portishead
N. Somerset
BS20 7DF
Tel: 01275 841188

PLOT A COURSE FOR.........
QUAY MARINAS

With their unique blend of superb yachting facilites Quay Marinas are internationally recognised as among the finest anywhere. All marinas offer a friendly welcome to yachtsmen and cater for every boating requirement.

BANGOR MARINA ....*Belfast Lough Tel: 02891 453297*
CONWY QUAYS MARINA ....*North Wales Tel: 01492 593000*
DEGANWY QUAYS MARINA ....*North Wales Tel: 01492 576888*
PENARTH QUAYS MARINA ....*Cardiff Bay Tel: 02920 705021*
PORTISHEAD QUAYS MARINA ....*Bristol Channel Tel: 02920 705021*
ROYAL QUAYS MARINA ....*North Shields Tel: 0191 272828*
RHU MARINA ....*Clyde Estuary Tel: 01436 820238*

2009/mg17/v

The NEW Portland Marina Open from April 2009 to berth holders and all visiting yachts

DEAN & REDDYHOFF
M A R I N A S

Premium quality berthing, accessed at all states of tide, excellent washroom facilities, value for money and unsurpassed customer service…

… the hallmark of all Dean & Reddyhoff Marinas.

Portland Marina
Brand new for 2009, a world class marina for a world class sailing destination!
Annual berths from just £410 per metre including VAT
Tel: 08454 30 2012

Weymouth Marina
Ideal stop off whilst cruising the South Coast.
Annual berths £407 per metre including VAT
Tel: 01305 767576

Haslar Marina
Only minutes from open water in the Solent.
Annual berths £445 per metre including VAT
Tel: 023 9260 1201

East Cowes Marina
Sheltered pontoon berths with all the Isle of Wight has to offer.
Annual berths £365 per metre including VAT
Tel: 01983 293983

www.deanreddyhoff.co.uk

2009/MG6/e

Sandpoint Marina (Dumbarton)	01389 762396
Saxon Wharf Marina	023 8033 9490
Seaport Marina	01463 725500
Seaton's Marina	028 703 832086
Shamrock Quay Marina	023 8022 9461
Sharpness Marine	01453 811476
Shepherds Wharf Boatyard Ltd	01983 297821
Shotley Marina	01473 788982
South Dock Marina	020 7252 2244
South Ferriby Marina	01652 635620
Southdown Marina	01752 823084
Southsea Marina	023 9282 2719
Sovereign Harbour Marina	01323 470099
Sparkes Marina	023 92463572
St Helier Marina	01534 447730
St Katharine Marina Ltd	0207 264 5312
St Peter Port Marinas	01481 720229
St Peter's Marina	0191 265 4472

Stromness Marina	07810 465825
Suffolk Yacht Harbour Ltd	01473 659240
Sunderland Marina	0191 514 4721
Sutton Harbour	01752 204702
Swansea Marina	01792 470310
Swanwick Marina	01489 884081
Titchmarsh Marina	01255 672185
Tollesbury Marina	01621 869202
Torpoint Yacht Harbour	01752 813658
Torquay Marina	01803 200210
Troon Yacht Haven	01292 315553
Victoria Marina	01481 725987
Walton Yacht Basin	01255 675873
Waterford City Marina	+353 51 309900
Weymouth Harbour	01305 838423
Weymouth Marina	01305 767576
Whitby Marina	01947 600165
Whitehaven Harbour Marina	01946 692435
Whitehills Marina	01261 861291
Windsor Marina	01753 853911

Wisbech Yacht Harbour	01945 588059
Woolverstone Marina	01473 780206
Yarmouth Harbour	01983 760321

MARINE CONSULTANTS AND SURVEYORS

Amble Boat Company Ltd Amble	01665 710267
Ark Surveys East Anglia/South Coast	01621 857065/01794 521957
Atkin and Associates Lymington	01590 688633
Barbican Yacht Agency Ltd Plymouth	01752 228855
Booth Marine Surveys, Graham Birchington-on-Sea	01843 843793
Bureau Maritime Ltd Maldon	01621 859181
Byrde & Associates Kimmeridge	01929 480064
Cannell & Associates, David M Wivenhoe	01206 823337
Clarke Designs LLP, Owen Dartmouth	01803 770495
Davies, Peter Wivenhoe	01206 823289
Down Marine Co Ltd Belfast	028 90480247
Green, James Plymouth	01752 660516
Greening Yacht Design Ltd, David Chichester	023 9263 1806
Hansing & Associates North Wales/Midlands	01248 671291
JP Services – Marine Safety & Training Chichester	01243 537552
Marintec Lymington	01590 683414
Norwood Marine Margate	01843 835711
Quay Consultants Ltd West Wittering	01243 673056
Scott Marine Surveyors & Consultants Conwy	01248 680759
Staton-Bevan, Tony Lymington	01590 645755
Swanwick Yacht Surveyors Southampton	01489 564822
Thomas, Stephen Southampton	023 8048 6273
Victoria Yacht Surveys Cornwall	0800 093 2113
Ward & McKenzie Woodbridge	01394 383222
Ward & McKenzie (North East) Pocklington	01759 304322
Yacht Designers & Surveyors Association Bordon	0845 0900 162

MARINE ENGINEERS

Allerton Engineering Lowestoft	01502 537870
APAS Engineering Ltd Southampton	023 8063 2558
Ardmair Boat Centre Ullapool	01854 612054

Arisaig Marine
Inverness-shire   01687 450224

Arun Craft Littlehampton 01903 723667

Attrill & Sons, H
Bembridge   01983 872319

Auto & Marine Services
Botley   01489 785009

Auto Marine Southsea   023 9282 5601

BJ Marine Ltd Bangor   028 9127 1434

Bristol Boat Ltd Bristol   01225 872032

Buzzard Marine Engineering
Yarmouth   01983 760707

C & B Marine Ltd
Chichester Marina   01243 511273

Caddy, Simon Falmouth Marina,
Falmouth   01326 372682

Caledonian Marine
Rhu Marina   01436 821184

Cardigan Outboards
Cardigan   01239 613966

Channel Islands Marine Ltd
Guernsey   01481 716880

Channel Islands Marine Ltd
Jersey   01534 767595

Clarence Marine Engineering
Gosport   023 9251 1555

Cook's Diesel Service Ltd
Faversham   01795 538553

Cragie Engineering
Kirkwall   01856 874680

Wartsila
Havant   023 9240 0121

Crinan Boatyard Ltd
Crinan   01546 830232

Cutler Marine Engineering, John
Emsworth   01243 375014

Dale Sailing Co Ltd
Milford Haven   01646 603110

Davis Marine Services
Ramsgate   01843 586172

Denney & Son, EL
Redcar   01642 483507

DH Marine (Shetland) Ltd
Shetland   01595 690618

Emark Marine Ltd
Emsworth   01243 375383

Evans Marine Engineering, Tony
Pwllheli   01758 703070

Fairways Marine Engineers
Maldon   01376 572866

Felton Marine Engineering
Brighton   01273 601779

Felton Marine Engineering
Eastbourne   01323 470211

Ferrypoint Boat Co
Youghal   +353 24 94232

Fettes & Rankine Engineering
Aberdeen   01224 573343

Fleetwood & Sons Ltd, Henry
Lossiemouth   01343 813015

Fleming Engineering, J
Stornoway   01851 703488

Floetree Ltd (Loch Lomond Marina)
Balloch   01389 752069

Fowey Harbour Marine Engineers
Fowey   01726 832806

Fox Marine Services Ltd
Jersey   01534 721312

Freeport Marine Jersey 01534 888100

French Marine Motors Ltd
Colchester   01206 302133

GH Douglas Marine Services
Fleetwood Harbour Village Marina,
Fleetwood   01253 877200

Golden Arrow Marine
Southampton   023 8071 0371

Goodchild Marine Services
Great Yarmouth   01493 782301

Goodwick Marine
Fishguard   01348 873955

Gosport Boat Yard
Gosport   023 9252 4811

Griffins Garage Dingle Marina,
Co Kerry   +353 66 91 51178

Hale Marine, Ron
Portsmouth   023 9273 2985

Hamnavoe Engineering
Stromness   01856 850576

Hampshire Marine Ltd
Stubbington   01329 665561

Harbour Engineering
Itchenor   01243 513454

Hardway Marine Store
Gosport   023 9258 0420

Hartlepool Marine Engineering
Hartlepool   01429 867883

Hayles, Harold
Yarmouth   01983 760373

Herm Seaway Marine Ltd
St Peter Port   01481 726829

HNP Engineers (Lerwick Ltd)
Lerwick   01595 692493

Home Marine Emsworth Yacht Harbour,
Emsworth   01243 374125

Hook Marine Ltd
Troon   01292 679500

Humphrey, Chris
Teignmouth   01626 772324

Instow Marine Services
Bideford   01271 861081

Jones (Boatbuilders), David
Chester   01244 390363

Keating Marine Engineering Ltd, Bill
Jersey   01534 733977

Kingston Marine Services
Cowes   01983 299385

Kippford Slipway Ltd
Dalbeattie   01556 620249

Lansdale Pannell Marine
Chichester   01243 512374

Lencraft Boats Ltd
Dungarvan   +353 58 68220

Lifeline Marine Services
Dolphin Haven, Poole   01202 669676

Llyn Marine Services
Pwllheli   01758 612606

Lynx Engineering
St Helens, Isle of Wight   01983 873711

M&G Marine Services
Mayflower International Marina, Plymouth
                               01752 563345

MacDonald & Co Ltd, JN
Glasgow   0141 334 6171

Mackay Marine Services
Aberdeen   01224 575772

Mainbrayce Marine
Alderney   01481 722772

Malakoff and Moore
Lerwick   01595 695544

**Mallaig Boat Building and
Engineering** Mallaig   01687 462304

Marindus Engineering
Kilmore Quay   +353 53 29794

Marine Engineering Looe
Brixham   01803 844777

Marine Engineering Looe
Looe   01503 263009

Marine General Engineers Beaucette
Marina, Guernsey   01481 245808

Marine Maintenance
Portsmouth   023 9260 2344

Marine Maintenance
Tollesbury   01621 860441

Marine Propulsion
Hayling Island   023 9246 1694

Marine & General Engineers
St. Sampsons Harbour, Guernsey
                               01481 245808

Marine-Trak Engineering Mylor Yacht
Harbour, Falmouth   01326 376588

Marlec Marine
Ramsgate   01843 592176

Martin (Marine) Ltd, Alec
Birkenhead   0151 652 1663

Medusa Marine Ipswich 01473 780090

Mobile Marine Engineering Liverpool
Marina, Liverpool   01565 733553

Motortech Marine Engineering
Portsmouth   023 9251 3200

Mount's Bay Engineering
Newlyn   01736 363095

MP Marine Maryport   01900 810299

New World Yacht Care
Helensburgh   01436 820586

North Western Automarine Engineers
Largs   01475 687139

Noss Marine Services
Dart Marina, Dartmouth   01803 833343

Owen Marine, Robert
Porthmadog   01766 513435

Pace, Andy Newhaven 01273 516010

**Penzance Dry Dock and Engineering
Co Ltd** Penzance   01736 363838

Pirie & Co, John S
Fraserburgh 01346 513314

Portavon Marine
Keynsham 0117 986 1626

Power Afloat, Elkins Boatyard
Christchurch 01202 489555

Powerplus Marine Cowes Yacht Haven,
Cowes 01983 200036

Pro-Marine Queen Anne's Battery
Marina, Plymouth 01752 267984

PT Marine Engineering
Hayling Island 023 9246 9332

QUAY MARINAS
A & W Building, The Docks,
Portishead, N. Somerset
BS20 7DF
Tel: (01275) 841188
Fax: (01275) 841189
e-mail: sriggs@quaymarinas.com
A wholly owned subsidary of Quay
Marinas, operate comprehensive yachting
facilities at 5 locations in the UK and are
marketing agents for Malahide Marina in
Dublin Bay. 2009/EXT3/e

R & M Marine
Portsmouth 023 9273 7555

R & S Engineering Dingle Marina,
Ireland +353 66 915 1189

Reddish Marine
Salcombe 01548 844094

Reynolds, Cliff
Hartlepool 01429 272049

RHP Marine
Cowes 01983 290421

River Tees Engineering & Welding Ltd
Middlesbrough 01642 226226

RK Marine Ltd Hamble 01489 583585

RK Marine Ltd
Swanwick 01489 583572

Rossiter Yachts Ltd
Christchurch 01202 483250

Ryan & Roberts Marine Services
Askeaton +353 61 392198

Salve Marine Ltd
Crosshaven +353 21 4831145

Seaguard Marine Engineering Ltd
Goodwick 01348 872976

Seamark-Nunn & Co
Felixstowe 01394 275327

Seaward Engineering
Glasgow 0141 632 4910

Seaway Marine
Gosport 023 9260 2722

Shearwater Engineering Services Ltd
Dunoon 01369 706666

Silvers Marina Ltd
Helensburgh 01436 831222

Starey Marine
Salcombe 01548 843655

Strickland Marine Engineering, Brian
Chichester 01243 513454

Tarbert Marine Arbroath 01241 872879

Tollesbury Marine Engineering
Tollesbury Marina,
Tollesbury 01621 869919

Troon Marine Services Ltd
Troon 01292 316180

Vasey Marine Engineering, Gordon
Fareham 07798 638625

Volspec Ltd Ipswich Marina,
Ipswich 01473 219651

Wallis, Peter Torquay Marina,
Torquay 01803 844777

WB Marine Chichester 01243 512857

West, Mick Brighton 01273 626656

West Point Marine Services
Fareham 01329 232881

Western Marine Power Ltd
Plymouth 01752 408804

Weymouth Marina Mechanical
Services Weymouth 01305 779379

Whittington, G Lady Bee Marine,
Shoreham 01273 593801

Whitewater Marine
Malahide +353 1 816 8473

Wigmore Wright Marine Services
Penarth Marina 029 2070 9983

Wright, M Manaccan 01326 231502

Wyko Industrial Services
Inverness 01463 224747

Yates Marine, Martin
Galgate 01524 751750

Ynys Marine
Cardigan 01239 613179

Yoldings Marine
Eastbourne 01323 470882

Youngboats
Faversham 01795 536176

1° West Marine Ltd
Portsmouth 023 9283 8335

MASTS, SPARS & RIGGING

1° Degree West Ltd
Portsmouth 02392 200670

A2 Rigging
Falmouth 01326 312209

Allspars Plymouth 01752 266766

Amble Boat Co Ltd
Morpeth 01665 710267

ATLANTIC SPARS LTD
Brixham 01803 843322
2008/M&WL13/e

Arun Canvas & Rigging
Littlehampton 1903 732561

Buchanan, Keith
St Mary's 01720 422037

Bussell & Co, WL
Weymouth 01305 785633

Carbospars Ltd Hamble 023 8045 6736

Cable & Rope Works
Pevensey 01323 763019

Coates Marine Ltd
Whitby 01947 604486

Composite Rigging
Southampton 023 8023 4488

Dauntless Boatyard Ltd
Canvey Island 01268 793782

Davies Marine Services
Ramsgate 01843 586172

Eurospars Ltd Plymouth 01752 550550

Exe Leisure Exeter 01392 879055

Fox's Marine Ipswich Ltd
Ipswich 01473 689111

Freeland Yacht Spars Ltd
Dorchester on Thames 01865 341277

Gordon, AD Portland 01305 821569

Harris Rigging Totnes 01803 840160

Heyn Engineering
Belfast 028 9035 0022

Holman Rigging
Chichester 01243 514000

Irish Spars and Rigging
Malahide +353 86 209 5996

Lowestoft Yacht Services
Lowestoft 01502 585535

Marine Resource Centre
Oban 01631 720291

Martin Leaning Masts & Rigging
Hayling 023 9237 1157

Mast & Rigging Services
Largs 01475 670110

Mast & Rigging Services
Largs 01475 670110

MP Marine Maryport 01900 810299

FRENCH MARINE MOTORS
4 Branches on the East Coast
Brightlingsea (Head Office)
61 - 63 Waterside, Brightlingsea, Essex, CO7 0AX
Tel: 01206 302133 / 01206 305233 Fax: 01206 305601
Email: info@frenchmarine.com
Walton-on-the-Naze (Essex)
Titchmarsh Marina, Coles Lane, Walton-on-the-naze, Essex, CO14 8SL
Tel/Fax: 01255 850303
Email: walton@frenchmarine.com
Levington (Suffolk)
Suffolk Yacht Harbour (Stratton Hall), Levington, Ipswich, Suffolk, IP10 0LN
Tel/Fax: 01473 659882
Email: suffolk@frenchmarine.com
Rackheath (Norfolk)
Unit 19, Wendover Road, Rackheath, Norfolk, NR13 6LR
Tel: 01603 722079 Fax: 01603 721311
Email: norfolk@frenchmarine.com

Specialists in:
• Marine engine repair
• Marine engine maintenance
• Prop shaft fabrication
• Stern gear fabrication
• Propeller repair - Fast turn around
• Engine Spares - all manufacturers supported
• Full Marine Chandlery
Suppliers of:
New and Second-hand engines and gearboxes,
marine installation equipment, propellers, stern tubes,
seacocks, exhaust hose, mufflers and fuel systems
Full range of chandlery stocked, ropes, paints, etc.
www.frenchmarine.com
2009/MG53/e

YANMAR · VOLVO PENTA · VETUS · MERCURY · YAMAHA · Perkins

MARINE SUPPLIES AND SERVICES GUIDE
MARINE ENGINEERS – MASTS, SPARS & RIGGING

Ocean Rigging Lymington	01590 676292
Owen Sails Oban	01631 720485
Premier Spars Poole	01202 677717
Pro Rig S Ireland	+353 87 298 3333
Rig Magic Ipswich	01473 655089
Rig Shop Southampton	023 8033 8341
Roberts Marine Ltd, S Liverpool	0151 707 8300
Sailspar Ltd Brightlingsea	01206 302679
Salcombe Boatstore Salcombe	01548 843708
Seldén Mast Ltd Southampton	01489 484000
Silvers Marina Ltd Helensburgh	01436 831222
Silverwood Yacht Services Ltd Portsmouth	023 9232 7067
Southern Spar Services Northam	023 8033 1714
Southern Masts & Rigging Brighton	01273 668902
Storrar Marine Store Newcastle upon Tyne	0191 266 1037
Tedfords Rigging & Rafts Belfast	028 9032 6763
TJ Rigging Conwy	07780 972411
TS Rigging Malden	01621 874861
Windjammer Marine Milford Marina	01646 699070
Yacht Rigging Services Plymouth	01752 226609
Yacht Shop, The Fleetwood	01253 879238
Yacht Solutions Ltd Portsmouth	023 9220 0670
XW Rigging Gosport	023 9251 3553
Z Spars UK Hadleigh	01473 822130
1° West Marine Ltd Portsmouth	023 9283 8335

NAVIGATION EQUIPMENT – GENERAL

Belson Design Ltd, Nick Southampton	077 6835 1330
B & G UK Romsey	01794 510010
Brown Son & Ferguson Ltd Glasgow	0141 429 1234
Cooke & Son Ltd, B Hull	01482 223454
Diverse Yacht Services Hamble	023 8045 3399
Dolphin Maritime Software Ltd Lancaster	01524 841946
Dubois Phillips & McCallum Ltd Liverpool	0151 236 2776
Eland Exeter	01392 255788
Garmin Romsey	01794 519944
Geonav UK Ltd Poole	0870 240 4575
Imray Laurie Norie and Wilson Ltd St Ives, Cambs	01480 462114
Kelvin Hughes Southampton	023 8063 4911
Lilley & Gillie Ltd, John North Shields	0191 257 2217

Marine Chart Services Wellingborough	01933 441629
PC Maritime Plymouth	01752 254205
Navimo UK Hedge End	01489 778850
Precision Navigation Romsey	01794 521079
Price & Co, WF Bristol	0117 929 2229
Raymarine Ltd Portsmouth	023 9269 3611
Robbins Marine Electronics Liverpool	0151 709 5431
Royal Institute of Navigation London	020 7591 3130
Sea Chest Nautical Bookshop Plymouth	01752 222012
Seath Instruments (1992) Ltd Lowestoft	01502 573811
Smith (Marine) Ltd, AM London	020 8529 6988
South Bank Marine Charts Ltd Grimsby	01472 361137
Southcoasting Navigators Devon	01626 335626
Stanford Charts Bristol	0117 929 9966
London	020 7836 1321
Manchester	0870 890 3730
Todd Chart Agency Ltd County Down	028 9146 6640
UK Hydrographic Office Taunton	01823 337900
Warsash Nautical Bookshop Warsash	01489 572384
Yachting Instruments Ltd Sturminster Newton	01258 817662

PAINT & OSMOSIS

Advanced Blast Cleaning Paint Tavistock	01822 617192/07970 407911
Blakes Paints Southampton	01489 864440
Herm Seaway Marine Ltd St Peter Port	01481 726829
Gillingham Marina	01634 280022
International Coatings Ltd Southampton	023 8022 6722
Marineware Ltd Southampton	023 8033 0208
NLB Marine Ardrossan	01563 521509
Pro-Boat Ltd Burnham on Crouch	01621 785455
Rustbuster Ltd Peterborough	0870 9090093
Smith & Son Ltd, EC Luton	01582 729721
SP Systems Isle of Wight	01983 828000
Teal & Mackrill Ltd Hull	01482 320194
Troon Marine Services Ltd Troon	01292 316180

PROPELLERS & STERNGEAR/REPAIRS

CJR Propulsion Ltd Southampton	023 8063 9366

Darglow Engineering Ltd Wareham	01929 556512
Gori Propellers Poole	01202 621631
Propeller Revolutions Poole	01202 671226
Sillette – Sonic Ltd Sutton	020 8337 7543
Vetus Den Ouden Ltd Southampton	023 8086 1033

RADIO COURSES / SCHOOLS

Bisham Abbey Sailing & Navigation School Bisham	01628 474960
East Coast Offshore Yachting – Les Rant Perry	01480 861381
Hamble School of Yachting Hamble	023 8045 6687
Pembrokeshire Cruising Neyland	01646 602500
Plymouth Sailing School Plymouth	01752 493377
Southern Sailing Swanwick	01489 575511
Start Point Sailing Kingsbridge	01548 810917

REEFING SYSTEMS

Atlantic Spars Ltd Brixham	01803 843322
Calibra Marine International Ltd Southampton	08702 400358
Eurospars Ltd Plymouth	01752 550550
Holman Rigging Chichester	01243 514000
Navimo UK Ltd Hedge End	01489 778850
Sea Teach Ltd Emsworth	01243 375774
Southern Spar Services Northam	023 8033 1714
Wragg, Chris Lymington	01590 677052
Z Spars UK Hadleigh	01473 822130

REPAIR MATERIALS AND ACCESSORIES

Akeron Ltd Southend on Sea	01702 297101
Howells & Son, KJ Poole	01202 665724
JB Timber Ltd North Ferriby	01482 631765
Robbins Timber Bristol	0117 9633136
Sika Ltd Welwyn Garden City	01707 394444
SP Systems Newport, Isle of Wight	01983 828000
Technix Rubber & Plastics Ltd Southampton	01489 789944
Tiflex Liskeard	01579 320808
Timage & Co Ltd Braintree	01376 343087
Trade Grade Products Ltd Poole	01202 820177
Wessex Resins & Adhesives Ltd Romsey	01794 521111

ROPE AND WIRE

Cable & Rope Works
Pevensey   01323 763019

Euro Rope Ltd
Scunthorpe   01724 280480

Marlow Ropes Hailsham 01323 444444

Mr Splice Leicester   0800 1697178

Spinlock Ltd Cowes   01983 295555

TJ Rigging Conwy   07780 972411

SAFETY EQUIPMENT

AB Marine Ltd
St Peter Port   01481 722378

Adec Marine Ltd
Croydon   020 8686 9717

Anchorwatch UK
Edinburgh 0131 447 5057

Avon Inflatables
Llanelli   01554 882000

Cosalt International Ltd
Aberdeen   01224 588327

Crewsaver Gosport   023 9252 8621

Glaslyn Marine Supplies Ltd
Porthmadog   01766 513545

Guardian Fire Ltd
Norwich   01603 787679

Hale Marine, Ron
Portsmouth   023 9273 2985

Herm Seaway Marine Ltd
St Peter Port   01481 722838

IBS Boats South Woodham Ferrers
                  01245 323211/425551

KTS Seasafety Kilkeel   028 41762655

McMurdo Pains Wessex
Portsmouth   023 9262 3900

Met Office Bracknell   0845 300 0300

Nationwide Marine Hire
Warrington   01925 245788

Norwest Marine Ltd
Liverpool   0151 207 2860

Ocean Safety So'ton   023 8072 0800

Navimo UK Ltd
Hedge End   01489 778850

RESTAURANTS/PUBS

the old forge
mainland britain's
remotest pub

real ales
famous prawn platters
open fire
folk music
hot showers
yummy seafood & game
fresh lattes & espressos

01687 462267

impromptu ceilidhs
bring your own instruments
            or use ours
yachties, trampers, dogs,
kids, musicians, anarchists
& politicians
welcome

inverie
knoydart
by mallaig

PH41 4PL

VHF ch.12
9 moorings
for hangers on
57deg.02'N
05deg.41'W

diesel driven email
www.theoldforge.co.uk
info@theoldforge.co.uk

2009/MD9/e

ADEC MARINE

Approved liferaft service station for South East.
Buy or hire new rafts. Complete range of safety
equipment for yachts including pyrotechnics.
Fire extinguishers – Lifejackets – Buoyancy aids

**4 Masons Avenue, Croydon,
Surrey CR0 9XS**
Tel: 020 8686 9717
Fax: 020 8680 9912
E-mail: sales@adecmarine.co.uk
Website: www.adecmarine.co.uk

Polymarine Ltd Conwy   01492 583322

Premium Liferaft Services
Burnham-on-Crouch   0800 243673

Ribeye Dartmouth   01803 832060

Secumar Swansea   01792 280545

South Eastern Marine Services Ltd
Basildon   01268 534427

Suffolk Sailing
Ipswich   01473 833010

Whitstable Marine
Whitstable   01227 262525

Winters Marine Ltd
Salcombe   01548 843580

SAILMAKERS & REPAIRS

Allison-Gray Dundee   01382 505888

Alsop Sailmakers, John
Salcombe   01548 843702

Arun Canvas & Rigging
Littlehampton   01903 732561

Arun Sails Chichester 01243 573185

Bank Sails, Bruce
Southampton   01489 582444

Barford Sails Weymouth 01305 768282

Batt Sails Bosham   01243 575505

Bissett and Ross
Aberdeen   01224 580659

Breaksea Sails Barry   01446 730785

Bristol Sails Bristol 0117 922 5080

Buchanan, Keith
St Mary's   01720 422037

C&J Marine Textiles
Chichester   01243 782629

Calibra Sails Dartmouth 01803 833094

Canard Sails Swansea   01792 367838

Coastal Covers
Portsmouth   023 9252 0200

Covercare Fareham   01329 311878

Crawford, Margaret
Kirkwall   01856 875692

Crusader Sails Poole   01202 670580

Cullen Sailmakers
Galway   +353 91 771991

Dawson (Sails), J
Port Dinorwic   01248 670103

Dolphin Sails Harwich 01255 243366

Doyle Sails Southampton 023 8033 2622

Downer International Sails & Chandlery
Dun Laoghaire   +353 1 280 0231
Duthie Marine Safety, Arthur
Glasgow   0141 429 4553
Dynamic Sails
Emsworth   01243 374495
East Coast Sails
Walton-on-the-Naze   01255 678353
Flew Sailmakers
Portchester   01329 822676
Fylde Coast Sailmaking Co
Fleetwood   01253 873476
Garland Sails Bristol   0117 935 3233
Goldfinch Sails
Whitstable   01227 272295
Gowen Ocean Sailmakers
West Mersea   01206 384412
Green Sailmakers, Paul
Plymouth   01752 660317
Henderson Sails & Covers
Southsea   023 9229 4700
Hood Sailmakers
Lymington   01590 675011
Hooper, A Plymouth   01752 830411
Hyde Sails Southampton 01489 563420
Jackson Yacht Services
Jersey   01534 743819
Jeckells and Son Ltd (Wroxham)
Wroxham   01603 782223
Jessail Ardrossan   01294 467311
JKA Sailmakers
Pwllheli   01758 613266
Kemp Sails Ltd
Wareham   01929 554308/554378
Lawrence Sailmakers, J
Brightlingsea   01206 302863
Leitch, WM Tarbert   01880 820287
Leith UK
Berwick on Tweed   01289 307264
Lodey Sails Newlyn   01736 719359
Lossie Sails
Lossiemouth   07989 956698
Lucas Sails Portchester 023 9237 3699
Malakoff and Moore
Lerwick   01595 695544
Malcolm Sails Fairlie   01475 568500
McCready and Co Ltd, J
Belfast   028 90232842
McKillop Sails, John
Kingsbridge   01548 852343
McKillop Sails (Sail Locker)
Ipswich   01255 678353
McNamara Sails, Michael
Great Yarmouth   01692 584186
McWilliam Sailmaker (Crosshaven)
Crosshaven   +353 21 4831505
Mitchell Sails Fowey   01726 833731
Montrose Rope and Sails
Montrose   01674 672657
Mountfield Sails
Hayling Island   023 9246 3720
Mouse Sails Holyhead   01407 763636
Nicholson Hughes Sails
Rosneath   01436 831356
North Sea Sails
Tollesbury   01621 869367

North West Sails
Keighley   01535 652949
Northrop Sails
Ramsgate   01843 851665
Ösen Sails Ltd
Plymouth   01752 563666
Owen Sails (Gourock)
Gourock   01475 636196
Owen Sails By Oban   01631 720485
Parker & Kay Sailmakers –
East Ipswich   01473 659878
Parker & Kay Sailmakers –
South Hamble   023 8045 8213
Penrose Sailmakers
Falmouth   01326 312705
Pinnell & Bax
Northampton   01604 592808
Pollard Marine
Port St Mary   01624 835831
Quantum Sails
Ipswich Haven Marina   01473 659878
Quantum-Parker & Kay Sailmakers
Hamble   023 8045 8213
Quay Sails (Poole) Ltd
Poole   01202 681128
Ratsey & Lapthorn
Isle of Wight   01983 294051
Ratsey Sailmakers, Stephen
Milford Haven   01646 601561
Relling One Design
Portland   01305 826555
Richardson Sails
Southampton   023 8045 5106
Rig Shop, The
Southampton   023 8033 8341
Rockall Sails
Chichester   01243 573185
Sail Locker
Woolverstone Marina   01473 780206
Sail Style Hayling Is   023 9246 3720
Sails & Canvas Exeter   01392 877527
Saltern Sail Co
West Cowes   01983 280014
Saltern Sail Company
Yarmouth   01983 760120
Sanders Sails
Lymington   01590 673981
Saturn Sails Largs   01475 689933
Scott & Co, Graham
St Peter Port   01481 259380
Shore Sailmakers
Swanwick   01489 589450
SKB Sails Falmouth   01326 372107
Sketrick Sailmakers Ltd
Killinchy   028 9754 1400
Storrar Marine Store
Newcastle upon Tyne   0191 266 1037
Suffolk Sails
Woodbridge   01394 386323
Sunset Sails Sligo   +353 71 62792
Teltale Sails Prestwick   01355 500001
Torquay Marina Sails and Canvas
Exeter   01392 877527
Trident UK Gateshead   0191 490 1736
UK McWilliam Cowes   01983 281100
Underwood Sails Queen Anne's
Battery, Plymouth   01752 229661

W Sails Leigh-on-Sea   01702 714550
Watson Sails
Dublin 13   +353 1 846 2206
WB Leitch and Son
Tarbert   01880 820287
Westaway Sails
Plymouth Yacht Haven   01752 892560
Wilkinson, Ursula
Brighton   01273 677758
Wilkinson Sails
Burnham-on-Crouch   01621 786770
Wilkinson Sails
Teynham   01795 521503
Yacht Shop, The
Fleetwood   01253 879238

SOLAR POWER

Ampair Ringwood   01425 480780
Barden UK Ltd Fareham 01489 570770
Marlec Engineering Co Ltd
Corby   01536 201588

SPRAYHOODS & DODGERS

A & B Textiles
Gillingham   01634 579686
Allison–Gray Dundee   01382 505888
Arton, Charles
Milford-on-Sea   01590 644682
Arun Canvas and Rigging Ltd
Littlehampton   01903 732561
Buchanan, Keith
St Mary's   01720 422037
C & J Marine Textiles
Chichester   01243 785485
Covercare Fareham   01329 311878
Covercraft Southampton 023 8033 8286
Jeckells and Son Ltd
Wroxham   01603 782223
Jessail Ardrossan   01294 467311
Lomond Boat Covers
Alexandria   01389 602734
Lucas Sails
Portchester   023 9237 3699
Poole Canvas Co Ltd
Poole   01202 677477
Saundersfoot Auto Marine
Saundersfoot   01834 812115
Teltale Sails Prestwick 01355 500001
Trident UK Gateshead   0191 490 1736

SURVEYORS AND NAVAL ARCHITECTS

Amble Boat Company Ltd
Amble   01665 710267
Ark Surveys East Anglia/South Coast
01621 857065/01794 521957
Atkin & Associates
Lymington   01590 688633
Barbican Yacht Agency Ltd
Plymouth   01752 228855
Battick, Lee
St Helier   01534 611143
Booth Marine Surveys, Graham
Birchington-on-Sea   01843 843793

Byrde & Associates
Kimmeridge | 01929 480064

Bureau Maritime Ltd
Maldon | 01621 859181

Cannell & Associates, David M
Wivenhoe | 01206 823337

Cardiff Commercial Boat Operators Ltd Cardiff | 029 2037 7872

CE Proof Hamble | 023 8045 3245

Clarke Designs LLP, Owen
Dartmouth | 01803 770495

Cox, David Penryn | 01326 340808

Davies, Peter N
Wivenhoe | 01206 823289

Down Marine Co Ltd
Belfast | 028 90480247

Evans, Martin
Kirby le Soken | 01255 677883

Goodall, JL
Whitby | 01947 604791

Green, James
Plymouth | 01752 660516

Greening Yacht Design Ltd, David
Chichester | 023 9263 1806

Hansing & Associates
North Wales/Midlands | 01248 671291

JP Services – Marine Safety & Training Chichester | 01243 537552

MacGregor, WA
Felixstowe | 01394 676034

Mahoney & Co, KPO
Co Cork | +353 21 477 6150

Norwood Marine
Margate | 01843 835711

Quay Consultants Ltd
West Wittering | 01243 673056

Scott Marine Surveyors & Consultants Conwy | 01492 573001

S Roberts Marine Ltd
Liverpool | 0151 707 8300

Staton-Bevan, Tony
Lymington 01590 645755/07850 315744

Swanwick Yacht Surveyors
Southampton | 01489 564822

Thomas, Stephen
Southampton | 023 8048 6273

Ward & McKenzie
Woodbridge | 01394 383222

Ward & McKenzie (North East)
Pocklington | 01759 304322

YDSA Yacht Designers & Surveyors Association Bordon | 0845 0900162

TAPE TECHNOLOGY

Adhesive Technologies
Braintree | 01376 346511

CC Marine Services (Rubbaweld) Ltd
London | 020 7402 4009

Trade Grade Products Ltd
Poole | 01202 820177

UK Epoxy Resins
Burscough | 01704 892364

3M United Kingdom plc
Bracknell | 01344 858315

TRANSPORT/YACHT DELIVERIES

Anglo European Boat Transport
Devon | 01803 868691

Boat Shifters
| 07733 344018/01326 210548

Convoi Exceptionnel Ltd
Hamble | 023 8045 3045

Debbage Yachting
Ipswich | 01473 601169

East Coast Offshore Yachting
| 01480 861381

Forrest Marine Ltd
Exeter | 08452 308335

Hainsworth's UK and Continental
Bingley | 01274 565925

Houghton Boat Transport
Tewkesbury | 07831 486710

Moonfleet Sailing
Poole | 01202 682269

Performance Yachting
Plymouth | 01752 565023

Peters & May Ltd
Southampton | 023 8048 0480

Reeder School of Seamanship, Mike
Lymington | 01590 674560

Seafix Boat Transfer
North Wales | 01766 514507

Sealand Boat Deliveries Ltd
Liverpool | 01254 705225

Shearwater Sailing
Southampton | 01962 775213

Southcoasting Navigators
Devon | 01626 335626

West Country Boat Transport
| 01566 785651

Wolff, David | 07659 550131

Sealand Boat Deliveries Ltd

Nationwide and worldwide yacht transport 36 years. Storage, salvage. lifting 24/7 ops room **01254 705225** fax 776582 ros@poptel.org www.btx.co.uk

2009/MD6/s

TUITION/SAILING SCHOOLS

Association of Scottish Yacht Charterers Argyll | 07787 363562
| 01880 820012

Bisham Abbey Sailing & Navigation School Bisham | 01628 474960

Blue Baker Yachts
Ipswich | 01473 780008

Britannia Sailing (East Coast)
Ipswich | 01473 787019

British Offshore Sailing School
Hamble | 023 8045 7733

Coastal Sea School
Weymouth | 0870 321 3271

Conwy School of Yachting
Conwy | 01492 572999

Corsair Sailing
Banstead | 01737 211466

Dart Sailing School
Dartmouth | 01803 833973

Dartmouth Sailing
Dartmouth | 01803 833399

Drake Sailing School
Plymouth | 01635 253009

East Anglian Sea School
Ipswich | 01473 659992

East Coast Offshore Yachting – Les Rant Perry | 01480 861381

Five Star Sailing
Southampton | 01489 885599

Gibraltar Sailing Centre
Gibraltar | 00350 78554

Go Sail Ltd East
Cowes | 01983 280220

Hamble School of Yachting
Hamble | 023 8045 6687

Haslar Sea School
Gosport | 023 9252 0099

Hobo Yachting
Southampton | 023 8033 4574

Hoylake Sailing School
Wirral | 0151 632 4664

Ibiza Sailing School | 07092 235 853

International Yachtmaster Academy
Southampton | 0800 515439

Island Sea School
Port Dinorwic | 01248 352330

JP Services – Marine Safety & Training Chichester | 01243 537552

Lymington Cruising School
Lymington | 01590 677478

Marine Leisure Association (MLA)
Southampton | 023 8029 3822

Menorca Cruising School
| 01995 679240

Moncur Sailing School, Bob
Newcastle upon Tyne | 0191 265 4472

Moonfleet Sailing Poole 01202 682269

National Marine Correspondence School Birkenhead | 0151 647 6777

Northshore King's Lynn 01485 210236

On Deck Sailing
Southampton | 023 8033 3887

Pembrokeshire Cruising
Neyland | 01646 602500

Performance Yachting
Plymouth | 01752 565023

Plain Sailing Dartmouth 01803 853843

Plymouth Sailing School
Plymouth | 01752 493377

Port Edgar Marina & Sailing School
Port Edgar | 0131 331 3330

Portsmouth Outdoor Centre
Portsmouth | 023 9266 3873

Portugal Sail & Power 01473 833001
Rainbow Sailing School
Swansea 01792 467813
Reeder School of Seamanship, Mike
Lymington 01590 674560
Safe Water Training Sea School Ltd
Wirral 0151 630 0466
Sail East Harwich 01473 689344
Sally Water Training
East Cowes 01983 299033
Sea 'N' Ski Portsmouth 023 9246 6041
Seafever 01342 316293
Solaris Mediterranean Sea School
01925 642909
Solent School of Yachting
Southampton 023 8045 7733
Southcoasting Navigators
Devon 01626 335626
Southern Sailing
Southampton 01489 575511
Start Point Sailing
Dartmouth 01548 810917
Sunsail
Port Solent/Largs 0870 770 6314
Team Sailing Gosport 023 9252 4370
The Dream Or Two Experience of Yachting Portsmouth 0800 970 7845
Tiller School of Navigation
Banstead 01737 211466
Workman Marine School
Portishead 01275 845844
Wride School of Sailing, Bob
North Ferriby 01482 635623

WATERSIDE ACCOMMODATION & RESTAURANTS

Abbey, The Penzance 01736 330680
Arun View Inn, The
Littlehampton 01903 722335
Baywatch on the Beach
Bembridge 01983 873259
Beaucette Marina Restaurant
Guernsey 01481 247066
Bella Napoli
Brighton Marina 01273 818577
Bembridge Coast Hotel
Bembridge 01983 873931
Budock Vean Hotel
Porth Navas Creek 01326 252100
Café Mozart Cowes 01983 293681
Caffé Uno Port Solent 023 9237 5227
Chandlers Bar & Bistro Queen Anne's Battery Marina, Plymouth 01752 257772
Chiquito Port Solent 023 9220 1181
Cruzzo Malahide Marina, Co Dublin +353 1 845 0599
Cullins Yard Bistro
Dover 01304 211666
Custom House, The
Poole 01202 676767
Dart Marina River Lounge
Dartmouth 01803 832580

Deer Leap, The Exmouth 01395 265030
Doghouse Swanwick Marina,
Hamble 01489 571602
Dolphin Restaurant
Gorey 01534 853370
Doune Knoydart 01687 462667
El Puertos
Penarth Marina 029 2070 5551
Falmouth Marina Marine Bar and Restaurant Falmouth 01326 313481
Ferry Boat Inn West Wick Marina,
Nr Chelmsford 01621 740208
Ferry Inn, The (restaurant)
Pembroke Dock 01646 682947
First and Last, The Braye,
Alderney 01481 823162
Fisherman's Wharf
Sandwich 01304 613636
Folly Inn Cowes 01983 297171
Gaffs Restaurant Fenit Harbour Marina,
County Kerry +353 66 71 36666
Godleys Hotel Fenit,
County Kerry +353 66 71 36108
Harbour Lights Restaurant
Walton on the Naze 01255 851887
Haven Bar and Bistro, The
Lymington Yacht Haven 01590 679971
Haven Hotel Poole 01202 707333
HMS Ganges Restaurant
Mylor Yacht Harbour 01326 374320
Jolly Sailor, The
Bursledon 023 8040 5557
Kames Hotel Argyll 01700 811489
Ketch Rigger, The Hamble Point Marina
Hamble 023 8045 5601
Kota Restaurant
Porthleven 01326 562407
La Cala Lady Bee Marina,
Shoreham 01273 597422
Le Nautique
St Peter Port 01481 721714
Lighter Inn, The
Topsham 01392 875439
Mariners Bistro Sparkes Marina,
Hayling Island 023 9246 9459
Mary Mouse II Haslar Marina,
Gosport 023 9252 5200

The Melfort Mermaid Moorings
Restaurant
56°16'08.79"N; 5°30'08.08" W
Come Hungry, Leave Happy
01852 200 324 / 333

Martha's Vineyard
Milford Haven 01646 697083
Master Builder's House Hotel
Buckler's Hard 01590 616253
Millstream Hotel
Bosham 01243 573234
Montagu Arms Hotel
Beaulieu 01590 612324
Olivo Port Solent 023 9220 1473
Oyster Quay Mercury Yacht Harbour,
Hamble 023 8045 7220
Paris Hotel Coverack 01326 280258
Pebble Beach, The
Gosport 023 9251 0789
Petit Champ Sark 01481 832046
Philip Leisure Group
Dartmouth 01803 833351
Priory Bay Hotel Seaview,
Isle of Wight 01983 613146
Quayside Hotel
Brixham 01803 855751
Queen's Hotel Kirkwall 01856 872200
Sails Dartmouth 01803 839281
Shananagans
Yarmouth 01983 760054
Shell Bay Seafood Restaurant
Poole Harbour 01929 450363
Simply Italian Sovereign Harbour,
Eastbourne 01323 470911
Slackwater Jacques
Port Solent 023 9278 0777
Spinnaker, The
Chichester Marina 01243 511032
Spit Sand Fort
The Solent 01329 242077
Steamboat Inn Lossiemouth Marina,
Lossiemouth 01343 812066
Taps Shamrock Quay,
Southampton 023 8022 8621
Tayvallich Inn, The
Argyll 01546 870282
Villa Adriana Newhaven Marina
Newhaven 01903 722335
Warehouse Brasserie, The
Poole 01202 677238
36 on the Quay
Emsworth 01243 375592

WEATHER INFO
Met Office Exeter 0870 900 0100

WOOD FITTINGS
Howells & Son, KJ
Poole 01202 665724
Onward Trading Co Ltd
Southampton 01489 885250
Robbins Timber
Bristol 0117 963 3136
Sheraton Marine Cabinet
Witney 01993 868275

YACHT BROKERS
ABC Powermarine
Beaumaris 01248 811413

ABYA Association of Brokers & Yacht Agents Bordon 0845 0900162

Adur Boat Sales
Southwick 01273 596680

Ancasta International Boat Sales
Southampton 023 8045 0000

Anglia Yacht Brokerage
Bury St Edmunds 01359 271747

Ardmair Boat Centre
Ullapool 01854 612054

Assured Boating Egham 01784 473300

Barbican Yacht Agency, The
Plymouth 01752 228855

Bates Wharf Marine Sales Ltd
01932 571141

BJ Marine
Bangor 028 9127 1434

Bluewater Horizons
Weymouth 01305 782080

Boatworks + Ltd
St Peter Port 01481 726071

Caley Marina Inverness 01463 236539

Calibra Marine International Ltd
Southampton 08702 400358

Clarke & Carter Interyacht Ltd
Ipswich/Burnham on Crouch
01473 659681/01621 785600

Coastal Leisure Ltd
Southampton 023 8033 2222

Dale Sailing Brokerage
Neyland 01646 603105

Deacons
Southampton 023 8040 2253

Exe Leisure
Essex Marina 01702 258190

Ferrypoint Boat Co
Youghal +353 24 94232

Gweek Quay Boatyard
Helston 01326 221657

International Barge & Yacht Brokers
Southampton 023 8045 5205

Iron Wharf Boatyard
Faversham 01795 537122

Jackson Yacht Services
Jersey 01534 743819

Kings Yacht Agency
Beaulieu/Southampton
01590 616316/023 8033 1533

Kippford Slipway Ltd
Dalbeattie 01556 620249

Knox-Johnston, Paul
Southsea 023 9286 4524

Lencraft Boats Ltd
Dungarvan +353 58 68220

Liberty Yachts Ltd
Plymouth 01752 227911

Lucas Yachting, Mike
Torquay 01803 212840

Network Yacht Brokers
Dartmouth 01803 834864

Network Yacht Brokers
Plymouth 01752 605377

New Horizon Yacht Agency
Guernsey 01481 726335

Oyster Brokerage Ltd
Ipswich 01473 602263

Pearn and Co, Norman
(Looe Boatyard) Looe 01503 262244

Performance Boat Company
Maidenhead 07768 464717

Peters Chandlery
Chichester 01243 511033

Portavon Marina
Keynsham 0117 986 1626

Prosser Marine Sales Ltd
Glasgow 0141 552 2005

Retreat Boatyard
Topsham 01392 874720

Scanyachts
Southampton 023 8045 5608

SD Marine Ltd
Southampton 023 8045 7278

Sea & Shore Ship Chandler
Dundee 01382 202666

South Pier Shipyard
St Helier 01534 519700

South West Yacht Brokers Group
Plymouth 01752 551991

Sunbird Marine Services
Fareham 01329 842613

Trafalgar Yacht Services
Fareham 01329 823577

Transworld Yachts
Hamble 023 8045 7704

WA Simpson Marine Ltd
Dundee 01382 566670

Walton Marine Sales
Brighton 01273 670707

Walton Marine Sales
Portishead 01275 840132

Walton Marine Sales
Wroxham 01603 781178

Watson Marine, Charles
Hamble 023 8045 6505

Western Marine
Dublin +353 1280 0321

Westways of Plymouth Ltd
Plymouth 01752 670770

Woodrolfe Brokerage
Maldon 01621 868494

Youngboats Faversham 01795 536176

YACHT CHARTERS & HOLIDAYS

Ardmair Boat Centre
Ullapool 01854 612054

Association of Scottish Yacht Charterers Argyll 01880 820012

Blue Baker Yachts
Ipswich 01473 780111/780008

Coastal Leisure Ltd
Southampton 023 8033 2222

Crusader Yachting
Turkey 01732 867321

Dartmouth Sailing
Dartmouth 01803 833399

Dartmouth Yacht Charters
Dartmouth 01803 883718

Doune Marine Mallaig 01687 462667

Four Seasons Yacht Charter
Gosport 023 9251 1789

Golden Black Sailing
Cornwall 01209 715757

Hamble Point Yacht Charters
Hamble 023 8045 7110

Haslar Marina & Victory Yacht Charters Gosport 023 9252 0099

Indulgence Charters
Wendover 01296 696006

Liberty Yachts West Country, Greece, Mallorca & Italy 01752 227911

Nautilus Yachting Mediterranean & Caribbean 01732 867445

Ondeck
Ryde 01983 612642

Patriot Charters & Sail School
Milford Haven 01437 741202

Plain Sailing Yacht Charters
Dartmouth 01803 853843

Portway Yacht Charters
Plymouth/Falmouth
01752 606999/01326 212320

Puffin Yachts
Port Solent 01483 420728

Rainbow Sailing School
Swansea 01792 467813

Sailing Holidays Ltd
Mediterranean 020 8459 8787

Sailing Holidays in Ireland
Kinsale +353 21 477 2927

Setsail Holidays Greece, Turkey, Croatia, Majorca 01787 310445

Shannon Sailing Ltd
Tipperary +353 67 24499

Sleat Marine Services
Isle of Skye 01471 844216

Smart Yachts
Mediterranean 01425 614804

Sunsail Worldwide 0870 770 0102

Templecraft Yacht Charters
Lewes 01273 812333

Top Yacht Charter Ltd
Worldwide 01243 520950

Victory Yacht Charters
Gosport 023 9252 0099

West Wales Yacht Charter
Pwllheli 07748 634869

Westways of Plymouth Ltd
Plymouth 01752 481200

39 North (Mediterranean)
Kingskerwell 07071 393939

YACHT CLUBS

Aberaeron YC
Aberdovey 01545 570077

Aberdeen and Stonehaven SC
Nr Inverurie 01569 764006

Aberdour BC
01383 860632

Abersoch Power BC
Abersoch 01758 712027

MARINE SUPPLIES AND SERVICES GUIDE

TUITION / SAILING SCHOOLS – YACHT CLUBS

Aberystwyth BC	
Aberystwyth	01970 624575
Aldeburgh YC	01728 452562
Alderney SC	01481 822959
Alexandra YC	
Southend-on-Sea	01702 340363
Arklow SC	+353 402 33100
Arun YC Littlehampton	01903 716016
Axe YC Axemouth	01297 20043
Ayr Yacht and CC	01292 476034
Ballyholme YC Bangor	028 91271467
Baltimore SC	+353 28 20426
Banff SC	01464 820308
Bantry Bay SC	+353 27 50081
Barry YC	01446 735511
Beaulieu River SC	
Brockenhurst	01590 616273
Bembridge SC	
Isle of Wight	01983 872237
Benfleet YC	
Canvey Island	01268 792278
Blackpool and Fleetwood YC	01253 884205
Blackwater SC Maldon	01621 853923
Blundellsands SC	0151 929 2101
Bosham SC Chichester	01243 572341
Brading Haven YC	
Isle of Wight	01983 872289
Bradwell CC	01621 892970
Bradwell Quay YC	
Wickford	01268 776539
Brancaster Staithe SC	01485 210249
Brandy Hole YC	
Hullbridge	01702 230320
Brightlingsea SC	
Colchester	01206 303275
Brighton Marina YC	
Peacehaven	01273 818711
Bristol Avon SC	01225 873472
Bristol Channel YC	
Swansea	01792 366000
Bristol Corinthian YC	
Axbridge	01934 732033
Brixham YC	01803 853332
Burnham Overy Staithe SC	01328 730961
Burnham-on-Crouch SC	01621 782812
Burnham-on-Sea SC	
Bridgwater	01278 792911
Burry Port YC	01554 833635
Cabot CC	01275 855207
Caernarfon SC (Menai Strait)	
Caernarfon	01286 672861
Campbeltown SC	01586 552488
Cardiff YC	029 2046 3697
Cardiff Bay YC	029 20226575
Carlingford Lough YC	
Rostrevor	028 4173 8604
Carrickfergus SC	
Whitehead	028 93 351402
Castle Cove SC	
Weymouth	01305 783708
Castlegate Marine Club	
Stockton on Tees	01642 583299
Chanonry SC Fortrose	01463 221415

Chichester Cruiser and Racing Club	01483 770391
Chichester YC	01243 512918
Christchurch SC	01202 483150
Clyde CC Glasgow	0141 221 2774
Co Antrim YC	
Carrickfergus	028 9337 2322
Cobnor Activities Centre Trust	01243 572791
Coleraine YC	028 703 44503
Colne YC Brightlingsea	01206 302594
Conwy YC Deganwy	01492 583690
Coquet YC	01665 710367
Corrib Rowing & YC	
Galway City	+353 91 564560
Cowes Combined Clubs	01983 295744
Cowes Corinthian YC	
Isle of Wight	01983 296333
Cowes Yachting	01983 280770
Cramond BC	0131 336 1356
Creeksea SC	
Burnham-on-Crouch	01245 320578
Crookhaven SC	087 2379997 mobile
Crouch YC	
Burnham-on-Crouch	01621 782252
Dale YC	01646 636362
Dartmouth YC	01803 832305
Deben YC Woodbridge	01394 384440
Dell Quay SC Chichester	01243 785080
Dingle SC	+353 66 51984
Douglas Bay YC	01624 673965
Dovey YC Aberdovey	01213 600008
Dun Laoghaire MYC	+353 1 288 938
Dunbar SC	
Cockburnspath	01368 86287
East Antrim BC	028 28 277204
East Belfast YC	028 9065 6283
East Cowes SC	01983 531687
East Dorset SC Poole	01202 706111
East Lothian YC	01620 892698
Eastney Cruising Association	
Portsmouth	023 92734103
Eling SC	023 80863987
Emsworth SC	01243 372850
Emsworth Slipper SC	01243 378881
Essex YC Southend	01702 478404
Exe SC (River Exe)	
Exmouth	01395 264607
Eyott SC Mayland	01245 320703
Fairlie YC	01294 213940
Falmouth Town SC	01326 373915
Falmouth Watersports Association	
Falmouth	01326 211223
Fareham Sailing & Motor BC	
Fareham	01329 280738
Felixstowe Ferry SC	01394 272466
Findhorn YC Findhorn	01309 690247
Fishguard Bay YC	
Lower Fishguard	01348 872866
Flushing SC Falmouth	01326 374043
Folkestone Yacht and Motor BC	
Folkestone	01303 251574
Forth Corinthian YC	
Haddington	0131 552 5939

Forth YCs Association	
Edinburgh	0131 552 3006
Fowey Gallants SC	01726 832335
Foynes YC Foynes	+353 69 91201
Galway Bay SC	+353 91 794527
Glasson SC Lancaster	01524 751089
Glenans Irish Sailing School	+353 1 6611481
Glenans Irish SC (Westport)	+353 98 26046
Gosport CC Gosport	02392 586838
Gravesend SC	01474 533974
Greenwich YC London	020 8858 7339
Grimsby and Cleethorpes YC	
Grimsby	01472 356678
Guernsey YC	
St Peter Port	01481 722838
Hamble River SC	
Southampton	023 80452070
Hampton Pier YC	
Herne Bay	01227 364749
Hardway SC Gosport	023 9258 1875
Hartlepool YC	01429 233423
Harwich Town SC	01255 503200
Hastings and St Leonards YC	
Hastings	01424 420656
Haven Ports YC	
Woodbridge	01473 659658
Hayling Ferry SC; Locks SC	
Hayling Island	023 80829833
Hayling Island SC	023 92463768
Helensburgh SC Rhu	01436 672778
Helensburgh	01436 821234
Helford River SC	
Helston	01326 231006
Herne Bay SC	01227 375650
Highcliffe SC	
Christchurch	01425 274874
Holyhead SC	01407 762526
Holywood YC	028 90423355
Hoo Ness YC Sidcup	01634 250052
Hornet SC Gosport	023 9258 0403
Howth YC	+353 1 832 2141
Hoylake SC Wirral	0151 632 2616
Hullbridge YC	01702 231797
Humber Yawl Club	01482 667224
Hurlingham YC London	020 8788 5547
Hurst Castle SC	01590 645589
Hythe SC Southampton	02380 846563
Hythe & Saltwood SC	01303 265178
Ilfracombe YC	01271 863969
Iniscealtra SC	
Limerick	+353 61 338347
Invergordon BC	01349 852265
Irish CC	+353 214870031
Island CC Salcombe	01548 531176
Island SC Isle of Wight	01983 296621
Island YC Canvey Island	01268 510360
Isle of Bute SC	
Rothesay	01700 502819
Isle of Man YC	
Port St Mary	01624 832088
Itchenor SC Chichester	01243 512400
Keyhaven YC	01590 642165
Killyleagh YC	028 4482 8250

Kircubbin SC	028 4273 8422	
Kirkcudbright SC	01557 331727	
Langstone SC Havant	023 9248 4577	
Largs SC Largs	01475 670000	
Larne Rowing & SC	028 2827 4573	
Lawrenny YC	01646 651212	
Leigh-on-Sea SC	01702 476788	
Lerwick BC	01595 696954	
Lilliput SC Poole	01202 740319	

**Littlehampton Sailing and Motor
Club** Littlehampton 01903 715859
Loch Ryan SC Stranraer 01776 706322
Lochaber YC Fort William 01397 772361
Locks SC Portsmouth 023 9282 9833
Looe SC 01503 262559
Lossiemouth CC
Fochabers 01348 812121
Lough Swilly YC Fahn +353 74 22377
Lowestoft CC 01502 574376
Lyme Regis Power BC 01297 443788
Lyme Regis SC 01297 442373
Lymington Town SC 0159 674514
Lympstone SC Exeter 01395 278792
Madoc YC Porthmadog 01766 512976
Malahide YC +353 1 845 3372
Maldon Little Ship Club
01621 854139
Manx Sailing & CC
Ramsey 01624 813494
Marchwood YC 023 80666141
Margate YC 01843 292602
Marina BC Pwllheli 01758 612271
Maryport YC 01228 560865
Mayflower SC Plymouth 01752 662526
Mayo SC (Rosmoney)
Rosmoney +353 98 27772
Medway YC Rochester 01634 718399
Menai Bridge BC
Beaumaris 01248 810583
Mengham Rythe SC
Hayling Island 023 92463337
Merioneth YC
Barmouth 01341 280000
Monkstone Cruising and SC
Swansea 01792 812229
Montrose SC Montrose 01674 672554
Mumbles YC Swansea 01792 369321
Mylor YC Falmouth 01326 374391
Nairn SC 01667 453897
National YC
Dun Laoghaire +353 1 280 5725
Netley SC Netley 023 80454272
New Quay YC
Aberdovey 01545 560516
Newhaven & Seaford SC
Seaford 01323 890077
Newport and Uskmouth SC
Cardiff 01633 271417
Newtownards SC 028 9181 3426
Neyland YC 01646 600267
North Devon YC
Bideford 01271 861390
North Fambridge Yacht Centre
01621 740370
North Haven YC Poole 01202 708830

**North of England Yachting
Association** Kirkwall 01856 872331
North Sunderland Marine Club
Sunderland 01665 721231
North Wales CC
Conwy 01492 593481
**North West Venturers YC
(Beaumaris)** Beaumaris 0161 2921943
Oban SC Ledaig by Oban
01631 563999
Orford SC Woodbridge 01394 450997
Orkney SC Kirkwall 01856 872331
Orwell YC Ipswich 01473 602288
Oulton Broad Yacht Station
01502 574946
Ouse Amateur SC
Kings Lynn 01553 772239
Paignton SC Paignton 01803 525817
Parkstone YC Poole 01202 743610
Peel Sailing and CC
Peel 01624 842390
Pembroke Haven YC 01646 684403
Pembrokeshire YC
Milford Haven 01646 692799
Penarth YC 029 20708196
Pentland Firth YC
Thurso 01847 891803
Penzance YC 01736 364989
Peterhead SC Ellon 01779 75527
Pin Mill SC
Woodbridge 01394 780271
Plym YC Plymouth 01752 404991
Poolbeg YC +353 1 660 4681
Poole YC 01202 672687
Porlock Weir SC
Watchet 01643 862702
Port Edgar YC Penicuik 0131 657 2854
Port Navas YC
Falmouth 01326 340065
Port of Falmouth Sailing Association
Falmouth 01326 372927
Portchester SC
Portchester 023 9237 6375
Porthcawl Harbour BC
Swansea 01656 655935
Porthmadog SC
Porthmadog 01766 513546
Portrush YC Portrush 028 7082 3932
Portsmouth SC 02392 820596
Prestwick SC Prestwick 01292 671117
Pwllheli SC Pwllheli 01758 613343
Queenborough YC
Queenborough 01795 663955
Quoile YC
Downpatrick 028 44 612266
R Towy BC Tenby 01267 241755
RAFYC 023 80452208
Redclyffe YC Poole 01929 557227
Restronguet SC
Falmouth 01326 374536
Ribble CC
Lytham St Anne's 01253 739983
River Wyre YC 01253 811948
RNSA (Plymouth) 01752 55123/83
Rochester CC 01634 841350

Rock Sailing and Water Ski Club
Wadebridge 01208 862431
Royal Dart YC
Dartmouth 01803 752496
Royal Motor YC Poole 01202 707227
Royal Anglesey YC (Beaumaris)
Anglesey 01248 810295
Royal Burnham YC
Burnham-on-Crouch 01621 782044
Royal Channel Islands YC (Jersey)
St Aubin 01534 745783
Royal Cinque Ports YC
Dover 01304 206262
**Royal Corinthian YC
(Burnham-on-Crouch)**
Burnham-on-Crouch 01621 782105
Royal Corinthian YC (Cowes)
Cowes 01983 292608
Royal Cork YC
Crosshaven +353 214 831023
Royal Cornwall YC (RCYC)
Falmouth 01326 312126
Royal Dorset YC
Weymouth 01305 786258
Royal Forth YC
Edinburgh 0131 552 3006
Royal Fowey YC Fowey 01726 833573
Royal Gourock YC
Gourock 01475 632983
Royal Highland YC
Connel 01852 300460
Royal Irish YC
Dun Laoghaire +353 1 280 9452
Royal London YC
Isle of Wight 019 83299727
Royal Lymington YC 01590 672677
Royal Mersey YC
Birkenhead 0151 645 3204
Royal Motor YC Poole 01202 707227
**Royal Naval Club and Royal Albert
YC** Portsmouth 023 9282 5924
Royal Naval Sailing Association
Gosport 023 9252 1100
Royal Norfolk & Suffolk YC
Lowestoft 01502 566726
Royal North of Ireland YC
028 90 428041
Royal Northern and Clyde YC
Rhu 01436 820322
Royal Northumberland YC
Blyth 01670 353636
Royal Plymouth Corinthian YC
Plymouth 01752 664327
Royal Scottish Motor YC
0141 881 1024
Royal Solent YC
Yarmouth 01983 760256
Royal Southampton YC
Southampton 023 8022 3352
Royal Southern YC
Southampton 023 8045 0300
Royal St George YC
Dun Laoghaire +353 1 280 1811
Royal Tay YC Dundee 01382 477133
Royal Temple YC
Ramsgate 01843 591766

Royal Torbay YC	Torquay	01803 292006
Royal Ulster YC	Bangor	028 91 270568
Royal Victoria YC	Fishbourne	01983 882325
Royal Welsh YC (Caernarfon)	Caernarfon	01286 672599
Royal Welsh YC	Aernarfon	01286 672599
Royal Western YC	Plymouth	01752 226299
Royal Yacht Squadron	Isle of Wight	01983 292191
Royal Yorkshire YC	Bridlington	01262 672041
Rye Harbour SC		01797 223136
Salcombe YC		01548 842593
Saltash SC		01752 845988
Scalloway BC Lerwick		01595 880409
Scarborough YC		01723 373821
Schull SC		+353 28 37352
Scillonian Sailing and BC	St Mary's	01720 277229
Seasalter SC	Whitstable	07773 189943
Seaview YC	Isle of Wight	01983 613268
Shoreham SC Henfield		01273 453078
Skerries SC	Carlingford Lough	+353 1 849 1233
Slaughden SC Duxford		01728 689036
Sligo YC Sligo		+353 71 77168
Solva Boat Owners Association	Fishguard	01437 721538
Solway YC	Kirkdudbright	01556 620312
South Caernarvonshire YC	Abersoch	01758 712338
South Cork SC		+353 28 36383
South Devon Sailing School	Newton Abbot	01626 52352
South Gare Marine Club - Sail Section Middlesbrough		01642 505630
South Shields SC		0191 456 5821
South Woodham Ferrers YC	Chelmsford	01245 325391
Southampton SC		023 8044 6575
Southwold SC		01986 784225
Sovereign Harbour YC	Eastbourne	01323 470888
St Helier YC		01534 721307/32229
St Mawes SC		01326 270686
Starcross Fishing & CC (River Exe)	Starcross	01626 891996
Starcross YC Exeter		01626 890470
Stoke SC Ipswich		01473 624989
Stornoway SC		01851 705412
Stour SC		01206 393924
Strangford Lough YC	Newtownards	028 97 541202
Strangford SC	Downpatrick	028 4488 1404
Strood YC Aylesford		01634 718261
Sunderland YC		0191 567 5133
Sunsail Portsmouth		023 92222224

Sussex YC	Shoreham-by-Sea	01273 464868
Swanage SC		01929 422987
Swansea Yacht & Sub-Aqua Club	Swansea	01792 469096
Tamar River SC	Plymouth	01752 362741
Tarbert Lochfyne YC		01880 820376
Tay Corinthian BC	Dundee	01382 553534
Tay YCs Association		01738 621860
Tees & Hartlepool YC		01429 233423
Tees SC	Aycliffe Village	01429 265400
Teifi BC - Cardigan Bay	Fishguard	01239 613846
Teign Corinthian YC	Teignmouth	01626 777699
Tenby SC		01834 842762
Tenby YC		01834 842762
Thames Estuary YC		01702 345967
Thorney Island SC		01243 371731
Thorpe Bay YC		01702 587563
Thurrock YC Grays		01375 373720
Tollesbury CC		01621 869561
Topsham SC		01392 877524
Torpoint Mosquito SC - Plymouth		01752 812508
Tralee SC		+353 66 36119
Troon CC		01292 311190
Troon YC		01292 315315
Tudor SC	Portsmouth	023 92662002
Tynemouth SC	Newcastle upon Tyne	0191 2572167
Up River YC	Hullbridge	01702 231654
Upnor SC		01634 718043
Wakering YC	Rochford	01702 530926
Waldringfield SC	Woodbridge	01394 283347
Walls Regatta Club	Lerwick	01595 809273
Walton & Frinton YC	Walton-on-the-Naze	01255 675526
Warrenpoint BC		028 4175 2137
Warsash SC	Southampton	01489 583575
Watchet Boat Owner Association	Watchet	01984 633736
Waterford Harbour SC	Dunmore East	+353 51 383389
Watermouth YC	Watchet	01271 865048
Wear Boating Association		0191 567 5313
Wells SC	Wells-next-the-sea	01328 711190
West Kirby SC		0151 625 5579
West Mersea YC	Colchester	01206 382947
Western Isles YC		01688 302371
Western YC	Kilrush	+353 87 2262885

Weston Bay YC	Portishead	07867 966429
Weston CC	Southampton	07905 557298
Weston SC	Southampton	023 80452527
Wexford HBC		+353 53 22039
Weymouth SC	Weymouth	01305 785481
Whitby YC		01947 603623
Whitstable YC		01227 272942
Wicklow SC		+353 404 67526
Witham SC	Boston	01205 363598
Wivenhoe SC	Colchester	01206 822132
Woodbridge CC		01394 386737
Wormit BC		01382 553878
Yarmouth SC		01983 760270
Yealm YC	Newton Ferrers	01752 872291
Youghal Sailing Club		+353 24 92447

YACHT DESIGNERS

Cannell & Associates, David M	Wivenhoe	01206 823337
Clarke Designs LLP, Owen	Dartmouth	01803 770495
Giles Naval Architects, Laurent	Lymington	01590 641777
Harvey Design, Ray	Barton on Sea	01425 613492
Jones Yacht Design, Stephen	Warsash	01489 576439
Wharram Designs, James	Truro	01872 864792
Wolstenholme Yacht Design	Coltishall	01603 737024

YACHT MANAGEMENT

Barbican Yacht Agency Ltd	Plymouth	01752 228855
Coastal Leisure Ltd	Southampton	023 8033 2222
O'Sullivan Boat Management	Dun Laoghaire	+353 86 829 6625
Swanwick Yacht Surveyors	Swanwick	01489 564822

YACHT VALETING

Blackwell, Craig	Co Meath	+353 87 677 9605
Bright 'N' Clean	South Coast	07789 494430
Clean It All	Nr Brixham	01803 844564
Kip Marina Inverkip		01475 521485
Mainstay Yacht Maintenance	Dartmouth	01803 839076
Marine Gleam	Lymington	0800 074 4672
Mobile Yacht Maintenance		07900 148806
Shipshape Hayling Is		023 9232 4500
Smith Boat Care, Paul	Isle of Wight	01983 754726